Hyperconnectivity and

in memory of my mother
Elizabeth Brubaker

Hyperconnectivity and Its Discontents

Rogers Brubaker

polity

First published in 2023 by Polity Press

Polity Press
65 Bridge Street
Cambridge CB2 1UR, UK

Polity Press
111 River Street
Hoboken, NJ 07030, USA

ISBN-13: 978-1-5095-5452-2
ISBN-13: 978-1-5095-5453-9(pb)

A catalogue record for this book is available from the British Library.

Library of Congress Control Number: 2022938892

Typeset in 11.5 on 14 Adobe Garamond
by Fakenham Prepress Solutions, Fakenham, Norfolk NR21 8NL
Printed and bound in the UK by TJ Books Limited

For further information on Polity, visit our website:
politybooks.com

MIX
Paper from
responsible sources
FSC
www.fsc.org   FSC® C013056

Contents

Preface

"The fox," wrote the ancient Greek poet Archilochus, "knows many things, but the hedgehog knows one big thing." In the figurative sense popularized by the philosopher and historian of ideas Isaiah Berlin, this dictum distinguishes writers who "relate everything to a single central vision" or "organizing principle" (the hedgehogs) from those who embrace "a vast variety of experiences and objects" without "seeking to fit them into ... [a] unitary inner vision" (the foxes).[1] This is the book of a fox. It has no overarching thesis to defend, no single conceptual prism to promote. It aims rather to provide a synoptic account of the sprawling, unruly, many-sided sociotechnical phenomenon I call digital hyperconnectivity, without squeezing it into the conceptual mold of a single big hedgehog-worthy idea. It aims to show how hyperconnectivity has transformed all aspects and spheres of social life, private and public, from the precincts of the self to the architecture of the economy and polity, and how these transformations, which have opened up so many new and exciting possibilities, are in other respects inimical to human freedom and flourishing.

The book grew out of an undergraduate seminar I had been teaching for a number of years in UCLA's Honors Collegium. The seminar invited students to think critically about the increasingly pervasive digital mediation of their everyday social experience and about the broader cultural, economic, and political transformations that had been set in motion, or accelerated, by digital hyperconnectivity. As I designed and redesigned the course for successive offerings, looking for appropriate readings, I did not find an integrated, encompassing account of digital hyperconnectivity that addressed both everyday experience and underlying structural transformations in a manner at once challenging and accessible. I hope that this is that book.

I began work on the book a year before the novel coronavirus brought normal life on the planet to a standstill. But the pandemic has made the project more opportune than ever. Its confinements, disruptions, and restrictions have sharply accelerated the digitalization of all spheres of life. They occasioned a sudden and massive shift to remote work, education, shopping, medicine, therapy, culture, entertainment, sociability, and more. None of these shifts will be anywhere near fully reversed. In all of these spheres, this abrupt and radical reorganization of social life was possible only because of preexisting digital infrastructures. Hyperconnectivity thus prepared us for the pandemic. Yet the pandemic, in turn, has prepared us for an even more fully digitally mediated future.

Before the pandemic, the immense and unaccountable power of Big Tech and the degradation of the digital public sphere had prompted heightened critical scrutiny. Much of the energy of this incipient "techlash" dissipated temporarily in the face of Covid-19. Big Tech was no longer an urgent problem; it was a keenly appreciated solution, allowing social life to continue online when it was suspended in the flesh. The pandemic was therefore a godsend for the tech giants. It offered a unique opportunity to open up new markets, experiment on a planetary scale, and remake the social world. It also offered an opportunity for redemption: tech firms could present themselves as working for the public good by partnering with governments and public health authorities. Mounting concerns about misinformation, to be sure, have kept platforms under pressure. The tech giants still face a series of antitrust and regulatory initiatives, some with a degree of bipartisan support. But whatever the fate of these initiatives, the power of Big Tech – cultural and political as well as economic – is likely only to increase further. And the "solutionist" ideology of Silicon Valley that Evgeny Morozov so brilliantly skewered a decade ago – the habit of thinking that all social and political problems have technological solutions – seems more firmly entrenched than ever.[2]

The book's broad scope and modest length oblige me to be ruthlessly selective as well as brutally concise, and they condemn me in advance to neglecting or at best merely scratching the surface of many important topics. The particular path I have charted through the vast territory I stake out is no doubt informed by my intellectual, moral, and political sensibilities. My account is therefore in some respects a personal and idiosyncratic one. But it is not only or primarily that: it is an effort to grasp the complexity of digital hyperconnectivity as a "total social fact" that powerfully structures the world in which we live.[3]

A book as wide-ranging as this one is obviously not based on primary research. It is a "quaternary" work, as Abram de Swaan memorably characterized a book of his own; it relies not only on a large body of more or less specialized secondary studies but also on synthetic "tertiary" works.[4] The literature on the various aspects of my subject – spanning the social sciences, media and communication studies, and science and technology studies – has become unsurveyably vast. I cannot of course pretend to have read, or even to be aware of, all of the relevant work. But the reader wishing to explore particular topics in greater depth will find abundant pointers to the literature (as well as amplifications and qualifications of the argument) in the endnotes.

Digital hyperconnectivity is a planetary-scale phenomenon, but it is configured very differently in different world regions and among different groups of users. Attentive readers may therefore wonder about my frequent use of first person plural pronouns. Who is this "we," they may ask, that is so casually invoked? The authorial "we" is a stylistic convenience, but a sociological fiction. "Our" relation to hyperconnectivity is a highly differentiated one, and "we" experience it in many different ways. Generational differences loom especially large, but differences of country, class, education, gender, religion, and race and ethnicity matter as well. It is not my aim to map out these differences, though they will come up from time to time in my discussion.

Yet I would offer a qualified defense of the authorial "we." Digital hyperconnectivity affects us in different ways, but it increasingly affects all of us. Even the relatively unconnected are drawn ineluctably into its orbit, as anytime-anywhere connectivity – minimally, the possession of a smartphone – becomes, in effect, a requirement of full citizenship. And the still more digitally mediated future that is being constructed by the great tech platforms is one that we will all inhabit. While users can remake platforms in unanticipated ways, increasingly powerful platforms also design, construct, and discipline their users. In certain respects, they can make the sociological fiction into a sociological fact.

Some parts of my argument, especially in parts of the politics chapter, address the American context specifically. But this is not a book about the US. The argument applies, for the most part, throughout the developed West, notwithstanding significant legal and institutional differences between Europe and the US, notably a much more robust data protection framework in Europe. And much of the argument applies beyond the West. I have not, however, been able to give the distinctive configuration of digital hyperconnectivity in China – the central role of the state, the specific characteristics of the giant Chinese tech platforms, and the even greater degree of digital mediation of everyday life – the attention it deserves. In the geopolitics of hyperconnectivity, China represents a major counterweight to the hegemony of the American tech giants elsewhere.[5]

A broadly critical account of digital hyperconnectivity by a sixty-five-year-old first-world university professor risks caricature as a "declinist" screed that frets dyspeptically about "kids these days," naïvely idealizes digitally unmediated face-to-face relations, and bathes the pre-digital public sphere in the warm but distorting glow of nostalgia. I hope that nothing in this book warrants such a reading. I readily acknowledge the many ways in which my own life – and the lives of billions of others worldwide – has been enriched by digital connectivity. My stance is indeed critical, but it is not uncritically critical: I have no interest in writing a jeremiad or a disconnectionist manifesto, and I underscore throughout the ambivalence of hyperconnectivity. For better or worse – for better *and* worse – we live in a world that is shaped and structured on every level and in every sphere of life by hyperconnectivity. The way forward is anything but clear. But there is no turning back.

Acknowledgments

My first thanks go to the students in successive versions of the course on digital hyperconnectivity that I have been teaching since 2015. Discussions with them gave me the chance to work out the ideas for this book before I knew that I was writing it; later, they were the first readers of most of my draft chapters. Talks at Yale University, UC Riverside, the University of Oslo, and the Central European University provided additional forums to test my ideas. For superb research assistance, I thank Morgan Boutilier and Alexander Ferrer. At Polity Press, I am very grateful for the support and encouragement of John Thompson.

I am greatly indebted to the friends, colleagues, students, and family members who discussed the project with me and commented on drafts at various stages. I am especially grateful to Wisam Alshaibi, Ben Brubaker, my sister Elizabeth Brubaker, Liana Grancea, Paul Starr, and Ori Schwarz for their detailed and illuminating comments, substantive and stylistic, on the entire manuscript; to Loïc Wacquant for characteristically sharp comments on two chapters; and to Sherry Turkle for valuable advice on the overall shape of the project. For helpful comments and encouragement I would like to thank Julia Adams, John Bowen, Sarah Boxer, Daniel Brubaker, Michael Cullina, Mitch Duneier, Jacob Foster, Pablo Geraldo, Bill Heffernan, Michael Ignatieff, Christian Joppke, Jaeeun Kim, Gail Kligman, John Laffey, Rebecca Lin, Richard Owens, Katya Rice, Juliane Vogel, Steve Wasserman, Andreas Wimmer, and Kaiting Zhou. Thanks also to Harry Cooper for suggesting the cover image by I. Rice Pereira.

After settling on my title, I discovered that it closely echoes a section heading ("Connectivity and Its Discontents") in Sherry Turkle's 2011 book *Alone Together: Why We Expect More from Technology and Less from Each Other*. Since I had read *Alone Together* years earlier, it's quite likely that I picked up the phrase on that initial reading (though I was also drawn to the title by my longstanding interest in Freud's *Civilization and*

Its Discontents). When I mentioned the echo to Turkle, she noted that she had also published a book I did not know called *Simulation and Its Discontents*. So the echo is a double one.

An earlier version of chapter 1 was published as "Digital Hyperconnectivity and the Self" in *Theory and Society* 49, nos. 5–6 (2020): 771–801.

Introduction

Digital hyperconnectivity is a defining fact of our time. The Silicon Valley dream of universal connection – the dream of connecting everyone and everything to everyone and everything else, everywhere and all the time – is rapidly becoming a reality. We are connected not only to (almost) everybody else and to an infinite universe of digital content, but also to an ever-denser network of material things. We inhabit not simply the Internet of Things, but the Internet of Everything.

All aspects of everyday experience have come to be mediated by connected devices and connective platforms: our social relationships, from the most casual to the most intimate; our forms of work and play; our ways of knowing the world, knowing others, and knowing ourselves; our experience of space and time; our practices of caring for our bodies, entertaining ourselves, and regulating our moods; our embodied habits and physiological rhythms; our commercial transactions; our inter-actions with things in our homes; and our engagement with cultural content of all kinds, from the merest ephemera to the most enduring fruits of human creativity. And the pandemic has dramatically intensified the digital mediation of everyday experience.

As more and more of our routine daily activities migrate onto digital platforms, they leave superabundant traces and imprints. These imprints are harvested, assembled, organized, and converted into data that can be commodified, exchanged, and aggregated into databases on hitherto unimaginable scales. Individually, the digital traces are worthless "data exhaust"; but integrated in databases and analyzed through cutting-edge computational techniques, the exhaust can be converted into gold.[1] This computational alchemy depends on connecting everything – even the most apparently trivial bits of digital detritus – to everything else. It has made data extraction and data-based surveillance central to social, cultural, economic, and political life; it has powerfully stimulated the development of machine learning and artificial intelligence; and it has

1

generated new modes of algorithmic governance that guide an ever-widening array of consequential decisions – and sometimes make such decisions without any human intervention at all.

Underlying and enabling both our experience of apparently immaterial, frictionless hyperconnectivity and the extraction, analysis, and valorization of digital data is a vast though largely invisible material substrate. This extraordinarily dense and sophisticated material infrastructure comprises the networks of interconnected routes – the fiber-optic freeways and last-mile local routes – along which an ever-growing volume of digital traffic travels; the ancillary machinery – the cell towers, the routers, the exchanges where the great networks meet – that keeps the traffic moving; the protocols that make sure the traffic gets to its destination; the enormous energy-hogging data centers that belie the ethereal imagery of "the cloud"; the vast array of connected end-user devices; and the hundreds of billions of networked sensors and tiny tracking and identifying tags that are embedded in our everyday objects and environments.[2]

In these experiential, data-extractive, and material dimensions – but also in its cultural, economic, legal, and political dimensions – digital hyperconnectivity is what anthropologist Marcel Mauss, writing about gift exchange in archaic societies, called a "total social fact," at once a legal, moral, political, domestic, religious, economic, aesthetic, and social structural phenomenon. Hyperconnectivity similarly "involve[s] the totality of society and its institutions."[3] It has colonized the self, reorganizing our attention and reshaping our ways of thinking, seeing, and feeling. It has recast social interactions, stretching them over space and time and channeling them into platform-friendly, surveillance-enhancing forms and formats. It has converted the whole of human culture into an unending stream of digital content, served to us by personalized algorithms. It has revolutionized economic life, giving birth to gigantic oligopolies with unprecedented power over our future. It has upended politics, fragmenting the public sphere; polarizing – and in some ways paralyzing – the citizenry; and strengthening populist challenges to mediating institutions.[4]

Hyperconnectivity and Its Discontents develops an interpretive account of these pervasive and unsettling changes, all of which have dramatically accelerated during the pandemic. The book casts a broad net, addressing transformations of selves, social interactions, culture, economics, and politics. I seek to illuminate the everyday experience of hyperconnectivity in each of these domains through the structural analysis of its underlying dynamics. I aim in this way to grasp hyperconnectivity as a total social fact that is central to late modernity.

* * *

Digital hyperconnectivity is a relatively new phenomenon. Large-scale digital connectivity goes back several decades: the explosive growth in internet use dates from the introduction of the first Web browser in 1993. (Electronic connectivity of course has a much longer history, dating from the mid-nineteenth century development of the telegraph.) But digital *hyper*connectivity, as I understand it, emerged only during the first half of the 2010s. In the space of just a few years, smartphone use and anywhere-anytime connectivity became nearly universal in the developed world. In the US, for example, the share of the population over age 14 with a smartphone soared from a mere 11 percent at the end of 2008 to 75 percent just six years later. This is also when social media use became widespread and normatively expected. Regular Facebook users amounted to only 14 percent of the US population at the end of 2008, but just three years later they made up more than half of the population (and a much higher fraction among younger people).[5] The extraction, aggregation, and monetization of vast troves of data from the traces of our digitally mediated activities; the great leaps in machine learning and artificial intelligence, trained on these immense data sets; the hypertrophy of digital surveillance; the development of cloud computing and high-speed mobile broadband infrastructure; the pervasive use of algorithmic sorting to govern what content we see online: these are all likewise relatively recent developments, emerging only in the new millennium and acquiring critical mass more recently still.

These transformations are not simply recent; they are ongoing. They are both deepening, as hyperconnectivity intensifies, and broadening, as it infiltrates new domains of life. Hyperconnectivity is a dynamic unfolding, not a static condition.[6] The fifth generation (5G) mobile networks presently being deployed, for example, afford much greater bandwidth, higher speeds, and lower latency than their 4G predecessors (themselves introduced to support mobile broadband only a decade earlier); they will greatly enhance augmented and virtual reality capabilities, central to emerging visions of the "metaverse." The self-expanding, self-transforming dynamism of hyperconnectivity became conspicuously visible during the pandemic, when the "great confinement" gave a massive impetus to the further digitalization of everything and anxieties about contagion accelerated the development and marketing of touchless technologies for a contactless future.[7]

What does the "hyper" in hyperconnectivity mean? When we think of digital hyperconnectivity, we are likely to think first of connections between people. The scale of such connectivity is indeed staggering. Facebook alone connects nearly 3 billion monthly active users, WhatsApp and Instagram over 2 billion each, Messenger 1.3 billion. (Many people of course use more than one of these apps, all owned by Meta.) YouTube has 2 billion users. China's WeChat has 1.25 billion, while TikTok, founded only in 2016, had already accumulated a billion by 2021, almost all of them since 2018. A billion – a thousand million – is a very large number. Obviously most people on these social media platforms have only relatively small numbers of friends or followers, and most use messaging platforms to communicate only with small numbers of others. But the immense scale of platform-mediated connectivity matters. Because social media connect not only close friends and family (what sociologists call strong ties) but wider circles of acquaintances (weak ties), and still wider circles of followers (nonreciprocal digital-only ties), content of all kinds – news, gossip, bits of culture, rumors, or misinformation – can spread very quickly to enormous numbers of people. Weak ties and ties of followership tend to branch out much more widely than strong ties, which tend to cluster around a cohesive core. Weak ties create links *between* different communities and networks; strong ties solidify relationships *within* communities and networks. Platform-mediated weak ties thus provide a social structural foundation for the viral diffusion of digital content, altering the dynamics of culture, politics, marketing, and amusement.

People are connected not only to other people. They are connected to organizations (social, political, religious, commercial, educational, medical, financial, and so on). They are connected to their "always-on, always-on-them" devices, which require continuous though largely habitual background attention.[8] They are connected to a densifying network of things in their environment. And they are connected to a dynamically updated infinity of digital content: information, news, commentary, games, music, video, entertainment, discussions about every imaginable topic, and the entire universe of human culture in the widest sense.

An increasing share of digital connectivity, however, does not directly involve people at all: it involves connections between things, operating through various forms of "machine to machine" communication. Such connections will proliferate even more rapidly under emerging 5G networks, which will support vastly greater numbers and densities of sensor-embedded devices. The consumer-facing "internet of things," with its connected wearables, thermostats, security systems, lighting systems, and other "smart home" appliances, offers the most familiar examples. But the "industrial internet of things," enabled by miniaturized sensors and uniquely identified RFID tags, is more profoundly transformative; it furthers the automation of production by allowing components and machines to communicate with one another without the mediation of a human operator.[9] Mobile payment systems, automated access to buildings or transit, automated inventory systems, and automated toll roads likewise depend on RFID tags. And wireless sensor networks are used for environmental, infrastructural, agricultural, medical, industrial, and military monitoring.

The "hyper" in hyperconnectivity is not only about the who and what of connectivity; it's also about the where and when. Anywhere-anytime connectivity has eroded the boundaries between previously distinct spheres of life, which used to have their own times and places. Yet in the future envisioned for us by Silicon Valley, connectivity is not just anywhere and any time; it is everywhere and always. Rearticulating Mark Weiser's early vision of "ubiquitous computing," current tech discourse on smart technologies sees connectivity and computing as becoming "ambient," inscribed in and distributed throughout the environment rather than concentrated in focal devices like smartphones.[10]

In their planetary scale and scope, widely ramifying pervasiveness, and dizzying speed, the transformations occasioned by digital hyperconnectivity exceed those set in motion by earlier revolutions in media and communication technology. The consequences of the invention and diffusion of print were certainly as pervasive, and they may have been more profound, but they took centuries to unfold. The telegraph and telephone eclipsed distance and knit the world together as never before, but these networks remained bound to particular places for a century and a half.[11] Television transformed everyday experience, culture, and politics, but digital hyperconnectivity has done the same, while at the same time penetrating more deeply into the organization of the self, fundamentally reorganizing modalities of social interaction, altering the basic structures of the economy, and engendering new modalities of algorithmic governance.

The revolution in digital connectivity has built on and subsumed previous media and communication revolutions, digitalizing and remediating existing media forms and combining print, photography, recorded sound, film, telegraph, telephone, radio, television, gaming, and computing into a single digitally networked omnimedia ecosystem.[12] This has enabled digital hyperconnectivity to develop into a kind of universal infrastructure of contemporary life, an infrastructure of communication, sociability, knowledge, culture, entertainment, news, politics, commerce, governance, and more. Telegraph, telephone, radio, and television, and before them the postal system: all these have been profoundly important infrastructures of communication. But the extraordinary pluripotentiality of the internet has made digital hyper-connectivity *meta-infrastructural*: it is an infrastructure on which almost all other sociotechnical infrastructures depend, including for example financial, industrial, and transportation infrastructures as well as utilities. It is this deeply infrastructural quality that gives hyperconnectivity its pervasive reach and transformative power.[13]

To emphasize the transformative power and permeative presence of hyperconnectivity – the ways in which it is ever more densely and intricately woven into every aspect of social life – is not to adopt a technologically determinist stance. My claim that hyperconnectivity has restructured all major domains of social life might seem to suggest otherwise. But this and similar highly abbreviated formulations are simply expository shortcuts, to which I resort so as to avoid cumbersome circumlocution. They stand in for more nuanced analyses. Digital hyperconnectivity is not a "thing"; it is not a "force"; it does not directly cause things to happen. It is an environment, a terrain, an ecology of communication;[14] a web of humans, machines, protocols, practices, and data; a complex sociotechnical assemblage comprising communication networks, computational procedures, material artifacts, social practices, embodied habits, organizational forms, economic incentives, and legal frameworks.[15] Networked digital technologies do not determine the uses we make of them, though they do have certain "affordances" that open up new possibilities and foreclose others, making some actions easier, others more difficult.[16] The social transformations set in motion by digital hyperconnectivity are not preordained by the nature of networked digital technologies themselves; they emerge rather from the ways in which these technologies and the practices that grow up around them are culturally understood, socially organized, legally regulated, and politically contested.[17]

I analyze these transformations in five domains, beginning with the experience-near territories of the self and social interaction and moving on to consider culture, economics, and politics. Chapter 1 addresses transformations of the self. I begin by reconsidering and reformulating early arguments about the Web as a medium of exploring and experimenting with the self and emancipating the self from social constraints. I then analyze the new modes of knowing and acting on the self that have emerged in an ecology of digital hyperconnectivity. These include new ways of seeing the self as an object, knowing the self through numbers, producing a digital self for others' consumption, and regulating mood and emotion. I conclude by analyzing the tension between reflexively governing oneself and being governed by sociotechnical systems. While hyperconnectivity has provided new resources for the late modern project of reflexive self-formation, it has also drawn the self into the service of opaque sociotechnical systems that objectify, quantify, produce, regulate, and govern the self from the outside.

Chapter 2 addresses social interactions. I show how digital hyperconnectivity – radicalizing changes introduced by earlier forms of electronically mediated communication – recasts the spatial and temporal frameworks of interaction, weaving the there and then into the here and now in new ways. I trace the proliferation of new forms of micro-sociality and their attendant micro-obligations, in both personal and professional contexts. I analyze the new regime of visibility and the new possibilities for (and conflicts over) the surveillance of friends, partners, and family members. And I consider the new forms of "platformed sociality" that format, channel, and manipulate social interaction, creating new forms of action (such as liking, friending, sharing, and following), steering us toward these actions, habituating us to the gratifications they provide, and inculcating in us the skills and dispositions the platforms need to grow and thrive. A brief coda addresses the accelerated shift towards disembodied interaction and contactless commerce during the pandemic.

Chapter 3 considers three hopeful claims commonly made about the cultural promise of digital hyperconnectivity. The promise of plenitude envisions instant, frictionless access to the entire cultural wealth of humanity. The promise of decommodification envisions the freeing of the production and consumption of culture from market constraints. The promise of democratization envisions broader, more active, and more self-directed popular participation in the production, circulation, and consumption of cultural goods. This threefold promise has been realized in certain respects. But it requires critical scrutiny. The digital cultural cornucopia, while exhilarating, has a flattening and homogenizing effect: culture is converted into "content" that tends to blur together as it flows through the same conduits and across the same interfaces in an endless stream. Many cultural goods have been made freely available, but the more far-reaching promise of decommodified cultural production remains largely unrealized: amateur cultural creativity is increasingly organized and mediated by commercial platforms, and users (even those who do not seek to monetize their content) are drawn into the competitive dynamics of the attention economy. New avenues of popular cultural participation have certainly opened up, and the power of gatekeepers has dramatically eroded, but cultural power remains extraordinarily concentrated, and winner-take-all (or winner-take-most) logics remain entrenched.

Chapter 4 addresses the emergence of the digital platform as a novel and increasingly dominant economic and organizational form, one that has reorganized sector after sector of social life including culture, entertainment, commerce, education, lodging, transportation, manufacturing, finance, medicine, journalism, public discussion, dating, and social interaction. I show how platforms function as rapidly scalable digital intermediaries, facilitating and coordinating frictionless interactions and transactions through carefully designed architectures of interaction and the extraction, control, and analysis of data. I argue that the power of the core platforms differs not just quantitatively but qualitatively from that of other platforms in entailing concentrated control over an array of infrastructural resources that have become indispensable for economic, social, cultural, and political life. I analyze the platform-driven changes in the ways in which digitally mediated labor is organized, carried out, and controlled. I conclude by considering the new techno-utopian vision of a radically decentralized economy built on blockchain technology.

Chapter 5 examines how hyperconnectivity has reshaped political life by transforming ways of knowing, ways of feeling, and ways of governing. It has altered ways of knowing the public world by proliferating channels of public discussion, weakening the authority of institutions that produce and disseminate knowledge, sowing suspicion about public knowledge claims, and eroding the foundations of a shared public world. Hyperconnectivity has altered regimes of public feeling by encouraging the expression and mobilization of moral outrage and thereby deepening partisan antipathy and polarization. And it has altered ways of governing by enabling new modalities of algorithmic regulation, public and private. The chapter concludes by highlighting the tension between the technocratic premises and modalities of algorithmic governance and the populist regimes of digitally mediated knowing and feeling.

The Conclusion shows how hyperconnectivity prepared us for the pandemic and how the pandemic, in turn, powerfully accelerated the digital mediation of every aspect of life, in ways that have not been and will not be reversed. It also reflects more broadly on the significance of digital hyperconnectivity. Taking as points of reference three dystopian visions – two mid-twentieth-century works of fiction and a recent work of social science – I consider how hyperconnectivity has enhanced technologies of control, technologies of distraction, and technologies of manipulation, all premised on the extraction and analysis of data, that is, on surveillance. In so doing, hyperconnectivity has empowered organizations to a much greater extent than individuals, and it has fostered the recentralization and reconcentration of power, reversing the decentralization and dispersion of power in the early years of the internet.

* * *

Cutting across the substantive chapters and linking them to one another are five themes to which I pay special attention throughout the book:

abundance, miniaturization, convenience, quantification, and discipline. These are not the only transverse themes that run through these pages; others include surveillance, data and datafication, algorithms, and platforms. But I want to sketch the contours of these five themes here, for they have been much less widely discussed.

Digital hyperconnectivity confronts us with promises and problems of abundance. Social theory, as Andrew Abbott has argued, has long been organized primarily around presumptions of scarcity.[18] Visions of technologically enabled material abundance, to be sure, have long been commonplace, and theorizations of new forms of post-scarcity politics have been circulating for half a century.[19] Yet abundance – and its normative cousin, excess – remains peripheral to social theory.

Digitally mediated abundance pervasively colors our everyday experience of the world. Observers had already called attention to information overload, communicative abundance, mediated experience, and the saturated self in the last decades of the twentieth century.[20] But anywhere-anytime access to everyone and everything has greatly intensified these forms of abundance. In the sphere of social relationships, we experience abundance in the ceaseless flow of messages on multiple channels; in the multiplication of friends and followers on social media platforms; in the unlimited supply of potential partners when we are dating; and in the proliferation of hyper-accessible visual material on social media showing us – and not just telling us about – the lives of others, in relation to which our own lives may seem pallid and unsatisfactory. The abundance of social information about our peers and about other social worlds situates our own experience and our sense of ourselves in a relentlessly comparative frame. The digitally mediated vistas of unlimited possibilities and alternative ways of life unsettle the here and now and heighten our sense of the provisional: the sense, already central to the experience of late modernity, that things could be otherwise.[21] What might be casts a perpetual shadow over what is.

Most strikingly, we encounter abundance in the infinity of digital content that is never more than a few clicks away.[22] Spotify hosts some 80 million songs, YouTube some 40 million channels, TikTok uncounted billions of videos. The infinite scroll is a key design feature of many social media feeds. We may revel in this exhilarating cornucopia, but we may also feel disoriented, adrift in a vast, flat, and featureless sea. It is not only that we may face the "paradox of choice": that an increased range of choice may decrease satisfaction.[23] It is also that abundance may erode value and meaning. The superabundance of digital memory artifacts, as Michael Sacasas has observed, "will not make us care more about those memories, they will make us care less."[24] The superabundance of music to stream, similarly, may undermine rather than stimulate desire.[25] And the superabundance of news, during times of crisis, makes it all too easy to engage in "doomscrolling."[26]

The abundance of digital goods – a consequence of the near-zero marginal cost of reproducing and distributing them – seemed to some observers to suspend the basic laws of economics, premised on scarcity. Business models of entire sectors – notably journalism and music – were rendered unviable. Giving things away for free became a key strategy for platform businesses seeking to scale quickly and benefit from network effects. Yet abundance creates its own scarcities. As Herbert Simon famously observed a half-century ago, "a wealth of information creates a poverty of attention."[27] The scarcity of the time and attention needed to process, consume, or even notice superabundant information and digital goods is at the core not only of the "attention economy" but also of what could be called the "attention polity." In every domain, there is too much information, too much culture, and too much communication chasing too little attention and too little time. This generates a fierce competition for attention and visibility in the social, cultural, and political fields as well as the economic sphere. It leaves us feeling chronically short of time and keenly aware of what we are missing. FOMO – the fear of missing out – is not a peculiarity of teenagers who spend too much time on social media; it is the inescapable condition of our time.

The abundance of information and communication has been central to the democratizing promise of digital connectivity. But today that promise seems hopelessly naïve. A cacophonous glut of information and pseudo-information, of claims and counter-claims, clogs the digital public sphere and generates a crisis of public knowledge.[28] Cast in the form of machine-analyzable data, however, superabundant information – including the staggering volume of digital traces generated as a byproduct of all digitally mediated activity – underwrites powerful new forms of knowledge and indeed transforms "what counts as knowledge."[29] Superabundant data have been central to advances in machine learning, to the emergence of the digital platform as a dominant economic form, and to ubiquitous and unprecedentedly powerful forms of governmental and commercial surveillance. The contrast between what is known *by* the public in the fractured public sphere and what is known *about* the public in the age of superabundant data and machine learning is striking.[30]

Miniaturization, my second crosscutting theme, is in some ways the flip side of abundance: digital objects and actions proliferate in part through their fragmentation. Insofar as the literature has been concerned with scale, it has focused on things getting bigger: big data, the rapid scalability of digital platforms, network effects that favor enormous size, and the immense power and global reach of the tech giants. But hyper-connectivity also makes things smaller. There is of course a large literature on nanotechnology and other aspects of *technical* miniaturization. But *social* miniaturization – the rearticulation of objects and activities into decomposable and recomposable bits – has been neglected.[31]

Among the affordances of digital objects and digitally mediated activities are their limitless divisibility, easy manipulability, and frictionless distributability. These affordances enable unbundling: items that were previously bound together in packages – newspapers, magazines, books, encyclopedias, record albums, jobs, or college degree programs – now circulate as individual articles, chapters, entries, songs, tasks, or courses. And these individual digital items can be further broken down into fragmentary bits, clips, and extracts that themselves circulate individually (often in remixed or at least recontextualized form). Miniature forms and formats such as memes, tweets, and TikToks gain cultural prominence, while micro-communication and micro-affirmations – the ultra-minimal text, the self-standing emoji, the "like" – proliferate on messaging and social media platforms. Microtask labor platforms allow firms to farm out tasks paying as little as a few cents each. "Micro-learning" initiatives serve up "byte-sized" educational content. Digital divisibility – along with the ease of switching between digitally mediated activities and objects that are all accessed through the same device – allows bits and pieces of news, games, entertainment, sociability, and work to be slotted into even the smallest of interstices between other activities.[32] Miniaturization thus contributes to the fragmentation of time and attention and to ubiquitous multitasking; it establishes the glance as the dominant mode of attention.[33]

Miniaturization is central to the digital economy. Digital platforms are organizational technologies of disaggregation and reaggregation. By breaking down activities or tasks into small units and reducing transaction costs to a minimum, platforms enable and encourage what would otherwise be inefficiently small transactions.[34] This holds not only for the microtask platforms mentioned above or for micro-entrepreneurship platforms like Uber and Airbnb. It also holds for noncommercial digitally networked peer production, best exemplified by Wikipedia, which depends on modularity (breaking a project down into smaller modules) and granularity (allowing people to participate with minimal investments of time and energy).[35] Digital payment infrastructures, especially those developed by Alibaba and TenCent in China, reduce the transaction costs of payments and enable micro-tipping for digital content. Micro-transactions allow game developers and publishers to make money even from increasingly popular "free-to-play" games by encouraging players to make small in-game payments for various decorative or functional upgrades. New forms of "tokenization" and "fractionalization" allow small investors to own and trade bits and pieces of digital assets. More fundamentally, digital advertising infrastructures use automated nano-auctions to determine nearly instantaneously which users will be shown which ads when searching on Google or scrolling through the Facebook newsfeed.[36]

Miniaturization also shapes the modalities of politics, governance, and power. Micro-communication platforms like Twitter (and increasingly TikTok), on which shards and fragments of discourse circulate in an often decontextualized manner, have transformed the temporality and the grammar of public discourse and restructured the public sphere. New forms of digital micro-engagement like signing online petitions or joining digital shaming campaigns – derided by some as forms of "clicktivism" – have altered understandings and practices of political participation and transformed the repertoires and trajectories of social movements; they have enabled rapid mobilization but eroded organizational capacities for sustained action.[37] Political campaigns enlist paid nano-influencers – seen as more engaged with their followers than mega-influencers are – as a way of tapping into networks defined by trust and familiarity.[38] Data-driven micro-targeting has migrated from the realm of commercial to that of political advertising. And governance itself is rendered more granular through data-driven "modulations" and personalized "micronudges."[39]

Convenience, my third transverse theme, has likewise been undertheorized. And understandably so: convenience would seem to be a dull subject, at home perhaps in the province of marketing, but distant from the concerns of social theory. Yet the seeming triviality of convenience should not blind us to its power. Convenience resets expectations, forms habits, and insinuates its way into our routines. And these expectations, habits, and routines are unobtrusively but powerfully world-transforming. We may lament the consequences of Amazon's retail dominance, for example, but the immense convenience it has trained us to expect and desire keeps us coming back for more. Click by convenient click, repeated trillions of times, we have co-constructed the immensely powerful platforms that today organize so much of our lives.[40]

Convenience reduces friction: it enables us to do quickly and quasi-automatically what would otherwise require time, thought, and effort. In a world of baffling complexity and relentless temporal pressures – complexity and pressures intensified, ironically, by the dynamism of hyperconnectivity itself and the superabundance of digital culture and communication – convenience becomes a cultural touchstone and an economic imperative.[41] In this respect as in others, digital technology is called upon to alleviate the very problems that it has itself aggravated.

The gospel of digital convenience celebrates instantaneity and frictionlessness. Milliseconds matter: already at the turn of the millennium, Google discovered that the additional half-second it took to display twenty-five results rather than the standard ten in response to a search query caused traffic to fall by 20 percent after a month.[42] Clicks count (and are counted) as well: Amazon's celebrated one-click technology marked a first major milestone in seamless e-commerce. The pursuit of instantaneity and frictionlessness is self-reinforcing: the expectations of immediacy to which hyperconnectivity has accustomed us sensitize us to even the smallest delays, while expectations of seamlessness magnify the smallest frictions. Next-day or even same-day delivery has been redefined as slow by startups promising low-fee, no-minimum delivery within half an hour. Covid has accelerated the drive toward frictionlessness and instantaneity. Touchless payment systems and contactless delivery have become commonplace. Shuttered retail outlets have been transformed into micro-fulfillment centers for ultra-fast delivery. Staffing shortages have increased the frictions associated with in-person shopping, pushing even the reluctant to shop online.[43]

The shift from the churning, exhilarating chaos of the open web to the tamed, orderly "walled gardens" of apps and platforms – and the fortunes of the companies that built them – was founded largely on convenience. Apps and platforms offer us convenience above all else: seamless shopping, anytime-anywhere culture and entertainment, instant political participation, and push-button reactions. They remove friction from friendship, communication, creativity, knowledge, contracting, investing, and education. They promise to make the physical world as frictionless as the digital. As former Uber CEO Travis Kalanick put it, "In a world where technology can deliver the ride you need within five minutes wherever you are in the world, just imagine all the other goods and services that you could one day get delivered quickly, safely, with just the single touch of a button."[44]

But these are by now old forms of convenience. The new frontiers of convenience are defined by attempts to gauge our moods and anticipate our needs and desires before we are even aware of them. They are defined by attempts to automate and outsource routine actions and decisions – reordering supplies, greeting Facebook friends on their birthdays, replying to routine communications, arranging meetings, or selecting the right music for the moment.[45] They mark a shift from making it easier for us to do things to making it unnecessary for us to do them at all.

Hyperconnectivity seems to offer us "a world where everything is organized for [our] convenience"[46] – a world that would free us from mental as well as physical drudgery. But the celebration of convenience is informed by an impoverished vision of human nature and politics, and the costs of convenience have become increasingly clear.[47] Frictionlessness degrades the public sphere, creates massive cyber-security vulnerabilities, and displaces and invisibilizes labor as well as the "enormous global networks of extraction, logistics, manufacture, and transportation, along with sites of disposal, salvage, and waste" on which the experience of frictionlessness depends.[48] Yet convenience remains powerfully entrenched in app and platform logics, enshrined in prevailing discourses, and engrained in our habits and expectations.

Quantification, my fourth unifying theme, has received much more attention in social theory; it has been central in recent decades to accounts of economic, cultural, and political modernity.[49] But digital hyperconnectivity has ushered in a new phase of intensified and generalized quantification. It has opened up new domains of quantification, including the territories of the self, the sphere of social interaction, and the domain of amateur creativity. And it has made quantification in every domain more pervasive. Since digital mediation renders the world as data, more and more aspects of the world can be quantified, and they can be quantified in continuous and automatic rather than episodic and deliberate fashion. Hyperconnectivity, in short, has made quantification universal and ubiquitous. The "avalanche of printed numbers" that Ian Hacking discerned in the third and fourth decades of the nineteenth century is nothing compared to the deluge of digital numbers with which, and by which, we live.[50]

Digital platforms have created vast new infrastructures of datafication and quantification. These infrastructures enable the automatic capture, storage, and analysis of every aspect of platform-mediated activity. Following the lead of the platforms, organizations of all kinds, public and private, subscribe to a cultural and institutional "data imperative": they seek to collect and store as much data as they can, even when they have no clear idea how the data can be used. Data extraction and storage are so cheap – and the data imperative so firmly embedded in the prevailing ideology of "dataism" – that they become the default option, requiring no special justification.[51]

The superabundant data thus accumulated feed into both visible and invisible practices of quantification. Metrics have thoroughly colonized the spaces of digital social interaction. Every Facebook and Instagram post is publicly rated by the number of likes (and, in the case of Facebook, other "reactions") and comments it has generated; every tweet by the number of likes, retweets, and quote tweets; and every Twitter and Instagram user by the number of followers. These metrics do not simply record and describe interactional patterns; by offering "immediate, vivid, and quantified evaluations of … conversational success," they motivate, organize, regulate, and gamify interaction.[52] But scores, ratings, and rankings have become ubiquitous in every sphere of life, not just in social media. Generalized metrics of social value or trustworthiness integrate across a variety of domains and data traces.[53] Trending algorithms quantify, and amplify, currently popular items of culture, news, and entertainment.[54] Fine-grained, real-time metrics connect advertisers, politicians, musicians, entertainers, live streamers, bloggers, vloggers, and content creators of all kinds directly and immediately to their online audiences. The ubiquity of such metrics has reorganized journalism by substituting the economic logic of measureable and monetizable popularity for the professional logic of trained editorial judgment; this has severely eroded the "wall of separation" between business and editorial operations and transformed the public sphere in a populist direction.

The "quantified self" movement promises a new form of self-knowledge through numbers, based on data streams derived from sensor-enabled self-tracking. But we have all become quantified selves. Even if we have no interest in self-tracking, we are relentlessly tracked and quantified in the background by sociotechnical systems. Our tastes are known by algorithms that may (like that of TikTok) seem uncannily accurate. Our traits and attitudes are probabilistically inferable from our data traces, enabling us to be individually targeted by commercial or political advertisers.[55] Our behaviors are predicted by algorithms that engage in price discrimination, allocate welfare benefits, guide bail and sentencing decisions, and distribute enforcement resources accordingly.[56] Predictive algorithms are not new: algorithmically generated credit scores, which seek to predict the likelihood that a borrower will repay a loan, go back to the mid-twentieth century. But the vast troves of digital data on which algorithms can now be trained have driven rapid advances in machine learning and enabled the proliferation of much more sophisticated algorithms that have become central not only to commerce but to practices of governance, both public and private.

Discipline, my final crosscutting theme, has figured centrally in traditions of social theory inspired by Foucault and, to a lesser extent, Elias and Weber. But it has not been widely discussed in connection with hyperconnectivity (although its close cousin in the Foucauldian tradition, surveillance, has of course been a key theme). In the influential view of Gilles Deleuze, "disciplinary societies" as understood by Foucault, dependent on enclosed spaces like families, schools, barracks, factories, hospitals, and prisons, have been yielding since the middle of the twentieth century to "societies of control," dependent on a continuous series of flexible "modulations," mediated by information technology.[57] But this contrast has been too sharply drawn. Digital platforms are themselves spaces of enclosure; they have corralled sector after sector of social life within the ambit of their surveillant gaze and governing regimes.[58] And the "universal modulation" that Deleuze identifies as central to control can alternatively be interpreted as enabling new and ultimately deeper forms of discipline. No longer limited to enclosed physical spaces and their corresponding blocks of time, digital disciplines operate more flexibly and continuously throughout the social field.[59]

One might even think of digital hyperconnectivity as the socio-technical matrix of a new "disciplinary revolution." Connective digital technologies and platforms, like the disciplinary technologies of the early modern era studied by Philip Gorski, discipline from within as much as from without; they work *in* the self as much as *on* the self. They form our subjectivities, shaping how we think and how we feel as much as how we behave.[60] They draw us into their orbits, condition us to desire the gratifications they provide, and channel our interactions into the surveyable, calculable, and manipulable forms and formats provided by digital platforms. They form a powerful and versatile "infrastructure of governance."[61]

The augmented powers and new forms of surveillance enabled by digital hyperconnectivity – government surveillance, workplace surveillance, commercial surveillance, social surveillance, and self-surveillance – all have disciplinary workings. They all partake of the disciplinary logic of panopticism, according to which, in Foucault's celebrated analysis, the individual who is "subjected to a field of visibility … assumes responsibility for the constraints of power," "makes them play spontaneously upon himself," and "becomes the principle of his own subjection."[62] They engender social discipline through new forms of self-discipline, social control through new forms of self-control. They create tractable, docile, predictable, trustworthy, and governable citizens and consumers.[63]

But digital infrastructures also enable modes of discipline that operate not indirectly, through the shaping of subjectivities, as in Foucault's understanding of disciplinary power, but directly, through the shaping of behavior. The digital mediation of more and more of social life enables neo-behaviorist forms of governance by nudge and automated, self-enforcing forms of governance by algorithm. Conduct on digital platforms is fully controllable by those who design and operate the digital architecture. Platform owners, for example, can automatically prevent certain actions (such as certain forms of speech) or exclude certain participants (such as those whose rating falls below a certain threshold). Disciplinary power in this sense operates through "generative" rules, which cannot be violated, and which operate independently of the consciousness of those whose conduct they govern, rather than through the more familiar "regulative" rules, which can be violated, and which work through the consciousness of those they regulate.[64]

By intensifying and automating processes of discipline, digital infrastructures of governance make social life – or at least certain platform-enclosed zones of social life – more orderly, more predictable, and more governable. Such digitally mediated disciplinary powers are a boon for platform capitalism and for digital authoritarianism, but they pose new kinds of threats to human freedom and flourishing. This is a challenge with which we have barely begun to grapple.

CHAPTER ONE

Selves

Digital hyperconnectivity has profoundly transformed the self. It has retrained us, reshaped our dispositions, and altered the basic rhythms of our being in the world. It has inflected our emotions, modified our neurochemistry – and perhaps even rewired our brains. It has reorganized our experience of space and time. It has transformed how we think, feel, desire, remember, and attend to the world and to one another. It has brought us into intimate relations with ever-more powerful, ever-more seductive devices. It has created new ways of knowing and imagining the self, new ways of seeing and assessing the self, new ways of presenting and performing the self. It has changed how we think about the self – and how we act upon the self. Hyperconnectivity, in sum, has created new ways of constructing a self. But it has also created new ways of being constructed as a self from the outside: new ways of being configured, represented, and governed as a self by sociotechnical systems.

Several traditions of social theory offer useful starting points for analyzing these transformations of the self. One rich tradition, from Charles Horton Cooley and George Herbert Mead through Erving Goffman and beyond, understands the self as a thoroughly social phenomenon, formed and sustained in and through ongoing social interaction and performative enactment.[1] How has hyperconnectivity transformed these deeply social processes of self-formation? If we come to know the self – and indeed to form the self – by seeing it from the outside, from the point of view of others, how does digitally mediated interaction introduce new ways of seeing the self from the outside? How does the "looking glass self" posited by Cooley change when the mirror in which we see ourselves reflected is a digital one? What new possibilities for the presentation of self – and the performative enactment and production of the self – emerge in digital contexts? In what sense is the self not just a social but – increasingly – a sociotechnical phenomenon?

A second tradition, associated with Anthony Giddens, understands the self in the "post-traditional" social environment of late modernity as a "reflexive project," for which the individual must assume responsibility. This is a project that requires continuous self-monitoring, critical self-interrogation, and ongoing choices "not only about how to act but who to be."[2] How has hyperconnectivity transformed this project? In what ways has it heightened the reflexivity of late modernity by generating new tools for self-monitoring, new forms of self-knowledge, and new styles of self-entrepreneurship? In what ways, conversely, might hyperconnectivity diminish reflexive self-making by enmeshing us in sociotechnical systems that nudge, manipulate, and discipline us?

A third tradition, inspired by the late work of Michel Foucault, likewise emphasizes reflexivity and active work on the self but focuses less on choice and more on practices or "technologies" of the self, "which permit individuals to effect by their own means or with the help of others a certain number of operations on their own bodies and souls, thoughts, conduct, and way of being," as a way of transforming themselves.[3] What new "technologies of the self," and what new resources for the "care of the self," have emerged under digital hyperconnectivity? What is the relation between these new technologies of the self and the new technologies of power and domination that have been enabled by hyperconnectivity?

I approach these questions obliquely rather than directly. Rather than analyze theories of the self, I focus on practices of the self. "Practices of the self" is a phrase associated with Foucault, but I use the expression in a looser, more general sense, in accordance with the broad "turn to practice" in social theory in recent decades.[4] I begin by considering two early lines of argument about the Web as a medium for exploring and emancipating the self. These arguments were initially developed in the 1990s, well before the era of hyperconnectivity; their limitations soon became evident, but they can be reformulated in ways that speak to the present. Subsequent sections show how hyperconnectivity has engendered new ways of objectifying, quantifying, producing, and regulating the self – considered both as *active, reflexive practices* and as *systemic, data- and algorithm-driven processes*. I conclude by reflecting on the broader implications of contemporary modes of governing the self and by underscoring how hyperconnectivity has colonized the territories of the self, conscripting the self into the service of techno-social systems.

Hyperconnectivity has transformed the self in complex and ambivalent ways. I want to resist the lure of a simple narrative of decline: a story of the betrayal of the heady liberatory promises of the early days of the Web. The themes of exploration and emancipation remain as pertinent today as they were a quarter century ago, though they are themselves complex and ambivalent. And the new practices of objectifying, quantifying, producing, regulating, and governing the self are likewise complex and ambivalent: they can be construed in ways that highlight the active, reflexive moment or the systemic, cybernetic, disciplinary moment. I seek to remain sensitive throughout to this complexity and ambivalence.

Exploring the self

Digital connectivity has been seen – and celebrated – by some theorists as having enlarged the space of possibilities for selfhood. It has been characterized as conducive to exploring and experimenting with the self and to emancipating the self from social constraints. In both respects connectivity has been understood as an empowering – or at least an expansive – ecology and technology of selfhood.

The themes of exploration and experimentation were first articulated a quarter century ago in discussions of virtual communities, chat rooms, and online role-playing games. In Sherry Turkle's influential account, the mutual anonymity characteristic of these contexts allows people to adopt and enact digital personas of their own choosing, to "express multiple and often unexplored aspects of the self, to play with their identity and to try out new ones." They can present and sustain their chosen selves – and those selves can be recognized and validated by others – without being constrained by the bodies they inhabit, the histories they incarnate, or the selves they enact offline. For avid participants, the interactional density of such virtual worlds can make them feel "more real than … real life."[5]

The selves enacted in such anonymous online contexts relate variously to offline selves. Some participants explore parts of their selves that are seldom or never expressed in "real life." Some present idealized versions of their offline selves. Some experiment with new identities – new gender or sexual identities, for example – as a way of gaining experience and confidence before coming out in real life. Some play with multiple online identities that may have little or no relation to offline selves.[6]

Writing in the mid-1990s, Turkle gave particular attention to participants who cycled through multiple online personas, thereby sustaining several selves in parallel. This "cycling-through," on Turkle's account, was emblematic of a broader postmodern experience of self. Participants in multiple virtual worlds were "pioneers" whose "experience of constructing selves in cyberspace will become increasingly important" in a postmodern "culture of simulation" in which identity is "multiple, heterogeneous, and fragmented."[7]

Later critics have challenged the extrapolation from the experience of such pioneers to the broader online experience. They have noted that role-playing gamers – disproportionately young, educated, technically sophisticated males – are not representative of the general online population. And role-playing games and virtual communities – though still an important niche for self-exploration – have become a much smaller part of the vast cosmos of online life.[8] More fundamentally, while anonymity remains important to certain forms of online activity, the entire ecosystem of digital hyperconnectivity turns increasingly on a sophisticated infrastructure of identification. For most people, the online self is an extension of the offline self, not an alternative to it.

Yet even if experimentation and play with multiple virtual identities in contexts of mutual anonymity are less representative of online activity than they were in the 1990s, the Web is more than ever an expansive space of self-exploration and self-formation – and not just for participants in virtual worlds, but for everyone. Surfing, searching, and lurking allow people to discover, explore, and find social support for a wide range of ways of being other than those available and approved in their immediate family and social environment.[9] But hyperconnectivity not only enables the self to venture out virtually into the world; it brings the world into the self. If earlier forms of media, television in particular, had generated a "saturated self," the web/social media/smartphone complex has generated a hyper-saturated self, inundating the self in a ceaseless and superabundant flow of "mediated experience" and "populating ... the self [with] multiple and disparate potentials for being."[10]

Hyperconnectivity furnishes all of us – not only those who are self-consciously exploring alternative ways of being – with an inexhaustible storehouse of "possible selves," which Hazel Markus and Paula Nurius define as "individuals' ideas of who they might become, what they would like to become, and what they are afraid of becoming." Possible selves often emerge directly from processes of social comparison: "what others are now, I could become."[11] By multiplying the occasions for social comparison, hyperconnectivity – and social media in particular – vastly enlarges the set of possible selves. This can be experienced as enriching, as widening the horizon of possible ways of being. But it can also be experienced as deeply unsettling. It may create a "virtual cacophony of potentials": as we incorporate a diversifying set of others into the self, their disparate desires and ways of thinking become our own, pulling us in differing directions and providing us differing and conflicting criteria of self-evaluation.[12] Here as elsewhere we see the ambivalence of abundance, which enriches and enlarges the self but at the same time threatens to fragment, paralyze, or dissolve it.

Emancipating the self

Digital connectivity has been understood as a technology not only of exploration but, in a more celebratory mode, of emancipation. The theme of emancipation, like that of exploration, emerged first in connection with virtual communities and role-playing games. Cyberutopian accounts heralded emancipation from the fixities of the body and from social hierarchies based on differentially valued bodies. In a 1987 essay about The Well, the storied early virtual community founded by Stewart Brand and Larry Brilliant, Howard Rheingold wrote that "because we cannot see one another, we are unable to form prejudices about others before we read what they have to say: Race, gender, age, national origin and physical appearance are not apparent unless a person wants to make such characteristics public."[13] In most early role-playing games and chat rooms, to be sure, people did identify by gender – and were often required to do so. But the fact that the online identification was not anchored in or guaranteed by the offline body seemed to some commentators to have the potential to disrupt the gender order more broadly.[14] Race received less attention than gender. But an early essay by cultural theorist Lisa Nakamura argued that the practice of "perform[ing] [oneself] solely through writing" can "enable a thought-provoking detachment of race from the body" and call into question "the essentialness of race as a category"; it has "the power to turn the theatricality [of role-playing games] into a truly innovative form of play, rather than a tired reiteration and reinstatement of the old hierarchies."[15]

The early optimism about the possibilities of emancipation from hierarchies and inequalities grounded in differentiated bodies was short-lived.[16] Role-playing games turned out to be spaces where gender norms and hierarchies were more often reproduced – sometimes in exaggerated form – than transcended.[17] And as Nakamura herself emphasized, "the internet is a place where race happens": even in chat spaces, when "physical bodies are hidden from other users, race has a way of asserting its presence in the language users employ, in the kinds of identities they construct, and in the ways they depict themselves online, both through language and through graphic images."[18] This disenchantment set in long before hyperconnectivity became the perfect petri dish for breeding the racism and misogyny of the alt-right.

Yet if hyperconnectivity has failed to emancipate or uncouple the self from the body, it has nonetheless contributed powerfully – for better or worse – to emancipating the self from family and local community. While emancipation from the body is a postmodernist dream, emancipation from family and community is a core narrative of sociological modernity: the long-running story of the progressive erosion of familial and communal control over the means of socialization in an increasingly literate, mobile, urban, and media-saturated world. Digital hyperconnectivity accelerates and intensifies this long-term development.[19]

The emancipatory potential of hyperconnectivity can be seen most clearly from the perspective of those to whom it poses the most acute threat. It is no accident that conservative religious communities – communities that seek to maintain their boundaries and reproduce their traditions in a secular world and to shield their members from the corrosive influences of the environing society and culture – regard the unfiltered internet and smartphone as particularly dangerous. As anthropologist Ayala Fader has shown in her study of ultra-orthodox Jewish communities in New York, the threat is not just that dangerous material like pornography becomes hyper-accessible; it is more insidious and ultimately deeper.

The danger is partly cognitive: for a community that prizes focus and memory in the study of Torah, the loss of capacity for concentration, as one rabbi put it, is a bigger threat to the holiness of the Jewish nation "than all the shmuts [filth] on the Internet." It is partly affective: the seductive appeal of the smartphone disrupts the affective economy of the community. As the rabbi remarked, "Too many of us ... love their iPhones. If they weren't embarrassed they would kiss them." But perhaps the greatest danger is social: the opportunities hyperconnectivity affords the questioning, doubting individual, struggling with forbidden thoughts, to share doubts, questions, and struggles under the cloak of anonymity with like-minded others, instead of simply struggling privately with one's own shame. As the rabbi complained, an internet forum allows such a person to "instantly [feel] that he has a support group. There are other people there who feel like him. Er iz dortn a normaler mentsh [There, in the forum, he is a normal guy.]"[20]

As a private anywhere-anytime portal to the internet, the smartphone is an *individualizing* technology: it circumvents the dense network of communal surveillance that is so central to the reproduction of ultra-orthodox or other conservative religious communities.[21] Yet as the rabbi's remark suggests, the smartphone – and hyperconnectivity more generally – can also be a *collectivizing* technology: it facilitates the emergence of counter-publics and alternative communities. In the case studied by Fader, a counter-public coalesced around an inter-linked set of anonymous blogs written by doubters that gave voice to widely shared but previously unarticulated concerns in the ultra-orthodox community.[22] In both individualizing and collectivizing ways, hyperconnectivity works to emancipate the self from family and local community.

As a collectivizing technology, hyperconnectivity helps overcome what social psychologists call "pluralistic ignorance" – a situation in which people mistakenly believe that their own beliefs differ from those of everyone else in the community. The overcoming of pluralistic ignorance is central to the ways in which hyperconnectivity has transformed politics.[23] But it is also important to the social shaping of selves.

In situations of pluralistic ignorance, individuals who feel like misfits, outsiders, or deviants – such as those harboring doubts in ultra-orthodox communities – remain isolated in that feeling; they wrongly believe their own situations are unique. By revealing the existence of like-minded others and enabling low-risk, low-cost communication with them, hyperconnectivity overcomes pluralistic ignorance and its attendant social isolation. It provides social support for alternative definitions of the self and alternative understandings of community. Self-understandings that are unrecognized, medicalized, or stigmatized in family and local community settings can be publicly articulated, recognized, and validated online as legitimate forms of selfhood. What are experienced as privatized personal failings in the context of family or local community can be rearticulated and reclaimed as publicly legitimated ways of being. Hyperconnectivity is thus a powerful technology of self-recognition and self-validation that opens up alternative paths to the social formation of the self.

When we think of emancipation, we almost invariably think first of emancipation from the constraints of conservative family and community milieux. But digital connectivity also provides resources for escaping the constraints of liberal or progressive family, community, or institutional milieux. The digital precincts in which precursors of the alt-right emerged, for example – notably the anonymous image-based message board 4chan – can be understood as emancipatory in this purely descriptive sense. They too helped overcome pluralistic ignorance and provided social support for an alternative style of selfhood, centered on provocation, transgression, and trolling.[24]

The emancipatory potential – or threat – of hyperconnectivity stands out in sharpest relief in sociologically "extreme" cases like that of conservative religious communities. But hyperconnectivity contributes to the emancipation of the self in a much more general, pervasive, and mundane way. The possibilities it affords for "anonymous sociality, critique, and exploration" redistribute control over the means of socialization from family, community, and local institutions – whose once-comprehensive socializing powers have already been greatly attenuated in the cultural and social structural contexts of late modernity – to a variety of mediated networks and communities and to the "infosphere" in general.[25] This cannot help but have an emancipatory working – provided, once again, that one understands that term in a purely descriptive sense.

* * *

The lines of argument I have considered in this and the preceding section converge in extending a classical story of sociological modernity.[26] They see digital connectivity as furthering and intensifying the long-run process of disembedding individuals from the unchosen, obligatory communities into which they were born and re-embedding them in looser, less encompassing and binding networks and communities of their own choosing.[27] Through this disembedding and re-embedding, the self becomes, more than ever, a reflexive project for which the individual must take responsibility.

This updated and extended version of a familiar story of individualization is compelling in many respects. But it remains too classically individualist. It does not capture what is specific about the sociotechnical dimensions of self-formation in an ecology of hyperconnectivity. It does not take account of the ways we construct – or co-construct with others – digital versions of ourselves. It does not take account of ubiquitous mobile connectivity, big data, pervasive quantification, algorithmic selfhood, or the powerful sociotechnical ensembles we call social media platforms. It does not take account of the disciplining or colonizing of the self by those sociotechnical systems. The sections that follow address these novel aspects of self-formation.

Objectifying the self

In George Herbert Mead's rich and subtle account of the social formation of the self in and through social interaction, a key moment involves seeing oneself from the outside. This requires "taking the role of the other." Children learn to do so in rudimentary ways in play, in somewhat more complex ways in structured games, and in considerably more elaborate ways when they take the view not only of particular others but of what Mead called the "generalized other." It is by taking the role of the other that one becomes an object to oneself. Such self-objectification is the basis for self-consciousness, and it is central to the process of becoming a self.[28]

Mead's account of the social formation of the self remains foundational to social psychology and to the symbolic interactionist tradition in sociology. Yet even as the literature on objectification and self-objectification burgeoned in psychology and sociology, it sharply narrowed in focus. Objectification came to refer for the most part to the ways in which girls and women are seen, assessed, represented, and treated – by men, by the media, and ultimately by themselves – as actually or potentially sexualized objects. And self-objectification came to designate the process through which girls and women turn the objectifying gaze back on themselves, internalize its standards of appraisal, and come to understand, evaluate, and act on themselves and their bodies in accordance with those standards.

Hyperconnectivity has given massive new impetus to this sexualizing form of objectification and self-objectification. It has ubiquitized pornography; multiplied new forms of self-objectifying digital sexuality, both commercial and non-commercial; and created online dating interfaces that are premised on visual self-objectification, inviting the user to "swipe right" or "swipe left" to signal interest or the lack thereof in response to a photograph. And even as the sexualizing, objectifying gaze has become more promiscuous, no longer aimed exclusively at women by heterosexual men, it remains profoundly gendered in its effects on bodily self-image and feelings of self-worth.[29]

But hyperconnectivity is a technology of objectification and self-objectification in a deeper and more general sense. It has radically transformed how objects exist in the world and how one becomes an object to oneself, to others, and to suprahuman knowledge systems. In so doing, it has created an entirely new techno-social infrastructure of selfhood: an entirely new ecology within which selves are formed and reformed.[30]

Digital mediation multiplies new ways of constructing and experiencing the self as an object. Most obviously, we objectify ourselves when we deliberately construct social media profiles, when we take and circulate selfies, or when we post on social media. More subtly, we continuously objectify ourselves – without any awareness of doing so – in the routine course of our everyday lives. As life moves online, it leaves an ever-expanding trail of digital objects in its wake. Digitally mediated action and interaction are in this sense *intrinsically objectifying*.[31] Every text, every email, every click of our browsing history, every app-mediated action, every sensor-recorded data point, every action and interaction on social media, even the most trivial "like" or retweet, leaves digital residues, many of which persist as digital objects.[32] These make us visible to ourselves and others in new ways; they allow us to see ourselves and our actions from the outside, as objects.[33] (These digital traces also allow us to be constructed as objects by algorithms deployed by platforms in their efforts to know who we are and to affect how we behave. The digital residues used for these purposes, which dwarf those that we ourselves use, remain invisible to us. They are fed into vast and opaque systems of data aggregation and analysis that enable the algorithmic objectification of the self, a theme I return to in the next section.)

Verbal and visual practices of representing the self as an object are in no way new. Writing has long been recognized as an important medium of self-formation; it is among other things a way of objectifying the self and seeing the self from the outside. The diary, in particular, has been analyzed by historians as a powerful technique of "writing the self," as has the letter. And self-portraiture has a long history.[34] In an ecology of hyperconnectivity, however, self-objectification is democratized, routinized, and banalized; it becomes an unmarked and unremarked quotidian habit of the many, required by platform-mediated sociability and woven into the fabric of everyday life, rather than a marked and distinctive practice of the few. This chronically objectifying and self-objectifying nature of everyday digitally mediated social life profoundly shapes the contemporary experience of selfhood.

We routinely create objectified digital representations of the self, sometimes through deliberate, self-conscious self-work, sometimes unselfconsciously. Once these representations are in place, we can see the self from the outside, as an object. (Many platforms specifically allow users to view their digital selves from the outside, as others see them.) The digital self that we see is a composite object: it includes not only the digital self-representations and self-traces that *we* have created, deliberately or unselfconsciously, but also *others'* digitally mediated responses, which are durably conjoined with our self-representations. When we look in the digital mirror, we see not only an image of ourselves, but also an image of ourselves as others see us. We see ourselves in a double refraction: as we have constructed our own digital selves, and as others have co-constructed our digital selves through their enduringly objectified digital responses.

Taking the point of view of the other therefore does not require – as it does for Mead – an imaginative displacement or cognitive shift. The point of view of the other is already there, encoded in the digital self. We can directly inspect others' objectified responses to our digital selves: their comments, likes, favorites, retweets, and so on. Since platforms quantify these responses, it is not only the point of view of *particular* others that is encoded in the digital self; it is also the point of view of a *generalized* other. And unlike Mead's generalized other, the digital generalized other is a *quantified and quantifying other*; it renders the digital self as a string of numbers, attached both to the global digital self (numbers of friends, followers, and so on) and to its particular objectified manifestations (numbers of comments and likes on the material we post or share).

In a final step in digital self-objectification, we turn the gaze of the digital generalized other back on ourselves.[35] As the literature on sexual objectification specifies, we internalize the objectifying gaze of the other and come to evaluate ourselves and orient our actions in accordance with its standards of appraisal. But the internalized objectifying gaze falls not only on our bodies, and it is not specifically sexualizing; it extends to every manifestation of our digital being.

The internalization of the external gaze alters our experience of the world, offline as well as online. As curators of the ever-changing exhibition of the digital self, we are ever alert to what might have digital value – to what might be effectively shareable or postable – as measured by the standards of the digital generalized other.[36] By internalizing its objectifying gaze, we not only assess ourselves and our digital performances after the fact according to its standards; we also assess our prospective digital performances by *anticipating* the judgment of the quantified other.

Hyperconnectivity thus proliferates objectified representations of the self; it creates new ways of seeing ourselves from the point of view of others; and it generalizes, democratizes, routinizes, and quantifies self-objectification by holding up to us a ubiquitous digital mirror that turns the digital gaze back on ourselves. I turn now to a closer examination of quantification.

Quantifying the self

In 2010, Gary Wolf published a *New York Times* op-ed on "The Data-Driven Life," extolling the new possibilities for seeking "self-knowledge through numbers." This and an article in *Wired* the previous year have been seen as the founding statements of what has come to be known as the "quantified self movement," a movement that promises to overcome the "vagaries of intuition" in the name of the objectivity of data by privileging numbers over words, instrumentation over introspection, the measurable over the ineffable, real-time feedback over long-term exploration, and the surfaces of the body over the depths of the soul.[37]

But the "quantified self" is less a movement than a moment, less an ideological project than an everyday practice. The vanguard of enthusiasts who have participated in the quantified self "community" or "movement" is a small minority in relation to those who have been drawn in less self-conscious, less overtly experimental ways into practices of self-quantification.[38] The "quantified self" is often taken to evoke the vanguard. But I take it to evoke the broader sociocultural moment in which practices of knowing the self through numbers have become a routine and taken-for-granted part of everyday life, emerging as the "authorized way to pursue self-knowledge in the networked society."[39]

The past decade has seen the proliferation of self-tracking devices and apps that use sensors to record a wide range of both biometric and behavioral data and prompt users to log other data at regular intervals. Biometric data include pulse, respiration, steps taken, sleep patterns, alcohol concentration, glucose levels, galvanic skin response, even penile thrusts. Behavioral data include patterns of speed, acceleration, braking, and other driving data; frequency, duration, and quality of social interaction (measured by recording and analyzing speech); and patterns of device use (such as screen time, app use, and websites visited). User-supplied data include reports on feelings, pain, energy levels, activities, spending, and the consumption of food, vitamins, fluids, alcohol, caffeine, and drugs. Together, these data allow users to systematically monitor exercise, sleep, diet, sex, mood, productivity, and a variety of other dimensions of health and well-being, on the premise that the knowledge thus gained can be enlisted in the service of fitness, health, happiness, and productivity.[40]

Disciplined forms of self-monitoring are of course not new.[41] Regimens of systematic self-scrutiny have been central to various religious traditions – and to their secularized descendants. Benjamin Franklin famously developed a system for the "daily examination" of his conduct, employing a grid in which each column represented a day of the week and each row one of thirteen virtues and "marking every evening the faults of the day" by placing a black spot – or occasionally two spots – in every category in which he found his conduct wanting.[42] And it was already a century ago that the widespread availability of the bathroom scale made the tracking of weight a routine practice.[43]

The affordances of hyperconnectivity, however, have led to the proliferation of forms of quantitative self-tracking. Innovations in sensor technology have vastly expanded the range of bodily and behavioral processes that can be tracked conveniently, unobtrusively, and inexpensively. Ubiquitous, always-connected mobile devices and cloud computing allow user input whenever prompted and give users access to their data anywhere and any time. Apps convert qualitative into quantitative data, identify correlations, and generate convenient visualizations of trends and relationships. And built-in integration with social media platforms allows self-tracking data to be readily shared with others, thereby harnessing an additional, social layer of motivation, also evident in the "gamification" of self-tracking.[44]

A decade ago, quantified self-tracking was for enthusiasts; in the near future, it may be for everyone. Whatever its value to the individual, self-tracking data are potentially valuable to insurance companies (who can set rates for auto, health, or life insurance based on individualized rather than aggregate data and penalize those unwilling to share personal data); to employers (who can encourage or even require employees to use fitness-monitoring apps in an effort to improve productivity, reduce healthcare costs, or discipline workers);[45] and to retailers (who can use such data to target customers more effectively). Beyond their potential monetary value, tracking data are of increasing interest to schools, some of which require students to participate in health- or fitness-tracking programs (or at least make it difficult to opt out of them). Such "pushed" or "imposed" forms of self-tracking raise broader questions about surveillance creep, privacy, and autonomy.[46]

But the self is increasingly quantified in ways that go well beyond self-tracking. In an ecology of communication dominated by social media platforms, *all* selves become quantified selves, nourished on a steady diet of numbers.[47] Quantification is built into the basic architecture of the platforms. Not only are numbers of followers featured prominently on social media platforms, but all activity on platforms – comments, likes, shares, favorites, retweets, even simple views – is relentlessly quantified and fed back to the user in a string of numbers.[48] On Facebook, for example, every post (and even every comment on a post) is quantified – in a manner visible to the poster and to everyone else who sees the post – by the number of people who have "reacted" to it as well as the number who have shared or commented on it.[49] In 2021, responding to concerns about adolescents' mental health, Facebook and Instagram started allowing users to hide "like" counts on posts. The company considered removing "like" counts altogether, but decided against doing so after finding that some users, notably aspiring and established influencers, were deeply invested in these metrics.[50]

Quantification involves commensuration: the establishment of a common metric that converts *unlike qualities* into *differing quantities*.[51] Facebook's "like" button – introduced within the site in 2009 and made available to external websites in 2010 as a way of integrating external content with Facebook – is an instrument of commensuration on a vast scale. Its implementation on millions of external websites (and the adoption of similar buttons on other major platforms) created a universally recognized metric of popularity: in effect a form of social currency that powers the "like economy."[52]

The massive work of commensuration performed by Facebook and other social media platforms enables and invites comparison on a double axis. It facilitates comparison across our own performances: we cannot help being attuned, consciously or unconsciously, to which of our posts – which of our online performances of self – are comparatively successful and which fall flat. That chronic attunement reshapes our self-understandings and self-appraisals, leading us to alter our performances in order to engage more effectively with our audiences. Commensuration also facilitates comparison across people: the social media environment makes us chronically aware of how we measure up against others; it renders visible our comparative visibility – or invisibility. The social media existence is an existence-for-others; we exist only insofar as others engage with our digital selves. The relentlessly quantifying ecosystem of social media takes the measure of our digital selves and places that measure in an inexorably comparative – and implicitly competitive – frame.[53]

Numbers are not only a means of *knowing* the self; they are a means of *governing* the self. Social media metrics do not simply reflect the world; they alter our relation to the world. They are "an engine, not a camera," as Donald MacKenzie said of financial models.[54] Continuous quantification contributes to the gamification of interaction; it deepens our engagement with social media, spurring us to seek to improve our numbers.[55] No matter how good those numbers, they can always be better: as in the case of other positional goods, defined by relative rather than absolute value, abundance is always at the same time experienced as scarcity.[56] The quantified self is therefore a restless and insatiable self.

The numbers I have been discussing so far enter into our experience in conspicuously visible ways: prominently displayed by our self-tracking reports and social media feeds, the numbers are inescapable. But these numbers are only the tip of the iceberg. Our selves are quantified, just as consequentially, in opaque and invisible ways, through data-analytic and computational procedures that construct digital representations or "data doubles" of the self.[57] We are tracked and quantified by others – by sociotechnical systems – much more thoroughly and relentlessly than we could ever hope to track and quantify ourselves.

These digital representations are made of data, assembled from the ever-expanding digital trail we leave behind us.[58] Even without computational procedures, the data trail contains a wealth of stunningly detailed information about our lives, including for example increasingly precise and comprehensive geolocation data. But beyond this, the data support a wide range of probabilistic inferences about who we are and how we are likely to behave. These inferences touch on the most intimate aspects of the self: personality traits, emotional states, sexual orientation, and the like.[59] Increasingly powerful machine learning algorithms, trained on ever-larger and richer data sets, have dramatically increased the accuracy of these inferences. A 2018 paper, for example, showed that a facial recognition algorithm could accurately distinguish between gay and heterosexual men 81 percent of the time, based on a single facial image, or 91 percent of the time, based on five images per person.[60]

Knowing the self through numbers is therefore not only a *reflexive practice*, a way in which the self is known from within; it is a *computational process*, a way in which the self is known from without. The external, computational knowledge of the self includes many things that we have forgotten and other things that we have never known. The socio-technical systems that assemble the data and make inferences from these data may have a fuller and more accurate representation of us than we have of ourselves – though it is important to recognize that these inferences and the data on which they are based may be riddled with errors.[61]

Producing the self

Erving Goffman's classic work on the presentation and performative enactment of the self in social interaction has been a rich source of inspiration for work on the digital presentation and performance of the self. While retaining Goffman's dramaturgical perspective and drawing on many of his key concepts – the distinction between "front stage" and "back stage" regions, for example, and the distinction between deliberately "giving" and unintentionally "giving off" information – researchers have highlighted certain distinctive features of self-presentation in online contexts. They have emphasized how asynchronous text-based communication, for example, facilitates the self-conscious "editing" of one's self-presentation and even allows for collaborative forms of self-presentation that enlist the help of others in real time. They have noted that the absence of the body-behavioral cues available in face-to-face communication not only makes it harder to assess others' self-presentations, but also makes it harder to grasp how others see us. They have observed that the anonymity characteristic of some online forums can allow for greater intimacy and self-disclosure, but may also license extreme incivility. And they have underscored the difficulties of practicing what Goffman called "audience segregation" on social media sites that "flatten multiple audiences into one" and thereby generate "context collapse."[62]

But hyperconnectivity not only introduces new ways to *present* the self; it affords new opportunities – and diffuses more widely a sense of obligation – to *produce* the self. The idea of becoming an "entrepreneur of oneself," as Foucault put it, has long been central to neoliberalism.[63] And the cultural obligation to work on the self, to treat the self as a reflexive project, has a longer history still; it can be construed as central to modernity. But ideals of self-work and self-production have found a vast new field of application – and taken on a new inflection – in an ecology of communication dominated by social media platforms.

In the 1980s and 1990s, prevailing accounts of the enterprising self stressed the proactive acquisition of human capital and the continuous retraining of the self to conform to the needs of a flexibilized post-Fordist economy, with its dynamically evolving division of labor.[64] The value of the enterprising self, in this context, was measured in the labor market. In the landscape of digital hyperconnectivity, self-entrepreneurship comes to mean not only improving the *corporeal* self as a *factor of production*, adapted to competition in the labor market, but producing the *digital* self as an *object of consumption*, adapted to competition in the social media market. In this new context, the value of the enterprising self is measured by the size of its audience. The digital self is no longer simply indexical, pointing to the "real" self that it represents; it acquires a value and significance of its own as a self to be consumed by others as part of their ongoing stream of media consumption.[65] The digital self thus no longer simply *represents* the neoliberal "self of value"; it *becomes* a self of value in its own right.

The paradigmatic self-entrepreneur of the digital age, practiced in the arts of producing the self, is the figure of the social media "influencer" or lifestyle blogger.[66] The influencer is a person who has cultivated a large social media following not by virtue of preexisting celebrity status but by producing and enacting a digital self that succeeds in engaging – and being consumed by – his or (more often) her followers. This self-production often involves the display, discussion, and endorsement of commercial products, from which the successful influencer can derive perks, sponsorships, and, for the fortunate few, a significant income. Influencers are thus involved in promoting and selling two kinds of products: the products they *promote*, and the products they directly *produce* for the immediate consumption of their followers – their digital selves. They *acquire* their influence by producing and marketing themselves; the fortunate few can then *monetize* their influence by promoting others' products.[67]

Social media influencers are an instance of the more general phenomenon of digital celebrity. Hyperconnectivity democratizes and universalizes celebrity; it makes new forms of micro-celebrity seemingly accessible to all.[68] Anyone, it seems, can become "Facebook famous" or "Instafamous," if only for Warhol's proverbial fifteen minutes. Social media provide everyone with a quantifiable and potentially expandable audience. As media studies scholar Alice Marwick has emphasized, digital micro-celebrity is defined not by numbers of followers, but by a particular set of practices: an audience-oriented, self-publicizing way of thinking and acting. Micro-celebrity can thus be practiced by anyone, regardless of the size of their following; it "becomes the default pose for much social media."[69] We are all micro-celebrities now.

The obligation to produce a digital self suitable for others' consumption – and capable of engaging and sustaining their attention in a media-saturated landscape – places a premium on developing and expressing a distinctive digital identity, a distinctive "brand." The idea of self-branding was first popularized in the late 1990s, well before the emergence of social media.[70] But it thrives in the ecology of hyperconnectivity. The pervasive quantification of visibility and popularity, the sheer superabundance of consumable content, and the intensified competition for attention compel us all, in some measure, to individualize the digital self. Even those who would be appalled by the idea of self-branding experience a structural pressure to produce a distinctive digital self-for-others, on pain of invisibility.[71]

The self-branding, self-marketing, and self-production practices required of the enterprising self might seem to mark the apotheosis of a narrowly market-oriented and competitive utilitarian individualism. Yet this style of self-work draws at the same time on a more expansive ideal of expressive individualism and personal authenticity that has long been integrated into the circuits of consumerist capitalism and into neoliberal understandings of selfhood.[72] The effectiveness of influencer marketing and lifestyle blogging, for example, depends crucially on the influencers and bloggers being perceived as authentic. Aspiring influencers are therefore obliged to work hard at producing and performing authenticity. Yet precisely the evidence of such work can expose them to the charge of inauthenticity: performances of authenticity must be self-concealing to be effective.[73] There is no way out of this double bind of authenticity.

It is not only would-be influencers who find themselves cross-pressured by the ideals of individuality and authenticity. Social media are a gigantic engine of communication, a technology of communicative superabundance.[74] No matter how much we communicate, how much we share, how much we express ourselves, we are always prompted to communicate more. And we are expected to have something distinctive to say. Social media at once heighten the demand for individuality and authenticity and make them more difficult to achieve. This is partly because of the sheer superabundance of communication: in such a crowded communicative field, it's at once imperative and nearly impossible to be distinctive. Moreover, the materials at our disposal to produce and perform a distinctive self are entirely generic: the bits of objectified culture that we recirculate, the generic photos, the familiar moves and gestures, the standardized formats and prescribed sequences made available by social media platforms.[75] And lingering cultural understandings of the authentic self as unfiltered and unmediated cast chronic doubt on the authenticity of digital selves constructed through curatorial practices and through the mediation of sociotechnical systems. In these conditions, as social media theorist Rob Horning has observed, "'becoming oneself' has turned into a crappy job – a compulsory low-paying, low-skill job" that leaves people feeling chronically underappreciated and beset by doubts about their authenticity.[76]

In a context in which the cultural obligation to produce the self as a distinctive, authentic individual is difficult to fulfill, the burdensome work of individualizing the self is turned over increasingly to algorithms. The "personalization" that is promised on every front – in the domains of search, shopping, health, news, advertising, learning, music, and entertainment – depends on ever more refined algorithmic constructions of individuality.[77] As it becomes more difficult to produce our digital selves as unique individuals, we are increasingly being produced as unique individuals from the outside. Individuality is redefined from a cultural practice and reflexive project to an algorithmic process. Our unique selfhood is no longer something for which we are wholly responsible; it is algorithmically guaranteed.

Algorithmic individuality reflects back to us a version of ourselves constructed not from the way others see us – as in Cooley's understanding of the "looking glass self" – but from our own data: our past choices, our habits, our likes.[78] This establishes a second feedback loop, distinct from the loop described earlier in which we alter our own behavior in response to, and in anticipation of, others' digitally mediated responses to our performances. This new feedback loop connects us not to others' responses but to our past selves. The algorithms train themselves on our data; they then train us by feeding us more of what they determine we like. They help us to remain the selves that we have revealed ourselves to be. They map out a space of our own for us to inhabit and discourage us from leaving that comfortable algorithmic home.

The task of becoming and being a self in late modernity – whether the self-monitoring, self-authoring, reflexive self described by Giddens or the enterprising, choosing, psychologically aware, self-governing self analyzed in the broadly Foucauldian account of Nikolas Rose – has been portrayed in the literature as an arduous one. Outsourcing individuation to algorithms takes some of the pressure off this task; it allows us to settle into the snug fit of an algorithmically tailored self. Algorithmic individuality combines the comforts of familiarity and the pleasures of self-recognition with the convenience of automation, while relieving us of some of the burdens and stresses of choice.

Regulating the self

Hyperconnectivity has transformed not only how we come to know ourselves and work on ourselves, and how we present ourselves and produce ourselves, but also how we regulate ourselves. It affords new resources – and prompts the development of new practices – for shifting or modulating our moods, monitoring and managing bodily states and processes, altering energy levels, inducing pleasurable experiences, relaxing body and mind, providing solace, and producing feelings of belonging. It generates new ways of conceptualizing, measuring, and pursuing well-being and new ways of dealing – effectively or ineffectively – with stress, pain, anxiety, loneliness, insomnia, depression, anger, and other unwanted physiological and emotional states. Having discussed new forms of measuring and tracking bodily and mental processes under the heading of quantification, I turn here to new ways of intervening in and regulating these processes, focusing especially on the regulation of mood and emotion.

Music has long served as a medium of self-regulation in this sense. As Tia DeNora has shown, music is a powerful "technology of self": "an accomplice in attaining, enhancing and maintaining desired states of feeling and bodily energy (such as relaxation); ... a vehicle [for moving] out of dispreferred states (such as stress or fatigue) ... [and] a resource for modulating and structuring the parameters of aesthetic agency – feeling, motivation, desire, comportment, action style, energy." It gives people "a medium in which to work through moods."[79] DeNora's *Music in Everyday Life* appeared in 2000, two decades after the Walkman first popularized mobile sonic bubbles, but before hyperconnectivity revolutionized the experience of listening to music (the first MP3 players had recently come on the market). The importance of music as a technology of physiological and emotional self-regulation has only increased since then. And much of what DeNora has to say about music holds equally, mutatis mutandis, for audiovisual materials more generally.

Consider for example the large and enthusiastic community of YouTubers devoted to producing and sharing videos that can trigger an "autonomous sensory meridian response" (ASMR). The term refers to a pleasurable tingling sensation on the skin, accompanied by feelings of mild euphoria, relaxation, and well-being. ASMR videos generally involve whispered communication and other quiet sounds that invite attentive listening. They are often recorded with a binaural microphone and listened to with headphones, which creates an immersive experience of proximity. The video component, generally secondary to the audio, shows a single person, often in extreme close-up, and often performing a repetitive task or playing, slowly and deliberately, the role of someone offering a personal service like a haircut or a medical check-up. ASMR videos enact routines of personal care and create a distinctive kind of "distant intimacy."[80] Participants report using ASMR videos to help them relax and to deal with stress, anxiety, and insomnia; some find they temporarily alleviate depression and chronic pain.[81] The popularity of ASMR videos has sparked interest in their possible therapeutic use, though evidence of their efficacy remains fragmentary and anecdotal.

Whether or not ASMR eventually receives experimental validation, ASMR users have developed a novel form of self-regulation that is at once emblematic of and strikingly antithetical to the socio-emotional world of hyperconnectivity. On the one hand, the entire ASMR phenomenon depends on the affordances of Web 2.0 and, more specifically, on the culture and the infrastructure of video sharing platforms like YouTube and Reddit.[82] ASMR videos became a "thing" – they acquired sociological reality – by virtue of being discovered, collected, discussed, labeled, shared, rated, and produced in the distinctive sociotechnical environment of these platforms. And they generate their impression of immediacy and intimacy at a digitally mediated double remove in both time and space.[83] On the other hand, ASMR videos regulate the self in a manner that stands in sharp contrast to the prevailing physiological, cognitive, and emotional rhythms of hyperconnectivity. They slow the self down rather than speeding it up; they soothe rather than stimulate; they offer quiet immersion rather than clamoring for attention. Indeed the ills to which they respond – stress, anxiety, and insomnia – have all arguably been exacerbated by the rhythms of hyperconnectivity. ASMR videos are a technology of self-regulation that responds to characteristic ways in which the self is *dysregulated*, physiologically and emotionally, in an ecology of hyperconnectivity.[84]

ASMR videos are part of a much broader phenomenon of the use of online resources – music, videos, games, social media feeds, and so on – for emotional and physiological self-regulation. The psychological literature has seen such practices as symptoms of "problematic Internet use."[85] Yet while some ways of using online resources to regulate moods are no doubt indeed problematic, this is surely too narrow a view. We all draw on online resources to modulate, alter, or regulate our moods and emotions. In addition to searching for information and advice on mood regulation and seeking out the immediate gratifications of online interaction, we use the affective powers of the immense wealth of online audio and visual materials, available anywhere and any time, to regulate our energy levels, alter our moods, cheer ourselves up, calm ourselves down, relieve stress or anxiety, distract ourselves, or simply stave off boredom.

The superabundance of such online resources, however, poses its own problems. Spotify claims to have "the right music for every mood and occasion" among its 80 million tracks, but how do we find it? And how do we find the right video for the right moment amidst the cornucopia of YouTube? The problem of choice in the face of superabundant content goes well beyond practices of self-regulation; as I will discuss in chapter 3, it is central to the workings of culture in an ecology of hyperconnectivity. Here I want simply to note that what may be experienced as a problem by individuals – finding the right music or video for physiological and emotional self-regulation – is increasingly understood as an opportunity by businesses.

As moods become increasingly "identifiable, addressable and manipulable" through big data, connective platforms, and new forms of surveillance, regulating the self becomes not only something we do, but something that that can be done to us.[86] The regulation of the self shifts from a self-reflexive individual practice to an algorithmically driven process. In the not too distant future, we will no longer face the burden of having to choose the "right music [or the right video] for every mood and moment": sensors and algorithms will detect our moods and deliver the right music or video without our having to search for it.[87] The regulation of the self will be outsourced to the sociotechnical systems in which we are enmeshed.

Automated mood-detecting and mood-regulating systems may still lie in the future, but we are already being powerfully regulated – and dysregulated – by sociotechnical systems. These systems have altered the basic rhythms of our everyday being: our attention habits, our sleep patterns, and our experience of time.[88] They have even altered our neurophysiology, deploying dopamine-dispensing notifications that cue possible future social rewards and thereby engage our "seeking" behavior and keep us checking our social media feeds and coming back for more.[89] The language of "addiction" remains controversial, both in the medical community and in broader public discussion.[90] But there is no doubt that social media platforms have been brilliantly engineered, in ways that exploit knowledge of our psychological vulnerabilities, to capture and sustain our attention. Nor is there any doubt that hyperconnectivity has been massively dysregulating for many people, disrupting everyday habits, exacerbating stress, anxiety, and low self-esteem, and interfering in a major way with work lives, social relationships, and the pursuit of goals.

Conclusion: Governing the self

Running through the four preceding sections – on objectifying, quantifying, producing, and regulating the self – is a tension between *reflexive practices* and *algorithmic processes*. A reflexive practice is something one does to oneself; the self is both subject and object. An algorithmic process constructs the self from the outside; the self is merely the object, not the subject. The tension is between objectifying oneself, quantifying oneself, producing oneself, and regulating oneself, on the one hand, and being algorithmically objectified, quantified, produced, and regulated, on the other. It is a tension between being an agent and being the recipient and target – and ultimately the product – of processes organized from the outside. It is a tension, in short, between governing oneself and being governed – and in significant ways constituted – by complex sociotechnical systems.

This corresponds roughly to the distinction drawn in the late work of Foucault between "technologies of the self" and "technologies of power." As noted at the beginning of the chapter, the former "permit individuals to effect by their own means or with the help of others a certain number of operations on their own bodies and souls, thoughts, conduct, and way of being," as a way of transforming themselves; the latter "determine the conduct of individuals and submit them to certain ends or domination."[91] Having perhaps "insisted too much," in earlier work, on the latter, Foucault devoted more attention in his late work to the former: to the "ascetical practices" that he characterized as involving the "labor of self on self."[92]

Hyperconnectivity has generated an array of new technologies of the self in this sense. These include exploring publicly unexpressed aspects of one's identity in anonymous online environments; blogging as a new form of public "self-writing"; lifelogging and self-tracking, insofar as these are oriented not simply to self-knowledge but to self-optimization; and posting curated content on social media sites.[93] All of these practices entail new forms of active work on the self by the self. In the complementary analytical idiom of Giddens, they contribute to making the self, more than ever, a reflexive project.

Beyond introducing specific new technologies of the self, hyperconnectivity has enlarged the realm of active self-governance in a more general way that deepens and intensifies neoliberal forms of governmentality. In Miller and Rose's loosely Foucauldian account of what they prefer to call "advanced liberal" strategies of government, individuals are construed as "subjects of responsibility, autonomy, and choice."[94] Such actively responsible, self-enterprising individuals are "not merely 'free to choose', but *obliged to be free*, to understand and enact their lives in terms of choice."[95] They can be governed "at a distance," "governed through their freedom to choose."[96]

Miller and Rose were writing in the 1990s, well before the era of hyperconnectivity. In the course of the last decade, however, the affinities between hyperconnectivity and neoliberal governmentality have come into sharp relief. I discussed above one such affinity: how hyperconnectivity has enabled – and rendered quasi-obligatory – new forms of self-entrepreneurship. Here I want to highlight another: how hyperconnectivity supports the neoliberal project of "responsibilizing" individuals as choosers.

In a context in which the empire of individual choice expands and choice is increasingly valorized in every domain – not just in the core domains of consumer choice but in the domains of health, lifestyle, relationships, schooling, public services, financial planning, risk management, insurance, and so on – hyperconnectivity provides a pervasive infrastructure for governing through choices and for training people to be responsible choosers. This infrastructure makes it easy for systems of governance to require choices; to record the choices that are made; to track individuals' behavior; and to reward them for making what are deemed responsible choices.[97] The infrastructure also makes it easy to generate and disseminate information (including quantitative indicators) about items in choice sets, thereby enabling individuals, in principle, to make "informed choices." Hyperconnectivity provides, in short, a training apparatus that seems admirably well suited to engineering neoliberal selves.

Yet even as hyperconnectivity proliferates the occasions for choice, requires us to be governed through the choices we make, and expands the range of choice in many contexts by bringing a universe of infinite digital possibility to our fingertips, it at the same time enframes and enmeshes choice in systems that preconfigure, circumscribe, formalize, gamify, routinize, and attenuate choice. The proliferation of choice goes hand in hand with the disciplining and in some contexts the emptying out of choice.[98] Devices like drop-down menus, for example, prespecify the acceptable alternatives. Personalized algorithmic filters shape the information we see and thereby often limit the range of what we can effectively or easily choose.[99] And choice architectures – including simple features like defaults – "nudge" people more or less strongly in particular directions. Cass Sunstein and Richard Thaler, the apostles of nudging, argue that the "libertarian paternalism" involved in nudging individuals toward "welfare-promoting" choices allows "public and private institutions to influence behavior while also respecting freedom of choice."[100] But the anthropologist Natasha Dow Schüll rightly underscores the tension between nudging and the neoliberal vision of governing people through their freedom to choose. Nudging, Schüll notes, "both presupposes and pushes against freedom. ... [It] falls somewhere between enterprise and submission, responsibility and discipline."[101]

At the limit, hyperconnectivity pushes not just toward circumscribing and guiding choice but toward making choice unnecessary. We see this in "autonomous search," which combines location data with knowledge of consumer habits to prompt users unbidden about a nearby bar, restaurant, pharmacy, or store. We see it in marketing strategies of "proactive personalization" or "anticipatory design," which promise "flow not friction" and "convenience not choice."[102] We see it in navigation software, which makes routing choices for drivers. We see it in subscription boxes that offer a personalized selection of clothes, food, or other goods at regular intervals, freeing the recipient from the choice-intensive burden of shopping.[103] We see it in "smart home" services that reorder supplies automatically or otherwise relieve the resident of making choices about routine home functioning or maintenance. We see it in the autoplay feature of many streaming services, which cues up a new video or song whenever the last one finishes.

Here we glimpse the contours of what might be called a *post-neoliberal self*. If the neoliberal self is governed through its choices, the post-neoliberal self is governed through its data. If the neoliberal self is constructed as a "subject of responsibility, autonomy, and choice," the post-neoliberal self is constructed as an object of knowledge, prediction, and control.[104] If the neoliberal self is produced in significant part through psychological expertise and through various forms of "governing the soul," the post-neoliberal self is produced through techno-social engineering and through the direct governing of behavior. If the neoliberal self is self-steering, the post-neoliberal self is steered by algorithmic systems.[105] If the neoliberal self is self-activated, self-reflexive, and entrepreneurial, the post-neoliberal self is conditioned to respond to increasingly pervasive and finely calibrated stimuli.[106] Returning to Foucault's distinction, if the neoliberal self is formed through technologies of the self, the post-neoliberal self is formed through technologies of power, "which determine the conduct of individuals and submit them to certain ends or domination."

This contrast is of course overdrawn. The full-blown post-neoliberal self is a figure on the horizon, not – yet – a familiar figure in our midst. For the time being, the empire of choice continues to expand, citizens of "advanced liberal" societies continue to be called upon to be self-activating and self-reflexive, and we continue to be governed for the most part at a distance, through the choices we make. Still, hyperconnectivity has enmeshed individuals in an ever-tighter web of algorithmic processes that objectify, quantify, produce, regulate, and govern the self. These processes do not simply work on pre-constituted selves from the outside; they enter into the constitution of the self and reshape its internal workings – its desires, its rhythms, its habits of attention, its modes of self-regulation. The ongoing social formation of the self is increasingly mediated by this web of algorithmic processes.

The sociotechnical, algorithmically mediated processes of self-formation are part of a larger political economy of the self. This is in some respects a familiar story. At least since the beginning of the advertising age, powerful economic actors have sought to reach inside the self, to engineer new desires and fantasies, to create new habits, to foster new styles, to alter ways of thinking and acting, to invent new ways of capturing and reorganizing our attention. For over half a century, these efforts have prompted concerns about new technologies of persuasion.[107]

So tech firms' efforts to reach inside the self are certainly not new. But their power to do so – grounded in the extraordinarily rich data they have extracted and in the unparalleled immediacy and intimacy of our relations with our devices – is unprecedented in scale, scope, and intensity.[108] It is a power less of persuasion than of insinuation. It is a power not only to capture and retain our attention but to regulate – and disrupt – our rhythms, to discern and alter our moods, and to reorganize our neurophysiology by dispensing dopamine hits on a schedule sufficiently unpredictable to keep us engaged, all on the basis of astonishingly comprehensive and fine-grained knowledge. Earlier efforts to reach inside the self – having at their disposal only the most fragmentary data and the crudest instruments of knowledge – were feeble by comparison. The self remained a largely unknown territory, and advertising was driven chiefly by conjecture. But the conquest of that unknown territory has advanced rapidly during the last decade, raising the prospect of a thoroughgoing colonization of the self.

The metaphor of colonization has several pertinent implications.[109] It suggests that the self is governed, increasingly, from the outside: a government *of* the self, but neither *by* the self nor *for* the self. It suggests that the self is vulnerable, with only weak defenses against the superior technology – and seductive blandishments – of the colonizing powers. It suggests that the territories of the self constitute a new frontier for the extraction of resources – vast troves of hitherto unexploited behavioral data – by external powers.[110] It suggests that the self has been disciplined by those powers, drawn into their administrative routines, habituated into yielding data to them, and conscripted into providing labor for them. It suggests that the self has been rendered legible, docile, predictable, and tractable, subject to neo-behaviorist regimes of behavior modification.[111] It suggests a form of rule that disguises itself as a service, one that purports simply to give us what we want and to "improve the user experience." It suggests – if one shifts from extractive to settlement colonies and stretches the metaphor a bit further – the populating of the self with wave after wave of new inhabitants, the flooding of the self with endless streams of "content," and the consequent transformation of individual and social imaginaries. In line with the notion of self-colonization, it suggests the enlisting of the self – the seduced, willing self – in its own colonization.

The "colonization of the self" is a potent and troubling metaphor. But it does not of course capture the whole story of the transformations of the self in an ecology of digital hyperconnectivity. As a "total social fact," hyperconnectivity contains many internal tensions; its affordances, as I have underscored throughout this chapter, are complex and ambivalent. Earlier themes of exploring and emancipating the self, reformulated to address the present conjuncture, remain pertinent. And a variety of new practices of the self – new ways of knowing the self and acting on the self – enrich the sense in which the late modern self is a reflexive project. Yet the reflexive practices of self-making have been increasingly overlaid by algorithmic processes that objectify, quantify, produce, regulate, and govern the self from the outside. This trajectory is sobering indeed.

CHAPTER TWO

Interactions

All kinds of social relationships – from the most intimate and enduring to the most impersonal and evanescent – have been recast as they have been drawn into the ecosystem of digital hyperconnectivity. Families, for example, can keep in touch as never before. This has been a great boon to far-flung, especially transnational families. But the ease of staying in constant touch has prompted concerns about children being "tethered" to their devices and, through them, to their parents (and friends) in ways that may make it harder to develop autonomous selves. And even as families are connected more closely through their devices, they are simultaneously pulled apart, each absorbed in the compelling elsewheres mediated by their devices. Families have also become the frontlines of chronic struggles over connectivity and surveillance, primed on the one hand by anxieties about overuse or "addiction" and on the other by fears of digitally mediated dangers.[1]

Friendship has been even more radically transformed. Social media platforms have re-engineered the territories of friendship, creating new ways for friends to hang out together, new regimes of visibility, and new forms of social currency. They have introduced new technologies of micro-validation and relentlessly comparative indicators of popularity. For younger people in particular, friendships are enacted largely through the mediation of mobile devices on social media sites, gaming platforms, and multimedia messaging apps. Friendship is conducted through an increasingly visual expressive language, with words supplemented, and sometimes replaced, by emojis, memes, GIFs, stickers, and mood-expressing selfies.

Dating practices and romantic and sexual relationships have also been reorganized. Online dating in all its forms – from the methodical search for a life partner to the casual scan for a hookup – has become the norm rather than the exception. But even people who meet offline often prefer digital messaging to face-to-face conversation for flirting or exploring a possible connection. People often feel more confident and less vulnerable online; with ample opportunity for composed self-presentation, they can maintain a stance of contrived casualness.[2] And hyperconnectivity has introduced new forms of digitally mediated sexuality.

I will have occasion to discuss family, friendship, and dating, as well as professional relationships, throughout this chapter. But I will organize my discussion by addressing four developments that cut across these relationship types: the reorganization of the space and time of interaction; the proliferation of micro-sociality and its attendant micro-obligations; the development of new forms of interpersonal surveillance in the context of heightened digital visibilities; and the engineering, programming, and automation of social interaction. I conclude by considering the accelerated shift towards disembodied, digitally mediated interaction and disembedded, contactless commerce during the pandemic.

The reorganization of space and time

Hyperconnectivity has profoundly transformed the space and time of interaction.[3] Most fundamentally, and most obviously, it has freed inter-action from the constraints of proximity and synchronicity. Interaction no longer depends on bringing people together in space or synchro-nizing them in time (although digital mediation also creates new ways of coordinating interaction in time and bringing people together in space). Communication technologies that bridge distance – the letter, the telegram, the telephone – have a long history.[4] Yet before the advent of mobile telephony, these distance-eclipsing technologies remained bound to place. Telegraph and telephone networks linked fixed places; letters (and telegrams) required physical addresses. Mobile telephones made communication more independent of place (though not fully independent, given high roaming costs for international calls), but they continued to require synchronization in time. Only after the turn of the millennium did the widespread adoption of texting allow routine asynchronous anyone-anytime-anywhere communication. And only in the last decade, as a result of the near-universal adoption of smartphones, social media, and multimedia messaging apps, has a much wider range of social interaction – including new forms of synchronous voice and video communication – become truly place-independent, freed from distance-related costs.

Hyperconnectivity not only *bypasses* physical copresence by creating new modes of interaction-at-a-distance; it also *overlays* and *transforms* the experience of copresence. It can enrich interaction with others in our immediate presence – acquaintances, friends, family, or lovers – by making available an additional channel of device-mediated communication, layered on top of the face-to-face channel.[5] But it can also attenuate interaction with copresent others by inviting us to redistribute attention and energy from the here and now to the inexhaustible elsewheres contained in our devices.[6] It is ultra-convenient and therefore chronically tempting to check for and respond to messages, even if this means turning our attention away from the local setting. And it is difficult to ignore the summons of incoming messages and notifications. As interactional norms and expectations are renegotiated, such divided attention and interactional multitasking become accepted and even expected; this legitimizes and thereby reinforces the habit of turning to our devices in the presence of others.[7]

Yet our devices do not simply provide a portal to elsewhere, an escape route from lulls in the here-and-now flow of interaction. They also connect us to an inexhaustible supply of resources for alleviating those lulls, a continually replenished fund of social currency that we can redeem by sharing the latest meme, the latest song or amusing video, the latest update from our friends. The same devices that relativize and weaken others' claims on our attention also sustain and enliven our interaction with them. Face-to-face interaction thus comes to depend on the very devices that threaten to hollow it out. We gain new interactional skills – new ways of integrating digital feeds into here-and-now sociability – even as we lose others, including the skill, and the motivation, to sustain face-to-face interaction without the help of those feeds.

Hyperconnectivity creates new forms of absent presence and present absence; it weaves together the there and then with the here and now.[8] Those who are physically absent can be rendered present in mediated yet compelling forms; those who are physically present may be cognitively, attentionally, or emotionally absent.[9] Interactional copresence becomes independent of physical copresence. As a result, face-to-face interaction loses its privileged position as the standard of value and touchstone of authenticity; it can no longer be considered, as it was by Goffman, the "primordial real thing" in relation to which forms of mediated inter-action – Goffman mentioned letters and phone calls – constitute only "reduced versions."[10]

Unlike ephemeral face-to-face encounters, which are clearly bounded in space and time, and which take place between mutually aware and mutually monitoring participants, digitally mediated interactions have no clear boundaries and no definitive set of participants. Because digitally mediated interactions are "self-documenting," leaving objec-tified and enduring traces, they are never definitively over; they may be joined later by those who were not initially parties to the interaction.[11] It follows that digitally mediated interactions have no stable contexts; they may be revived in new contexts and take on new meanings for new audiences. This open-endedness of digitally mediated interaction increases the scope of accountability: one can be held accountable in a new context – that of employment, for example – for digitally mediated interaction that was initially directed to a different audience in a different context, sometimes many years earlier. Many of the controversies bound up with current debates over "cancel culture" pivot on this extended accountability.

Hyperconnectivity transforms the meaning and experience not only of physical copresence but of place and space more generally. Here one should distinguish between the concrete, meaningful social reality of place and the abstract, measurable frame of space.[12] The chronic access to elsewhere that hyperconnectivity affords weakens the phenom-enological hold and binding power of place, which ceases to provide a shared horizon of orientation for interaction. At the same time, location-tracking technology makes spatial proximity relevant in new ways. We become addressable – by proximate friends or potential dates, by navigation systems, and especially by advertisers – by our precisely quantifiable position in space, not by our qualitative location in a place.[13]

The ubiquity of mobile devices accelerates the privatization of public space that commentators on the Walkman and mobile phones have long described.[14] Using one's phone – a reflexive action in almost any public space – signals unapproachability and discourages interaction. In univer-sities, for example, an eerie silence prevails among students gathering in or outside a classroom before the class begins; all occupy the same space, but each is somewhere else. Conversation among copresent students becomes a marked and unexpected activity, set off against the norm of parallel interaction, all with their own devices.

As public space is privatized, private space is opened up to a range of more public activities. The boundaries between the home and the outside world have always been permeable, especially in the age of electronic media. But hyperconnectivity greatly increases that permeability.[15] The device-filled home contains a set of portals linking household members individually to multiple elsewheres. The home becomes a place of work, shopping, individualized entertainment, keeping up with social media, and hanging out with spatially dispersed friends. All this was true before the pandemic. But the confinements of the pandemic dramatically accelerated the inversion of public and private. As Drew Austin observed, it was precisely in the "private" space of the home that we were now living "the most public version of our lives," including work, education, and politics as well as shopping, entertainment, and socializing, while offline "public" space outside the home could become, paradoxically, a kind of "private," "sheltered" refuge from the relentless mediation of large-scale sociotechnical systems.[16]

The temporal and spatial boundaries between work and non-work have also blurred.[17] The sequestration of work – its confinement to specific times and places – had developed in the nineteenth century and peaked, in the US, after the Second World War, before subsequently beginning a long and gradual decline. Anytime-anywhere connectivity and the increasing digital mediation of both work and non-work activities have sharply accelerated this decline. They have enabled working time – for work involving the manipulation of symbols rather than the manipulation of things – to be distributed across multiple places: the home, vehicles of all sorts, cafes, airports, hotels, and vacation spots as well as the dedicated workplace. And they have made workplaces sites of multiple temporal streams of activity in addition to working time itself: time devoted to interacting with family, friends, or partners, or to the infinite array of things one can do, discreetly, on a phone or computer.[18] (In intensively surveilled workplaces, to be sure, employees have far more circumscribed opportunities to attend to non-work matters: their browsing activities or keystrokes may be monitored, and video surveillance may limit their ability to use their phones.)[19]

The distribution of digitally mediated work across multiple places was temporarily interrupted by the lockdown phase of the pandemic; the home, for many, became the sole place of work. But the long arc of the pandemic has accelerated the liberation of work from spatial and temporal enclosures, including the home as well as the workplace. The massive legitimation and normalization of remote work during the pandemic has reset baseline expectations. Many companies, not just in the tech industry, have committed themselves to allowing remote or hybrid work post-pandemic. Remote work need not be done at home: many forms of remote work, like other digitally mediated activities, can be distributed across multiple places and times. The ranks of self-styled digital nomads, working from campgrounds, temporary apartments, coffee shops, and co-working spaces, can be expected to swell.[20]

The anywhere-anytime logic of hyperconnectivity tends to erode all spatial and temporal boundaries, not just those that once separated work from domestic life. It reinforces broader structural trends towards the deinstitutionalization of both place and time. Socially defined places and times cease to contain sharply bounded and distinctive flows of activity; they lose much of their power to orient action. There is no longer "a time and a place for everything." Institutionally defined places and times give way to individually constructed and negotiated spatial and temporal arrangements. This can be experienced as empowering, but it can also be experienced as burdensome, requiring more work of coordination and negotiation.[21]

Digital mediation contributes powerfully to the fragmentation of time. Digitally mediated activities can not only be distributed across multiple places; they can also be broken up into multiple temporal segments. This is true not only for work but also for activities like shopping, consuming news and entertainment, playing mobile games, and scrolling through social media feeds.[22] And asynchronous social interactions, by their very nature, are segmented into very small units that can be widely distributed across time.

Of course many offline and non-digital activities, too, can be segmented: we can dip in and out of a physical book, pause a video tape, or interrupt a conversation. But the fragmentation of online digital activities is aided by the fact that such activities are not equipment-, place-, or time-dependent. A single all-purpose connected device serves as the hub of all digital activities, facilitating frictionless switching between them. Since that device is everywhere and always at hand, we can easily employ "underutilized" time – time spent walking, driving, waiting in line, and so on – with some digital activity-fragment. The minimal units of asynchronous communication or media consumption, in particular, are easy to fit in anywhere and any time. The smallest nooks and crannies of "empty" time – the time on an elevator, the time between sets at the gym, even the time at a stoplight, for those not otherwise texting while driving – become opportunities for watching a TikTok or checking one's messages.[23] And time that has not been filled up with digital content becomes harder to tolerate.

The possibility of efficiently "packing" digital activity-fragments into available slots of empty or underutilized time should in principle relieve time pressure elsewhere. But the temporal fragmentation and frictionless hyper-convenience of digital interaction (and digital activity more generally) lead us to undertake more activities overall as well as to increase the temporal density of activity through rapid cycling, multitasking, and "multicommunicating" (engaging in more than one conversation at a time). They therefore contribute in practice to the acceleration of the tempo of life and the intensification of time pressure – a theme I return to in the next section.[24]

A final aspect of temporal fragmentation concerns the state of continuous interruptibility that we have come to inhabit. Asynchronous digital communication contributes to this interruptibility in a paradoxical way. By definition, asynchronous communication requires no coordination in time. The temporal flexibility it affords should allow us, in principle, to attend to incoming messages at our convenience, without interrupting other activities. But in practice, asynchronous communication chronically intrudes on ongoing activity (including face-to-face interaction).

The reasons for this intrusiveness are social, not technological. Widely shared expectations about immediate reachability and responsiveness lead us to treat incoming messages as legitimate and relatively urgent claims on our attention. The fact that we can read and respond to messages quickly, with seemingly minimal diversion of attention from ongoing activity or interaction, reinforces our openness to incoming summonses. Over time, a state of continuous interruptibility has come to be taken for granted; indeed for many, incoming messages and notifications are no longer experienced as disruptive or interruptive at all.

My initial observation about hyperconnectivity freeing interaction from the constraints of place and time therefore requires qualification. Many technically asynchronous modes of digital interaction are socially understood as *semi-synchronous*. Unlike synchronous face-to-face or voice-to-voice interaction, semi-synchronous interaction is not fully coordinated in time; participants are not fully copresent with one another. But unlike truly asynchronous interaction, semi-synchronous interaction does require temporal coordination, given prevailing expectations about reachability and responsiveness.[25]

In general, then, digitally mediated interaction transcends the constraints of place much more fully than it does those of time. The proliferation of time-sensitive, semi-synchronous interaction – and the consequent routinization of interruption – contributes to the further fragmentation of time. It also contributes to the sense that our time is not our own. This is a final paradoxical aspect of the reorganization of time in a regime of hyperconnectivity: by furthering the deinstitutionalization and individualization of time, hyperconnectivity increases our temporal autonomy, giving us more control over our time; yet by enmeshing us in networks of expectations about reachability and responsiveness, it curtails that autonomy.[26]

The proliferation of micro-sociality

Hyperconnectivity has freed interaction not only from the constraints of place and (albeit less fully) time, but also from those of cost and effort. The infrastructure of high-speed networks, mobile devices, social media platforms, and messaging apps has made digitally mediated interaction frictionless. Social media have made people easy to find, follow, and interact with. With its nearly 3 billion users, Facebook serves as a kind of planetary directory. Messaging apps like WhatsApp, WeChat, and Facebook Messenger, each with over a billion users, have made anytime-anywhere multimedia interaction essentially free as well as hyper-convenient for anyone with internet access.

The connective infrastructure not only enables and facilitates interaction; it directly invites and stimulates interaction. Social media platforms continually prompt and instigate activity in order to generate new content and thereby keep users engaged, retain their attention, capture their data, and expose them to advertising.[27] Facebook nudges users to activity through various prompts and notifications, including the mobile app's injunction to "write something."[28] The "like" button, originating on Facebook but implemented across the Web, invites users to "engage" with content and, when clicked, "set[s] a chain of inter-action in motion."[29] Snapchat encourages interaction through a variety of emojis, notably by marking and quantifying "streaks" – consecutive days on which two users have exchanged snaps (photos or videos) – and reminding users when a streak is about to end. Dating sites prompt users to communicate with those to whom they have been algorithmically matched. Workplace communication platforms also facilitate, invite, and stimulate interaction.

All this has led to the explosive growth of digitally mediated inter-action in an expanding range of forms. What was once limited to the medium of text now includes images, audio, video, and proliferating sets of emojis, stickers, and GIFs, deployable separately or in combination.[30] One can interact in asynchronous, semi-synchronous, and synchronous modes on a great variety of multimedia messaging apps and social media and workplace communication platforms. This interactional abundance can be a blessing. It can enrich intimate relationships, add new registers to friendship, sustain family ties across great distances, create new expressive possibilities and nuances, facilitate organizational communication, and generate a sense of quasi-continuous "connected presence."[31] But it can also be a burden, in both personal and professional contexts.

The burdens of communicative abundance stem from the prolif-eration of what I will call micro-sociality. Ultra-minimal communicative acts such as liking a social media post or sending a single emoji, photo, or GIF are obvious examples. But as I noted above, asynchronous (and semi-synchronous) online interaction is by its very nature segmented into small, often very small units. One study found that the average text message comprises just fifty-one characters;[32] the increasing use of graphical devices in messaging apps makes for even shorter messages. Another study found that respondents distinguished two formats for text messages – "mini letters" and "one-liners" – and that nearly 80 percent of the messages counted as "one-liners."[33] In an ecology dominated by newer and snappier forms of digital communication, email is associated with relatively long-form communication. But even email teems with micro-sociality: a Google study of several million pairs of emails and replies showed that a quarter of all replies used no more than twenty characters.[34]

Some digital micro-sociality has a practical purpose such as coordinating activity, seeking information, or requesting a service. A great deal of such micro-sociality, however, exemplifies what anthropologist Bronisław Malinowski called "phatic communion": aimless small talk that has a social "grooming" or bonding function.[35] Such phatic communication – the "insistent psalmody of short expressive messages," in Licoppe and Smoreda's evocative formulation – proliferates in an ecology of hyperconnectivity, which facilitates and promotes precisely this kind of communication for communication's sake, in which the content of the message is less important than the mere fact of connecting.[36]

Taken individually, acts of micro-social communication are not in the least burdensome. Their very convenience and frictionlessness, after all, have enabled micro-sociality to multiply by lowering the threshold for communication. In the aggregate, however, superabundant digital sociality can indeed be a burden.

The proliferation of digital micro-communication brings in its train a proliferation of micro-decisions. In synchronous face-to-face or voice-to-voice interaction, the individual turns of talk are embedded in a single more or less continuous flow. But asynchronous digital interaction is disembedded – lifted out of the flow of synchronous interaction – and broken up into a series of separate micro-communicative acts. Each of these acts presents a choice – even if the choice is as trivial as whether or not to "like" a friend's post. And each choice provides an opportunity for reflection, however minimal, about whether to respond, what to say, and how to say it.[37] These choices and opportunities for reflection may be welcomed. Young people often report that they would "rather text than talk" precisely because texting allows them to "edit" what they say and manage their self-presentation.[38] Yet the proliferation of micro-decisions requires cognitive and sometimes emotional resources and can be experienced as stressful. Superabundant digital micro-sociality, moreover, leads to a "task-based perception of interaction," even in personal contexts, in which social media or messaging app indicators remind users of the "number of tasks to be completed."[39]

Semi-synchronous digital interaction may shade over into a nearly continuous exchange that leaves little or no room for choice or reflection about how to respond. Even in this semi-synchronous form, though, the sheer volume of digital micro-sociality can be overwhelming. In workplaces that use communication platforms like Slack, for example, a common complaint concerns the vastly increased volume of communication they generate. Built around real-time group chat functions that are supposed to enable more effective teamwork, Slack has been marketed in part as a solution to the overload generated by the overflowing email inbox. But it has generated its own form of communication overload. Slack's "amazing ease-of-use," according to one user, is precisely the problem: it lowers the threshold for communication and thereby invites anyone to jump in at any time with any half-baked thought or humorous GIF. And it prioritizes (as does group chat in general) rapid rather than well-considered responses (necessary if one is to have the chance of being heard before the conversation moves on) and brief rather than longer and more complex interventions.[40] By encouraging people to "hang out" at the virtual water cooler, Slack can help integrate people working at home into a common team culture. But this creates what another disaffected Slack user, formerly enamored of the platform, called "a self-perpetuating feedback loop: the more everyone's hanging out, the more conversations take place. The more conversations, the more everyone's expected to participate."[41] Keeping up with the ceaseless flow can be stressful: a steady stream of notifications is always calling users away from other tasks, yet they hesitate to turn notifications off lest they miss out on something. And when they are away from their screens, on vacation, or in a different time zone, they feel pressured to try to catch up on what they have missed, since all conversations remain persistently available.

Keeping up with the flow can be stressful in personal life as well. Social media platforms multiply the number of friends and the interactional burdens of keeping up with them. The aggregate burden increases even though platforms also provide efficient, streamlined means of keeping up, paradigmatically the "like" button that makes "paying attention to friends a one-click sentiment."[42] Social media platforms are *designed* to proliferate micro-sociality – to keep us posting and commenting, liking and sharing, tweeting and retweeting. Their success in doing so is indicated by the profusion of popular advice for avoiding or mitigating social media overload or burnout. The multiplication of group chats – enabled by the shift from SMS to messaging apps that accommodate multi-party as well as dyadic interaction – has further augmented the sheer volume of micro-sociality. Active users who belong to many groups may send over a hundred messages per day and are exposed to far more.[43] The dynamic in personal and business contexts is the same: the convenience and frictionlessness of digital interaction generate a super-abundant flow of micro-communication, which can in turn prompt a sense of stress and overload. Stress is exacerbated by expectations of continuous and immediate availability. These expectations exercise a form of "soft coercion" that makes us accountable for and anxious about being unreachable.[44]

In response to the superabundance of digital micro-communication, users seek to "manag[e] the communication environment" by means of "constant and habitual interactions, not with other individuals through communication devices, but with the devices and platforms themselves," which are constantly monitored, in the background, for indicators of incoming messages. Users describe being anxious about indicators of unread messages; even if they cannot respond to them until later, many feel obliged to glance at the messages, if only to make the indicator disappear. The habit of constant background monitoring and checking leads to a "partial displacement of attention away from the quality and content of interaction" to the interface itself; users end up interacting almost as much with their devices as with the people who can be reached through them.[45]

The proliferation of interactional micro-obligations suggests that a key element of the classical sociological story of modernization may require rethinking.[46] As I discussed in the previous chapter, that story emphasizes the progressive disembedding and emancipation of individuals from the bonds of family and local community. Hyperconnectivity has furthered that disembedding and emancipation in many ways, opening up new avenues of self-exploration and offering cultural, psychological, and social support for those seeking to escape the constraints of family and community. At the same time, however, it has enmeshed individuals in a dense network of expectations, norms, and obligations. As a result, the hyperconnected individual is far from unencumbered by social bonds and demands. In contrast to the "mobility narrative" central to modernizationist accounts, as Keith Hampton has argued, hyperconnected individuals don't shed their social ties when they move through different social, occupational, and geographic spaces. By enabling "relational persistence" and "sustained awareness," hyperconnectivity embeds the individual in a "persistent-pervasive community" that "resembles a hybrid of preindustrial and urban-industrial community structures."[47]

The regime of visibility

A key aspect of the "persistent-pervasive community" enabled by hyperconnectivity is that interactions unfold in a field of superabundant visibility. Digitally mediated interaction, to be sure, does not allow for the finely calibrated mutual visual monitoring of facial expressions and bodily gestures that is central to face-to-face interaction. My concern here, however, is not with this "situated visibility of copresence," but with digitally mediated forms of visibility.[48] The field of mediated visibility is not limited to what can be directly seen and known in real time or to what can be seen and known through the mediation of still or moving images. It extends to what can be known through the mediation of words and numbers, what can be sensed and made known by devices (such as sensor-equipped tracking devices or cameras paired with facial recognition systems), and what can be inferred by algorithms from the digital traces harvested by platforms. The realm of the visible thus goes far beyond what the human eye can see; it includes all that can be watched, tracked, monitored, and surveilled. The word surveillance comes from the French *veiller*, to watch; the field of digitally mediated visibility is thus the field of surveillance, the field of what can be watched. And that field has expanded exponentially in an ecology of hyperconnectivity.[49]

When we think of surveillance, we may think first of centralized, top-down modes of government surveillance. (Etymologically, to surveil means not simply to watch, but to watch from above.) And indeed government surveillance has expanded dramatically in the era of hyperconnectivity, from the digital dragnet of the National Security Agency through the tight digital mesh emerging in China to the growing law

61

enforcement interest worldwide in facial recognition software, touted inter alia by Amazon for its ability to monitor "all faces in group photos, crowded events, and public places such as airports."[50]

Or we may think first of commercial surveillance, which has expanded even more dramatically under hyperconnectivity. Surveillance – the extraction, storage, aggregation, and analysis of ever more fine-grained data about ever more aspects of user behavior – has become the dominant business model of the internet. As Maciej Cegłowski noted, the surest way to convince venture capitalists to invest in an internet startup is to tell them a story about why the company could one day be immensely profitable, and the most effective way to tell this kind of story has been to propose ever more intensive forms of surveillance, enabling more effective forms of targeted advertisement.[51]

We are less likely to think of interpersonal surveillance: the ways people watch one another. Interpersonal surveillance has always been central to social life. But it too has expanded dramatically – and taken on new forms – as a result of the new regime of digitally mediated visibility.[52] For most of human history, interpersonal surveillance – even surreptitious forms like eavesdropping – required copresence.[53] Even as organizational practices of remote monitoring through surveillance cameras and other devices developed, routine interpersonal surveillance remained tied to copresence. But hyperconnectivity has freed interpersonal surveillance – as it has interaction in general – from the constraints of proximity and synchronicity. The field of social visibility is no longer limited to the here and now; it extends to events occurring long ago and far away.

Hyperconnectivity has also freed interpersonal surveillance from the constraints of ephemerality. The situated visibility of copresent face-to-face interaction is evanescent; it lives on only in unreliable and decaying memory traces. But the digital objects through which people become visible to one another – with significant exceptions, notably much of what is exchanged on Snapchat and audio conversations on platforms like Clubhouse – are enduring rather than ephemeral; they can be closely and repeatedly scrutinized.[54]

Digital objects are not only persistent; they are searchable, and they can be accessed anywhere and any time in a private and unobtrusive manner.[55] The combination of persistence, searchability, and private anytime-anywhere accessibility makes social surveillance easy, convenient, and unembarrassing. It requires no special arrangements, no special equipment, and no special social skills or tact (which may be required when undertaking social surveillance in the course of face-to-face interaction).

Much interpersonal digital surveillance takes place through social media platforms. Social media are of course a major vector of commercial surveillance and an increasingly significant resource for government surveillance as well. But they are also a vast engine of interpersonal surveillance. The whole point of social media is to make people visible to one another (and to the platform itself) in new ways. The architecture of social media is designed to promote, as well as to document and quantify, visibility; the ideology of social media, which invokes sharing and openness ("making the world more open and connected"), is an ideology of visibility and transparency ("you have [only] one identity") as well as connectedness.[56] And for users, visibility to other users is a feature, not a bug. Users may worry about certain forms of unwanted visibility, but they worry more about the threat of *invisibility*.[57]

Social media surveillance is often surreptitious in one sense: it is often done without the target being aware of being watched by that particular watcher at that particular moment.[58] Terms like "Facebook stalking" indicate a certain unease about this surreptitiousness.[59] Yet social media surveillance is not surreptitious in another important sense: the targets know perfectly well – indeed ardently hope – that they are being watched, even if they don't know who may be watching at any given moment. This awareness of and desire for surveillance distinguishes social media surveillance from eavesdropping, in which information is "stolen by the receiver" rather than "donated by the sender." As Alice Marwick notes, the information on social media sites is indeed "'donated' by the sender," precisely in the hope that it will be seen. Social media-based interpersonal surveillance is thus characterized by a considerable degree of mutuality and reciprocity: users watch others and are watched by them in turn.[60] (Social media surveillance, to be sure, is not always mutual and reciprocal. It is more often reciprocal on Facebook, where the elementary relation is reciprocal "friendship," than on sites like Instagram and Twitter, where the elementary relation is followership, which may or may not be reciprocal.)

What is rendered visible on social media is of course anything but an unfiltered view of social life. While copresent surveillance can glean information from the body-behavioral cues unintentionally "given off" by the target, social media surveillance relies to a much greater degree on information that is deliberately and often strategically "given."[61] Watchers are no doubt aware on some level that the picture they form of the "lives of others" is skewed by selective and carefully curated self-presentation. Yet social psychologists have shown that social media users are nonetheless vulnerable to the sense that others are happier, more active, more social, and more attractive than they themselves are.[62]

Social comparison – comparing oneself to others in order to assess oneself – is a universal part of social life. But social media make social comparison both salient and inescapable. A vast and ever-humming engine of social comparison, social media continually incite users to compare themselves with their peers and supply superabundant material for such comparisons. Social media users constantly see – rather than simply hearing about – what others have been doing, where they have been, how they look, and with whom they are hanging out. They are constantly confronted with their own and others' metrics – numbers of friends, followers, likes, retweets, and so on – and they cannot help interpreting these metrics in comparative perspective.

Social psychologists distinguish between upward and downward social comparisons: in the former, others are judged superior to oneself on some relevant dimension; in the latter, they are judged inferior. Selective sharing, accentuating the positive and downplaying the negative, means that social media specifically foster upward social comparison. Research has shown that upward comparison – when the target is similar to oneself and the domain of comparison is relevant to one's self-understanding – tends to promote envy. Social media are thus a gigantic machine for the generation of envy.[63]

Social media surveillance is practiced not only in a diffuse and wide-angled manner, as a way of keeping track of friends, but also in a more deliberate and narrowly targeted manner, as a way of discovering information about a particular person. The abundant digital visibility of a prospective romantic interest – a prolific Twitter or Instagram presence, or a Facebook trail that might go back a decade or more – can yield an extraordinarily rich and detailed trove of information. But the field of interpersonal digital visibility extends far beyond what is made available on social media. Public records that used to languish in obscurity because of the time and effort required to obtain them are now not only digitized; they are systematically harvested, aggregated, and integrated into comprehensive searchable databases by commercial data brokers.[64] Some public records data can be found simply through more or less assiduous Googling. But for a modest fee, anyone can access "background check" or "people search" services that yield detailed data on age, residence, marriage, divorce, relatives, real estate transactions, bankruptcy proceedings, tax liens, political affiliations and contributions, employment history, address history, phone numbers, criminal records, civil judgments, known aliases, sex offender status, and more. Online dating has created a new demand for such services on the part of those concerned about scamming, fraud, and false or misleading online self-presentation. But such services can be used to perpetrate as well as to detect fraud.[65] And they are routinely used by "doxxers" to shame, harass, and sometimes threaten political opponents by publishing personal information about them. The revolution in the effective accessibility of public records is thus another disturbing aspect of digital over-visibility.[66]

New digital visibilities have altered the relationships between romantic partners and between parents and children. Social media make partners' lives – and their interactions with others – much more visible to one another and vastly expand partners' opportunities to watch one another in an unobtrusive manner.[67] Such watching may be entirely benign. But for those inclined to insecurity or jealousy, the visibility of a partner's interaction with others on social media – and the ambiguity that results from the lack of context – provides rich soil on which suspicions may grow.[68] Dozens of overt spyware apps, as well as hundreds of dual-use apps that can be configured to allow covert interpersonal surveillance, cater to those who suspect their partners of cheating.[69]

As phones become increasingly central to the ecology of intimacy, they are freighted with symbolic meaning. Phones are conduits of mobile intimacy, but they are also foci of suspicion.[70] Some couples opt for maximal transparency and share passwords, treating this as an indicator of trust. For others, however, such transparency is incompatible with privacy and autonomy and signals a lack of trust.[71]

The phone becomes a symbolically charged object – and a focus of negotiations and struggles over surveillance – in relations between parents and children as well.[72] Such negotiations and struggles are not confined to phones: they embrace all devices through which the internet and social media are accessed, as well as special-purpose surveillance tools like GPS devices for tracking children deemed too young for smartphones.[73] But surveillance struggles have focused increasingly on phones, precisely because they are more private and less visible to parents than desktop or laptop computers or gaming consoles.

Negotiations and struggles over surveillance pivot on the appropriate scope of visibility. What parts of children's device-mediated social lives should be visible to parents? Their whereabouts? Their browsing history? The content of their messaging and social media activity? All of this and more can be monitored by the large and growing set of surveillance products that are marketed to parents, appealing to their anxieties about the dangers facing their children, online and off. As part of a "contract" associated with the child's first smartphone, parents may require that the child be reachable at all times.[74] They may even require children to share the passwords to their phones, computers, and social media and messaging accounts.

The stakes of struggles over visibility are high: they pit parents' fundamental desire – and obligation – to protect their children from harm against children's equally fundamental desire – and need – to assert and develop their autonomy.[75] In a world that is understood as full of risks and dangers, parents can be made to feel negligent and irresponsible if they do not micro-monitor their children. The knowledge that one *can* intensively monitor one's children – and that one can be in touch with them any time and anywhere – leads easily to the thought that one *ought* to do so. This facilitates a kind of "surveillance creep" in the family, analogous to surveillance creep in other domains.[76] Marketers of surveillance products promise "peace of mind" to parents. But peace of mind is elusive. Precisely the extension of visibility and the expectation of anytime-anywhere reachability generate new anxieties about remaining zones of opacity and moments of unreachability. Surveillance can thus intensify rather than assuage anxieties.[77]

Recent years have seen a gathering reaction against digital over-visibility and over-sharing. Private messaging platforms have been

66

growing much more rapidly than public social media platforms; in 2019 Facebook aligned itself with this trend, pledging to help bring about a "shift to private, encrypted services where people can be confident what they say to each other stays secure and their messages and content won't stick around forever."[78] Yet even as the growth trajectory of social media has leveled off – inevitably, as saturation levels have been reached in key markets – public social media show no sign of disappearing or even shrinking. Private messaging platforms, moreover, generate their own forms of hyper-visibility. By recording, fixing, and storing interactions by default, they make the past visible and accessible in new ways. The multimedia archive of a relationship's digital past may serve simply as an aide-mémoire or a focus of nostalgia. But it can also be mobilized as evidence in arguments and enlisted in efforts to hold others to account, and it may even find its way into legal proceedings.[79] Even if platforms begin to shift away from storing all content indefinitely by default, ephemeral communication remains the exception.[80] The new forms of interpersonal surveillance engendered by hyperconnectivity will no doubt continue to evolve; but they are more likely to intensify than to attenuate in the foreseeable future.

Programmed sociality

Digitally mediated interactions on social media platforms are hyper-visible not only to participants, but also to the platforms themselves. Since platforms own and control the material infrastructure, the code, and the data through which interactions occur, they are in a position to capture and analyze the digital traces of all platform-mediated activities. This asymmetrical visibility, together with full control of the architecture of interaction, enables platforms to engineer, program, and discipline interaction in new ways.

Social media platforms are not simply neutral conduits for inter-action, any more than they are neutral conduits for the flow of news, gossip, rumors, or cultural content.[81] Just as platforms shape, select, and curate the flow of content, so too they shape, stimulate, and modulate the flow of interaction. They do so by channeling interaction into codeable, countable, surveillable, computable, and therefore manipu-lable forms. Behind Facebook's claim in the late 2000s to be making the Web "more social," as media scholar José van Dijck has argued, lay the undeclared aim of "making sociality technical": "Sociality coded by technology renders people's activities formal, manageable, and manipulable, enabling platforms to engineer the sociality in people's everyday routines."[82]

The most well-known instances of the direct manipulation of sociality by Facebook were two large-scale experiments demonstrating that both voting behavior and emotional expression in Facebook posts could be shaped by altering the information to which users were exposed in their newsfeeds. Users seeing profile pictures of Facebook friends who had voted were themselves more likely to vote; and users exposed to positive (or negative) messages were more likely to post positive (or negative) messages themselves. These experiments – carried out without the consent required by experiments in academic settings – were controversial; but at least they were made public after the fact.[83] Apart from these high-profile social science experiments, driven by particular research questions, hyperconnectivity allows data-rich platforms to engage in continuous, fully automated experimentation without any public reporting or disclosure.[84] As a data scientist who used to work for Facebook and Google noted, there is nothing surprising about such experimentation: "the fundamental purpose of most people at Facebook working on data is to influence and alter people's moods and behavior. They are doing it all the time to make you like stories more, to click on more ads, to spend more time on the site."[85]

Facebook's social influence and emotional contagion experiments demonstrated a troubling capacity for subtle, utterly nontransparent forms of behavior modification on a vast scale.[86] But Facebook routinely programs and disciplines sociality in much more mundane ways. The forms of social interaction that can be undertaken on Facebook are limited to a small set of predefined and preformatted actions. One can construct a profile by entering information into a grid of prespecified categories. One can extend or accept a friend request. One can post a status update. One can share a photo or video or tag people in pictures shared by others. One can comment on content shared by a friend or "react" to it with Like, Love, Haha, Wow, Sad, or Angry emojis.[87] The discipline imposed by Facebook's carefully templated forms of self-presentation and its limited palette of possible actions has been central to Facebook's commercial success; it helps to explain why Facebook flourished while the less disciplined MySpace floundered.[88]

Facebook not only makes available particular actions; it prompts and incites users to undertake them. It prompts users to add friends through its "people you may know" feature (which relies on its knowledge of the friends of one's friends). It asks users "what's on your mind?" and prompts them to "add to your story" by sharing a photo or video or writing something. It reminds users of friends' birthdays and serves up memories. It invites users to engage with friends' content through the one-click convenience of the "like" button (or other "reaction" emojis). Its relentless metrics are designed to deepen engagement and incite further activity. And by algorithmically governing which of one's friends, and which of their activities, show up in a user's newsfeed, "mak[ing] certain people more visible than others," Facebook steers and curates social interactions. In all these ways, Facebook programs and engineers our sociality; it "becomes an active agent participating in the performance of friendship."[89]

The sociality that is enacted on social media platforms is so limited in form and format that much of it can be quite successfully performed by machines, specifically by social bots – automated software that is programmed to perform all the actions that a human user can perform on the platforms. Social bots "share pictures, post status updates and Tweets, enter into conversations with other SNS users, and make and accept friend and follower requests."[90] They even analyze pictures and videos posted by others so as to be able to comment on them. Such social bots already have a massive presence on Twitter and – perhaps more surprisingly – on Instagram and Facebook. In the reduced-cue environments of social media platforms, which lack the rich panoply of real-time vocal and body-behavioral cues available in face-to-face settings, many social bots are able to pass as human.[91] The success of social bots thus depends on the "radical reduction" of human sociality effected by social media platforms: "for these machines to work, we ourselves have to be trained to be machinelike."[92]

The ability of many social bots to pass as human creates disturbing possibilities for deception and manipulation.[93] These possibilities first came to broad public attention in the aftermath of the 2016 American presidential election campaign, when studies suggested that bots on

Twitter had played a significant role in fomenting polarization and disseminating misinformation.[94] The concerns will become more acute as increasingly sophisticated AI-powered natural language-generating models enable bots to pass as human in more open-ended discursive contexts.[95] My interest here, however, is in the broader ways in which sociality is being programmed, engineered, rationalized, and automated in an ecology of hyperconnectivity, not just in sophisticated political or commercial operations, but also – and more relevant for this chapter – in everyday social contexts.

Consider some ways in which routine digital micro-sociality has been partly automated. One app developer wrote code that "liked" all the photos posted on the Instagram accounts he followed – and found that friends appreciated this.[96] A less idiosyncratic example is the automation of birthday greetings on Facebook, a service provided by numerous apps. The pitch for one such app, BirthdayFb, is twofold: the app allows the user to "configure and forget – set a message once for a friend and it will be sent every year on his birthday"; and it "feels personal – unlike other similar apps, the messages [don't] have any link backs or advertisement text so nobody will know you are relying on a tool."[97] Birthday greeting apps offer a technological solution to a problem created by technology. The only reason one might be interested in such an app is that Facebook *already* automates birthday reminders. Regular Facebook users can therefore be expected to know about their friends' birthdays and can be held accountable for failing to offer birthday wishes. This leads to the overproduction and concomitant devaluation of birthday greetings – a classic example of the proliferation of burdensome micro-sociality. The dozens and sometimes hundreds of perfunctory greetings that pile up on birthdays are differentiated largely by the number of exclamation points deployed, by their capitalization conventions, and by the emojis added for seasoning. The recipient of such greetings, knowing that they have been prompted by Facebook's reminders, can derive only limited satisfaction from them. When micro-sociality becomes a chore – a form of drudgery – it is no wonder that some welcome the opportunity of outsourcing it to software.[98]

Online dating is another focus of automation efforts. Especially on the high-volume, swipe-intensive Tinder, digital abundance has made the preliminaries involved in online dating a matter of drudgery. One male San Francisco software engineer, frustrated by the amount of right-swiping required to generate matches with women – men tend to right-swipe fairly indiscriminately on Tinder, while women are much more selective – wrote some elementary code that would swipe automatically, send a standardized sequence of messages, and seek to schedule coffee dates with matches.[99] A more ambitious initiative used neural networks and facial recognition to learn a user's visual preferences and, in later iterations of the app, to send introductory messages based on contextual information gleaned from the match's profile picture.[100] The app was shut down at the request of Tinder. But dating sites themselves, including Tinder, have been investing heavily in data science and machine learning. They have access to vast troves of data, not only from their own sites, but also, in some cases, from their users' social media feeds, from which they make inferences about personality, lifestyle, and interactional style.[101] With data on what people do rather than what they say they do – as in the questionnaire-based matching model conventionally used by dating sites – data-oriented dating sites envision being able to automate the early stages of dating. Tinder co-founder Sean Rad sketched a scenario in which Tinder would know so much about whom a user is likely to be interested in that an automated Tinder assistant might say, "You know, Sean, there's a beautiful girl, someone that you're going to find very attractive down the street. You have a lot of things in common and your common friend is Justin and you're both free Thursday night and there's this great concert that you both want to go out to and can I set up a date? And here is a little bit more about her."[102]

A much more widely used form of automation is Google's Smart Reply, which brings the convenience of one-click replies to email and messaging. Why type when you can simply click? Why ponder what to say when you can acquiesce in an automated suggestion? First introduced in Gmail, and subsequently made available in all Android messaging apps, Smart Reply uses machine learning, trained on a large corpus of data, to predict replies to emails or messages, taking advantage of the fact that, even on email, many replies comprise just a few words or perhaps just an emoji. These predictions enable Smart Reply to propose three possible replies, made up of text and/or emojis; if one of these seems appropriate, the user simply taps on it to reply. Over time, Smart Reply adapts to the user's communication style, promising to "give you better responses the more you use it. So if you're more of a 'thanks!' than a 'thanks.' person, we'll suggest the response that's, well, more you!"[103]

A more experimental form of semi-automated sociability, developed by computer scientist Miaomiao Wen and a team of Microsoft researchers, involves "computer-aided humor." The system suggests "possibly funny images" to include in a digital conversation, based on the previous text and images used. If one of the suggested images seems to work, the user can click to include it (and add text if desired); the other user is then prompted with possible images to use in reply. The project initially focused on suggestions for humorous text, but the researchers found that suggesting images worked better, both because images are more ambiguous and open to interpretation than text and because computers can quickly scan large databases for potentially relevant images and make such images quick and easy to insert into an ongoing digital conversation. The program can search for potentially funny emotional reaction images and GIFs, based on one of five emotions – anger, disgust, joy, sadness, or surprise – it detects in the text; and it can generate a meme by combining the text from the last utterance in the conversation with a popular meme template. Users found the system to be engaging; they felt they could "express their own sense of humor" more than they could with plain chat or with a system in which the computer automatically inserted an image rather than proposing a set of possibly relevant images for the user to draw on as appropriate. A system like this, developed as a research project, could easily be integrated into messaging apps or social media platforms.[104]

The automation of birthday greetings, dating preliminaries, routine emailing and messaging, and even humorous exchange is premised on a logic of convenience. Automation, we are told, can save us time, spare us the cognitive burden of thinking, and emancipate us from the drudgery of repetitive tasks. It can make interaction faster, more efficient, and more frictionless. But do we always want interaction to be fast, efficient, and frictionless? Is there not something to be said for friction? For slowing down? Even, perhaps, for inefficiency?[105] Should we not be concerned by the corporate colonization of everyday communication, a new form of the colonization of the lifeworld analyzed by Jürgen Habermas?[106]

Beyond the logic of convenience, automation opens up possibilities, at once fascinating and disturbing, for entirely new forms of digital sociality. I consider just one example, though the field is vast, including all forms of social robots and chatbots, from digital playmates for children to digital companions for the elderly, socially assistive robots to support rehabilitation and training, and AI-driven forms of cognitive-behavioral therapy.[107] In 2015, after her close friend Roman died suddenly at a young age, software developer Eugenia Kuyda, whose company had developed a bot for making restaurant reservations, decided to create a memorial chatbot for her friend. Trained on Roman's text messages, the bot responds to messages in a manner that Kuyda hoped would evoke his distinctive texting voice.[108] The bot was made publicly available, and people who did not know Roman nonetheless found it meaningful to interact with the bot. This led the company to launch Replika in 2017; during the pandemic, the company claimed to have over 10 million users.

Replika is pitched not as a task-oriented digital assistant but as an empathic conversational digital companion, as "the AI companion who cares": "If you're feeling down, or anxious, or you just need someone to talk to, your Replika is here for you 24/7."[109] Replika will even offer to call you if you are unhappy. Part of a new generation of "emotionally aware chatbots," Replika is part digital friend, part life coach or wellness counselor, part journaling software, and, most distinctively, part – as the name suggests – digital representation of the user.[110] Replika asks the user direct and often intimate questions about mood, thoughts, memories, dreams, aspirations, and the like. Some users find themselves opening up to it in a way they would not do with an actual friend or therapist. The more the user interacts with it, the better it gets to know the user – and the more it becomes *like* the user. The digital avatar thus created can chat with the user's friends or with their Replika avatars. But it seems to be mainly used for chatting with oneself. Replika can be experienced as better than a real friend, because it's always fascinated by the user, and it's not judging her: it's a digital alter-ego, not a digital superego. Tempting though it is to dismiss Replika as a vehicle for digital narcissism, it can also be seen, more charitably, as "an experiment in human-bot interaction."[111]

The engineering of sociality is still in its infancy; the examples discussed here are only baby steps. But the field is developing very quickly. There seems little doubt that sophisticated forms of robotic sociality are a matter not of science fiction but of the relatively proximate future. What does this mean for our understandings of sociality? What might it mean for a machine to understand us and to respond appropriately, not just in severely limited contexts like customer service but in open-ended exchange? In what sense can we speak of "emotionally aware" artificial intelligence? Can we properly speak of machines exhibiting empathy?[112] What might it mean to have relationships of friendship or even love – as imagined by the 2013 film *Her* – with machines? How should we think about interaction with "appealing, intelligent, servile robots who make us feel special and cared for"? These are questions that are moving out of laboratories and into life.[113]

Coda: Losing touch

The early phase of the pandemic rent the fabric of routine social interaction. Sites of conviviality were shuttered. Commensality was curtailed. Workplace and schoolyard sociability collapsed as work and education went remote. Friends could not assemble to hang out; families could not congregate to celebrate or mourn. Nursing homes and hospitals banned visitors. Residential colleges rigidly limited in-person gatherings. Screen-to-screen or mask-to-mask replaced face-to-face sociability. Greetings dispensed with handshakes, kisses, and hugs. The pandemic thus imposed an unprecedented regime of distancing and touchlessness.

This rupture concealed an underlying continuity. Already before the pandemic, the online universe had become a world unto itself, a space in which the hyperconnected could live nearly all of their lives. If mobile connectivity had initially encouraged people to leave the house, hyperconnectivity had enabled them to stay home.[114] The plenitude of the online universe – the ever-widening range of content that could be accessed, activities that could be undertaken, and wants and needs that could be satisfied – had made it less and less necessary for the hyperconnected to go anywhere. It was this that made lockdowns thinkable.

Still, the lockdowns radically recast the parameters of interaction. Entire domains of previously face-to-face interaction – in personal, professional, educational, cultural, entertainment, and therapeutic contexts – were abruptly transferred to videoconferencing platforms such as Zoom. These platforms certainly helped sustain social relationships, and people made creative use of them; they organized games, workouts, lessons, happy hours, dinner parties, dates, synchronized TV and film watching, and much more. But many users found the platforms unsettling and exhausting. One key problem with Zoom is that "the body is but isn't there."[115] Users see partial images of others' bodies, but the bodies do not occupy a shared space and are therefore not mutually oriented. Gestures that are oriented to a shared space in face-to-face communication (such as gaze direction or pointing) are rendered meaningless. Deprived not only of touch but of the full range of body-behavioral cues, users cannot experience the shared focus that is generated by mutual monitoring and mutual orientation in situations of copresence. Zoom users are relentlessly exposed to the gaze of others, yet eye contact is not aligned (when looking at the image of an interlocutor on the screen, users are not looking into the camera and thus do not appear, to that interlocutor, to be making eye contact). Even more disconcerting, users are continually exposed to their own mirror image (unless they change the default settings). And they are more constrained in their mobility than they would be in face-to-face conversation.

Although people returned eagerly to in-person sociability as restrictions eased, the shift to video-mediated interaction-at-a-distance has not been and certainly will not be fully reversed. And looking to the future, Big Tech is betting heavily on investments in virtual reality (VR) and augmented reality (AR). Developments in VR and AR – given major new impetus during the pandemic – will allow distant interaction partners, represented by photorealistic avatars or even holographic projections, to occupy a shared virtual or digitally augmented space. The wager of Facebook/Meta in particular is that this respatialization of digitally mediated interaction will enable participants to feel more fully "present" with one another and that people will therefore be eager to hang out and interact with their friends, families, and colleagues in the digitally engineered spaces of the "metaverse," which Mark Zuckerberg has characterized as an "embodied internet." I take up the idea of the metaverse, as envisioned by Facebook/Meta and many other tech companies, in the Conclusion. Suffice it to say here that interaction in which the body is present for others only as a digital avatar or a holograph – and touch is experienced, if at all, only through the mediation of haptic gloves – is "embodied" in a highly attenuated sense that depends on simulation and privileges sight over other senses. The metaverse can thus be understood as the consolidation and culmination of what philosopher Richard Kearney has called the "age of excarnation."[116]

Interaction was not only *recast* during the pandemic; it was increasingly *bypassed*. Commercial transactions that had been embedded in face-to-face interactions, however cursory, were disembedded as they moved online. Such disembedding has a long pre-pandemic history in the development of e-commerce over the last three decades. But it accelerated sharply during the pandemic. Not only did online shopping surge; it also became fully disembedded from any human interaction as contactless delivery systems replaced the in-person handoff of packages. And even when commercial interactions remain face-to-face, they are no longer touch-to-touch: the rapid adoption of contactless payment systems during the pandemic means that neither cash nor credit cards need be exchanged.

Contactless transactions had been gaining ground for reasons of convenience and economy – and sometimes for cultural reasons as well – before the pandemic. In South Korea, for example, the idea of "untact" – a portmanteau of the prefix "un" and "contact" – had been deployed in marketing discourse both as a productivity-boosting way of dealing with a shrinking labor force and as a way of appealing to tech-savvy young people drawn to the prospect of streamlined, interaction-free transactions. But the concept acquired a much higher profile during the pandemic, when the promotion of untact industries became official government policy.[117] "Contactless" and "touchless" became key marketing buzzwords in the West as well, as anxieties about contagion reinforced techno-futurist visions of frictionless transactions.

The social disembedding and (from the point of view of the consumer) physical disembodying of commerce no doubt make transactions more streamlined, efficient, and hygienic. But in de-socializing and sanitizing commerce, in rendering it friction-free and contactless, they also risk making life as a whole more transactional. And they risk further invisibilizing the labor that undergirds and sustains what appears to the user as a world of frictionless transactions, on-demand delivery, and immediate gratifications.[118] In losing touch, we risk losing touch with the messiness and complexity of our world – and with our own embodied humanity.

CHAPTER THREE

Culture

Even as the bloom of enchantment with hyperconnectivity has faded in other domains – especially in the domains of economics and politics – it remains fresh in the domain of culture. On this still enchanted understanding, everyone has at their fingertips an infinitely rich and varied universe of cultural products. Barriers to access have fallen; the inexhaustible wealth of human culture is freely available to all. Individuals are not simply enriched as consumers of culture; they are empowered as producers, publishers, and distributors. Culture is increasingly shared rather than bought and sold. New cultural forms and innovative cultural practices have proliferated. Ever-expanding circles of people are actively, collaboratively, and creatively involved in the production, circulation, and consumption of culture.

The cultural promise of connectivity is threefold: it is a promise of abundance, decommodification, and democratization. The three notions are related, but it is helpful to distinguish them analytically. The promise of abundance is that of frictionless access to the whole of human culture. It takes little effort to imagine a universal digital library that would enable everyone to access – everywhere and all the time – every recorded product of human creativity in the spheres of music, literature, film and video, photography, scholarship, and so on, as well as digital representations of all the material cultural artifacts of the world's museums and archives.[1] Already today, the sheer superabundance of cultural products one can access, either for free or with a modestly priced subscription, is dizzying. The abundance on offer, moreover, is a differentiated abundance: the "long tail" of digital inventories – unlike brick and mortar stores, with their scarce shelf space – accommodates niche as well as mass or mainstream tastes.[2] Who could fail to be moved by the exhilarating horizon of possibilities opened up by this digital cultural cornucopia?

The promise of decommodification is that the production and consumption of culture can be liberated from the constraints of the market. The near-zero cost of copying and distributing digital cultural objects has removed many of them from the circuits of market exchange. This has happened in part through piracy or more or less legally dubious forms of file-sharing. But more importantly, those who hold the property rights have often been willing to distribute digital cultural objects for free as a business strategy.[3] And digital connectivity has fostered the growth of a "nonproprietary" mode of "commons-based peer production" – most clearly exemplified by Wikipedia and open-source software – that relies neither on "market signals [nor] managerial commands."[4] Amidst the ongoing commodification of more and more spheres of life, the internet has seemed, on techno-utopian accounts, to be the great exception, creating spaces governed by the logic of the gift, rather than that of the commodity.[5]

The promise of democratization is that centralized, top-down modes of cultural production are being replaced by decentralized, participatory modes. The increasing sophistication and decreasing cost of digital tools for the production of photography, video, and music, for example, have democratized cultural creativity by revitalizing amateur cultural production (and often blurring the distinction between professional and amateur).[6] More generally, universally accessible tools for "cutting, pasting, rendering, annotating, and commenting" have democratized participation in the process of shaping and reshaping cultural meanings and thereby vastly expanded the realm of "semiotic democracy."[7] These tools – enabling a transition from a "read/only" mode of engagement with cultural products to a "read/write" mode – work not just with text but with audio and visual materials; they are the basis for a broadly participatory multimedia remix culture.[8] The division between active producers and passive consumers, moreover, has been blurred in the figure of the "prosumer," whose active participation in the production of cultural content has been enabled by the interactive forms and formats of Web 2.0.[9] Cultural evaluation, too, has been democratized as user reviews and ratings have displaced professional critics and gatekeepers.

Dissenting voices, to be sure, have questioned this vision of digital abundance, decommodification, and democratization. Yet the cultural promise of hyperconnectivity remains powerful and seductive. In certain respects, indeed, the promise has already been realized. But the manner in which it has been realized, as well as the ways in which it remains unrealized, calls for critical scrutiny. Digital cultural abundance can be overwhelming and at times even impoverishing: as we struggle to keep abreast of the voluminous and accelerating flow of cultural content, drawn by the perpetual lure of the new, we come to know less and less about more and more. Decommodification in some areas has been overshadowed by recommodification in others. Democratization has flattened and in certain respects homogenized the cultural landscape, enshrining popularity as the sole measure of cultural value. I address abundance, decommodification, and democratization in turn. I begin, though, with a more general discussion of how we encounter and engage culture in the context of digital hyperconnectivity.

When culture becomes "content": The ambivalence of abundance

For more than a century, "culture" has been one of the most contested terms in the human sciences. I will not wade into these debates. Suffice it to say that I will not be concerned here with culture in the all-encompassing meaning that has been central to anthropology and influential in sociology as well, referring to the totality of socially patterned ways of understanding the world and orienting oneself in the world. I will be concerned instead – as will be evident from the preceding paragraphs – with culture in a much more limited and specific sense: with the changing ways in which we create, encounter, and engage cultural goods, products, or objects.

But what do we mean by *cultural* goods, products, or objects? What is cultural about them? How can we distinguish a discrete bit of culture from a discrete bit of something else? I do not want to get bogged down in a definitional quagmire here. But as a rough first approximation, we can treat cultural goods as those that we engage with, attend to, enjoy, value, or "consume" for their own sake, rather than as a means to some other end. More specifically, they are goods that we value and engage primarily for the sake of the symbolic, expressive, or aesthetic gratifications they afford.[10] These include not only such prototypically "cultural" goods as songs, movies, novels, and performances but also things like sporting events, games, jokes, and memes.

Digital hyperconnectivity has profoundly altered how we create, encounter, and engage cultural goods. It has recast old cultural goods in new forms, assembled them into vast digital storehouses, and made them available any time and anywhere. And it has called into being entirely new kinds of cultural goods and practices, from the sharing of user-generated textual, audio, and/or visual content on digital platforms to the live streaming of video games, from massively multiplayer online role-playing games to crowdsourced undertakings like Wikipedia, from new forms of cultural remixing exemplified by internet memes and TikToks to new visual languages based on GIFs, emojis, and stickers.

Most fundamentally, for my purposes, hyperconnectivity has demate-rialized many categories of cultural goods, transforming them into digital objects.[11] A vast, intricate, and expensive material infrastructure, to be sure, is required to store, circulate, and access these digital objects. And as the characteristics of these objects change (as more videos circulate, for example), the material infrastructure must be upgraded (to increase bandwidth, for example).

Yet dematerialization is nonetheless crucial. Cultural goods that were previously inscribed onto materials such as paper, vinyl, magnetic tape, and celluloid film and inseparably embedded in physical containers such as books, magazines, newspapers, record albums, and audio and video tapes have been pried loose from those containers. They may still be packaged and distributed in those physical vehicles, as remains true for the substantial majority of books. But even in that case, the cultural good itself – the content of the book – exists as a digital object that is both conceptually and physically separable from its material envelope.[12]

Like other digital objects, digital cultural goods share a set of key properties – or "affordances," as students of technology call them – that have radically transformed how they are produced, distributed, and consumed. These affordances can be traced back to the fact that digital cultural objects are made out of bits rather than atoms.[13] They can therefore be copied with perfect fidelity. They can be transmitted frictionlessly and instantaneously. They are weightless and take up no space. They are non-rivalrous: they can be shared without diminishing the amount or quality of the good available for others. They are often though not always non-excludable: when they are provided to some users, it is hard (since they can be so easily copied) to keep others from enjoying them as well.[14] They can be manipulated with simple, widely available tools. They can be produced at much lower cost than material cultural goods.

The affordances of digital objects are conjoined with those of mobile hyperconnectivity. Ubiquitous, always-on connectivity means that digital cultural objects – like all other digital content – can be delivered and consumed anywhere and any time. Since connected devices serve increasingly as means of cultural production, and not simply of cultural consumption, a wide range of digital cultural goods (TikTok videos, for example) can also be produced and shared anywhere and any time.

The paired affordances of digital objects and mobile hyperconnectivity underlie and enable the staggering abundance of digital cultural goods. (They also underlie the partial decommodification and democratization of culture, as I will discuss in subsequent sections.) Because digital cultural goods take up essentially no space, they can be stored in unlimited quantities at minimal cost. Because they are weightless and frictionlessly transmissible, their marginal cost of distribution is near zero. Because they are perfectly and instantaneously replicable, they can be reproduced essentially for free. The digitization of non-digital cultural objects is extremely inexpensive as well, since the object, once digitized, is infinitely replicable and frictionlessly distributable.

Inexpensive digitization and the negligible marginal cost of storage, replication, and distribution enable and incentivize the accumulation and bundling of immense stocks of cultural content.[15] Spotify, for example, hosts 80 million songs, while 500 hours of new videos are uploaded to YouTube every minute, all made accessible for free (with ads) or for a small fee (without ads) to some 400 million Spotify users and 2 billion YouTube users.[16] It is not only the stocks of digital cultural goods that are superabundant, but also the flows. On Spotify and YouTube, for example, the autoplay feature, enabled by default, ensures that the music – and the video – never stops. Another widely implemented form of digital abundance is the infinite scroll: new content is dynamically loaded as the user scrolls, without the user having to click "next page" or take any other action. No matter how long one scrolls, one never reaches the end; the user may be exhausted, but the feed is inexhaustible. Particularly well adapted to mobile devices, the infinite scroll harnesses psychological knowledge – of dopamine loops, variable reinforcement schedules, and the lure of the unknown – to capture and hold users' attention.[17] In TikTok's algorithmically governed "for you" mode, for example, the user never even has to click "play"; a new video starts to play every time one scrolls just a bit further.

TikTok illustrates a further aspect of digital abundance: the shrinking of digital cultural goods. Hyperconnectivity has not only furthered the fragmentation of time, as noted in the previous chapter, but also enabled and incentivized the production and circulation of ever-smaller bits of digital stuff that can be used to fill up the smallest fragments of unused time. These include not only new forms of asynchronous micro-sociality but also new forms of micro-culture and micro-entertainment.[18] Vine led the way with six-second videos; TikTok succeeded spectacularly with its fifteen-second format; and Google has responded with its fifteen-second YouTube Shorts. Designed to be viewed on phones, these can be consumed on the go, anywhere and any time. Memes are another key form of digital micro-culture. Shifman has persuasively argued that internet memes are not individual digital items; they are rather collections of related items, created in reference to one another.[19] But it is the individual variants – the images or ultra-short videos into which complex meanings are condensed – that we encounter and appreciate, one at a time, not the collection as a whole (even though our appreciation of any given individual item depends on our familiarity with related items).

Our experience of cultural goods is shaped by the affordances not only of the goods themselves but also of the distribution systems through which we access them. Non-digital cultural goods were and are distributed through a variety of different delivery systems and spaces, many of them tailored to the particular kind of good being delivered. For tangible goods (or intangible goods embedded in tangible vehicles, as in the case of physical books), these include bookstores and other retail stores, libraries, galleries, and museums. For intangible goods that take the form of events, they include informal spaces where people gather for privately coordinated activities and institutionalized spaces such as movie theaters, stadiums, performance venues, and all kinds of sites where "experiences" are staged and consumed.[20] These differentiated packaging and delivery systems help keep non-digital cultural goods distinct from one another and from other sorts of non-digital goods.

Unlike the differentiated distribution of non-digital goods, the superabundant flow of digital cultural goods is delivered through a single general-purpose system. That delivery system is shared by all other digital content – weather forecasts, traffic reports, financial transactions, messages from friends and families, news, porn, shopping, social media feeds, and so on. Everything flows through the same pipes and reaches us through the same screens of the same receivers, be they phones, tablets, laptops, or desktops. Moreover, different streams of cultural content draw on similar audiovisual codes and communicational conventions. Since all digital cultural goods flow through the same conduits, devices, and interfaces and share similar codes and conventions – and since they also share these conduits, devices, interfaces, codes, and formats with all other digital content – they tend to blur together in the continuous flow of content.[21]

The reformatting of culture as content thus erodes the distinctiveness, integrity, and boundaries of digital cultural goods. Temporally and spatially separate and distinct encounters with non-digital cultural goods yield to continuous, blurred, device-mediated, anytime-anywhere exposure to the ceaseless cultural flow. There are no specific times and places for digital culture. Music, in particular, becomes ubiquitous, since it can accompany us anywhere and any time, in the background, regardless of what we are attending to in the foreground; it can envelope us in a perpetual sonic cocoon.[22] But all forms of digital culture tend toward the ubiquitous; we encounter digital culture as it washes over us in a never-ending flow.

The superabundant stocks and ceaseless flow of digital cultural content – hyper-accessible, device-mediated, and ubiquitous – fundamentally reshape our mode of engagement with cultural goods. They invite and facilitate browsing, scanning, skimming, grazing, sampling, skipping, and shuffling. As the volume of accessible culture increases and the size of cultural units shrinks, the pace of circulation accelerates; we encounter more culture than ever, but we engage it more superficially.[23] We surf on the cultural froth.

As our mode of engagement with cultural objects changes, so do our habits, expectations, and capacities.[24] We acquire new capacities but lose old ones – or never develop them in the first place. Reskilling and deskilling go hand in hand. The range of our cultural references expands as the span of our attention shrinks. We become efficient processors, capable of registering a tremendous range of cultural stimuli and keeping abreast of shifting constellations of cultural references; this helps us display a kind of digital-age cultural literacy, based more on knowingness than on knowledgeability.[25] We are chronically distracted, but we become more agile and nimble, skilled at making lateral associations and maneuvering amidst the accelerating flow. We become so agile that we may opt to further accelerate the flow of content, listening to podcasts and watching YouTube videos at speeds up to twice the original.[26] But our capacity for sustained engagement is diminished.

Material cultural objects slow us down; their materiality creates friction. We cannot jump instantaneously from one book, one film (at a movie theatre), one live performance to another. Digital cultural objects speed us up; their immateriality eliminates friction. We *can* jump nearly instantaneously from one musical track, one streaming film, one TikTok to another.

The frictionless hyper-accessibility of superabundant digital content tends to diminish the value and significance of any given cultural object. And it tends to diminish our investment in any particular object. Our chronic awareness of alternatives – the endless supply of new items on the horizons of our attention – increases the opportunity cost of staying with any given item; and the frictionless accessibility of the alternatives renders negligible the cost of switching.

Frictionless superabundance may even lead to a crisis of desire, as Eric Drott has argued with respect to music streaming services.[27] Such services were initially predicated on a "database logic" that promised unfettered access. But unlimited access may undermine desire and leave listeners paralyzed. Streaming services therefore seek to recreate scarcity in new forms; they have invested heavily in recommendation and curation systems that promise to identify and deliver "your song, right here, right now," as a Pandora commercial put it.[28] This striking shift from emphasizing access to "any song, any time, anywhere" to suggesting that there is only one right song for every moment testifies eloquently to the ambivalence of abundance.

That ambivalence predates hyperconnectivity. Nearly twenty years ago, psychologist Barry Schwartz popularized the idea that, in many domains of life, an "overabundance of choice" reduces rather than enhances well-being. The internet figured only glancingly in Schwartz's account. But hyperconnectivity – a great engine for the generation of abundance and the proliferation of choice – has made the ambivalence of abundance more acute than ever.[29]

Some relish the choices offered by cultural superabundance; they enjoy exploring the inexhaustible landscape of possibilities. But doing so can be strenuous, and it requires certain skills and dispositions. For many, the path of least resistance is to go with the programmed flow and accept the algorithmically personalized offerings of "automated culture."[30] The data-nourished dream of music streaming services, for example, is to relieve the listener of the burdens of choice altogether: the "ultimate interface" is one in which "you hit play and you don't have to do anything else."[31] With enough data, the service aspires to deliver the right song for every moment by matching the music to the listener's sensor-gleaned, algorithmically inferred mood, location, activity, and context. As the algorithms get better, the temptation to simply let oneself be carried along by the programmed flow can only grow stronger.[32]

Here we again encounter the tension between the choice-expanding, choice-demanding aspects of hyperconnectivity and the guiding or bypassing of choice through nudging or through algorithms that make decisions for us.[33] In the domain of culture, hyperconnectivity increases the burdens of choice by making a vast universe of cultural goods frictionlessly accessible; but it also proposes to alleviate those burdens by matching us with the right content. In this as in other domains, hyperconnectivity provides solutions to the very problems it has itself exacerbated.

Even apart from the burdens of choice, collective cultural abundance may itself paradoxically entail a kind of individual cultural impoverishment. This was noted long before the digital age by the social theorist Georg Simmel, who underscored the "atrophy of individual culture through the hypertrophy of objective culture."[34] As the accumulated cultural products of humanity – Simmel's "objective culture" – loom ever larger, the fraction of this collective cultural wealth that any individual can appropriate becomes vanishingly small, and the individual becomes ever more insignificant as a locus of embodied culture.

Hyperconnectivity accentuates this tension between collective abundance and individual impoverishment. It does so by making collective cultural wealth visible, proximate, and accessible. That wealth appears to us as simply there for the taking. But the taking takes time, and time is the ultimate scarcity. Even as we accelerate our cultural consumption and process more and more cultural items per unit of time, a world of superabundant possibility confronts us brutally with our own finitude. "A wealth of information" – to quote again Herbert Simon's pithy observation – "creates a poverty of attention."[35] The collective digital abundance of which we are reminded at every turn can make us feel individually poorer, since we are hyper-aware of what we are missing.

Decommodification or recommodification?

The promise of decommodification is premised in part on abundance. The conditions that underlie digital abundance – the properties of bits and network infrastructures that allow near zero-marginal-cost copying, storage, and distribution of digital objects on an immense scale – also make it unnecessary to attach price tags to many digital cultural objects. Price signals are a mechanism for coordinating action in a context of scarcity, and individual prices serve as measures of relative scarcity.[36] If a particular good is in superabundant supply, its price tends toward zero.[37] And in a context of general digital abundance, prices lose their signaling, coordinating function.

For the consumer, the suspension of the price mechanism indeed represents a decommodification of culture. An immense world of digital cultural objects appears as freely accessible on demand; it is experienced as – and is expected to be – a world of "free culture."[38] This marks an important shift in the way people experience culture. But it amounts to a very limited form of decommodification. In the first place, consumers *do* pay for many professionally produced digital cultural goods. For the most part, to be sure, they pay for bundles or subscriptions rather than for individual cultural goods (though people are also willing to pay individually, given convenience and low transaction costs, for particular items, for example, to rent individual films). And people may experience this bundled mode of accessing digital culture as quasi-decommodified, since what is commodified is not the cultural goods themselves (to which subscribers enjoy unmetered, non-price-regulated access), but the service provided by the aggregator. This is most clear in the case of Spotify, which provides an advertisement-supported free option that allows listeners to access the full range of content, albeit with lower audio quality. The commodity offered by Spotify is therefore not access to the music, but rather a more enjoyable listening experience.[39]

Yet in view of the warnings about the existential threat posed to the music and film industries by freely accessible digital content, it is striking how successful subscription-based services have been at getting people to pay for professionally produced culture. Contrary to expectations, people have shown themselves quite willing to pay for the quality, quantity, convenience, security, user-friendly interface, and social media integration they offer. Spotify, notably, has amassed over 180 million paid subscribers, notwithstanding the availability of its free option; Netflix has 220 million. Clearly, one cannot speak of the decommodification of digital culture in general, even if users experience streaming services as quasi-decommodified.

Moreover, even when firms provide free access to digital goods, as many digital platforms have done, they do so as part of a business strategy. Chris Anderson's popular book *Free: The Future of a Radical Price* was aimed precisely at businesses; it expressly promoted making digital goods free as a way of making money, whether through direct cross-subsidies, "freemium" models, or two-sided markets (in which firms provide free content to consumers while selling advertisers access to the consumers).[40]

The broader and more radical promise of decommodification is not about making cultural *consumption* free of charge; it is about freeing cultural *production* from the constraints of the market. Toward the beginning of his 2006 magnum opus *The Wealth of Networks*, Yochai Benkler observed that previous revolutions in technologies of communication over the last century and a half had worked to "concentrate and commercialize" the production of culture. But digital connectivity, Benkler argued, held out the promise of reversing this double trend. "[E]merging models of information and cultural production, radically decentralized and based on emergent patterns of cooperation and sharing, are beginning to take on an ever-larger role in how we produce ... information, knowledge, and culture."[41]

Enthusiasts invariably cite Wikipedia for demonstrating the possibilities for decentralized, collaborative, non-market-oriented cultural production. Its evident unevenness and limitations notwithstanding, Wikipedia is indeed a magnificent example of such "commons-based peer production," as Benkler termed it, and one that managed to win over many initially skeptical critics. Open-source software is another oft-cited example.[42] Yet as Benkler himself felt obliged to acknowledge in a somewhat melancholy retrospective piece, "expansion of the domain of nonmarket production has stalled."[43] Wikipedia and open-source software remain islands of fully decommodified cultural production in an immense sea in which few undertakings are fully insulated from market logics.

There are of course expansive terrains of amateur cultural production and circulation in which many users share their own creations – photos, fanfiction, poetry, music, videos, commentary, and so forth – without any expectation or hope of monetary reward. But these terrains have become deeply embedded in a commercial ecosystem of tightly interconnected digital platforms, dominated by the largest and most powerful corporations on the planet. Like so many other domains of social life, amateur cultural creativity is increasingly mediated by – and dependent on – digital platforms that seek to commodify and profit from the activities of their users.[44]

Even when users themselves have no commercial interests or aspirations, they are conscripted into circuits of commercial production. This happens in two main ways. On the one hand, as noted above in connection with two-sided markets, platforms extract data from users in return for the free or cross-subsidized services they provide, and they monetize those data by selling targeted ads or by selling the data to data brokers. On the other hand, platforms extract value from users' activities: they profit both from the primary content that users create and share and from the secondary circulation of and engagement with others' content – the "small acts of engagement" (likes, comments, and so on) through which that content is made more visible and thereby more valuable.[45] Many commentators have interpreted this as a form of unpaid and exploited labor; others reject treating as labor what may be subjectively experienced as enjoyable or playful activity.[46] But either way, users and user-generated content are deeply implicated in processes of commodification.

Digital platforms do not simply exploit users; they also transform users. They not only possess immense economic (and political) power; they also enjoy immense cultural power. That cultural power enables platforms to shape users' aspirations and subjectivities and to socialize them into market or quasi-market logics. Platforms inculcate attunement and attachment to the currency of attention and the signals of value that currency conveys. They encourage and legitimize self-branding and self-commodification. Even users uninterested in monetization are inexorably drawn into the comparative and competitive dynamics of the attention economy. On pain of digital invisibility and non-existence, they orient their cultural production to that which will command attention: to signals of what will "sell," even if no monetary prices are involved.

Platforms also directly promote strategies of monetization. They nurture fantasies of fame and fortune, focused on the alluring figure of the social media influencer. Success on the scale of the top influencers is as distant a dream as that of movie stardom in an earlier era. But like that earlier dream, it is powerfully resonant and inspiring. And there are growing opportunities for some degree of monetization. Already in 2016, some 2.5 million people were making some money from YouTube;[47] more recently, the other major platforms have been introducing or expanding monetization opportunities. Yet with remuneration rates declining steeply as the volume of content chasing ad revenue has exploded, the vast majority of YouTube content creators earn very little.[48] By the calculation of one researcher, even those at the threshold of the top 3 percent of YouTube channels earn only about $1,400 per month for their 1.4 million monthly views.[49]

Nonetheless, the widely diffused aspiration to "get paid to do what you love" and platforms' eagerness to monetize user-generated content have come together to create an "emerging proto-industry based on previously amateur creators professionalising and engaging in content innovation and media entrepreneurship across multiple social media platforms to aggregate global fan communities and incubate their own media brands." A key component of this proto-industry is the growing array of commercial intermediaries that position themselves between content creators and platforms, offering to help the former professionalize their operations and monetize their content, in return for a share of their ad revenues.[50]

The emergence of this "social media entertainment" industry has no doubt empowered content creators in some respects and opened up new micro-entrepreneurship opportunities for them, even if it has been disempowering in other respects, rendering their labor precarious and contingent.[51] But that emergence is also a sign of the increasingly close intertwining of digital culture and commerce. By one reckoning, 40 percent of all Instagram accounts with more than 15,000 followers – some half million in all – belong to influencers.[52] As brands turn increasingly to "influencer marketing" in an effort to reach younger audiences, platforms have been seeking to make user-generated cultural content more seamlessly "shoppable," for example by enabling within-app purchases of items tagged in influencers' posts on Instagram. In accordance with the central mantra of e-commerce, such initiatives seek to "remove friction" from the shopping experience.[53]

The commodification of digital culture extends to terrains and practices self-consciously defined in opposition to mainstream commercial culture. The initially esoteric memetic language first developed and popularized in the anonymous subcultural space of self-identifying internet trolls – in which everything is done "for the lulz": for "the joy of disrupting another's emotional equilibrium" – has itself been commercially appropriated.[54] Memes have become a major marketing strategy. This is yet another instance of the infinite absorptive power of capitalism and of what Thomas Frank called the "commodification of deviance." "Cool capitalism" thrives on the "incorporation of disaffection."[55]

The promise of cultural decommodification, in sum, remains unrealized. Enthusiastic celebration of cooperative modes of unlocking the "wealth of networks" has given way to disillusioned critiques of proprietary strategies for extracting wealth *from* networks. Wikipedia, once heralded as a model for decentralized and decommodified intellectual and cultural production, now appears as sui generis and non-replicable. Decentralization and decommercialization have yielded to recentralization and recommercialization. User-generated cultural production is flourishing, but it is "subsumed under the wider economic regime of 'platform capitalism.'"[56] Cultural production is ever more finely attuned to signals of what will attract attention, and attention is ever more pervasively measured and monetized. Platforms find new "ways to commercialize the smallest particles of our time and attention."[57] Far from freeing culture from commerce, hyperconnectivity has brought commerce and culture together in an ever-tighter embrace.

Democratization: Participation, creativity, power

Celebrants of cultural democratization have pointed to a number of ways in which hyperconnectivity has enabled broader, more active, and more self-directed popular participation in the production, circulation, and consumption of cultural goods.[58] Inexpensive and user-friendly digital tools for editing and manipulating text, images, and sounds have broadened access to the means of cultural production. Gatekeeper-free digital platforms and tools for frictionless sharing have expanded access to the means of cultural circulation. And the eclipse of critics and institutionalized cultural intermediaries has emancipated consumers from the cultural tutelage of professional tastemakers and enabled them to direct their own cultural consumption.[59]

The argument about the democratization of cultural *production* turns on overcoming barriers to access: barriers of cost on the one hand, barriers of skill on the other. The tools used in digital cultural production – in the domain of print but even more strikingly in the domains of music, image, and video production – have become much more accessible in this double sense: much cheaper and also much easier to use. Many tools for editing and manipulating text, sound, images, and videos are free and require no special skill or training to use. This has indisputably broadened access to the means of cultural production.[60] And digital platforms have provided gatekeeper-free and cost-free spaces in which to publish – to make public – one's creations.

But the promise of the democratization of cultural production is not simply a quantitative promise of increased access. It concerns not only *how many* people participate in the production of cultural goods, but *how* people participate.[61] It is a qualitative promise of the democratization of active, meaningful forms of cultural production – a promise, in short, of the democratization of cultural creativity.

Whether hyperconnectivity has fostered cultural democratization in this qualitative sense is not obvious. TikTok, for example, has contributed powerfully to the democratization of cultural production among young people. About half of young Americans use the platform, and one survey found that over half of "engaged" users had themselves uploaded a video.[62] TikTok is also undoubtedly an important site of vernacular cultural creativity. It enables and invites the pointed, witty, playful, allusive, zany, and endlessly inventive combination of video, music, and text.[63] TikTok has created a wildly successful form of micro-entertainment that engages the creative energies of its billion-plus users.

Yet the creative energies of TikTok users are circumscribed, channeled, and templated by the architecture of the platform.[64] The platform's success in enlisting consumers as producers depends on its making production astoundingly easy. One can create a new video – the vast majority of which, reflecting the memetic logic of the platform, riff on existing videos – in a matter of seconds, with a few taps on the screen: grab a song extract (from an existing video or a library of pre-cut extracts), choose a filter, shoot the video, select a cool "effect" (providing distortions, clones, "green screen" backgrounds, augmented reality effects that interact with the videographer's environment, and so on), add a few hashtags, and post. One can of course invest a lot of time and skill in crafting a TikTok video, but neither time nor skill is required. TikTok "enables everyone to be a creator."[65] But it does so, arguably, through the automation and deskilling of creative labor.

Jean Burgess has identified a key tension in technology design between "usability" and "hackability," the former emphasizing "easy access to a predetermined set of simple operations," the latter open-ended manipu-lability and scope for "complex experimentation."[66] TikTok and many other digital tools and platforms encourage broad participation in the production of culture by opting for extreme usability. Broadening cultural participation by radically redefining and simplifying what it means to participate is certainly not new: the brilliant slogan "you push the button, we do the rest" was coined in 1888 by George Eastman to market the new Kodak portable camera to a mass public.[67] Yet the cultural dominance of the iPhone – and more generally the displacement of the open internet by "walled gardens" and apps focused on stream-lining and simplifying the user experience – has taken the "triumph of seamless usability" to a new level, in the sphere of cultural production as well as consumption.[68] This "tyranny of convenience" should sensitize us to what may be lost – alongside all that is gained – when democratization proceeds through deskilling.[69] A democratization of culture worthy of its name, one might argue, would promote the development of skills and capacities rather than minimize the need for them.

In a celebratory 2005 account of the participatory efflorescence enabled by the Web, Kevin Kelly envisioned a near future in which nearly "everyone alive will ... write a song, author a book, make a video, craft a weblog, and code a program."[70] But what will it mean to "write a song" when automation, deskilling, and frictionless convenience are pushed even further? Already today, the AI music company Amper promises to help customers "create your own original music in seconds."[71] That the creativity involved is rather attenuated, amounting to editing and tweaking the music generated by the AI, did not stop Amper co-founder Drew Silverstein from evangelizing in a TED talk about how AI can "democratize music" by enabling "anyone to express their creativity through music."[72] There are no doubt important ways in which creativity can indeed be exercised and developed in and through interactions with AI. Yet marketing pitches about the democratization of creativity – pitches that were central to Kodak, have been central to Apple,[73] and are central to TikTok and many other digital platforms – warrant a certain critical skepticism. Such skepticism would seem to be all the more important when those pitches serve to harness and, arguably, exploit vernacular creativity by enclosing it within the regulated, surveilled, and commodified space of the platform.[74]

The argument about the democratization of access to the means of cultural *circulation* turns on the decline of gatekeepers. Many digital platforms are open to all comers and welcome all user contributions. Open platforms do, to be sure, bar certain kinds of content that they deem unacceptable or inappropriate.[75] But these platforms are not otherwise selective: they employ no gatekeepers who filter contributions based on judgments of quality or marketability. Users, moreover, can not only publish their own materials without the mediation of editorial gatekeepers; they can also recirculate others' materials. The eclipse of gatekeepers and the rise of open digital platforms have created new ways for content and talent to emerge and circulate. They have redistributed cultural power – so goes the argument – from elite cultural intermediaries and large cultural firms and organizations to ordinary people. The argument about the democratizing effects of the eclipse of gatekeepers is thus ultimately an argument about power.

Digital hyperconnectivity has indeed enabled ordinary people to publish their materials – to make them publicly available – without gatekeeper intervention. But making something publicly available on a digital platform does not mean that it will be seen. Anybody can speak, in the digital cultural sphere, but nobody may be listening. In an increasingly saturated cultural environment, this problem is all too familiar to those hoping to gain some visibility.[76] There may be no gatekeeper at the point of publication, but there is a gatekeeper, albeit a non-human one, at the point of circulation. Who sees what – in the domain of culture as well as that of news, commentary, and political speech – is governed by opaque and proprietary algorithms.

It is therefore misleading to speak of the democratization of the means of cultural circulation. The means of circulation are algorithmic, and they are not subject to democratic accountability or control. Ordinary people have gained access to the means of publication, but they have *not* gained access to the means of circulation. Nor can one speak of a redistribution or deconcentration of cultural power. Hyperconnectivity has arguably further concentrated cultural power. The giant platforms have accumulated immense cultural and political as well as economic power. Their cultural power is a kind of meta-power: a power to shape the distribution of cultural power by designing and controlling the architectures of visibility that determine who sees what.[77] Not only is cultural power highly concentrated *in* platforms; the cultural power distributed *through* platforms and their regimes of visibility is also highly concentrated.

It was widely anticipated that, on the newly level playing field of digital culture, the cultural and economic logic of the blockbuster would yield to a more egalitarian distribution of attention. This, it was thought, would enable small and previously unknown cultural producers to thrive, each with their own niche audience. Instead, researchers have found that the distribution of attention remains highly unequal across a wide range of digital contexts, ensuring the hyper-visibility of a few and the invisibility or near-invisibility of the great majority. The winner-take-all (or winner-take-most) logic, sustained in part by algorithms that ratify and reinforce what is already popular, remains as entrenched as ever.[78]

The argument about the democratization of cultural *consumption*, finally, is partly an argument about access. Digital cultural abundance – and the partial decommodification of consumption it has enabled – broadens access to goods that were once scarce or expensive. And digital platforms, bypassing traditional intermediaries, promise access to those previously excluded or intimidated by a lack of cultural capital.[79] But the more interesting argument is about making cultural consumption autonomously self-directed and active rather than other-directed and passive.

That argument goes something like this. Digitally mediated cultural abundance, together with the massive erosion in the power of professional tastemakers, empowers the public; it enables and invites people to take charge of their own cultural consumption.[80] Instead of being fed from above a limited diet of standardized cultural products, everyone – not just a minority of highly educated cultural omnivores – can now craft a varied and customized cultural diet reflecting their own tastes and preferences. People create these customized diets not on their own or as members of an undifferentiated mass public but as participants in differentiated niche taste publics. Members of these publics – an individual may belong to several such publics – share the work of "curation": the work of "seeking, arranging, choosing, and contextualizing." This collective work is carried out in networked virtual public spaces, in which participants exchange discoveries, suggestions, and assessments.[81] The democratization of consumption and the democratization of evaluation therefore go hand-in-hand: cultural consumption becomes democratically self-directed insofar as members of niche publics share the curatorial work of discovery and appraisal.

Vigorously participatory curatorial subcultures certainly exist. Yet however attractive in principle the vision of universal participatory curatorship, it is too exigent to have broad appeal in practice. Curation entails "time- and energy-consuming labor that must be expended before the pleasure of viewing [or listening or reading] can occur"; it therefore "requires more intentionality and less spontaneity" than other ways of discovering content.[82] It is therefore no surprise that most people, most of the time, would prefer to leave much of the hard work of curation to others – or to algorithms. People do enjoy sharing their discoveries with friends, and they may at least occasionally rate, review, and comment on items on digital cultural platforms. But sustained curatorial participation in niche communities of consumption is itself a niche activity, not a universal practice.

For most, the pleasures of digital cultural consumption are uncoupled from the exertions of curatorship. Today's digital consumers are no longer being fed a limited diet of standardized cultural products, but they are still being fed. Consumption may be personalized, but it would be a stretch, in most cases, to call it self-directed, and it is not necessarily more active than pre-digital forms of "mass" cultural consumption.[83] Even so enthusiastic a proponent of participatory digital culture as Benkler has been obliged to acknowledge the continued "prevalence of the culture of passive consumption."[84] Spotify, as noted above, invested heavily in its own curation services – both algorithmic and human – after finding that many of its listeners were baffled by superabundance, burdened by excessive choice, and uninterested in charting their own paths through the digital wilderness.[85] And while TikTok has successfully recruited users as producers, it has also perfected a fully passivized mode of consumption: its algorithmic "For You" feed offers what many find an irresistibly gratifying and uncannily personalized stream of videos that requires no choice whatsoever by the consumer – indeed no involvement at all beyond the occasional tap on a heart icon and the flick of a finger that allows one to skip the rest of an unengaging video.

One might, to be sure, look at the democratization of cultural consumption from a different point of view. Instead of insisting on autonomously self-directed and actively participatory consumption, one might be more concerned with emancipating people from the cultural tutelage of critics and other elite cultural intermediaries and enabling them to consume what they like and want. And while the emancipation of popular cultural consumption from elite tutelage began long before the internet era,[86] hyperconnectivity has accelerated this process by undermining the power of professional critics and elite gatekeepers.[87] From this perspective, one might be tempted to understand algorithms like that of TikTok – or the trending algorithms that invite us to consume what others are consuming – as democratizing.

Yet just as participation, understood purely quantitatively, cannot be the sole criterion by which to assess the democratization of cultural production, so popularity cannot be the sole touchstone for assessing the democratization of cultural consumption. And just as a robustly democratic politics of cultural production would enable people to develop their skills and capacities, so a democratic politics of cultural consumption would enable people to develop their tastes, interests, and knowledge. A democratic cultural politics, in short, would be developmentalist, oriented to learning, growth, and discovery, rather than presentist. All kinds of resources made available by digital hyperconnectivity could support such a developmentalist cultural politics. But the algorithms that feed us what we like or register what is popular – and thereby performatively amplify that popularity – are oriented to the here and now.

Moreover, as critic Rob Horning has argued with respect to TikTok, algorithms do not simply discern what we want and serve it to us; they train us to want what they can serve us. Successful platforms do not just discover what consumers want; they produce the consumers – and the forms of consumer desire – that they need.[88] Of course, this is not specific to the digital economy; it is an abiding feature of capitalism, understood as a system not only of satisfying but of generating wants. To the extent that preferences are endogenous, shaped by the systems that claim simply to respond to them, the satisfaction of preferences cannot serve as an independent normative standard. When algorithms that are portrayed as responding to our desires are in fact tuned to optimizing – and thereby monetizing – our "engagement" with the platform, there is no reason to regard such algorithmically organized cultural consumption as democratic.[89]

* * *

Of the three cultural promises of connectivity considered in this chapter, the promise of abundance has doubtless been most fully realized. But digital cultural abundance, its manifold delights notwithstanding, has turned out to be a mixed blessing. Individual cultural goods lose their distinctiveness and integrity as they blur together in a vast and undifferentiated stream of digital content, all flowing through the same pipes and flickering across the same screens. The superabundant stocks and accelerating flows feed us more culture than ever but diminish our capacity for sustained engagement. The overabundance of choice may overwhelm rather than empower us; it may tempt us to go with the programmed flow and outsource our choices to algorithms, which may know our tastes better than we ourselves do – and may indeed powerfully shape our tastes.

The promise of decommodification is the least well realized. To be sure, much of digital culture is freely accessible to anyone with an internet connection; abundance has indeed made the price mechanism irrelevant in some contexts. But even content to which no price tag is attached is paid for in some manner, not least through platforms' monetization of our attention and our data. More fundamentally, even where cultural consumption has been decommodified, cultural production is driven chiefly by market logics; the alternative logic of commons-based peer production, in which high hopes had been invested, remains marginal, shining exceptions like Wikipedia notwithstanding. Amateur cultural creativity is increasingly mediated by and dependent on profit-seeking platforms, while the culture of self-branding and the rise of the influencer have aligned the social media attention economy ever more closely with the commercial economy.

If the promise of democratization means a broadening popular participation in the production, circulation, and evaluation of cultural goods and a more participatory form of consumption, then hyperconnectivity has undoubtedly been democratizing. It has increased the numbers and widened the range of those involved in creating, publishing, distributing, and assessing cultural goods, and it has opened up new modes of participatory cultural consumption. But the promise of cultural democratization is not simply about increased participation. It is also about the democratization of creativity, the redistribution of cultural power, and the active self-direction of cultural consumption. These are more difficult to assess, but there are grounds for skepticism about whether hyperconnectivity has been democratizing in these respects.

CHAPTER FOUR

Economics

It is no small irony that the economic transformations that emplaced oligopolistic tech giants at the commanding heights of the US and the global economy were accompanied and abetted by a self-consciously "alternative," anti-corporate ethos and discourse with roots in what historian Fred Turner called the "new communalist" strand of late 1960s counterculture. In Turner's compelling account of the path "from counterculture to cyberculture," the new communalists rejected political action and embraced "technology and the transformation of consciousness as the primary sources of social change." Their most enduring achievement was to legitimize information technology by dissociating it from the loathed military-industrial complex and associating it instead with personal growth and social renewal. The techno-utopian discourse of the new communalists promised creativity in lieu of conformity, self-expression in lieu of soullessness, collaboration in lieu of competition. It envisioned not just a new economy but a new society that would be egalitarian, decentralized, and harmonious. This discourse built a bridge between new communalist countercultural ideals and Silicon Valley entrepreneurship by way of the Whole Earth Catalog, the WELL (a celebrated early virtual community of the 1980s), and the techno-enthusiasts of *Wired* magazine in the 1990s.[1]

Turner's book ends with the collapse of the dot-com bubble. But the story he traced continued to unfold. The various commercial undertakings associated with Web 2.0 wrapped themselves in a mantle cut from similar cloth. They recast consumers as co-creators and invoked community, connectedness, authenticity, participation, empowerment, and openness along with creativity, collaboration, and self-expression.[2] The mission statement of Facebook (now Meta), for example, promises to "give people the power to build community and bring the world closer together."[3]

Amidst this welter of ideals, one stands out for its versatility, resonance, and metaphorical linking power. This is the idea and ideal of "sharing." More than any other term, "sharing" captured the public imagination by knitting together disparate digitally mediated practices and infusing them with the warm glow of countercultural values of equality, mutuality, and community and therapeutic ideals of openness and intimacy.[4] The practices range from the circulation and recirculation of digital objects (as in Napster-era file-sharing and the sharing of content on social media sites) through the unrecompensed participation in a digitally coordinated common task (as in Wikipedia or open-source software development) to the digitally coordinated "sharing" of underutilized material objects (such as cars, homes, or tools). Even the communication of user-supplied personal information to advertisers has been called "sharing."[5]

The "sharing economy" came to stand not just for this set of practices but for a broader and more fundamental shift – or set of interrelated shifts – in economic and social organization held to have been occasioned by hyperconnectivity: from ownership to access, from selfishness to solidarity, from centralization to decentralization, from alienated labor to micro-entrepreneurship, from wastefulness to sustainability, from isolation to conviviality, from the sclerotic corporation to the dynamic crowd, from individualistic competition to networked collaboration, and from the separation of producer and consumer to their fusion in the "prosumer" or "produser." Various versions of this transformation have been articulated – and celebrated – not only in corporate rhetoric, boosterish business literature, and popular accounts but also in academic social theory.[6]

In the burgeoning literature on economic aspects of hyperconnectivity, many analysts have recognized that "sharing" is a problematic and in many respects misleading term. They may place "sharing" in scare quotes to distance themselves from its connotations;[7] they may seek to distinguish "true" sharing from "pseudo-sharing";[8] or they may comment on the ideological and in certain respects obfuscatory work done by the term.[9] Yet many continue to take "the sharing economy" as their object of analysis, no doubt because of the momentum acquired by the concept at the intersection of corporate, journalistic, and scholarly discourses as well as the undeniable resonance of "sharing" to a generation that has grown up sharing digital objects online.[10]

Others, however, have categorically rejected the sharing economy perspective. The most generative alternative perspective has focused on the digital platform as a novel economic and social-organizational form.[11] "Platform" had long been used in the computer industry to designate a base (such as an operating system) on top of which other programs could be written.[12] In the Web 2.0 context, the term became much more widely used, carrying with it vernacular associations both literal ("a raised level surface on which people or things can stand") and figurative (a "ground, foundation, or basis" for something else). "Platform" has thereby come to suggest an "open, neutral, egalitarian and progressive" infrastructure for activity, "promising to support those who stand on it" and enabling without directing or constraining their activities.[13]

Thus "platform," like "sharing," is an ideologically loaded term; its vernacular resonances have been strategically harnessed by tech companies.[14] But to a much greater extent than the concept of "sharing," the concept of "platform" (and associated terms like "platformization," "platform capitalism," and "platform society") has acquired a clear set of analytical meanings, sharply distinct from the vernacular meanings, that have powerful analytical traction on the economic and social transformations occasioned by hyperconnectivity.[15]

I begin this chapter, then, by addressing the digital platform as an innovative economic and social-organizational form. I next consider the immense infrastructural power – the concentrated control over the digital facilities that have become indispensable for economic, social, cultural, and political life – held by the dominant platforms. And I analyze how digital platforms have transformed labor and employment by introducing new ways of coordinating and contracting for labor, new ways of directing and controlling labor, and new ways of inducing and exploiting (unpaid) labor. A brief coda addresses the new wave of techno-utopian discourse that celebrates the transformative power of blockchain technology.

Platforms

Digital platforms can be characterized most succinctly by highlighting five properties. First, platforms are *intermediaries*. The internet figures in the public imagination as a technology of immediacy and therefore as a "populist" technology: a technology that connects people directly, allowing them to "cut out the middleman."[16] "Disintermediation" became a buzzword for this process in the 1990s as commentators analyzed, and celebrated, how the net enabled businesses, social movements, politicians, and ordinary people to bypass intermediaries of all kinds and connect directly with customers, audiences, like-minded others, or exchange partners.[17] Many digital businesses continue to trade on the rhetoric of directness.[18] But that rhetoric masks the reality of new intermediaries; disintermediation often involves re-intermediation.[19] Digital connectivity does not eliminate intermediaries; it replaces one set of intermediaries with another.[20] The major new intermediaries – even if they would often prefer to remain unrecognized as such – are platforms.

As intermediaries, platforms position themselves between two or more parties (or between parties and things those parties are interested in), and they mediate the connections between them.[21] In the simplest configuration, transactional platforms such as Uber, Airbnb, Etsy, eBay, Amazon Marketplace, and TaskRabbit position themselves between buyers and sellers, charging a fee for the transactions they enable and coordinate. Google Search positions itself between users, web content, and advertisers, providing users with relevant content and advertisers with relevant users. YouTube and Spotify position themselves between audiences, cultural content, content creators (or rights-holders), and advertisers. In a slightly more complex configuration, Facebook positions itself between users who create content, users who consume content (the two categories of course overlap), advertisers, and third-party software developers, who use application programming interfaces (APIs) to access platform data and build new tools that enhance the functionality and attractiveness of the platform for users.[22] Educational platforms position themselves between students, curricular materials, teachers, and administrators. Industrial platforms position themselves between clients (manufacturing businesses) and third-party firms, providing data from the operations of the former to the latter, which enable them to develop tailored applications and services for the former.[23]

In all of these cases, the "betweenness" of platforms means that much of the work they do – enabled by sophisticated algorithms and fine-grained data – involves matching.[24] Transactional platforms match buyers with sellers; content-hosting (or content-organizing) platforms match users with content; and "innovation platforms" match users with "complementors" (often software developers) who create "complementary" products and services on the programmable technological base of the platform.[25]

Second, platforms seek to make platform-mediated action and interaction *frictionless*. Frictionlessness sustains the illusion of immediacy. But it also reduces transaction costs to an absolute minimum. Transaction costs include search costs: the cost of finding a service provider, a romantic partner, a material good, an item of cultural consumption, or a piece of information. For economic exchanges, they may also include negotiation costs (the cost of coming to an agreement on the terms of the exchange) and monitoring costs (the cost of making sure the transaction is carried out as agreed).[26] Platforms reduce search costs by bringing people, things, and information together in a single space and using sophisticated matching algorithms to connect them.[27] They reduce negotiation costs through standardized pricing, contracts, insurance, and so on. They reduce monitoring costs through ratings-based reputational systems, which help overcome problems of asymmetric information, lack of trust, and opportunism.

Streamlined, frictionless platform interfaces call into being many kinds of interactions and transactions that would not otherwise have occurred. This is especially the case for micro-interactions and micro-transactions that were previously unthinkable because of prohibitively high transaction costs. In line with the miniaturization I have emphasized throughout the book, platforms allow users to "slice up time and space into smaller units" on both supply and demand sides, making practicable "short-term rentals, a few minutes of personal assistance, [or] a couple of hours of furniture installation."[28] From a microsociological perspective, as discussed in chapter 2, frictionless platforms facilitate miniaturized forms of "phatic" communication that enable friends and intimates to feel a sense of "connected presence" even when apart (though they also contribute to the burdensome proliferation of interactional micro-obligations). From a microeconomic perspective, platforms awaken "dormant capital" – underutilized physical resources such as cars or spare bedrooms and underutilized human capital and labor power – and put "idle capacity to work," thereby realizing efficiency gains. As legal scholar Orly Lobel put it, "in a systemic way, the market ...

is perfecting [itself]."[29] However problematic this teleological formulation, the direct talk of market logic is at least less mystifying than the language of "sharing." But if transactional platforms enable the market to perfect itself, they threaten to do so by devouring the social: the transactionalization and monetization of everything that digital platforms enable may be a market utopia, but it is a social dystopia. Even Lobel admits to qualms: "the platform tilts the balance away from altruistic/communal interactions to marketable/commodified exchanges. ... The platform takes the saying that everything, and *everyone*, has a price quite literally."[30]

Third, platforms are *architectures of interaction*. In keeping with the etymological connotations of an open, level surface, platforms present themselves as neutral facilitators. But this self-representation obscures how they shape and structure rather than simply enable and facilitate interactions. For this reason, van Dijck has suggested that platforms are more accurately characterized as mediators than as intermediaries.[31] As sole authors and owners of the software through which interaction occurs, platforms are in a position to specify and control the forms and formats of interaction between the parties they bring together. One can therefore think of platforms as carefully designed architectures of interaction and as "regulatory structures" or "governance systems" that "deeply structure the rules and parameters of action."[32] As in other cases in which "code is law," as Lessig famously put it, "governance is effectively embedded in the code itself."[33]

As architectures of interaction, platforms pre-specify the range of possible actions; they open up certain possibilities and close off others. As I discussed in chapter 2, for example, Facebook and other social media platforms are spaces of "programmed sociality," offering their users limited palettes of possible actions.[34] This is not to say that platform architecture fully determines the range of possible uses: the generativity of platforms depends on a certain openness and indeterminacy. But that generativity exists in tension with the high degree of control that platforms can and do exercise over the kinds of things that can be done or said in the spaces that they govern.[35] Even platforms that are designed for open-ended communication (as opposed to those that seek to facilitate specific transactions) are in fact tightly regulated spaces.[36] This came into sharp focus during the pandemic and especially in the aftermath of the US 2020 elections when major social media platforms became much more aggressive about flagging and removing certain content and banning certain participants, culminating in Twitter's lifetime ban on Donald Trump.

Fourth, platforms *extract, process, and control data.* Like all digitally mediated activity, platform-mediated activity leaves digital traces. As architectures of interaction, platforms are designed to preserve these traces and turn them into data. Platforms' sole ownership of the means and medium of interaction enables them to unilaterally capture, control, and exploit these data. No special effort is needed to gather the data; the data can be captured automatically, simply by saving the digital traces, though these must then be aggregated, processed, and analyzed. Yet data are no longer understood as incidental byproducts of platform-mediated activity, as worthless "data exhaust," in Kenneth Cukier's phrase. Ongoing processes of "datafication" and an emerging ideology of "dataism" have made the capture, analysis, and valorization of data a central axis – arguably *the* central axis – of the platform economy.[37] "Data is the new oil" has become a business cliché, and as *The Economist* observed, "even industrial giants such as GE and Siemens" – backers of the two most prominent industrial platforms – "now sell themselves as data firms."[38] Persistent doubts and uncertainties in many quarters about the usefulness of the data being collected have done nothing to weaken the cultural "data imperative" to which, increasingly, all organizations are subjected.[39]

Of the vast troves of data captured by platforms – often with only the thinnest veneer of consent, if even that – a portion serves directly to improve the algorithms that match users with exchange partners, goods, or information. But far more data can be captured – and therefore *are* captured – than can be put to use improving the experience of individual users. On Shoshana Zuboff's influential account, Google's initial discovery and exploitation of this "behavioral surplus," at a moment of urgent need to raise revenue during the dot-com bust, was the foundational moment in the development of "surveillance capitalism."[40] Some companies – Google/Alphabet and Facebook/Meta, with spectacular success – use these surplus data to sell targeted advertisements. Others sell data to brokers. Startups assign data a starring role in the stories they spin to investors about how their ever more fine-grained data will make their ads more effective in the future.[41] Increasingly, data are used to train machine learning algorithms and drive advances in artificial intelligence.

Fifth, platforms have demonstrated a striking ability to *scale rapidly*. The affordances of digital objects are central to this scalability. Rapid growth requires neither expanding physical plant nor hiring large numbers of employees, and the necessary digital infrastructure – not just additional servers, but entire suites of modularly designed scalable software – can be rented on demand through Amazon Web Services or other cloud providers, which in effect serve as platforms for the construction of platforms.[42]

Network effects are also central to platform scalability. Network effects are often illustrated with respect to telecommunication networks: such networks are useless if there is hardly anyone to talk to; they become more valuable the more nodes or users there are in the network.[43] Digital platforms involve a distinctive kind of network effect, known as an indirect network effect. Unlike the direct network effects that result from growth in a single category of users, as in the case of a telephone or messaging app network, indirect network effects benefit *one* category of users as a result of growth in *another* category. Thus Open Table diners in a particular area benefit from an increase in the number of participating restaurants, and vice versa.[44] People interested in watching YouTube videos benefit from an increase in the number of those uploading videos, and vice versa. Airbnb hosts benefit from an increase in the number of those looking for short-term rentals, and vice versa. Once a critical mass of both categories of users is reached, indirect network effects can make growth self-sustaining.[45] Network effects and self-sustaining growth create winner-take-all or winner-take-most dynamics. Many sectors are dominated by a single firm. Google is overwhelmingly dominant in search, Google's YouTube in video sharing, Amazon in e-commerce, Facebook/Meta in social media and messaging, and Google and Apple in app stores for their respective mobile operating systems.

Infrastructural power

Taken together, the properties outlined above give successful digital platforms great power. But the power of the core "GAFAM" platforms

– Google (Alphabet), Amazon, Facebook (Meta), Apple, and Microsoft – differs not only quantitatively but also qualitatively from that of other platforms.[46] Their power is not only economic but social, cultural, and political. In all of these respects their power is fundamentally *infrastructural*: it entails the concentrated private control over digital infrastructures that have become or are becoming indispensable for economic, social, cultural, and political life.

When we think about infrastructure, we tend to think first about large-scale sociotechnical systems, paradigmatically public utility systems that provide water, sewage treatment, electricity, and gas or transportation systems such as port facilities or road and rail networks.[47] But what is it that makes such systems and networks infrastructural? Four features are worth underscoring. First, infrastructures are *foundational*: they are substrates that enable and constrain what can be built on top of them. They are often invisible or taken for granted, emerging from the background and coming into focus only when they break down.[48] Second, infrastructures are very widely used, often to the point of being *ubiquitous*. Their widespread use reflects the fact that infrastructures tend to be shareable: use by one party does not interfere with use by another. In economic terms, they are (to some degree) non-rivalrous; they can therefore be thought of as public goods or club goods.[49] Third, infrastructures are *generalized*: even when they have a specific primary purpose, they enable a broad range of secondary uses and activities.[50] Lastly, and most importantly for my purposes, infrastructures are facilities that have come to be understood as *indispensable*: not as indispensable for some specific activity, but as more broadly indispensable for life as we know it. Reflecting on the heterogeneity of phenomena widely considered infrastructural, Paul Edwards observed that "'infrastructure' is best defined negatively, as those systems without which contemporary societies cannot function."[51]

The internet as a whole is readily understood as infrastructural in this fourfold sense.[52] Many of the systems established by tech giants have likewise become infrastructural.[53] Some of these are user-facing services like search engines, web browsers, messaging apps, social media systems, email systems, video-hosting systems, app stores, digital wallets, geolocation and navigation systems, and e-commerce platforms. Others, more removed from everyday view, include ad-serving services, identification services, payment services, desktop/laptop and mobile operating systems, machine learning and artificial intelligence systems, warehouse automation, delivery logistics, and web hosting, data-analytic, and cloud computing services. And the dominant platforms are making huge investments in systems that are not yet infrastructural –not yet indispensable for the functioning of society – but likely to become so in the near future: natural language chatbots, voice user interfaces, smart home systems, driverless cars, urban governance systems, micro-payment systems and digital currencies, and augmented and virtual reality services.

Platforms exercise infrastructural power insofar as they control these and other foundational, ubiquitous, generalized, and increasingly indis-pensable sociotechnical facilities.[54] These facilities form crucial parts of today's *commercial infrastructure*: businesses of all kinds, for example, depend on identification, payment, advertising, data-analytic, and cloud computing services, as well as the basic business software suites. They have also become part of our *cognitive, cultural, and social infrastructure*: everyday life as we know it has come to depend massively on search engines, video and music streaming services, and social media and messaging platforms.

The infrastructural power of platforms is highly concentrated. Consider illustratively Amazon, Google/Alphabet, and Facebook/Meta. Amazon alone controls key parts of the infrastructure of commerce in the US.[55] This has been the company's vision all along: building not "an online bookstore or an online retailer, but rather a 'utility' that would become essential to commerce."[56] Amazon's Marketplace platform has become just such an essential utility for its perhaps 2 million active vendors. The indispensability of the platform reflects the company's enormous customer base, the immense success of its Prime program in attracting and retaining customers (150 million in the US alone), its vast and burgeoning network of fulfillment centers, and its warehouse automation and sophisticated logistics systems. Vendors hoping not only to reach a broad audience but to offer the expedited shipping that Amazon has conditioned buyers to expect have no choice but to sell their products on Marketplace.[57] No other platform can offer remotely comparable reach or infrastructural support. Vendors' dependence on the Marketplace platform makes them vulnerable to unilateral actions taken by Amazon, including changing the terms of access, downplaying their visibility in search results, forcing them off the platform, or, as happened for several weeks early in the pandemic, suspending fulfillment services for Marketplace products it deemed "non-essential."[58] Vendors are also vulnerable to direct competition from Amazon's own private label brands.[59]

Amazon's infrastructural power extends well beyond Marketplace. The immense delivery system it has built up now ships 5 billion parcels per year in the US and will soon be in a position to challenge UPS and FedEx on their own turf by offering shipping services to others.[60] Amazon remains by far the dominant provider of cloud computing services despite competition from Microsoft and Google. The company's Alexa remains the leader among digital voice assistants. Kindle has enabled Amazon to dominate the e-book market. Amazon is an increasingly close second behind Netflix in video streaming. And it has become the third largest player in digital advertising, though still well behind Google and Facebook. Although Amazon's share of all e-commerce fell during the pandemic as e-commerce in general soared, the pandemic left Amazon stronger than ever: the company doubled its workforce, hiring half a million employees, and nearly doubled its capital expenditures.[61] If ubiquity and indispensability are key aspects of infrastructure, Amazon has certainly made itself infrastructural. Its infrastructural power seems firmly entrenched: no other platform – apart from the other infrastructural giants – can hope to come anywhere close to the immense infrastructural investments Amazon has been able to make, thanks to investors who have been more interested in growth and dominance than in immediate profit.[62]

Google's infrastructural power is grounded in its domination of search. Nothing is more foundational, ubiquitous, generalized, taken-for-granted, or indispensable, in an era of digital hyperconnectivity, than the search engine. Already in 2008, writing about the "Googlization of our lives," Geert Lovink could observe that "search is the way we now live."[63] Domination of search confers power over the means of digital visibility. This power over who sees what is shared, to be sure, with all algorithms that help us cope with digital superabundance by steering us toward relevant content. But Google's overwhelmingly dominant general-purpose search engine, still the universal gateway to the Web, holds a unique degree of infrastructural power, with far-reaching impli-cations for commerce, culture, politics, and understandings of the world.

In a deeper sense, Google's infrastructural power is grounded in its extraction, control, and analysis of vast quantities of data. As observed above, the extraction and analysis of data are central to all digital platforms. But data have been even more central to Google. Through search, Google gained access to all the data on the open web, as well as to all the behavioral data gleaned from its users' queries and their responses to the search results the algorithm served up. But this was just the beginning. Google has sought not just to passively record but to actively extract ever more data. The data come in the first instance from the users of its many ubiquitous apps, no fewer than nine of which have more than a billion users: Search, Gmail, YouTube, Photos, Maps, Chrome, Android, Drive, and Google Play Store. But Google also extracts data from the physical world, most notably by digitizing 40 million books and mapping the world's streets.

The unparalleled troves of data have enabled Google/Alphabet to learn continuously from user behavior, to revolutionize and subsequently dominate the market for digital advertising,[64] and, most important in the long run, to make cutting edge advances in machine learning and artificial intelligence in key infrastructural domains such as translation, speech recognition, natural language processing, image recognition, computer vision, and autonomous vehicles. Thanks to the company's fabulous wealth and unrivaled computing infrastructure, Alphabet's AI, robotics, and autonomous vehicle subsidiaries have been able to outbid competitors for top talent and have positioned Alphabet as the leading power in AI, which has become increasingly central to infrastructural power.

The infrastructural power of Facebook/Meta rests on the extraor-dinary reach of its social media and messaging apps as well as its data-extracting and data-analyzing capabilities.[65] Facebook itself reaches nearly 3 billion people, WhatsApp and Instagram over 2 billion each, Messenger 1.3 billion; together (since many people of course use more than one of these apps) they reach some 3.5 billion users.[66] Yet enormous though Facebook/Meta is, it wants to be bigger. "The real goal," as Mark Zuckerberg noted, "is to connect everyone in the world and help people map out everything that there is."[67] The company expects growth to be concentrated in private, encrypted messaging rather than in the public or semi-public sharing of permanently viewable material.[68] Yet even though the global user base of its surveillance-rich flagship platform has recently stagnated, erasing hundreds of billions of dollars from the company's pandemic-inflated market capitalization, Facebook remains an indispensable infrastructure of sociability, thanks to inertia, network effects, and lack of data portability and interoperability with other platforms.

The Facebook/Meta ecosystem comprises infrastructures not only of sociability but also, increasingly, of commerce and politics. As an infrastructure of commerce, Facebook is used by more than 200 million businesses to communicate with potential customers. Its incomparably rich data on users enable it to offer sophisticated targeting capabilities to its more than 10 million advertisers.[69] And the company has been integrating shopping and an array of other services ever more seamlessly into its platforms. As an infrastructure of politics, Facebook is a crucial medium of political communication, news, and public discussion. As such, it has come under fire for short-circuiting deliberation, facilitating the flow of mis- and disinformation, amplifying polarization, and promoting the use of nontransparent and unaccountable micro-targeted political advertisements. Given the scale at which Facebook operates, its efforts to curb misinformation and to flag or remove otherwise objectionable content, like those of other platforms, have themselves become important – and contested – parts of the infrastructure of politics.[70]

Facebook/Meta's ambitions are totalizing: it wants to become "the operating system of our lives."[71] Taking China's WeChat – the "everything app" – as its model, the company aspires to enclose more and more of everyday life within its platforms.[72] It wants to make it possible to take care of routine tasks and activities – paying a bill, scheduling a medical appointment, ordering a meal, buying a movie ticket, making travel arrangements, and so on – without ever leaving its family of applications.[73] Looking further forward, the company is investing heavily in new services that it foresees becoming "ubiquitous utilities that 1 billion or 2 billion or more people are going to want to use."[74] It has made a big bet that virtual reality and augmented reality – highlighted in the company's 2021 rebranding as the key to the emerging "metaverse"

– might become the basis for the next big computing platform, a successor to the smartphone.[75]

* * *

I noted above that "platform," like "sharing," is an ideologically laden term; it suggests a raised level surface that will lift everyone up equally, providing a new and elevated foundation for their activities. Clearly, that egalitarian promise has not been realized. To the extent that platforms have a leveling effect, it involves the leveling of the "platformed masses" in the face of the platform powers, recalling Max Weber's observation that bureaucracy has historically promoted the "leveling of the governed in the face of the governing and bureaucratically articulated group."[76] Contrary to their promise, platforms have concentrated rather than distributed power.

As the sketches above suggest, the great platforms exercise entrenched private power over core economic, social, political, cultural, and cognitive infrastructures. That power has been largely unaccountable, especially in the US.[77] Until the last few years, platform power largely escaped serious public scrutiny, even as the tech giants, flush with cash, entrenched their power further by buying up threatening competitors.[78] Facebook's acquisitions of Instagram in 2012 and WhatsApp in 2014, for example, faced no objections from the Federal Trade Commission.

A key reason for the longstanding lack of serious scrutiny is that the giant platforms are not, strictly speaking, monopolies. They do of course exercise overwhelmingly dominant power over particular sectors (Google in general-purpose search, for example, Facebook in social media and messaging, and Amazon in general-purpose e-commerce). Yet they compete vigorously with one another over key infrastructural positions: cloud computing, virtual and augmented reality, voice interfaces, natural language processing, autonomous vehicles, and more.[79] And they have not behaved in the way monopolists – according to orthodox economic theory – are supposed to behave: they have not raised prices for consumers. Governed by the distinctive economic logics of digital scale and multisided platforms, they have continued to subsidize consumers, as Amazon does through Prime, in order to reap benefits of scale, and to offer products free of charge, as Google and Facebook do, so as to make the platform more valuable and attractive to advertisers.

The fact that platforms are widely seen – not only by economists but by consumers themselves – as enhancing rather than diminishing consumer welfare means that antitrust doctrine, as it has been prevailingly understood since the 1980s, has offered little leverage to those seeking to curb the power of the giant platforms.[80] In the dominant Chicago School paradigm of antitrust theory, consumer welfare is the decisive criterion; concentrated "market power is not inherently harmful and instead may result from and generate efficiencies." Absent evidence of harm to consumers in the form of higher prices, considerations of concentrated power or anticompetitive behavior have been seen as irrelevant.[81]

In recent years, however, the political and legal climate has shifted dramatically. As public concern about concentrated tech power has grown, new approaches to antitrust law and platform regulation have emerged. "Neo-Brandeisian" analyses by legal scholars have sought to broaden the scope of antitrust analysis by focusing on the "structure and dynamics of markets" rather than on narrow measures of price and efficiency.[82] Neo-Brandeisians have also sought to recover the spirit of the progressive-era critique of great concentrations of private power;[83] they see such concentrations as posing "not just [an] economic, but a political problem of domination – the accumulation of arbitrary authority unchecked by the ordinary mechanisms of political accountability."[84] They have proposed diverse remedies. Some have called for treating platforms as "public utilities" or "essential facilities" and regulating them accordingly.[85] Others have argued for heightened scrutiny of mergers in the future and for breaking up concentrated power achieved through anticompetitive mergers in the past (requiring Facebook, for example, to divest itself of Instagram and WhatsApp).[86] Still others favor the "structural separation" between platforms (such as Amazon's Marketplace or Apple's and Google's App Stores) and the businesses selling things on those platforms, so as to prevent the platform giants from competing directly, as they presently do, against other sellers on their platforms.[87]

Informed in part by these academic analyses, regulators have adopted a much more aggressive posture, while legislators have proposed sweeping reforms. The challenge to the power of Big Tech is one of the few issues to have found some bipartisan backing. The Trump administration filed antitrust cases against Google and Facebook in late 2020. Separate Justice

Department probes are investigating Apple, Amazon, and Facebook. Lina Khan, a legal scholar whose work has been central to the neo-Brandeisian rethinking of antitrust law and policy, was appointed by Biden to head the Federal Trade Commission.[88] And a package of bills, introduced in the House in 2021, would prohibit acquisitions that entrench market power, facilitate the breaking up of the tech giants, bar a range of practices deemed anticompetitive, and require platforms to allow users to switch platforms, and move their data along with them, while still being able to communicate with their contacts who remain on the platform. The fate of these bills is uncertain at this writing, but they are a striking indicator of the sharp change in climate.

Regardless of how these legal and political struggles play out, digital platforms of all kinds and at all scales – not just the GAFAM megaplatforms – are likely to continue to take a leading role in restructuring sector after sector of economic and social life. Platforms have transformed or are in the course of transforming culture and entertainment, commerce, education, lodging, transportation, manufacturing, finance, medicine, journalism, political discourse, social interaction, dating, service work, and even, recursively, platform-building itself.[89] There is every reason to think that they will continue to reorganize the social world to conform to their economic and sociotechnical logics.

Labor

The enclosure of more and more of social life within the embrace of digital platforms has transformed labor in three main ways. It has generated new ways of *coordinating* and *contracting for* labor outside standard employment frameworks. It has transformed the labor process itself, generating new ways of *directing* and *controlling* labor, both within and outside standard employment relations. And it has generated new ways of *inducing* and *exploiting* labor – or at least value-generating activity – on the part of platform users. I consider each of these in turn.

Platforms organize and coordinate labor by matching businesses and individuals who want things done with individuals who are willing and able to do them. The most salient feature of platform-mediated matching is its flexibility. Platforms disassemble labor arrangements and reassemble them in new forms. They "taskify" labor, unbundling and disembedding it from the jobs within which it had been packaged. They match people not with stable, ongoing *positions* or *jobs* but with delimited *tasks* or *projects*.[90] They thereby enable businesses and individuals to summon labor in the precise quantity and quality, and at the precise time, when they need it. This just-in-time and just-enough logic, central to the "on-demand economy," carries to a new level the longstanding trend toward the flexible organization of labor in post-Fordist capitalism.

One key to flexibility is miniaturization: platforms make it possible to purchase ever smaller bits of labor. This is especially true for labor that is not only digitally arranged but digitally executed. Many large and complex digital tasks are easily divisible: they can be broken down into tiny fragments and reassembled once the tasks have been completed. The largest and best-known platform for such crowdsourced nano-tasks is Amazon Mechanical Turk, where most tasks pay 10 cents or less, and some "penny tasks" as little as 1 cent.[91] In accordance with the logic of temporal fragmentation discussed in chapter 2, nano-task platforms' mobile interfaces allow users to monetize the smallest slivers of their free time by completing tasks in the interstices of their days. Companies use such platforms to frictionlessly outsource certain simple and repetitive tasks that cannot (yet) be fully automated, including moderating content, transcribing audio recordings, and, perhaps most important, tagging objects in photos or videos (once tagged, the data can be used to train machine object recognition algorithms).[92]

Labor carried out in person can't be sliced up quite so finely, not least because providers need to travel in order to perform the service. But the sharp reduction in transaction costs enabled by digital platforms has made it ultra-convenient to contract on an as-needed basis for minimal in-person services as well: delivery services, assembling goods, minor repairs, an hour of care work, and so on.[93]

Not all platform-coordinated labor, to be sure, takes the form of unskilled digital nano-tasks or minimal in-person services. Some platforms, notably Upwork, as well as a variety of smaller, sector-specific professional platforms, focus on matching digital projects of varying duration with skilled freelancers.[94] But here too the logic of flexibility and concomitant cost savings reigns supreme. The flexibility promised by Upwork – that of "swiftly onboarding talent on-demand and quickly releasing contingent workers when required"[95] – enables firms to shift certain risks and costs to workers. It gives new impetus to the outsourcing of work, accelerating the move away from stable employment relationships and the forms of social protection they provide.[96] Since digitalizable tasks, even the most urgent and time-sensitive ones, can be carried out anywhere with good digital infrastructure, the global reach of Upwork and other digital labor platforms also promotes the offshoring of work, bringing providers worldwide into competition with one another. This opens up new opportunities for providers in emerging economies, beyond those available in their local labor markets, but it puts downward pressure on wages elsewhere.[97] Some platform providers – those with relatively scarce skills that are in high demand – can flourish as relatively-high-earning freelancers. But they are the exception in an emerging global labor market for digital services.

Platform enthusiasts – and platforms themselves – tout the flexibility platforms give providers as well as those hiring them. They herald the "end of employment" and the emergence of a "networked society of micro-entrepreneurs" in its stead.[98] Freed from the constraints of bureaucratic employment, providers, on celebratory accounts, can choose when and how much to work as well as which of the tasks or projects on offer they will undertake. They can serve as their own boss, define their own pace of work, and flexibly combine work with other activities. Ethnographic studies have shown that this discourse of flexibility and independence does indeed resonate with many providers.[99] But the promise of flexibility often turns out to be illusory. The flexibility once enjoyed by providers on the TaskRabbit platform, for example, vanished once providers were required to accept at least 85 percent of work offers.[100] Many platforms' algorithms favor providers who make themselves available all the time and accept all work offers; this pressures other providers to do the same. And the formal freedom to determine one's schedule means little when insufficient work is available or when providers depend on the platform for their living.[101]

New forms of precarious platform-mediated labor outside standard employment arrangements arise not only directly, through platforms that bring together buyers and sellers of *services*. They also arise indirectly, through platforms that bring together buyers and sellers of *goods* and through platforms that bring together the producers and consumers of user-generated *content*. Low barriers to entry have induced millions to try their luck selling goods on platforms such as Amazon Marketplace, Etsy, and eBay. Even though these platforms involve the exchange of goods, not labor, they indirectly but powerfully reshape patterns of labor by inducing many people to work – on a supplementary basis or even full time – as home-based retail micro-entrepreneurs. Airbnb has similarly generated a new form of platform-mediated labor. And platforms such as YouTube and Instagram, by introducing opportunities for monetization, have prompted large numbers of users to try their hand at making a living, or at least earning supplementary income, from creating and circulating content.[102] Here the entrepreneurial model of the self discussed in chapter 1 converges with literal self-entrepreneurship.

Platforms have not only generated new ways of arranging for labor outside standard employment relations; they have also generated new ways of directing and controlling labor, both within and outside regular employment. These have been succinctly captured in the notion of "algorithmic management,"[103] denoting the techniques used to govern, supervise, and manage labor in automated or semi-automated ways, with minimal intervention from human supervisors. Such techniques were pioneered by labor platforms, which needed to scale quickly and possessed the data infrastructures that enabled algorithmic governance. But they have spread well beyond the gig economy and beyond platform businesses in general, driven by advancing datafication and by an interest in cutting costs and rationalizing the use of labor resources.

As a recent review suggested, algorithms are increasingly central to directing, evaluating, and disciplining workers.[104] They *direct* workers, often in frustratingly opaque ways, by prompting them to take certain actions or make certain decisions and by restricting the flow of information or the range of actions available to them. In the much-studied case of Uber, for example, algorithms assign rides to drivers and give the drivers just fifteen seconds to accept or reject the trip. Crucially, drivers are not told the trip's destination and thus cannot strategize over which trips to accept. This makes the matching of riders and drivers more efficient. Like similar information asymmetries on food delivery platforms, however, it substantially abridges the autonomy of the worker, which is central to the ideology of platform work.[105]

Outside the platform economy, algorithms are widely used to implement flexible scheduling, notably in retail and service sectors.

"Demand forecasting" algorithms integrate detailed historical sales data and external information (about weather, holidays, or local events, for example) to predict visits and sales at particular times and to adjust staffing needs accordingly, sometimes at the last minute. Such top-down modes of automated scheduling demand flexibility *of* workers – who are obliged to accept high levels of uncertainty about their work hours as well as disruptive schedules – but offer no flexibility *to* workers.[106]

Algorithmic systems *evaluate* workers by capturing data generated by every aspect of digitally mediated work processes, enlisting customers in the rating of workers,[107] and deploying sensors to record an increasingly wide range of data including physical movements (of warehouse workers, for example), detailed driving data (in the delivery and trucking sector), communication patterns among workers, and even health and exercise data.[108] Algorithmic evaluation, in short, depends on pervasive digital surveillance. The routinization and normalization of such surveillance are the foundation of what has come to be known in the business world as "people analytics," which promises that fine-grained data and algorithms can free managerial decision-making from bias, subjectivity, and the vagaries of intuition.[109] Algorithmic evaluations are central to the hiring process as well: the semi-automated hiring platforms that are used by most large companies sort, filter, and exclude candidates according to algorithmic assessments of their value as prospective workers.[110]

Algorithmic management systems *discipline* workers most strikingly through their power to swiftly and seamlessly dismiss underperforming workers – sometimes without any human intervention at all – and recruit new ones to take their place.[111] Many platforms automatically "deactivate" workers if their ratings fall below a certain threshold or if they underperform in other ways (for example by accepting too few tasks in the specified period); other platforms algorithmically steer work away from underperforming workers. Discipline and termination are less fully automated outside the platform economy. But as digital surveillance proliferates, managers' decisions to discipline or fire workers are increasingly informed by data analytics.[112] Other disciplinary mechanisms of algorithmic management systems include making performance data continuously available to workers and managers in real time, rewarding high-performing workers, monitoring employee health and fitness, and using gamification methods to motivate workers.[113]

The new ways of coordinating and contracting for labor on the one hand and monitoring and disciplining labor on the other have profoundly transformed the experience of labor. They have reorganized labor not only *outside* but also *within* standard employment relations. They have done so through a logic of decomposition and recomposition. Both labor platforms and algorithmic management platforms disassemble jobs into projects and tasks. In the former case, decomposition makes it possible to contract for individual projects and tasks on an as-needed basis. In the latter, an even more minute decomposition enables a neo-Taylorist form of datafied and algorithmically driven scientific management, premised on granular monitoring, measurement, evaluation, and discipline. In both cases, the ultimate aim is a more flexible and efficient deployment of labor: rationalization in the interest of cost-saving. Taylor himself had characterized the "task idea" – the idea of analyzing labor into small tasks and specifying "not only what is to be done but how it is to be done and the exact time allowed for doing it" – as "the most prominent single element in modern scientific management."[114] Digital platforms have developed the "task idea" – with its potential deskilling implications – beyond anything Taylor could have dreamed of.

Both labor and algorithmic management platforms also contribute to making work more precarious: work becomes more "uncertain, unstable, and insecure," and workers assume more of the risks of work and enjoy fewer benefits and legal protections.[115] Digital platforms (and digitalization more broadly) are only one of several factors – alongside de-unionization, financialization, and globalization – contributing to precarity.[116] But they make their own distinctive contribution by lowering the transaction costs of outsourcing and offshoring, as well as those of micro-entrepreneurship; increasing income insecurity through downward pressure on wages; destabilizing working hours even within regular employment contexts; and subjecting workers to opaque and unpredictable regimes of algorithmic assessment and control.[117]

The third aspect of the transformation of labor in a world of digital platforms stands apart from the first two, even if it is related to them at the abstract level of extracting value from platforms. This concerns the ways in which platforms have been able to induce and exploit the labor of their users (or at least value-generating activity: whether such activity should be called "labor" remains controversial). In an influential early contribution, written before the emergence of social media, Tiziana Terranova characterized activities such as creating websites, serving as "community leaders" on AOL, or co-constructing virtual spaces as "free labor," meaning by "free" both unpaid (and exploited) and freely offered (and enjoyed).[118] The notion of unpaid and exploited labor came to seem especially apt once platforms that depend on user-generated content started making large amounts of money. Such content is obviously critical to the economic success of Facebook, Instagram, YouTube, TikTok, and other platforms. Without it, there would be no audience to whom advertisements could be shown. And the business model of these platforms is almost exclusively advertisement-based: Facebook, for example, derives about 98 percent of its revenue – well over $100 billion in 2021 – from ads. Not only the creation and posting of content but also all kinds of other user activities that create value for platforms have been subsumed under the concept of free labor: liking, sharing, and commenting on content; rating and reviewing goods, services, and cultural items; tagging images; and contributing to fan communities. The concept has been broadened still further to include not only activities that enrich the experience of other platform users but also activities like providing data or even passively allowing data – and therefore value – to be captured by platforms.[119]

Some writers have criticized the extension of the concept of exploited labor to all activities that generate value for platforms, without regard for the meaning of the activities to those undertaking them. They note that many platform-mediated activities such as creating and engaging with content are understood and experienced as enjoyable forms of expression, play, or sociability, and that it is awkward to fold these into the notion of exploited labor.[120] Extending the notion of labor to include processes of automated data and metadata extraction that require no activity whatsoever from the user – save, for example, searching for something on Google, scrolling through a social media feed, or communicating with "smart" objects in one's home – feels like even more of a stretch.

Yet platforms have indisputably been remarkably successful in putting users "to work" for them, even if – and precisely *because* – users do not experience their platform-mediated activities as work. They have been remarkably successful, that is, in inducing, and profiting from, a wide range of user activities that yield valuable data and generate the content that makes the platforms more attractive to other users and therefore also to advertisers.

Beyond this vast domain of uncompensated yet value-creating user activity that is not experienced as labor, a new terrain has emerged on which users *do* think of their activity as labor – as "productive, purposeful, task-oriented, and value-generating" – and *may* receive compensation.[121] This is the terrain, touched on in chapter 3, of what has been called "consignment labor" or "aspirational labor." "Consignment labor" denotes the practice of providing content to a platform "in the hope of attracting an audience or consumers so that the content can be monetized," a practice in which the content creator "bears all the risks"; it also includes the labor of app developers on Apple's App Store or Google Play or authors who self-publish through Amazon's Kindle Direct Publishing. "Aspirational labor" – a concept developed in a study of fashion, beauty, and lifestyle bloggers and vloggers – designates (largely) uncompensated labor that is inspired by the "ideal of [eventually] getting paid to do what you love" and by the "prospect of a career where labor and leisure coexist."[122]

These conceptualizations point in somewhat different directions, but each highlights the fact that users create content for platforms such as YouTube, Instagram, Twitch, or TikTok in the hope of monetizing it through advertising, subscriptions, donations, tips, sponsored posts, or brand partnerships. As platforms have embraced the idea of monetization and developed new ways of compensating content creators,[123] the earlier scholarly concern with unpaid labor has broadened to take into account the "continuum of unpaid, micro-paid, and poorly paid" activity.[124] The continuum, to be sure, extends to well paid work: some content creators with substantial followings, like some platform freelancers with relatively scarce skills, have managed to secure good and steady incomes. But the compensation received by the great majority of content creators remains minimal. Even those who do manage to scrape together a living, or hope to be able to do so, find themselves working very long hours, not only in producing content but in the "relational labor" of engaging with their audiences across multiple platforms.[125] This again points to the limits of flexibility for workers: increased flexibility about *where* to work may go hand in hand with decreased flexibility about *when* to work.[126]

Consignment labor and aspirational labor, like other forms of platform-mediated labor, remain precarious – vulnerable to sudden changes in platform design and algorithms – even for those few who are relatively successful.[127]

As platforms have reshaped social life in sector after sector, they have profoundly transformed how labor is organized, carried out, and controlled. They have done so most conspicuously by introducing new ways of coordinating and contracting for labor – including both in-person services and remote work – *outside* standard employment relations. In-person ride-hailing and delivery services have come to epitomize such "disruptive" forms of platform-organized labor; but remote work platforms have a far greater potential to disrupt standard employment and to circumvent its costly benefits, protections, and inflexibilities by taskifying, outsourcing, and offshoring digital or digitalizable labor. Less conspicuously but just as importantly, platforms and their algorithms have become increasingly central to directing, evaluating, and disciplining labor *within* standard employment relations. And social media platforms have managed to enlist and orchestrate their users in the generally unpaid (or underpaid) work of making the platforms attractive for other users and for advertisers. Platforms thus increasingly orchestrate both our work and our play – in important part by blurring the lines between the two.

Coda: Blockchain utopianism

I began this chapter by showing how the key Web 2.0 idea – and ideology – of "sharing" carried forward into the new millennium elements of the techno-utopian discourse associated with "new communalist" countercultural ideals of the late 1960s. The notion of the "sharing economy," I noted, came to stand for a fundamental shift in economic and social organization enabled by hyperconnectivity. In the last few years, a new techno-utopian discourse about fundamental economic and social transformation enabled by digital technology has coalesced around cryptocurrencies, non-fungible tokens (NFTs), decentralized finance (DeFi), and decentralized autonomous organizations (DAOs), sometimes subsumed under the overarching rubric of "Web 3."[128] This discourse gained much broader public traction during the pandemic, particularly after an NFT certifying "ownership" of a purely digital artwork sold for $69 million at Christie's in March 2021 at the same time that the value of Bitcoin reached dizzying highs close to $60,000. A full discussion of these emerging digital forms is beyond the scope of this chapter. But it's worth briefly considering the vision that underlies and animates the new discourse.

Cryptocurrencies, NFTs, DeFi, and DAOs are all built on blockchain or similar forms of distributed ledger technology. Ledgers are a key part of economic infrastructure; they record and establish facts about ownership, identity, commitments, and transactions. Blockchain is fundamentally a new kind of ledger technology. Simply put, it is a distributed digital ledger that uses cryptographic algorithms to ensure the secure and durable recording and authentication of transactions without the need for any central authority or trusted intermediary.[129] The decentralization and disintermediation promised by blockchain are touted by its proponents as the key to its transformative potential. They are seen as allowing for digital currencies and financial transactions without banks as intermediaries; digital authentication of identity, ownership, and authority without states as intermediaries; coordinated economic projects without firms as intermediaries; and self-executing "smart" contracts without accountants, auditors, and lawyers as intermediaries.[130] By virtue of this capacity to enable organizationally unmediated transactions and projects, blockchain is held to emancipate and empower individuals vis-a-vis political and economic organizations and intermediaries of all kinds.

In its populist and egalitarian tone, its promise to empower ordinary people, and its celebration of decentralization, micro-entrepreneurship, universal transactionalization, and disruptive disintermediation, the new discourse echoes elements of Web 2.0 discourse (and earlier internet-era discourse).[131] But there are harder-edge libertarian and anarcho-capitalist elements in the crypto and blockchain discourse.[132] And there are other striking differences. While the great tech platforms were the *authors* of much of the Web 2.0 discourse, they are among the key *targets* of the new discourse, figuring as centralized organizational intermediaries ripe for disruption.[133] While the "sharing economy" was premised on extending the reach of trust between strangers, blockchain dispenses with the need for trust altogether: it is the perfect instrument for the trustless medium that the Web has become.[134] And while the discourse of "sharing" envisioned a "post-ownership" society, blockchain enthusiasts envision the proliferation of ownership through the "tokenization" and "securitization" of an ever-broader range of undertakings and assets, opening up new possibilities for fractional micro-ownership. This celebration of the financialization and commodification of everything contrasts strikingly with earlier utopian visions of the internet as a space of nonmarket exchange.

Public discussion of the transformative potential of blockchain is highly polarized. Evangelists liken blockchain to the internet itself, casting it as a world-changing "technology of freedom."[135] They have succeeded in mobilizing significant numbers of tech-savvy enthusiasts to design and participate in a rapidly proliferating array of blockchain-based initiatives. And public interest soared along with the value of cryptocurrencies, the total market capitalization of which exceeded $3 trillion at peak valuations of late 2021. For most people, hoping to strike it rich or afraid of missing out on the next big thing, cryptocurrencies and other digital assets are simply an investment vehicle. Many involved in building the blockchain ecosystem, however, have also been drawn in by a heady sense of excitement – recalling the early days of the Web – about working on an open frontier, creating something new, and challenging powerful, sclerotic incumbents. They feel themselves part of something like a social movement, animated by utopian energies, and framed by a populist, anti-institutional vision that many find resonant at a moment of declining trust in and disenchantment with government and financial institutions on the one hand and entrenched tech oligopolies on the other.

Skeptics – and there are many – see blockchain as a massively overhyped technology. They deplore and deride the staggering energy costs of Bitcoin "mining" and note that cryptocurrencies fail to perform any of the basic functions of a currency: serving as a unit of account, a widely accepted means of payment, and a stable store of value.[136] They underscore blockchain's technical problems of scalability and argue that considerations of cost and efficiency make centralized systems inescapable for large-scale data management. They observe that the promise of full disintermediation is belied by the emergence of new intermediaries (such as cryptocurrency exchanges), the promise of decentralization by new forms of centralization (such as the extreme concentration of Bitcoin mining operations).[137] They characterize cryptocurrency and other digital asset markets – delinked from any form of productive economic activity – as pure vehicles of speculation, sustainable, like pyramid schemes, only so long as a substantial stream of new participants can be drawn in.[138] The populist rhetoric, in their view, is a cynical ploy, allowing experienced and well-resourced players to profit from inexperienced newcomers. Skeptics characterize Web 3 discourse as performative and self-referential: "spin all the way down," as Evgeny Morozov put it.[139]

Whatever the fate of cryptocurrency markets, blockchain technology, broadly understood, seems likely to be here to stay. Many large corporations are developing blockchain-based systems for purposes like tracking inventory or shipments and managing supply chains. And the tech giants are offering "blockchain-as-a-service" to business clients. But these private and "permissioned" forms of blockchain are not radically disruptive: they do not eliminate the need for trusted intermediaries, they may remain under centralized control, and they are easily integrated into the existing social, legal, and economic order. The utopian promise of blockchain may be tamed and domesticated, just as the utopian promise of the early internet was. It is worth remembering that the apparently radically decentralizing technology of the early internet ended up supporting unprecedented concentrations of power. Skepticism is therefore warranted towards claims about the intrinsically decentralizing and democratizing consequences of blockchain.[140]

CHAPTER FIVE

Politics

Ever since the advent of mass democracy, commentators have feared that new communications technologies and media formats would undermine democratic citizenship. In late nineteenth-century America, concerns focused on the sensationalism of "yellow journalism," the newly inexpensive mass-circulation newspapers whose reporting – in reckless disregard of facts – helped push the United States into war with Spain in 1898. A critical cartoon from that era even used the phrase "fake news."[1] The emergence of radio as a mass medium in the 1920s and 1930s – by 1940 radio reached more than 80 percent of American households – occasioned concerns about manipulation and demagogy as well as hopes about the medium's democratizing potential. And radio was in fact skillfully exploited by populist demagogues such as Huey Long and Charles Coughlin.[2] Television initially seemed to possess even greater power as a vehicle of charismatic leadership. In the West, early concerns were allayed by (mainly American) research suggesting that television exercised only minimal direct persuasive effects. More recent research, however, considering a wider range of cases, has challenged this consensus and renewed concerns about television as a particularly potent medium for personalistic leaders.[3]

Digital connectivity, by contrast, seemed full of democratic promise. From the 1980s through the middle of the last decade, it generated more enthusiasm than anxiety. The shift from unidirectional mass communication to multidirectional "mass self-communication" – so the story went – would inform and empower ordinary citizens, give voice to the previously voiceless, bypass sclerotic, elite-dominated institutional gatekeepers, facilitate lateral communication and collective action, hold governments and powerful actors accountable, and make politics more transparent and responsive. It would promote more participatory forms of citizenship, bring previously excluded or marginalized groups into the polity, and contribute to undermining authoritarian regimes. In short, it would enhance rather than diminish democratic citizenship.[4]

This story got many elements right. Citizenship has indeed become more participatory, for many, as ordinary citizens have joined public conversations in new ways and in unprecedented numbers. Hyperconnectivity has eroded the power of many institutional gatekeepers, notably "legacy" media institutions and political parties. Social media platforms have created powerful new channels for lateral communication, lowered the cost of coordination, and enabled collective action. They have made it easier for previously marginalized groups – including, however, exponents of extreme views – to amplify their voices and gain followings. New forms of "sousveillance" enabled by the ubiquity of mobile, connected, camera-equipped devices and by new forms of public documentation have rendered certain forms of speech and action by powerful people and organizations more visible and accountable. And Facebook and Twitter have been celebrated for their key role in toppling dictatorial regimes during the Arab Spring and in enabling and energizing new forms of "connective action" and new kinds of "horizontal" social movements, exemplified by the Occupy movements around the globe, the Gezi Park protests in Turkey, and the *Indignados* in Spain.[5]

Yet the optimistic narrative got other things badly wrong. Instead of connecting the public and making politics more transparent, hyperconnectivity has fragmented the public and made politics more opaque. Micro-targeting practices – utterly nontransparent, premised on surveillance, and guided by sophisticated behavioral science – have diffused from the realm of commerce to that of politics, making effective use of Facebook's formidable platform for customized advertisements.[6] Opaque algorithms determine who sees what news; in the name of personalization, they contribute to privatizing the public sphere. Encrypted messenger services like Facebook/Meta's WhatsApp allow political campaigns, especially in the developing world, to mobilize – and all too often to mobilize fear, hatred, and misinformation – while avoiding public visibility and accountability.[7]

Since the middle of the last decade, the digital dream of renewing democratic citizenship has been challenged and partly overshadowed by a digital nightmare of undermining democratic citizenship through short-circuiting reasoned deliberation, spreading pernicious rumors, disseminating fake news, nurturing conspiracy theories, intensifying polarization, multiplying public shaming, manipulating fears and anxieties, and incubating extremism. And authoritarian regimes, though initially unprepared for the nimbleness and creativity of digitally mediated opposition movements, have long since learned to monitor, disrupt, and counter such movements; the most sophisticated such regimes, led by China, have entrenched their power through massively enhanced capacities for digital surveillance.

Digital nightmares, to be sure, can be as distorting – and as seductive – as digital dreams. Blaming hyperconnectivity, or social media in particular, for contemporary political ills is too easy by far.[8] All the ills just noted have histories that long antedate hyperconnectivity. And as I have argued throughout the book, digital hyperconnectivity is not a force that causes things to happen: it is an environment – or more precisely, a complex environment of environments – in which certain actions become easier (or are made possible or even thinkable in the first place), while other actions become more difficult. A nuanced account must show how particular features of this environment enable and incentivize some forms of activity while discouraging others.

This chapter will address transformations of politics by considering regimes of knowing, regimes of feeling, and regimes of governing. By *regimes of knowing* I mean the ways in which people acquire politically relevant knowledge – or what they take to be knowledge – and the stances they take toward knowledge claims that are advanced in the public sphere. I will argue that hyperconnectivity undermines the authority of "legacy" institutions that produce and disseminate knowledge, strengthens populist stances toward knowledge, and erodes the foundations of a shared public world. By *regimes of feeling* (separable only analytically, not empirically, from regimes of knowing), I mean to invoke the "structures of feeling" about public matters that are patterned by sociotechnical environments as well as the "feeling rules" that legitimate certain ways of experiencing and expressing feeling.[9] I will argue that hyperconnectivity rewards the expression and mobilization of outrage and thereby contributes to what political scientists have called affective polarization. By *regimes of governing* I mean the new modalities of algorithmic governance, based on machine learning, that have been enabled by hyperconnectivity and, in particular, by the enormous volume of data generated by the ever-growing apparatus of digital surveillance. I will argue that algorithmic governance has fundamentally transformed the business of rule and the exercise of power by public agencies and private platforms, not least by enabling the fully automated exercise of power. I conclude by considering the tension between these technocratic modes of governance and the populist regimes of knowing and feeling fostered by hyperconnectivity.

Regimes of knowing

Epistemic issues – concerns about truth and falsehood; about information, misinformation, and disinformation; about science and expertise and their limits; about rumor and conspiracy theories; about how we claim to know what we know – have become increasingly central to the study of politics in recent years. They have also become increasingly central to political debates and struggles themselves. Claims have proliferated about what "science" tells us, about what "the experts" got wrong, about "fake news" and "alternative facts." Political struggles concern not just who *gets* what or who *is* what but who *knows, thinks, or believes* what and on what grounds: the politics of interest and the politics of identity are increasingly bound up with the politics of knowledge.[10]

Concerns about who knows or believes what, and about how people come to believe what they believe, are not new. Worries about the ignorance of "the people" have long informed elite anxieties about democracy. These anxieties go back as far as Plato, and they have been chronic ever since the late nineteenth-century emergence of mass democracy in tandem with the mass media. Hyperconnectivity, however, has made these concerns much more salient.

The emerging regime of hyperconnectivity initially inspired optimism about public knowledge. It encouraged people to think of politically relevant knowledge, as of other knowledge, in terms of discrete, searchable, decontextualized, freely communicable bits of *information*. In the political domain, as in the domain of culture, it was assumed that such information "wants to be free" and that digital connectivity would unlock it, liberating it from scarcity and from artificial restraints on its circulation. Information would be abundant, easily discoverable, and universally accessible. The flow of information, moreover, would be lateral, not simply vertical; citizens would be empowered to produce and disseminate as well as consume information. The possibilities of "citizen journalism," for example, attracted considerable interest in the 2000s.[11] The free flow of information in all directions, it was assumed, would not only make politics more transparent and citizens better informed; it would also make politicians, parties, and other organizations better informed about and therefore more responsive to the views and preferences of their constituents.[12]

Even as this optimistic view came to seem hopelessly naïve, the focus on discrete bits of information remained. Only now the emphasis was placed on the abundant and unimpeded flow of misinformation and disinformation. Research suggesting that misinformation may circulate farther and faster than correct information gave the issue a new urgency.[13] Discussions of misinformation intensified during the pandemic and reached a fever pitch in the US in the aftermath of the 2020 presidential election. In response, the major social media platforms dramatically altered their content moderation policies; they adopted a sharply more interventionist stance, culminating in Twitter's sensational announcement of a lifetime ban on President Trump on January 8, 2021.

The question of misinformation – how to define and identify it, and what to do about it – is evidently of great importance. But it has been extensively discussed.[14] Here I want to address a different question: how the ecology of digital hyperconnectivity has reshaped ways of knowing the public world by reinforcing suspicion and distrust and eroding the foundations of a shared public world. Hyperconnectivity is not solely or even primarily responsible for these developments. Challenges to the authority of mainstream knowledge-producing and knowledge-disseminating institutions – science, medicine, universities, government, and journalism – have been gathering force for half a century. These challenges – part of a broader "participatory turn" in politics, culture, and society – are rooted in longstanding developments in the cultural politics of knowledge.[15] These include the decline of deference; the suspicion of insular forms of expert judgment; the valorization of various forms of lay expertise;[16] and the growing sense, especially in health and lifestyle domains, that people must educate themselves and take responsibility for arbitrating between competing expert claims.[17] All of these can be seen, for better or worse, as aspects of a long-term process of cultural and epistemic democratization.

Yet hyperconnectivity, here as elsewhere a potent accelerant and amplifier, has intensified all of these developments. Three features of the environment of hyperconnectivity are worth highlighting in connection with the politics of knowledge: abundance, flatness, and immediacy. (I touch briefly at the end of the section on two other features that will loom even larger in the future: the manipulability of digital objects and the rapidly increasing power of machine learning.) By "abundance" I mean not only the abundance of information (or misinformation), but also the abundance of conflicting knowledge claims. By "flatness" I mean that knowledge claims of the most varied provenance, unfiltered by gatekeepers, jostle side-by-side for our attention and assent on what is experienced as a relatively unstructured and level playing field. The digital public sphere is of course not in fact a level playing field; there are enormous differences in the ability to make one's voice heard. But the openness of the digital environment means that all knowledge claims, along with all other digital content, flow through the same conduits and circulate in a decontextualized manner. This exerts a homogenizing, leveling effect (just as it does in the cultural domain, as I argued in chapter 3). It places the wildest and most implausible claims on the same plane and in the same frame as those generated by mainstream knowledge-producing and knowledge-disseminating institutions. By "immediacy," finally, I mean the sense of having institutionally unmediated, direct access to information. Who needs the specialized institutions that generate, test, certify, transmit, filter, and disseminate knowledge when one has Google? (That Google provides not direct but rather algorithmically mediated access to "the world's information" tends to be blissfully ignored.)[18]

As noted above, abundance has figured centrally in information-focused accounts, both optimistic and pessimistic. But the focus on information is too limiting. Abundance alters not just *what* we know, by providing us with vastly more information (or misinformation); it alters *how* we know what we (think we) know. It alters our relation or stance toward knowledge claims. By exposing us continuously to a welter of conflicting knowledge claims – claims that, in a flat knowledge space, may appear to be on the same plane – digitally mediated abundance tends to inculcate or reinforce doubt, suspicion, and distrust. It thereby contributes to weakening the authority of the institutions that produce and disseminate public knowledge, journalism in particular. This mood of heightened distrust can engender a kind of generalized skepticism toward public knowledge claims, as virtually every knowledge claim about public affairs is shadowed by a cloud of suspicion. This can contribute to a feeling of paralysis, to a sense that nothing can reliably be known about controversial public matters. And it can contribute to a demobilizing cynicism.[19]

Abundance is a general and inescapable feature of the landscape of hyperconnectivity. But as Zeynep Tufekci has argued, it can also be wielded as a weapon. In a flat knowledge space, abundance can be enlisted as a deliberate strategy of distraction and obfuscation and as a means of promoting distrust and producing "resignation, cynicism, and a sense of disempowerment." In the digital public sphere, where it is difficult to simply block information, authoritarian regimes can effectively suppress information or dilute and disrupt its impact "by creating an ever-bigger glut of mashed-up truth and falsehood to foment confusion and distraction." This strategy is especially potent in the absence of trusted institutional intermediaries to which citizens can turn to assess the credibility of knowledge claims. The instrumentalization of abundance need not aim to persuade; it may aim simply to overwhelm. The result may be a paralyzing, demobilizing "sense ... that the truth is simply unknowable."[20]

The weaponization of abundance is not confined to authoritarian regimes. The strategy was given its classic formulation by Steve Bannon, in conversation with Michael Lewis in early 2018: "The Democrats don't matter. ... The real opposition is the media. And the way to deal with them is to flood the zone with shit."[21] Bannon was no longer President Trump's chief strategist at that time, but there is no better description of Trump's own skillful media practice.

Yet while digitally mediated abundance tends to erode trust, it does not do so uniformly. Distrust in "traditional" institutionalized media often goes hand in hand with trust in less institutionalized sources of knowledge.[22] In an environment of seemingly immediate access to information and knowledge, abundance can heighten confidence in individuals' own judgment, including their judgment about which purveyors of public knowledge claims to trust. It can thereby contribute to what has been called "epistemic hubris": unwarranted confidence in one's beliefs about policy-related matters.[23] The experience of immediacy, in other words, can work against the disorienting effects that can be produced by abundance and flatness. Individuals may feel that they enjoy immediate access not only to an abundance of unstructured information and conflicting knowledge claims, but to an abundance of audio, visual, textual, and even statistical "evidence" or "proof" that they may understand as validating or invalidating particular public knowledge claims. Abundance in connection with immediacy can thus be polarizing rather than paralyzing; it can produce contending certainties, as those who already hold strong views hew to them even more strongly, seeing their own views as abundantly confirmed and opposing views as abundantly discredited.

During the pandemic, for example, citizens had direct digital access not only to an abundance of conflicting claims and opinions but also to an enormous glut of anecdotes, reportage, data, and research findings.[24] Numerous tracking projects conveyed daily updates and trends on cases, deaths, tests, and hospitalizations. Many sites allowed users to download and explore the data on their own. And voluminous streams of new research were freely accessible on preprint servers – not only published work, but also papers that had not yet been peer-reviewed.

This evidentiary glut gave many citizens the sense that they were in a position to assess the knowledge claims made by experts and others. It was easy to track the sharp oscillations in expert opinion. It was easy for some to find not just anecdotes and news stories but abundant data and research that could be taken (or mistaken) as suggesting, or even "proving," that "the experts" got things massively wrong in this way or that. And it was just as easy for others to find abundant evidence strengthening their conviction that critics of expert-legitimated measures were ignoring the dictates of capital-s Science and endangering the public.

Hyperconnectivity has made it much easier for us to inhabit radically different public worlds. The public worlds we inhabit are constituted in significant part by what we know or believe about them. And what we have known or believed about Covid-19 – not only about what should be done, but about the most basic descriptive facts – has been radically discrepant. Apart from a brief moment in the early spring of 2020, there has been no shared definition of the situation. Was Covid-19 "the greatest existential threat in our lifetimes," or was it no more dangerous than a bad flu season?[25] Did the lockdowns save more than 3 million lives in Europe?[26] Or were they not only medically ineffective and economically devastating but likely to have disastrous health consequences, especially in poor countries, inter alia by disrupting childhood immunization programs?[27] Was the rapid development and deployment of vaccines a remarkable and unprecedented scientific and medical achievement, or were the vaccines ineffective and more dangerous than the disease they were supposed to prevent?[28]

Sharp disagreements about how to define and make sense of the pandemic would no doubt have flourished in a less connected communication ecosystem. But polarization in what people claim to know or believe about the public world – an increasingly important dimension of political polarization – has been deepened, and democratized, in a digitally hyperconnected environment. Thanks to the flood of hyper-accessible "evidence," and the ease of sharing and discussing it on social media, polarization has become participatory: it has become much easier for "ordinary" people to contribute to the polarization of public knowledge.

Already a century ago, to be sure, Walter Lippman could observe that while people "live in the same world, ... they think and feel in different ones." And even if mid-twentieth-century systems of mass communication did support a widely shared public world, the binding power of that world had been weakened long before hyperconnectivity. In the US, for example, the proliferation of alternative channels for the construction of public worlds, including talk radio and cable news channels, had long been eroding the public binding power of network news.[29] But the fragmentation of the public world and the proliferation of rival epistemic, moral, and political worlds have been carried much further in an environment of digital hyperconnectivity.

One symptom of this is the proliferation and mainstreaming of what are often considered conspiracy theories. Again, this is not a new development; but it has been amplified and accelerated by hyperconnectivity. In the structurally flat, culturally populist digital public sphere, such theories circulate alongside and compete on increasingly equal or even superior footing with institutionally legitimated knowledge claims. The digital mediatization of reality and the pervasive awareness of the alterability of digital objects have heightened already chronic and widespread suspicions of manipulation by and through the media. At the same time, however, the immediate and abundant access to alternative knowledge claims – especially those purporting to debunk mainstream views – has enhanced the sense many people have of being able to look behind manipulated, staged, "official" versions of reality.[30]

The abundance, structural flatness, and anti-institutional immediacy of the digital environment have strengthened both individualist stances toward public knowledge claims (by making it easier – or seeming to make it easier – to think for oneself or to "do the research") and populist stances (by heightening skepticism of the complex and opaque workings of institutions and increasing access to and interest in forms of "counter-knowledge" that challenge established bodies of knowledge).[31] In both ways, hyperconnectivity has further undermined the already weakened cultural authority and deference once enjoyed by mainstream knowledge-producing and knowledge-disseminating institutions. In so doing, it has invited – and directly stimulated – the proliferation of competing public worlds. It has provided a robust infrastructure for such worlds that facilitates the production and circulation of a seemingly limitless supply of engaging, compelling, world-sustaining content.

Digital media have often been blamed for contributing to "post-truth politics."[32] But as Michael Sacasas has argued, the contemporary digital environment encourages not the abandonment but the proliferation of truth claims. It facilitates the emergence and multiplication of digitally mediated subcultures that, in the disembodied hothouse atmosphere of "symbolic exchange structured by carefully calibrated architectures of reward and approbation," may develop into "cultures in the strong sense," committed not just to "alternative moral orders" but to "alternative realities." The radically discrepant perspectives on public phenomena thus generated are not just differences of interpretation; they are differences about the most basic facts. The upshot, for Sacasas, is that "we are all conspiracy theorizers now" in the sense that we all hold certain beliefs that many others consider "not just mistaken but preposterous and paranoid."[33]

Two additional features of the knowledge environment of hyperconnectivity, already very much in evidence, are likely to be increasingly salient in the near future. One, touched on in passing above, is the unlimited manipulability of digital objects; the other is the rapidly increasing power of machine learning. These two come together in intensifying concerns about the authenticity of digital objects. Generative machine learning models can be used to create synthetic images, text, and audio that appear extremely convincing. And even if fully synthesized video remains a much more difficult challenge, it is already possible to create "deepfake" videos that seamlessly swap faces so as to purportedly show one person doing or saying something another person was actually doing or saying. In the absence of effective countermeasures, the widespread ability to make up textual, audio, and visual "evidence" – easily, cheaply, and convincingly – will substantially undermine the integrity of digital evidence. This can only further aggravate the forms of epistemic disarray I have described.

One class of generative models – so-called large language models, trained on enormous corpora of text – can already produce plausible-sounding new articles on any theme imaginable. As such models improve further, the texts they generate will be increasingly difficult to distinguish from texts written by humans, and the present difficulty distinguishing bot-generated from human tweets will extend to longer-form writing.[34] Propaganda will be largely automated – and therefore much cheaper – as well as much harder to trace (since the ability to create new content at scale will remove telltale evidence of copying and recycling that currently helps researchers identify propaganda operations). Many platforms are likely to respond by limiting posts to accounts with verified identities, or at least validated pseudonyms; this may be indispensable, but it will further increase platform control over public discourse.[35]

Regimes of feeling

In recent decades, the "affective turn" in the human sciences has led scholars to pay increasing attention to affect, feeling, and emotion in social, economic, and political life.[36] In the study of politics, which had been dominated during the second half of the twentieth century by rationalist approaches, researchers have come to emphasize the critical role of emotion in such phenomena as social movements, charismatic leadership, populist discontent, and ethnic, religious, and nationalist conflict.[37]

In seeking to grasp the affective dimension of political life, scholars have stressed the potency of the media in mobilizing feeling. Even pre-electronic media – notably the sensationalist reporting of the early mass-circulation newspapers – could stir up strong and politically conse-quential feelings. But electronic media, television in particular, have been understood as more emotionally engaging and mobilizing. One important mechanism of engagement involves "parasocial" relation-ships: the illusion of a close and mutual social relationship that audience members may develop with a television personality. The literature on such relationships has stressed their psychological dynamics and later their commercial implications. But scholars have recently begun to explore the political significance of feelings of identification and pseudo-intimacy with public figures.[38] More generally, political scientists and media scholars have long been concerned with the affective aspects of the "mediatization of politics." This literature, like that on parasocial relationships, developed in the television era, but its contemporary relevance is obvious: it specifies how political communication must conform increasingly to "media logics," themselves increasingly commer-cialized, that favor conflict, drama, spectacle, negativity, simplification, personalization, emotionalization, and entertainment.[39]

More recently, attention has turned to the specific role of digital media in mobilizing political affect.[40] Just as hyperconnectivity initially inspired optimism about new forms of public knowledge, so – under the influence of the Arab Spring and the Occupy movements – it inspired optimism about the mobilization of feeling as well. Manuel Castells' hopeful account of the horizontal and participatory social movements enabled by digital networks, for example, pivoted on the political mobilization of affect. Collective action is "rooted in outrage, propelled by enthusiasm and motivated by hope." The emergence of these shared feelings, precipitated by "learning of an unbearable event suffered by someone with whom they identify," is facilitated by the new ecology of networked digital communication: "the fastest and most autonomous, interactive, reprogrammable and self-expanding means of commu-nication in history."[41] Zizi Papacharissi's equally hopeful account of "affective publics" argued that "public displays of affect" on Twitter enable processes of "affective attunement" that allow people to "feel their place into a developing story." Papacharissi joined other critics of rationalistic Habermasian understandings of the public sphere in her appreciation of the power of an affectively driven politics to disrupt "dominant political narratives" and open up new political possibilities.[42] In the second half of the last decade, however, in a digital media landscape dominated by Trump, hyperconnectivity came to be associated with politically toxic emotions – hatred, contempt, anger, disgust, and fear – and with divisive practices of digital shaming, trolling, bullying, and cancelling.[43] Instead of the affective attunement emphasized by Papacharissi, hyperconnectivity seemed to promote affective discord.

I want to focus here on one aspect of the mobilization of toxic political affect: how hyperconnectivity enables and incentivizes the production, circulation, and experience of outrage. I am particularly interested in what social psychologists call moral outrage, directed against those seen as violating some kind of moral, social, or political norm. (What those norms are and what counts as a violation are of course deeply contested, especially when one moves away from basic moral norms into the domain of social and political norms, all the more so in a polarized political environment.)

Moral outrage, to be sure, is an ambivalent emotion; it is not always toxic.[44] It can motivate and energize by focusing attention and emotional energy on something that is perceived as intolerable or unjust and channeling action toward remedying it.[45] But the outrage I am concerned with here, although articulated and justified in moral terms, is directed against members of a political outgroup, not, or not only, against a putatively intolerable or unjust state of affairs. It is strongly associated with the "other-condemning" emotions of anger, contempt, and disgust.[46] It is also associated with a desire to hold others accountable or to punish them. The expression of outrage, while not abusive in and of itself, shades over easily into abuse and harassment, which may involve personal insults, extreme profanity or obscenity, divulging of personal information, or even direct threats. When harassment is sparked by moral outrage, it is often felt to be justified.[47]

The mobilization of outrage against political opponents is not new, and it cannot be blamed on the internet. In the US, outrage has been available as a strategy for capturing attention since the early days of mass-circulation newspapers. And it was broadcast media, after regulatory restrictions were relaxed in the 1980s and 1990s, that made the mobilization of outrage a recognizable – and reliably profitable – genre, central to the business model of conservative talk radio in the 1990s and of Fox News in the 2000s.[48] But digital hyperconnectivity has supercharged the production and circulation of moral outrage.

Hyperconnectivity provides an especially propitious environment for outrage in three respects. First, the algorithms that govern the circulation and visibility of digital content are optimized for engagement. And moral outrage is distinctively (though not uniquely) engaging: it captures attention both because of its moral framing (moral stimuli in general being attention-getting) and because of the expression of intense emotionality.[49] Content producers, both organizations and individuals, therefore have incentives – economic and political in the case of profit- and power-seeking organizations, psychological in the case of attention-seeking individuals – to generate and circulate content that expresses outrage. Incentives to produce engaging content long predate hyperconnectivity.[50] But techniques for monitoring and measuring attention and optimizing content for engagement have become ubiquitously deployed and vastly more sophisticated in the era of universal surveillance, big data, and continuous A/B testing. So while commercial media undertakings have always sought to engage audiences, newly fine-grained data on what drives engagement, and newly sophisticated algorithmic means of optimizing for engagement, mean that these incentives now channel content producers more directly and powerfully toward the expression of moral outrage (as well as toward other forms of measurably and demonstrably engaging content). And the ubiquitous user-facing metrics of social media platforms, saliently reporting likes, shares, retweets, and so on, channel individual contributions in the same direction.[51]

Second, the superabundance of digital content affords an inexhaustible and hyper-accessible reservoir of material for those seeking to mobilize moral outrage. Considerable research and commentary have highlighted the role of fake news or misinformation in fueling outrage.[52] But purveyors of moral outrage need not resort to fabrication. The abundance of real material – new stories, documents, tweets, TikToks, and so on

– that nontrivial segments of the population will find outrageous makes fabrication unnecessary.[53] In the hyper-integrated, fully nationalized, easily searchable digital media space of a very large country, there is never any shortage of outrage-inducing material.[54] In a country with more than a hundred thousand K-12 schools, for example, and in a context in which K-12 education has become a key site of conflict over racism and wokeness, it's easy, as Matthew Yglesias has observed, to generate an endless stream of outrage-mobilizing stories about racist incidents on the one hand or "woke administrators out of control" on the other without having to make things up.[55] This is obviously not to deny the importance of misinformation in the digital public sphere. But it is to argue that the outrage machine does not depend on wholesale invention, even if it does depend on taking things out of context, selective quotation, and tendentious framing.[56]

The self-documenting nature of interaction on platforms like Facebook and Twitter, moreover, contributes to the inexhaustible supply of outrage-inducing material by making an enduring digital record of the interaction visible to broad audiences with heterogeneous political and moral commitments.[57] The expression of outrage itself becomes part of this objectified, publicly visible digital record. This contributes to the further proliferation of outrage, since the documented public expression of outrage often provokes counter-outrage that expresses outrage about the expression of outrage.[58]

Third, the affordances of digital communication networks have democratized the production and circulation of moral outrage (just as they have democratized the production of polarized public knowledge). Outrage is no longer simply mobilized from above; it is co-produced from below in a participatory manner. The participatory affordances allow outrage to take the form of a self-propagating chain, as outrage begets further outrage. One-click convenience enables frictionless participation in ongoing digitally mediated expressions of moral outrage, whether by signing an online petition or commenting on, retweeting, sharing, or liking others' expressions of outrage.[59] Initiating a chain of moral outrage – by posting and commenting on a news story, for example, or character-izing someone else's tweet or post as outrageous – is equally convenient and frictionless. As the costs of expressing outrage have plummeted – not only because digital frictionlessness reduces to negligible the time and effort required, but also because the digital remove from the target reduces the emotional costs of expressing outrage – the threshold for what is deemed outrageous has declined, allowing for the proliferation of forms of micro-outrage.[60] Here again we see digitally mediated minia-turization at work – both in the emergence of ultra-minimal forms of political participation (which have occasioned complaints about "clicktivism" and "slacktivism") and in the lowered bar for considering something outrageous.

Social media networks not only reduce the costs of expressing moral outrage; they provide new benefits for doing so.[61] They assemble audiences for anyone wishing to broadcast, and they provide immediate, salient, unambiguous, quantified, and highly gratifying social feedback. They thereby provide the perfect environment for "moral grand-standing"– audience-directed moral talk that seeks to enhance one's status within a group or network.[62] And just as anyone can become a digital micro-celebrity, so anyone can have their own grandstand, since moral grandstanding, like micro-celebrityhood, is defined not by the number of followers one has but by the fact that one is performing for an audience.

This somewhat abstract discussion can be made more concrete by considering how public shaming – in which coordinated expressions of moral outrage are focused on a particular perceived transgression of a particular individual – has been transformed by hyperconnec-tivity.[63] Face-to-face public shaming, in modern Western contexts, is ordinarily bounded in time and space. The shamer and the target stand in an immediate relationship: in the paradigmatic case, the shamer has personally witnessed the conduct deemed shameworthy and directly confronts the target. Although the shaming is observed by others – this is what makes it public – and although knowledge of the shaming may travel through gossip to others not immediately present for it, neither the conduct that occasioned the shaming nor the shaming itself is objectified in any enduring form.

Contemporary digital public shaming is no longer bounded in time and space. Both the action deemed shameworthy and the shaming itself are objectified and enduring. The offending action may have been captured as a photograph or audio or video recording by others, or it may have existed from the beginning in objectified form (a tweet, for example). In either case, it is part of a vast searchable archive. Objectification and digitization enable anyone, anywhere to participate in the shaming without having any knowledge of or connection to the target. The resultant impersonality and anonymity make it easy to pile on. Objectification and digitization also enable the shaming to happen at any time. The archive never forgets, and it can be searched for traces from the past that, recontextualized in terms of the standards of the present, may allow retrospective shaming.[64]

Digitally amplified outrage contributes to what Anton Jäger has called "hyper-politics," and it powerfully reinforces preexisting patterns of polarization.[65] It contributes specifically to reinforcing "affective polarization," defined by antipathy toward the opposing party.[66] The irony is that social media intensify polarization in important part by exaggerating its extent. By contributing to what political scientists have called "false polarization," social media end up contributing to real polarization. More precisely, by contributing to false *ideological* polarization, social media contribute to real *affective* polarization.[67] The voices of outrage on social media platforms are amplified by our tendency to pay more attention to moral and emotional stimuli when scanning a social media feed;[68] by the fact that people who post frequently on political topics are more partisan, more polarized, and more inclined to outrage than others;[69] and by algorithms that boost the circulation of engaging material. The voices of outrage not only *drown* out others; they *drive* out others, as more quiet and moderate voices, disgusted by the toxic atmosphere, drop out of the discussion.[70] Social media therefore yield a distorted picture of the distribution of political views, a picture that represents the public as much more deeply divided, and much more clustered towards the extremes, than it actually is. To moderate partisans, this makes the opposing party seem more extreme and threatening, and it can thereby increase antipathy toward that party. Misrepresentations of the degree of polarization, themselves polarizing, can thus come to be self-fulfilling.[71]

Regimes of governing

The new ways of governing made possible by hyperconnectivity are in certain respects antithetical to the new ways of knowing and feeling discussed above. If the new modes of knowing and feeling are deeply politicized, the new modes of data-intensive and algorithmically guided governance seem at first to be strikingly depoliticized, promising, as Evgeny Morozov sardonically observed, a "utopia of politics without politics."[72] If the new regimes of knowing and feeling can be described as populist and participatory, the new regimes of governing are technocratic. If the new landscapes of knowing and feeling are unruly and chaotic, the new landscapes of governance seem orderly, coordinated, and disciplined.

By regimes of governing, I mean the new modalities of algorithmic governance that have been enabled by hyperconnectivity. Although still in early stages of development, these have been widely adopted by under-resourced and overburdened government agencies in recent years, driven by the availability – and ideological celebration – of data and by promises of insight, efficiency, objectivity, and cost savings.[73] In the criminal justice system, for example, algorithmically computed "risk scores" guide bail, sentencing, and parole decisions.[74] "Predictive policing" algorithms channel policing resources toward particular geographic areas or toward persons deemed "at risk" of committing or becoming the victim of a crime.[75] Similar predictive algorithms direct attention to children deemed at risk of abuse and to persons deemed at risk of suicide.[76] Agencies such as the Internal Revenue Service, the Securities and Exchange Commission, and the Environmental Protection Agency focus scarce enforcement resources on algorithmically flagged potential violations.[77] Algorithms streamline the processing of applications for disability benefits (and appeals of denials of benefits) by selecting for expedited treatment applications and appeals that are deemed most likely to succeed.[78] Natural language processing algorithms digest and assess enormous volumes of comments on proposed changes in regulations.[79] The list could be extended indefinitely.[80]

Algorithmic *governance* is not restricted to *governments*. It is in fact much more developed in the private sector, especially by the great tech platforms themselves.[81] The platforms, after all, have the data and machine learning expertise to employ forms of algorithmic governance that are much more sophisticated than those used in the public sector. And platforms are indisputably involved in the business of governing. In the most obvious sense, as we saw in the last chapter, they govern the activities of their users through their design and control of the digital architectures that determine what can be done on and through the platforms. But their governing power extends to public life more broadly. They provide increasingly indispensable infrastructures not only of sociability and entertainment but of knowledge, commerce, labor, and politics. Most crucially, for the purposes of this chapter, they govern who sees what and therefore, in some measure, who knows or believes what and who feels what.[82] Regimes of governing thus operate in part through regimes of knowing and feeling. Platforms also govern, in an increasingly interventionist manner, who can *say* what in the digital public sphere. Although the giant platforms are owned and operated by private companies, they clearly exercise public functions.[83]

For all their variousness, these new modalities of governance all rely on vast quantities of data; on ubiquitous surveillance to generate the data; on sophisticated forms of quantification to render digital traces as analyzable data; on algorithms that make predictions or classifications and make or recommend decisions; and on machine learning to create and train the algorithms. Governance through data, surveillance, and quantification, to be sure, has a long history. The word "statistics" is derived from French and German terms that initially designated the study of states and statecraft, and a rich literature, much of it Foucauldian in inspiration, has analyzed the "avalanche of printed numbers" that had already become central to governance by the early nineteenth century.[84]

But algorithmic governance based on machine learning is new. Machine learning requires enormous amounts of data in order to train classificatory and predictive algorithms, and data of the requisite magnitude have become routinely available only in the context of hyperconnectivity. The data come partly from the digitalization of originally non-digital data – books, images, and public records of all kinds. But they come mainly, and increasingly, from the never-resting engines of digital surveillance, which expressly solicit previously undreamt of volumes of data from users and surreptitiously vacuum up traces of all digitally mediated activity. The superabundance of digital data not only enables machine learning to develop with unprecedented rapidity; it also vastly increases the demand for machine learning algorithms, since only such algorithms are capable of making sense of overwhelming volumes of data. Data superabundance thus drives both the demand for and the supply of machine learning-based algorithmic governance. It also accounts for the circular, bootstrapping quality of machine learning in the era of big data: machine learning algorithms learn from superabundant data how to learn from superabundant data.[85]

The new regimes of governing, in short, depend on new ways of knowing and learning. These new ways of "seeing like a state" are powered by machine learning models that have been trained on the unimaginably large data sets that are generated by continuous and ubiquitous digital surveillance.[86] It's worth underscoring how these modes of *organizational* knowing differ from the new modes of *individual* knowing discussed in the first section of this chapter. For individuals, digital abundance often obscures more than it reveals: it is overwhelming and chaotic, at least as far as knowledge of public affairs is concerned, and it tends to reinforce epistemic distrust, cynicism, and polarization. For organizations, digital abundance, once algorithmically analyzed, reveals what was previously obscure; it discloses previously hidden patterns and forms of order. While the attention-grabbing and outrage-inducing *optimization for engagement* that algorithmically structures realms of popular knowing and feeling makes public reality appear chaotic, unknowable, and ungovernable, the *optimization for prediction* that structures organizational ways of knowing promises to make social life more minutely knowable – and more governable – than ever.[87] As Shoshana Zuboff has observed, there is an "abyss between what we know and what is known about us" by data-rich organizations.[88] That power functions through the control and manipulation of knowledge is not a new insight, but hyperconnectivity has made this insight more pertinent than ever.[89]

Algorithmic governance is riven by three fundamental tensions.[90] The first is between the claim to objectivity and counterclaims of bias. The ways in which algorithms can encode and perpetuate bias have been the focus of a great deal of recent debate and research. The irony is that algorithmic governance has been promoted precisely as a means of *overcoming* well-known biases in human decision-making. Nor is this mere marketing rhetoric: there is evidence that algorithms can indeed be more accurate, consistent, and impartial than human decision-makers in certain respects.[91] But there is also ample evidence of bias. Algorithms have no God's-eye view of the world: what they take account of, and how, is determined by a series of human choices. They depend, in particular, on the data on which they are trained. If the historical data used to train predictive policing algorithms reflect racial inequalities in policing, for example, those inequalities will be carried over into the algorithm in ways that can reinforce the racialization of policing.[92] A growing literature addresses strategies for countering potential sources of algorithmic bias and ways of enlisting algorithms in efforts to combat discrimination.[93]

The second tension is between opacity and transparency. In democratic settings, it is expected that legal, administrative, and political decisions will be explained and justified and that the process of arriving at them will be transparent. Explainability and transparency are understood as central to accountability. Algorithmic determinations, however, are generally opaque, and it is often difficult or impossible to explain or justify them.[94] A certain degree of opacity, moreover, may be necessary in order to prevent algorithms from being easily gamed (even though opacity is not sufficient to prevent efforts at gaming, as indicated by the enormous market for search engine optimization services).[95] These difficulties notwithstanding, an emerging literature explores ways of increasing transparency and legal and political accountability through disclosure (explaining a model's inputs and outputs, ranking inputs by how important they are in the model, and explaining the choices made in the design and testing of the model); design constraints (prohibiting the use of certain especially complex and uninterpretable methods); or benchmarking (requiring the non-algorithmic processing of a sample of cases and the comparison of the results to algorithmic determinations of the same cases).[96]

The final tension is between automaticity and human agency and autonomy. At present, most algorithmic governance systems generate recommendations, leaving humans to make the decisions. As algorithms have become more powerful and sophisticated, however, they have encroached on the space for discretion. Even where algorithms nominally only recommend courses of action, it becomes increasingly difficult in practice for humans – public officials, for example – to override the algorithmic recommendation.[97] As people cease to take full responsibility for complex decisions, they lose certain skills and capacities.[98] And as levels of automaticity increase, as they will surely do as a result of computational advances, cost pressures, and habituation to algorithmic decision-making, the tension between automaticity and human agency and autonomy will become more pronounced. As algorithmic systems become more autonomous, humans risk becoming less so.

But it is not just the agency and autonomy of bureaucratic and other decision-makers that are eroded; it is the agency and autonomy of the governed. Automated forms of algorithmic governance are distinctive in being potentially self-enforcing. To be sure, not all forms of algorithmic governance are self-enforcing. Algorithmic determinations that prompt interventions by police or child protection officials, for example, are not self-enforcing. The algorithmic determination is one thing; the human intervention, even if guided by the algorithmic determination, is another. But the algorithmic governance of digitally mediated social action can indeed be self-enforcing. And as more and more of social life becomes digitally mediated, the field of potentially fully automated, self-enforcing governance expands dramatically.

As Ori Schwarz has argued, self-enforcing systems of algorithmic governance do not establish rules and specify penalties for violating them; digital mediation enables them to pre-empt violations altogether. This transforms the nature of power, which is now "generative" rather than "regulative": it can directly produce social reality and govern people's conduct from the outside, bypassing rather than seeking to influence their will and consciousness.[99] As I noted in my discussion of the algorithmic disciplining of labor, gig workers' accounts can be automatically deactivated if their rating falls below a certain level. Or a car could be remotely disabled if the owner falls behind on payments.[100] This new modality of automated algorithmic power, proceeding through the direct governing of behavior rather than through the shaping of consciousness, corresponds to what Zuboff calls the computational "tuning" or "herding" of behavior.[101] And it contributes to the emergence of what I called in chapter 1 the "post-neoliberal self": a self governed not in and through its choices, but in and through automated procedures that make choice unnecessary or impossible.

Consider algorithmic systems of content moderation on digital platforms. These have developed rapidly in recent years in response to advances in machine learning, the sheer scale of offending content (Facebook reports removing millions of pieces of content every day from its platforms), the challenge of the early phase of the pandemic (when most human moderators were sent home), and the intensi-fying demand for platforms to intervene more aggressively against hate speech, bullying, racism, terrorism, pornography, misinformation, disinformation, conspiracy theory, and copyright infringement.[102] Until recently, humans have played two key roles in large-scale content moder-ation systems. The unpaid labor of social media's enormous user base has been mobilized to flag problematic content; and armies of (poorly) paid workers have been hired to review the flagged content and make decisions on removal. But algorithms have been displacing humans on both fronts. The vast majority of content determined to be in violation of Facebook's policies is now discovered by algorithms before having been flagged by users.[103] And an increasing share of this algorithmically *flagged* content is also algorithmically *removed* without human review.[104] Further moves in this direction are likely, both because of the economic and human costs of having human operators review enormous quantities of disturbing material and because, with every determination they make, human moderators are training algorithms to make themselves dispensable.[105]

In a world of more fully automated ex ante content moder-ation, private platforms will wield enormous, opaque, and largely unaccountable algorithmic power over *all* platform-mediated speech, public and private. Unlike human moderators, whose attention is limited, algorithms can scrutinize all content.[106] And as automated algorithmic content moderation comes to be taken for granted as part of the basic infrastructure of platform-mediated communication, the ultimately political nature of definitions of terrorism, hate speech, bullying, and so on risks being hidden beneath a patina of machine-guaranteed objectivity.[107]

The immense power of platforms over public speech, to be sure, does not depend on automated algorithmic control alone. The decisions to ban President Trump from Facebook and Twitter were not made by algorithms. But they *were* self-enforcing. Trump could not violate the bans; he was directly and materially excluded by the platform software itself.[108] Whatever one's views on the merits or likely consequences of the bans, they certainly brought into sharp focus the distinctive affordances of digitally mediated power over speech and the extraordinary concen-tration of such power in the hands of a few giant platforms.

Coda: Between populism and technocracy

The technocratic quality of new regimes of algorithmic governance stands in stark contrast to the populist cast, participatory logics, and hyper-politicizing and polarizing tendencies of new regimes of digitally mediated knowing and feeling. I turn in conclusion to a broader consideration of the ways in which hyperconnectivity can promote both populism and its seeming antithesis, technocracy.

Digital hyperconnectivity accentuates the chronic populism of late modern societies in two main ways.[109] First, it is a technology – and an ideology – of *immediacy*. It enables (or seems to enable) direct connections between people – and between people and "the world's information," as Google puts it – by bypassing or disrupting institutional intermediaries of all kinds: gatekeepers in the realm of culture, credentialed experts in the realm of knowledge, middlemen in the realm of economics, and the press and parties in the realm of politics. Hyperconnectivity promises to connect audiences directly to creators, buyers directly to sellers, citizens directly to political leaders.[110]

Complete disintermediation, as noted in chapter 4, is a myth: hyperconnectivity simply replaces conspicuously visible intermediaries with self-invisibilizing ones. Digital platforms remain intermediaries even when they minimize or disavow that role and present themselves as neutral conduits and facilitators.[111] Yet the promise of immediacy is not entirely illusory. The bypassing or weakening of existing intermediaries is real and important. Digitally mediated connections can *feel* direct and immediate, and President Trump's connection with his legions of Twitter followers *was* more direct and immediate than the usual, more filtered and institutionally mediated connections between politicians and citizens. Citizens' relation to public knowledge claims, though algorithmically filtered, is indeed more immediate than it was when public knowledge was more thoroughly organized by institutions. The ideology of disintermediation is powerfully attractive to many, and it is precisely a populist ideology. For populism is itself an ideology of immediacy.[112] It promises to empower ordinary people by disempowering mediating institutions and their comfortably ensconced elites. In the political sphere, it is an ideology that delegitimizes political parties, trade unions, professional expertise, courts, and the mainstream media and demands an immediate or direct relation between "the people" and the exercise of power.

Second, hyperconnectivity contributes to the *popularization* of culture and politics. It does so in one sense by making cultural and political activity more attractive and engaging, by opening up new and more accessible forms and arenas of cultural and political participation, and by broadening the range of those actively involved as producers or "prosumers" of culture and as participants in the expanded and fragmented public sphere. Digital platforms – raised level surfaces, as suggested by the term's architectural connotations, which have been adroitly harnessed by platform owners – promise to make visible the previously invisible, to give voice to the previously voiceless.[113] And they have in fact done so, even if the digital surfaces they have created are in no sense level playing fields. They have made it easier for those outside the cultural or political mainstream, including the disaffected citizens to whom populist politicians often appeal, to create spaces of communication and mutual recognition with like-minded others and to establish a public presence.[114]

The networked digital public sphere contributes to popularization in a second sense by making calculations of popularity – and representations of what "the people" as a whole or some particular public like, want, prefer, and believe – more central to culture and politics. Technologies of continuous and granular quantification render "the people" visible and knowable and feed those objectified representations back to the public in new ways. Digitally mediated ways of consulting constituencies and registering their preferences have been at the forefront of digital democracy initiatives.[115] And renderings of the popular have become central to the everyday workings of culture and politics. Ubiquitous "trending" algorithms, for example, do not simply register what is popular for a particular "calculated public" at a particular moment: in recording and diffusing signals of popularity, they amplify those signals and reinforce the popularity that they register.[116] The digitally networked public sphere not only registers the popular: it foregrounds and accentuates the popular, and it enshrines the popular as the ultimate arbiter of value.[117]

Hyperconnectivity contributes to popularization in a final sense by strongly favoring popular – in the sense of "low" rather than "high"

– cultural and political styles.[118] "Low" styles are "raw" and crude (yet "warm" and unrestrained); "high" styles are refined and cultivated (yet cool and reserved). "Low" styles are attention-seeking and taboo-breaking; they flout the constraints and restraints of polite speech and political correctness. They incline toward confrontation, emotion-alization, personalization, and hyper-simplification. Such "low" styles, already favored, as noted above, by the pre-digital mediatization of politics, are even more strongly selected for in the highly competitive digital attention economy – and in what might be called the "attention polity."[119] They have the best chance of breaking through the glut of superabundant digital content.

The ecology of hyperconnectivity thus has deep affinities with the logic of populism. It offers (seemingly) unmediated alternatives to insti-tutional mediation, affords new forms of popular participation, makes popularity the measure of all things, and valorizes popular cultural and political styles. In the cultural domain, it erodes the power of gatekeepers, engenders new forms of popular creativity, and universalizes metrics that amplify as well as record popularity. In the political sphere, it allows "ordinary" people – disaffected citizens in particular – to be addressed in a (relatively) immediate and direct manner; it facilitates the emergence and coalescence of counter-publics styling themselves in opposition to the mainstream; and it rewards the "low" political styles that are best suited to mobilizing against "the elite" and against the rules and practices of the establishment.

At the same time, however, the new modes of algorithmic governance enabled by hyperconnectivity are deeply technocratic. Algorithmic governance, like technocratic governance in general, is premised on specialized knowledge: in this case, on the knowledge that is encoded in and generated by complex computational procedures that analyze large volumes of data. The justification for entrusting decision-making to such procedures is that the correlational and predictive knowledge they generate – and their capacity to find the optimal solutions for precisely defined problems – is superior to the knowledge and optimizing capabil-ities of even the most experienced and highly trained humans.

Technocratic ideals also underlie and animate the broader spirit of "technological solutionism" that is central to the "technological imaginary" of Silicon Valley.[120] Solutionist thinking, like technocracy in general, is depoliticizing. It seeks to transform social, political, administrative, and judicial problems into technical problems that have technically rational solutions. It subscribes to the idea that "most problems, when properly understood, are ... amenable to the logic of statistical analysis and optimization."[121] It thus exemplifies the "assimilation of politics to engineering" that Michael Oakeshott saw as characteristic of rationalist politics in general.[122]

Technocracy and populism are generally understood to be antithetical, defined in antagonistic opposition to one another. While technocracy entrusts decision-making powers to experts (or to expert-designed knowledge procedures like algorithms), populism distrusts the claims of expertise in politics. And while technocracy is depoliticizing, seeking to insulate decision-making from popular and specifically populist interference, populism is generally re-politicizing; it claims to reassert political control over issues that are seen as having been illegitimately removed from the domain of democratic decision-making and entrusted to democratically unaccountable bureaucrats, experts, or courts.[123] As decision-making by unaccountable algorithms (and by the unaccountable platforms or experts that design them) becomes increasingly important – especially if algorithmic governance becomes more visible and intrusive – one might therefore expect it to become similarly vulnerable to populist challenge.

Yet there are reasons to believe that algorithmic governance may remain insulated from such challenge. As noted above, for example, content moderation on major platforms became both more automated and more visible and intrusive during the pandemic and during and after the 2020 US election. This did prompt user complaints about censorship and liberal bias. Yet while some users voted with their feet, migrating to alternative platforms, the more automated and aggressive content moderation did not generate a populist challenge to algorithmic content moderation per se. Algorithms are not only unaccountable; they are in a sense unaddressable. Unlike courts, bureaucratic agencies, or expert panels that publish their rulings and recommendations, they do not make easy targets. Algorithms are self-invisibilizing, protected by their opacity. They are also protected by the fact that they work in a granular, case-specific manner. Algorithmic governance has indeed become an important focus of contestation. But the contestation is carried out in a technical idiom: specialized knowledge *of* algorithms is required in order to contest the specialized knowledge encoded *in* algorithms.

More fundamentally, as Christopher Bickerton and Carlo Invernizzi Accetti have argued, the reciprocal and apparently mutually constitutive antagonism of populism and technocracy conceals an underlying complementarity and even an affinity: both are opposed to the complex and messy institutional mediations of party democracy and its procedural understanding of political legitimacy. As the structural foundations of party democracy have eroded over the course of the last half-century, political competition has come to be structured increasingly by a "technopopulist" political logic, characterized by conjoined appeals to "the people" and to problem-solving "competence."[124]

Bickerton and Invernizzi Accetti are not concerned with new communications technologies; the "techno" in their "technopopulism" refers to technocracy, not to technology.[125] Yet digital hyperconnectivity powerfully reinforces the synthesis of populism and technocracy that they describe. As a technology and ideology of immediacy, it exacerbates the very crisis of institutional mediation to which it claims to respond; it contributes in particular to the hollowing out of parties and of the press as mediating institutions. As a technology of the popular, it generates new ways of mobilizing, consulting, and measuring "the people" and new ways of claiming to act on their behalf. And as a technology of knowledge, it affords new ways of knowing, acting upon, and governing the social world, new ways of recasting social problems as technical problems. If technopopulist appeals to "the people" and to expertise increasingly "structure our politics and shape our experience of democracy," as Bickerton and Invernizzi Accetti argue in the final sentence of their book, hyperconnectivity increasingly structures and shapes appeals to "the people" and to expertise.[126] The "techno" in technopopulism may thus indeed refer to technology as well as to technocracy.

Conclusion

A book like this one can have no proper conclusion. The dynamism of digital hyperconnectivity remains undiminished: there is no stable point from which one can look back and take stock. During the writing of this book, the pandemic accelerated the transformations I was analyzing; it provided a powerful impetus for broadening and deepening digital mediation in every sphere of life. I begin these concluding reflections by considering how the pandemic enabled digital platforms to extend and intensify their already encompassing embrace. I then reflect more broadly on the significance of hyperconnectivity, considering three dystopian visions – two drawn from fiction, one from social science – that highlight the ways in which hyperconnectivity has enhanced technologies of control, technologies of distraction, and technologies of manipulation.

Hyperconnectivity prepared us remarkably well for the pandemic. As Ian Bogost wrote just before lockdowns were imposed in the US, many had already been voluntarily dwelling in a kind of digital quarantine: "Never before in human history has it been so easy to do so much without going anywhere."[1] For some, digital technology had already induced a habit of social distancing, a regime of disembodied, contactless sociability, shopping, entertainment, work, education, even sex. Had this digital infrastructure not already been in place, the lockdowns that were imposed worldwide would have been unthinkable.[2] Hyperconnectivity, then, profoundly shaped the response to the pandemic, and it introduced a fundamental new axis of inequality: between the digitally privileged (who could go fully remote with only minimal inconvenience while keeping their jobs and minimizing their risk of exposure) and the in-person "essential workers" (who made the fully remote life of the digitally privileged possible) as well as the minimally or inadequately connected and those without the skills and experience to adapt to an online-only life.

The pandemic could therefore be seen as "the ideal proof-of-concept for the particular utopia that the tech industry has tried to build."[3] But it was not just an occasion to showcase the existing infrastructure; it was an opportunity to reimagine the future. A crisis, the saying goes, is a terrible thing to waste, and the great tech platforms had no intention of letting this one go unexploited. In the only slightly hyperbolic words of theorist of "disaster capitalism" Naomi Klein, they used the pandemic as a "living laboratory" in which to work out and test their vision for "a permanent – and highly profitable – no-touch future."[4] And by invoking the specter of a digitally ascendant China, they could plead for government support for that vision. As former Google CEO Eric Schmidt put it in a *Wall Street Journal* op-ed early in the pandemic, "If we are to build a future economy and education system based on tele-everything, we need a fully connected population and ultrafast infrastructure. The government must make a massive investment … to convert the nation's digital infra-structure to cloud-based platforms and link them with a 5G network."[5]

Consider briefly four domains in which the pandemic opened up new opportunities for intensified digital mediation: health and medicine, education, entertainment, and work. Before the pandemic, the tech giants and other tech companies had already been investing heavily in the health and medical sector. They had been training the public in self-tracking, vacuuming up data, and positioning themselves as indis-pensable partners in medical research and the broader health and medical field.[6] But the pandemic was a breakthrough moment for digitally mediated telehealth services of all kinds (previously limited by regulatory and insurance restrictions). And tech initiatives – including the primarily telehealth platform Amazon Care, advertising "No appointments, no waiting rooms" – are presuming that the vast new telehealth market will be here to stay.[7]

The pandemic was also a breakthrough moment for the giant tech platforms as key players in public health. They alone could muster the geolocation data to assess aggregate compliance with social distancing measures. They alone were in a position to support automated digital contact tracing.[8] They alone had the infrastructural power to implement digital "passports," widely used in Europe and elsewhere to restrict access to certain venues and facilities to the vaccinated and/or recently tested. They alone had the automated tools needed to combat what was deemed misinformation about Covid-19 vaccines and other pandemic-related matters, marking a sharp increase in platform censorship of content deemed problematic. They alone could afford to spend lavishly on a series of techno-philanthropic initiatives.[9] At a moment when platforms were on the defensive in the face of a developing "techlash," the pandemic provided a welcome occasion for high-profile efforts to re-legitimize themselves – and their data-extractive, surveillance-based business models – as acting in the public interest.[10]

The crisis that disrupted schooling for as many as a billion and a half students worldwide was seen – and seized – as an opportunity by the educational technology (edtech) sector. Like health tech, edtech had been gaining ground long before Covid-19. But the pandemic presented an extraordinary opportunity for a digital great leap forward – and an opportunity to sideline concerns about privacy and tracking. The tech giants – especially Microsoft, Google, and Amazon – and smaller firms like Zoom were able to offer free tools to help school systems, teachers, students, and families meet the immediate and urgent need for continuity in instruction. By thus being in a position to "deliver solutions at international scale, at speed, and for free," the great platform companies could emplace themselves at the heart of the educational enterprise. They could hope to make themselves indispensable, as key providers of infrastructural services, not only during the pandemic but after. By allying with foundations, intergovernmental organizations, and government agencies at various scales, the tech platforms could turn the crisis into an opportunity to "reimagine" education and "shape education systems for the future" – a future of data-centered, software-mediated, putatively personalized, partly privatized, and surveillance-intensive teaching, assessment, and management.[11]

The sudden disruption of in-person events afforded a similar chance to reimagine live entertainment.[12] Gaming platforms had been experimenting with digitally mediated live concerts before the pandemic; one on Fortnite drew more than 10 million viewers, profiting from the fact that the immensely popular platform had become a social space as much as a video game.[13] And live streaming of video games and other content (including, recently, music) on Twitch and other platforms had been gaining ground for a decade as a new form of interactive "networked broadcasting."[14] As in the educational field, however, the pandemic offered an unprecedented opportunity. Virtual concerts quickly became ubiquitous. Initially, as in education, platforms provided a short-term solution to an immediate problem, a way of reconnecting performers and audiences on an ad hoc basis. But again as in education, the pandemic offered the opportunity to redefine what "live" music – or "live" events more generally – might mean in the longer term. Platforms sought to define liveness in terms of virtual copresence, interactivity, and immersiveness: occupying the same virtual space with others at the same time, being able to interact on voice or text chat not only laterally (among audience participants) but sometimes also vertically (between performers and audience), and being viscerally transported to and absorbed in the event (as virtual reality technology becomes more widely used).[15] Live digital events could thereby be promoted not as a poor substitute for but as a rich complement to in-person events.[16]

Even as in-person concerts have resumed, digital liveness is clearly here to stay. In this and other domains, we see a ratchet effect, as much of the ground gained by digital initiatives during the pandemic is not ceded in its aftermath. Like their edtech counterparts, music tech entrepreneurs envision a hybrid future with a central and expanding role for digitally mediated experience. This is framed in terms of broadening and democratizing access to musical experiences. But it is driven by vistas of vast new markets. During the pandemic, most digital events were free or inexpensive. But if millions or even tens of millions can attend a digital event – the spectacular Travis Scott event in Fortnite early in the pandemic drew 28 million unique visitors to its five performances – the economics of scalability hold out an irresistible promise of monetization, not only in the domain of digital live music, but also in the broader domain of the digital experience economy.[17]

Just as the pandemic prompted efforts to reimagine education and redefine live entertainment, so it prompted efforts to reinvent collaborative work and conferencing. The existing digital infrastructure allowed a remarkably seamless transition to remote work. But that infrastructure was manifestly unsatisfactory in some respects, especially for meetings and collaborative work. The lack of a shared space hindered interactive work, cut off access to many of the cues available in copresent interaction and contributed, as noted in chapter 2, to widely felt "Zoom fatigue."[18]

The pandemic therefore presented an exceptional opportunity – both for giant tech firms and for small augmented and virtual reality startups – not simply to facilitate remote work during the Covid-19 crisis but to reimagine the future of work. Like "liveness" in the domain of music, "presence" would no longer depend on physical proximity: AR and VR tools, in emerging 5G environments, would allow people to interact in a shared virtual (or mixed physical and virtual) space in a way that would capture gesture, gaze, and directional sound, create a convincing sense of presence, and eventually provide "a better experience than face-to-face meetings."[19] Tech-supported remote work has found favor with many companies: persuaded by the pandemic experience that productivity need not suffer, and happy to shrink their office footprints, numerous companies have promised their employees permanent remote or hybrid work opportunities.

Alongside these efforts to reimagine and restructure medicine and public health, education, entertainment, and work, the pandemic gave new impetus to grander efforts to reimagine social life in its entirety. Central to these efforts has been the concept of the metaverse: a persistent, distance-transcending, all-encompassing virtual or digitally augmented space in which a full range of leisure, social, and work activities and interactions could take place. The concept goes back to Neal Stephenson's 1992 novel *Snow Crash*, and it has long been used by VR enthusiasts and tech journalists. During the pandemic, however, as activities of all kinds moved into virtual spaces, and as platforms like Fortnite became more than ever places to hang out and do things other than play the video game itself, the notion of the metaverse came to resonate with a broader public.

Metaverse-talk went mainstream after Mark Zuckerberg repositioned Facebook as a metaverse company in a carefully orchestrated series of communications in the summer and fall of 2021, culminating in the renaming of the company as Meta. Facebook/Meta certainly doesn't have the field to itself: Microsoft, Apple, Google, and game manufacturers Epic Games (maker of Fortnite) and Roblox, among others, have been laying out their own visions of the metaverse during the pandemic and investing heavily in AR, VR, and virtual spaces.[20] But it was Facebook's highly visible rebranding that launched "metaverse" into broad public circulation.

In Zuckerberg's vision, at once grandiose and vague, the metaverse is "an embodied internet, where instead of just viewing content[,] you are in it."[21] This immersiveness is what underwrites the feeling of being "present" with others, and this robust sense of presence – ironically enough, given the ways in which Facebook has recast social interaction on a planetary scale – is the touchstone to which Zuckerberg returns again and again. The phone will no longer be our primary interface with the digital; instead we will have more "natural" ways of interacting digitally. Just how VR headsets will feel "natural" is not clear, since, in addition to being bulky and uncomfortable at present, they work by completely shutting out the immediate physical world. AR is more promising in this respect: although high-performance AR glasses are currently expensive and clunky, continued miniaturization will no doubt eventually yield powerful AR glasses that will be much cheaper and sleeker, perhaps even indistinguishable from ordinary eyeglasses.

The key audience for metaverse talk, though, is not users; it is actual and potential investors. Zuckerberg and his competitors are framing the metaverse as the "next big thing": a new computing and communication platform that, as the eventual successor to the mobile internet, will open up a multi-trillion-dollar economy.[22] Of course a lot of the metaverse talk is hype. But hype backed by $10 billion a year in investment on the part of Facebook alone – an amount the company says will increase over time – is more than mere hype. Ten billion here, ten billion there, and pretty soon you're talking real money. Others, as noted, are investing heavily as well. These investments, and the technical advances they will enable, will certainly transform modes of digital connectivity, and it seems safe to say that VR and especially AR will play an important role in this transformation. For Facebook and its competitors, the immersiveness promised by improved VR and AR technologies is an opportunity to capture yet more of our attention and track us still more thoroughly. In the dystopian musing of technology critic Rob Horning, the metaverse is an opportunity to make the internet "even more invasive and all subsuming." AR allows people to be "perpetually inundated with ads and branded content. ... Many of these companies want you to eventually wear their augmented-reality glasses so that you literally see the reality they want you to see."[23]

Metaverse enthusiasts, as Brian Merchant has noted, rarely reflect on the concept's origins in dystopian cyberpunk science fiction. In

Stephenson's *Snow Crash*, the metaverse – a 3-D virtual world, accessed by donning VR goggles, in which users appear and act as avatars – is "addictive, violent, and an enabler of our worst impulses"; but "it is necessary, because the real world has become so unbearable."[24] In Ernest Cline's 2011 *Ready Player One*, the virtual world (called the Oasis) is likewise an escape from a world mired in environmental and economic crisis. It requires no great leap of the imagination to think that the attractiveness of the current metaverse-in-the-making (to consumers, that is: the business market for AR and VR services is likely to be quite different) might similarly be inversely proportional to that of the opportunities enjoyed in the "real world."

Just this possibility, albeit without explicit reference to the metaverse, was raised by tech entrepreneur and venture capitalist Marc Andreessen. Responding to an interviewer's question about the hazards of over-connectivity, Andreessen dismissed the question as "a great example of what I call Reality Privilege":

A small percent of people live in a real-world environment that is rich, even overflowing, with glorious substance, beautiful settings, plentiful stimulation, and many fascinating people to talk to, and to work with, and to date. These are also *all* of the people who get to ask probing questions like yours. Everyone else, the vast majority of humanity, lacks Reality Privilege – their online world is, or will be, immeasurably richer and more fulfilling than most of the physical and social environment around them in the quote-unquote real world.

Andreessen denied that this was a dystopian view: "we should build – and we are building – online worlds that make life and work and love wonderful for everyone, no matter what level of reality deprivation they find themselves in."[25]

Andreessen's remark is nonetheless chilling, and it points to an eventual reversal of the digital divide as generally understood.[26] The pandemic, to be sure, has underscored the importance of ongoing inequalities of digital access and skills. To take just one obvious example, children without broadband or laptops – or without much in the way of digital literacy – were hugely disadvantaged by the sudden shift to remote schooling. In the long run, however, we may see the emergence of a new digital divide that is in a sense the opposite of the conventional one: the poor may experience not insufficient but excessive digital connectivity. Signs of this are already evident. The children of harried and overworked poor (and often single) parents, without access to high-quality child care, are more likely to be left to their own devices in a literal rather than metaphorical sense and soothed with digital pacifiers, while the children of wealthy parents – especially, ironically, the children of Silicon Valley professionals and executives – are more likely to be read to, to participate in device-free enrichment activities or summer camps, or even to have nannies who have been obliged to sign no-device contracts.[27] As the range of digital services and experiences increases and their cost decreases, this incipient reversal of the digital divide will become more pronounced. It is easy to imagine a future in which the poor will suffer from digital excess, while the rich frequent curated enclaves of digital scarcity. The poor may be relegated to digital entertainment, virtual experiences, AI-powered therapy, and robotic companions, while the rich will continue to enjoy the varied and gratifying in-person experiences that only they, as the "reality-privileged," can afford.

* * *

Writing in 1985, media theorist and cultural critic Neal Postman bookended his influential *Amusing Ourselves to Death* by juxtaposing two dystopian novelistic visions from the first half of the twentieth century: Orwell's *1984*, published in 1949, and Huxley's *Brave New World*, which appeared in 1932. Both were visions of dictatorship, but the visions were very different. Orwell envisioned a brutal dictatorship turning on fear, coercion, and ubiquitous surveillance; Huxley, a gentle dictatorship turning on pleasure, conditioning, and distraction.

For Postman, concerned with the effects of television on cultural and political life, Huxley's vision was the more pertinent. But the hypertrophy of surveillance enabled by hyperconnectivity has revived interest in Orwell's. In the US, the Snowden revelations indicated that contemporary forms of government surveillance exceeded in their reach and technological sophistication anything Orwell could have imagined.[28] And the Pentagon's "Total Information Awareness" program certainly had an Orwellian ring to it. Yet while the ever-denser web of state and commercial surveillance in the US is deeply concerning, it is in China's frontier Xinjiang region that Orwell's vision seems more powerfully prescient.

The brutally tightening grip of police control over the Uyghur and other non-Han Muslim population of the region in recent years – framed after some attacks by Uyghurs on Han civilians as part of a "People's War on Terror" – pivots on an extraordinarily invasive system of surveillance, involving cutting-edge digital technology as well as intrusive in-person monitoring. Attention has focused, for good reason, on the mass internment of hundreds of thousands and possibly a million or more in brutal conditions in a network of re-education camps.[29] But the entire Muslim population of Xinjiang, numbering some 14 million, is subject to hyper-intensive surveillance, and the region has become a laboratory for the development and deployment of surveillance technologies, protocols, and practices that Chinese tech companies, working in close public–private partnerships with the state, are eagerly seeking to export to the rest of the world.[30] These include AI-trained facial recognition systems (and the comprehensive, compulsory databases of photos and biometric information that give such systems their power); iris scanning and other biometric recognition systems that promise to be still more accurate than face recognition; "smart gates" that control access to public spaces by matching faces against scanned ID cards and police blacklists; closely spaced checkpoints that monitor and control movement in urban space and enforce "digital enclosures"; ubiquitous "smart" surveillance cameras; compulsory tracking software that residents are obliged to install on their phones; flagging of suspicious contacts, travel patterns, and consumption expenditures; emotion and affect recognition systems to monitor detainees in camps; and systems for storing, retrieving, and searching the huge volumes of surveillance data.

While Xinjiang represents the leading edge of intensive surveillance, China as a whole is rapidly developing a sophisticated system of digital surveillance. The much-discussed "social credit system" is a big part of this, as are the facial recognition systems and surveillance cameras that have been intensively deployed in Xinjiang. The drastic heightening of digital surveillance in China's attempt to pursue a zero-Covid policy, moreover, is very likely to survive the pandemic. This is a dynamic familiar from the history of surveillance creep in the West as well, where innovations introduced during emergencies tend to persist afterwards.[31]

The key innovation has been the quasi-compulsory, smartphone-based "health code" app. (The app is not formally compulsory, but everyday life is very difficult without it.) Drawing on user-input data and a non-transparent range of other surveillance data, an opaque algorithm determines the level of Covid-19 risk that each individual has been exposed to and assigns one of three corresponding QR codes: green (unrestricted), yellow (one-week quarantine), or red (two-week quarantine). People must scan or display their health code in order to access public places like restaurants or public transport. The system was put in place quickly, with little discussion or scrutiny, and no evidence of its public health efficacy. As legal scholar Wanshu Cong has argued, its usefulness to the state "lies not in its accuracy and reliability but simply in its being used at a societal scale": this in itself creates a powerful new tool of social control and discipline with potential applicability far beyond the pandemic.[32]

It is surely wrong to draw too sharp a line between surveillance practices in China and those of liberal democratic countries. Facial recognition technology, for example, is in great demand by law enforcement agencies in the US and other countries; surveillance cameras have long been a fixture in British public life and elsewhere; key aspects of the social credit system are commonplace in the West; and the pandemic sharply intensified surveillance practices in many Western countries.[33] That said, the Chinese government obviously has a much freer hand in designing and implementing systems of surveillance. There has been pushback, for example, against the use of facial recognition systems in the US, responding to concerns about racial bias, while significant data protection requirements have slowed down the rollout of such systems in the EU. Taken on its own, the grim vision of *1984*, formed under the impress of totalitarian regimes, has limited purchase on the complex and contested landscape of digital surveillance in liberal democracies – not because surveillance is not a crucial issue, but because it is configured in very different ways than those envisioned by Orwell.[34]

In certain respects, Huxley's dystopian vision has greater purchase on hyperconnectivity in contemporary liberal settings. *Brave New World* turns not on repression or surveillance – its limitations notwithstanding, *1984* was far more prescient about surveillance – but on a ceaseless flow of immediate gratifications, engrossing experiences, and compelling distractions. These are qualities provided in abundance by hyperconnectivity,

and promised in still greater abundance for the metaverse. (In an anticipation of the metaverse, the distractions of *Brave New World* include
the "feelies," a cinematic virtual reality experience, modeled on "talkies,"
which had become a sensation just before the book was published, but
enriched with tactile and olfactory dimensions to enhance the sense of
presence.)

Huxley's is a world of sexual abundance, general happiness, and
harmless mood-enhancing drugs. It is also a (benign) dictatorship, a
rigorously caste-stratified social order, and a thoroughly engineered and
hyper-conformist society that allows no individuality of thought or
feeling. The connection to the present lies not so much in these details,
resonant though some of them are, but in the regime's ways of catering
to and exploiting what Huxley would later call humankind's "almost
infinite appetite for distractions."[35] The novel's characters are granted no
respite from distraction, "no leisure from pleasure, not a moment to sit
down and think," as the disabused Mustapha Mond, the governor of one
of the World State's ten regions, observes. There is no space for solitude:
as Mond later remarks, "people never are alone now. ... We make them
hate solitude; and we arrange their lives so that it's almost impossible for
them ever to have it."[36] Reflecting on the novel in 1958, a quarter century
after its publication, Huxley emphasized that the "non-stop distractions"
divert its characters from "paying too much attention to the realities of
the social and political situation."[37] Like many critics of mass culture,
Huxley fretted that the similarly non-stop distractions afforded by the
mid-century mass media – and afforded in vastly greater measure by
networked digital media today – could undermine democratic liberties
by sapping the vigilance and habits of mind needed to preserve them.[38]
And he worried that a "really efficient totalitarian state" of the sort
gestured toward in his novel would not need to rely on coercion because
it could make its inhabitants "love their servitude" through a combination of conditioning, drugs, and distraction.[39]

1984 and *Brave New World* are both dystopias of the state.
Notwithstanding their perspicacity on surveillance and distraction, the
centrality of the state in both works limits their relevance as touchstones
for understanding where we are and where we might be going. The
tradition of cyberpunk science fiction since the 1980s is more pertinent
in this respect: the state is in retreat in cyberpunk novels and films, while

giant corporations exercise ruthless and unbridled power. And the genre's trademark mix of "high tech and low life" has kept the cyberpunk imagination attuned to the digital cutting edge. But I want to counterpose to the state-centered dystopian visions of *1984* and *Brave New World* the economically driven dystopian vision that informs a recent work of nonfiction: Shoshana Zuboff's 2019 *The Age of Surveillance Capitalism*. (This counterposition is perhaps not as far-fetched as it might at first seem: Orwell and Huxley, after all, were critics and social theorists as well as fiction writers, and there are elements in Zuboff's book that could be characterized as "social science fiction.")[40]

At the heart of surveillance capitalism, on Zuboff's account, is the extraction of digital behavioral data from every phase and form of human experience, online and (increasingly) off. With the help of machine learning, these data generate a continuous stream of marketable and actionable nano-predictions about our future behavior. These predictions constitute a deeply asymmetrical form of knowledge: surveillance capitalists "have the means to know everything about us, but we can know little about them."[41] We are transparent; they are opaque. The asymmetries of knowledge translate into asymmetries of power, for "automated machine processes not only *know* our behavior but also *shape* our behavior at scale" through control over the "means of behavioral modification."[42] Such "instrumentarian power" is a "creature of the market," not of the state.[43] And while instrumentarian power is "totalizing," taking all of human life as the province of its data extraction and the field of its application, it is in key respects antithetical to totalitarian power. Unlike totalitarianism – and unlike the "soft" dictatorship envisioned by Huxley – instrumentarian power is indifferent to ideology and to all of our "meanings and motives"; it works not through the "engineering of souls" but through the "engineering of behavior."[44] Instrumentarian power "does not care what we think, feel, or do" so long as the "ubiquitous sensate, networked, computational infrastructure" (which Zuboff, with a nod to Orwell, calls "Big Other") can "observe, render, datafy, and instrumentalize" our conduct.[45]

If one abstracts from the particulars of their dystopian visions, Orwell, Huxley, and Zuboff suggest in different ways how hyperconnectivity enhances *technologies of control, technologies of distraction*, and *technologies of manipulation*. It enhances technologies of control by providing an infrastructure for unilateral and authoritarian modes of governance, public and private. Not all modes of digital governance, to be sure, are unilateral or authoritarian. My point is not that there is an intrinsic affinity between the digital and the authoritarian (any more than there is, as many long claimed, between the digital and the democratic). It is rather that the affordances of hyperconnectivity offer unprecedentedly powerful and supple resources for projects of control.[46] This was anticipated three decades ago by Gilles Deleuze's brief but prescient comments on the "societies of control" that he saw as succeeding the "disciplinary societies" analyzed by Foucault. Governance in societies of control would be effected not through enclosure, as in disciplinary societies, but through "modulation":

> what is important is no longer either a signature or a number, but a code ... a *password*. ... The conception of a control mechanism, giving the position of any element within an open environment at any given instant ..., is not necessarily one of science fiction. Felix Guattari has imagined a city where one would be able to leave one's apartment, one's street, one's neighborhood, thanks to one's ... electronic card that raises a given barrier; but the card could just as easily be rejected on a given day or between certain hours; what counts is not the barrier but the computer that tracks each person's position – licit or illicit – and effects a universal modulation.[47]

This hypothetical example of data-mediated modulation rather precisely anticipated contemporary forms of movement control through QR codes. But we need not accept Deleuze's opposition of control and discipline. On a broader understanding of discipline, not restricted to physically enclosed spaces like the prison, the factory, or the school, digitally enabled modes of "modulatory" control do not supersede discipline; they extend and deepen discipline by making it more flexible and pervasive. Digital enclosures serve as spaces of discipline just as physical enclosures did. And platformization in every domain of life – as well as the making of the metaverse – can be seen as a movement toward digital enclosure: a movement to enclose more and more of social life within the surveillant and modulatory embrace of the platform.[48]

Hyperconnectivity enhances technologies of distraction by providing an infrastructure for capturing, diverting, and retaining our attention.

In an environment of scarce attention (in relation to superabundant content) and sophisticated techniques for mobilizing, measuring, and monetizing it, a continuous, high-stakes struggle for attention plays out in every sphere of life. This struggle pits those who seek to capture our attention against one another; but it also pits them in the aggregate against our efforts to concentrate, to stay on task, to deploy our attention in a manner that enables us to pursue our own ends. The major contestants in the former struggle meet on more or less equal terms. But the latter struggle is grossly unequal: on one side a "brilliant and well-funded army [of] designers and engineers," on the other a weakly defended target, biologically programmed to respond to salient stimuli in our visual and auditory fields.[49] Small wonder then that we are such poor custodians of our own attention and that we find ourselves chronically "distracted from distraction by distraction," to borrow T. S. Eliot's memorable formulation.[50] Distraction is a human universal propensity; but it is undeniably exacerbated by hyperconnectivity. The contemporary ecology of communication makes it much easier to be distracted from our immediate tasks, from larger projects and purposes, and, as Huxley suggested, from the social and political world.

Hyperconnectivity enhances technologies of manipulation, finally, by providing an infrastructure for activating, prompting, nudging, tuning, herding, and channeling conduct: an infrastructure for behavior modification at scale. Guided by continuous automated experimentation and neo-behaviorist "conditioning," which hyperconnectivity makes possible, scalable, and inexpensive, behavioral engineering moves out of the laboratory and into the world.[51] Unlike digital technologies of control that are focused on particular individuals (such as QR codes at access points that bar some while letting others pass), digital technologies of manipulation do not directly or coercively determine what any single *individual* can do; instead, by adjusting the "choice architecture," digital environment, or digital content to which people are exposed, they shape *aggregate* patterns of behavior by increasing the probability that individuals will act in some commercially, politically, or otherwise desired way (clicking on an advertisement or headline, making a purchase or a charitable contribution, spending more time on a site, voting for a candidate, and so on). The manipulation may be "personalized," i.e., differentiated according to what is known about different individuals, but it is still oriented to aggregate outcomes.

Digitally enhanced technologies of control, distraction, and manipulation – and the contemporary version of the Huxleyian as much as the Orwellian or Zuboffian vision – are all premised on ubiquitous surveillance. They are all premised, that is, on the exercise of power through the accumulation of knowledge. Surveillant control depends on knowing who we are and how we measure up: who matches what criteria, who has what score or rating, and who falls into what category. This knowledge allows digital gates and checkpoints to directly govern who gets access to what opportunities, goods, or services. Surveillant distraction depends on knowing in fine-grained detail what we like, how we interact with digital content, even what kind of mood we are in. This knowledge allows platforms and content purveyors to capture our attention and keep us engaged. Surveillant manipulation depends on knowing our tastes, preferences, and personality traits as well as how we respond to experimentally varied stimuli. This knowledge allows behavioral engineers to nudge us more effectively. The knowledge that undergirds technologies of control, distraction, and manipulation, as Zuboff underscores, is "*about* us, but ... not *for* us" and not accessible *to* us. This foundational "epistemic inequality" entails that we are being used as "means to others' ends":[52] as means, above all, to the commercial ends of the great tech companies that are designing our digital future – and designing us to desire that future.[53]

* * *

Digital hyperconnectivity cannot of course be reduced to the technologies of control, distraction, and manipulation that have flourished under its auspices. As a many-sided social phenomenon, it is too large, too unruly, and too internally contradictory to be neatly subsumable under a selective and one-sided conceptual rubric like this one. Even among critical and pessimistic accounts, there are numerous alternative lenses through which hyperconnectivity can be viewed, bringing into focus processes such as automation, platformization, and infrastructuralization.[54] And techno-optimistic accounts, such as the blockchain utopianism I discussed in chapter 4, have continued to flourish even as the public has soured on Big Tech.[55]

Although my own stance is certainly critical and pessimistic, I have tried to remain sensitive throughout to the ambivalence of hyperconnectivity. As I have observed, hyperconnectivity affords news ways of exploring the self and emancipating the self – for better or worse – from forms of social control rooted in family and local community. It has opened up new modes of reflexively knowing, regulating, and governing the self, even as it also creates new ways of being known, regulated, and governed from the outside. It provides new possibilities for sustaining friendships, families, and love relationships at a distance, and it has enriched communicative repertoires and engendered new modalities of communication and new forms of "connected presence." It has brought the infinite wealth of human cultural creativity within the immediate reach of anyone with an internet connection and opened up new avenues for popular participation in the production, circulation, and evaluation of cultural goods. It has created new opportunities for micro-entrepreneurship and flexible forms of remote work. And it has undermined the power of institutional gatekeepers and opened up public conversations to new voices. Hyperconnectivity can therefore feel empowering – and it *is* in fact empowering – in all these ways and more.

Yet while hyperconnectivity has empowered individuals in certain respects, it has also – more profoundly and pervasively – empowered organizations: specifically, the organizations that are in a position to extract and analyze data and that therefore possess the means of control, distraction, and manipulation. And while digital connectivity initially contributed to the decentralization and dispersion of power, the regime of *hyper*connectivity that has been consolidated in the last decade has entailed an immense recentralization and reconcentration of power.

The accelerating digitalization of life during the pandemic has confronted us with large and difficult questions about the shape – and the shaping – of our digital future. There is nothing about digital technology or connective networks per se that will determine that shape. This goes against the grain of the technological "inevitabilism" that is prevalent in the tech industry: the idea that technological change has its own dynamic that escapes human choice.[56] But digital hyperconnectivity is not a technological fact alone. It is also, inescapably, a psychological, social, cultural, economic, political, and legal fact: a total social fact, to take up once again Marcel Mauss's term. It is an immensely complex sociotechnical phenomenon, comprising psychological dispositions and habits, social practices, cultural understandings, economic organization, political contestation, governance structures, and legal and regulatory frameworks as well as hardware, software, protocols, and the vast material infrastructure of "cloud" computing and connectivity.

This complexity means that digital hyperconnectivity is not fated to be organized in any particular way. As Paul Starr has shown in his historical account of the emergence of the modern media, media systems are shaped by "constitutive choices" that set developments on particular paths.[57] The ecosystem of digital communication could have been configured differently at key junctures in the past, and it could be configured differently in the future. Advertising – and the immense investments in surveillance and data extraction that hold out the promise of more effective advertising in the future – did not have to become the default business model of the internet.[58] Strict privacy protections could have barred the long-term storage of behavioral data (and thereby limited the reach of behavioral micro-targeting).[59] The distinctively broad American provisions of the 1990s that shield digital "intermediaries" (by virtue of not being considered "publishers") from liability for the speech of their users – and that have allowed the social media platforms that emerged in the 2000s to present themselves as intermediaries and enjoy the benefits of this immunity – might have been drawn more narrowly.[60]

At this writing, Facebook, Google, Amazon, and Apple are all the focus of high-profile public scrutiny and high-stakes legal, political, and regulatory struggles in the US, featuring multiple antitrust lawsuits, far-reaching legislative proposals, and regulatory agencies headed by longstanding critics of Big Tech. They are also the targets of major new legislative initiatives in Europe, which already has a much stricter regulatory regime. How these struggles will play out cannot be predicted. As critics have noted, however, antitrust and regulation are no panaceas. Breaking up the tech giants (as a Federal Trade Commission lawsuit seeks to do with Facebook by undoing its acquisition of Instagram and WhatsApp) would not alter the underlying economic logic, while regulation is slow, inefficient, and subject to capture by the regulated.

Outside of the limelight, many other initiatives have been brewing in recent years. Nobel prize-winning economist Paul Romer, for example, has proposed a graduated tax on targeted digital ads, the rate increasing with the size of the company, as a way of nudging companies toward subscription-based business models.[61] And tech entrepreneur turned public policy professor Ethan Zuckerman has been promoting the idea that revenues from such a tax or from other sources could be used to stimulate the development of different forms of "public service digital media" that could eventually coalesce into a "digital public infrastructure." Key projects might include "auditable and transparent search and discovery tools"; advertising networks that would not rely on surveillance; and an ecosystem of alternative, smaller-scale social media networks that could moderate content in accordance with the purposes and norms of particular communities – instead of herding billions of people across the world into a single network operating by a single set of rules.[62]

In a deeply fractured political environment, in which polarization is aggravated by the existing private digital infrastructure, will it be possible to construct a public digital infrastructure that could alleviate the crisis of public knowledge and support rather than undermine a democratic public sphere? Can emerging alternative platforms develop into something more than interesting but marginal experiments? Will newer generations of users reclaim zones of privacy or simply take ubiquitous surveillance for granted? Can the private platforms that organize and mediate almost every sphere of life be made more accountable to public values? I do not pretend to have the answers to these and similar questions. But they are questions we can ill afford to neglect.

Notes

Preface

1 Berlin 1953: 1.
2 Morozov 2013a. On the ways in which the pandemic strengthened technological "solutionist" ways of thinking, see Morozov 2020.
3 I borrow the notion of a "total social fact" – taken up in the Introduction – from Marcel Mauss 2002 [1925].
4 De Swaan 1988: xviii.
5 In recent years, Russia has also been developing the legal framework and technical infrastructure for greatly enhanced state control over the internet (Epifanova 2020); that control was of course radically intensified after the invasion of Ukraine. Other countries, too, have recently begun to assert their "digital sovereignty"; see McCabe and Satariano 2022.

Introduction

1 Converting data exhaust into gold: Kenneth Cukier, quoted in Zuboff 2019: 68. On digital traces generally, see especially Harcourt 2015.
2 On the material infrastructure underlying digital hyperconnectivity, see Bratton 2015. On the materiality of cloud computing specifically, see Monserrate 2022. For an accessible overview of the environmental costs of hyperconnectivity, see Crawford 2021, chapter 1.
3 Mauss 2002 [1925]: 100–1.
4 Other institutions that have been profoundly transformed by digital hyperconnectivity include childhood (Twenge 2017; Danby et al. 2018), education (Williamson 2021), religion (Campbell and Tsuria 2021), sexuality (Nash and Gorman-Murray 2019), and war (Ford and Hoskins 2022); the list could be extended indefinitely.
5 Share of the population with a smartphone: https://www.comscore.com/Insights/Blog/US-Smartphone-Penetration-Surpassed-80-Percent-in-2016. Facebook users: https://www.nickburcher.com/2012/01/facebook-usage-statistics-by-country.html.
6 For a critique of static notions of an overarching "digital era," with reference to the challenges of studying digital politics that arise from successive and ongoing transformations in the political affordances of digital connectivity, see Karpf 2020. For a succinct account of the transformation of the internet from a highly decentralized "integrated system of open systems" to a "platform for the reconcentration of power," see Benkler 2016.
7 On the development of "touchless technology," see Greely 2020.
8 "Always-on, always-on-them" devices: Turkle 2008. On continuous background attention to devices, see Burchell 2015.
9 On the ever-denser connectivity of an ever-wider range of ever-smaller networked things, with special reference to the issue of addressability, see Bratton 2015, especially pp. 191ff. On the industrial internet of things in the context of platform capitalism, see Srnicek 2017: 65. RFID tags – the acronym stands for radio-frequency identification – are tiny devices that use electromagnetic fields to identify and track material objects. On their significance as an invisible "infrastructure of identification," see Frith 2019.

10 "The most profound technologies," wrote Weiser (1991: 94), "are those that disappear. They weave themselves into the fabric of everyday life until they are indistinguishable from it." On the ways in which Weiser's vision of ubiquitous computing has subsequently been recycled and repurposed, see Hong 2021.

11 On the "mobile revolution," see Rainie and Wellman 2012, chapter 4.

12 On the concept of remediation, see Bolter and Grusin 1999.

13 I return to the theme of infrastructure in chapter 4; see pp. 106ff.

14 The notion of an "ecology of communication" was first developed by Altheide 1994. For an accessible introduction to the "media ecology" approach, see Strate 2008.

15 The legal frameworks governing digital hyperconnectivity are largely beyond the scope of my analysis. For a sustained and influential analysis, see Cohen 2019.

16 On the notion of affordances, in the context of an attempt to stake out a position in the sociological study of technology between radical constructivism and technological determinism, see Hutchby 2001.

17 Paul Starr's emphasis on the "constitutive choices" that channel the long-term development of media systems in particular directions (Starr 2004) applies equally to the development of digital hyperconnectivity. On the key "design choices" that have shaped and reshaped the internet, see Benkler 2016; for a critique of "internet-centrism," the tendency to endow the internet with a kind of ahistorical essence, see Morozov 2013a: 15–62.

18 Abbott (2014: 1) calls for a reorientation of social theory around the "central problematic of … dealing with excess."

19 On "post-scarcity society" and its characteristic forms of politics, see Giddens 1995; on post-materialist politics, see Inglehart 1977.

20 On communicative abundance, see Keane 1999; on mediated experience, Giddens 1991: 23ff and Thompson 1995: 228ff; on the saturated self, Gergen 1991.

21 On the counterfactual quality of experience in late modernity, see Giddens 1991: 29.

22 On the "digital plenitude," see Bolter 2019. A near-infinity of material goods is also just a few clicks away: an estimated 12 million different items are sold by Amazon itself, and hundreds of millions of other items are offered on the Amazon platform by other sellers.

23 On the paradox of choice, see Schwartz 2004.

24 Sacasas 2013.

25 On musical abundance and the ways in which streaming platforms have sought to re-institute forms of scarcity, see Drott 2018: 330ff.

26 The term "doomscrolling" was coined in 2018 and popularized during the pandemic; for an initial scholarly treatment, see Sharma et al. 2022.

27 Simon 1971: 40.

28 For a sophisticated account of various forms of "infoglut," see Andrejevic 2013. On digital abundance and the crisis of public knowledge, see Brubaker 2017a. On the weaponization of digital abundance as a form of censorship, see Tufekci 2017: 227ff.

29 Hong 2020: 1.

30 Zuboff 2020. On the exponential growth of data in the context of a broad philosophical account of the information revolution, see Floridi 2014: 13ff.

31 An exchange with Loïc Wacquant helped clarify my thinking about miniaturization.

32 On mobile news platforms and the shifting of news consumption toward brief interstitial moments, see Carlson 2020: 239. On likewise interstitial casual mobile game play, see Hjorth and Richardson 2011.

33 On the glance as the characteristic mode of seeing in the attention economy, with special reference to Instagram, see Zulli 2018.

34 On platforms' capacity to shrink the size of transactions, see Lobel 2016: 108–9.

35 On the modularity and granularity of digitally networked peer production, see Benkler 2006: 100–1.

36 On digital advertising infrastructure, see MacKenzie 2022.

37 On new forms of "connective action," see Bennett and Segerberg 2013; on the ambivalent affordances of hyperconnectivity for social movements, see Tufekci 2017.

38 On political nano-influencers, see Joseff et al. 2020.

39 The notion of "modulation" was proposed by Deleuze in his influential short piece on "societies of control" (1992); I take this up in my discussion of discipline below. On "governance by micronudge," see Schüll 2016.

40 On the cumulative effect of trillions of micro-choices, see Frischmann and Selinger 2018: 265–6.

41 As a marketing pitch, convenience goes back to the 1960s, when the term first acquired its associations with time: saving time, but also flexibly shifting and coordinating time. On convenience in relation to complexities of temporal ordering in contemporary society, see Shove 2012: 298ff.

42 The Google experiment is reported by Hindman 2018: 1–2. There was no evidence that users simply felt overwhelmed by the larger numbers of results.

43 On the turn toward on-demand delivery, see Austin 2021b; Nguyen 2022.

44 Kalanick is quoted in Kosoff 2015.

45 One journalist tried out Google's "smart reply" feature by limiting himself entirely to replies proposed by Google – choosing one of three proposed replies in response to every incoming message – for a week, and none of his correspondents noted anything unusual; see O'Reilly 2019.

46 Alex Pentland, quoted in Zuboff 2019: 429.

47 For general critiques of ideals of frictionless convenience, see Sacasas 2011; Morozov 2013a, 2013b; Wu 2018b.

48 On frictionlessness and cybersecurity vulnerabilities, see Roose 2018; on the displacement of friction, see Pendergrast 2019.

49 For a survey of recent literature on quantification, see Mennicken and Espeland 2019. Until recently, the social theory literature on quantification has been largely separate from that on digital connectivity. Jerry Muller's 2018 book on the "tyranny of metrics," for example, barely mentions digital connectivity or big data. And the literature on big data and algorithmic governance did not engage the general social theory literature on quantification. Recent contributions, however, have begun to bring these literatures together: see notably Fourcade and Healy 2017; Mau 2019; Mennicken and Salais 2022.

50 On the "avalanche of printed numbers," see Hacking 1982.

51 On datafication, see van Dijck et al. 2018: 33ff. On the "data imperative," see Fourcade and Healy 2017, especially pp. 13–16. On "dataism," see van Dijck 2014.

52 On Twitter's gamification of conversation, see C. T. Nguyen 2021; the quotation is from p. 411.

53 On the potential development of a calculable summary measure of "Übercapital," drawing on the full range of digital data traces about an individual, see Fourcade and Healy 2017: 18; on the notion of digital social capital as a kind of "metacapital," operative across fields, see Schwarz 2021: 98ff. On Chinese cities' experimentation with generalized, cross-domain "social credit scores," which go well beyond considerations of economic creditworthiness, see Liu 2019: 25–7.

54 On trending algorithms, see Gillespie 2016.

55 On "computational politics," see Tufekci 2014a.

56 On algorithmic price discrimination, see Bar-Gill 2019. For a sociological perspective on the paradoxes involved in algorithmic predictions, see Rona-Tas 2020.

57 On "societies of control," see Deleuze 1992.

58 On digital enclosure, see Andrejevic 2007: 1ff, 105ff.

59 On control as extending rather than replacing discipline, see Williams 2015: 212; Weinberg 2018: 68–9.

60 On the disciplinary power of Facebook and the shaping of a participatory subjectivity, see Bucher 2018: 88–9.

61 On the early modern "disciplinary revolution" and its contribution to the development of a new "infrastructure of governance," see Gorski 2003.

62 Foucault 1995: 202–3.

63 On digital modulation and surveillance as generating predictable citizen-consumers, see Cohen 2013: 1917.

64 On the novel and distinctive properties of digitally mediated power, see Schwarz 2021, chapter 5.

Chapter 1: Selves

1 Foundational accounts of the self as a social phenomenon include Cooley 1902; Mead 1934; Goffman 1956, 1959.

2 Giddens 1991: 14, 75, 81; see also Thompson 1995, chapter 7; Beck and Beck-Gernsheim 2002.

3 Foucault 1988: 18.

4 On the "turn to practice" in social theory, see Schatzki et al. 2001.

5 Turkle 1995; the quotations are from pp. 12 and 10.

6 On online experimentation with identity as a form of "serious play," see Turkle 2011: 212ff.

7 Turkle 1996: 157.

8 Robinson 2007: 94, 101–3; Tufekci 2013a: 36.

9 Zhao 2005: 392–5.

10 The quotation is from Gergen 1991: 69, italics omitted. On the "saturated self," see ibid. On "mediated experience," see Giddens 1991: 23–7 and Thompson 1995: 211f, 225ff.

11 On "possible selves," see Markus and Nurius 1986; the quotations are from p. 954.

12 Gergen 1991: 68–73; the quotation is from p. 73.

13 The essay is reprinted in Rheingold 2008.

14 Dickel 1995.

15 Nakamura's 1995 essay is reprinted in Nakamura 2002; the quotations are from pp. 35 and 49.

16 Marwick (2005: 37–47) provides a useful overview of "critical cyberculture studies" and its challenge to the notion of cyberspace as intrinsically liberatory.

17 Bell 2001: 124–5.

18 Nakamura 2002: xi, 31.

19 Hampton and Wellman 2018: 647.

20 Fader 2017b; the quotations are from pp. 193–4.

21 On the smartphone as an instrument for circumventing communal surveillance in conservative religious communities, see Deutsch 2009: 8.

22 On counter-publics in the ultra-orthodox case, see Fader 2017a.

23 On the significance of overcoming pluralistic ignorance for social movements and politics, see Tufekci 2017: 25–6.

24 On the online milieux out of which the alt-right emerged, see Nagle 2017.

25 "Anonymous sociality, critique, and exploration": Fader 2017b: 187. On the "infosphere," see Floridi 2014.

26 Some formulations of these arguments have a postmodern inflection (Gergen 1991; Turkle 1995). But there is no hard and fast line between characterizations of postmodernity and characterizations of contemporary modernity. Many aspects of the alleged postmodern

condition are treated by theorists like Giddens (1991) or Beck et al. (1994) as aspects of "late," "high," or "reflexive" modernity.

27 For a clear account of such disembedding and re-embedding, developing the notion of "networked individualism," see Rainie and Wellman 2012. The authors criticize as sociologically unfounded laments about the alleged contribution of digital connectivity to the "destruction of community" (pp. 117–31). But Calhoun's (1998) cautionary reflections about the notion of "community without propinquity" remain pertinent.

28 Mead 1934.

29 On pressures on adolescent girls and young women towards sexualizing self-objectification online, see Mascheroni et al. 2015; Bell et al. 2018.

30 My concern here is not with the initial formation of self in early childhood – although digital technologies of objectification figure increasingly in that process as well – but rather with the ongoing process of the social shaping and reshaping of selves. On digital media infrastructures as central to childhood socialization, see Couldry and Hepp 2017: 149ff.

31 Some platforms, to be sure, do not objectify users' interactions. Photos sent by Snapchat, for example, disappear after ten seconds (though users can alter this default setting). But objectification is the prevailing option, thanks to the cheap and declining cost of preserving digital traces and the various actual or ostensible benefits of doing so. And even when communication is designed to be evanescent to users, as with Snapchat, the business model of the platform depends on turning digital traces into monetizable data-objects.

32 See Harcourt 2015: 1ff.

33 On the consequences of this abundant objectification for the dynamics and micro-politics of interaction, see Schwarz 2021, chapter 2. I take up this theme in the next chapter; see pp. 61ff.

34 On the diary, see Heehs 2013; on the letter, Foucault 1983; on self-portraiture, Hall 2014. For comparative reflections on self-formation through letters around 1800 and through digitally mediated written communication today, see Erk 2019. On new resources that become available for narrating and representing the self in changing media environments, see Couldry and Hepp 2017: 157ff.

35 On the digital gaze, see Floridi 2014: 73–4.

36 On new modes of alertness and attentiveness to experiences that might be converted into enduring, shareable digital objects, see Schwarz 2012. Similarly, on the "Facebook eye," which leads us to experience things, even when we are not connected, with a view to their postability and likely interest to an audience, see Jurgenson 2012; Jurgenson 2019: 12, 27–8, 36–8.

37 Wolf 2009, 2010.

38 On "everyday self-trackers," see Didžiokaitė et al. 2018. On enthusiastic participants in the quantified self community, see Nafus and Sherman 2014; Sharon 2017; Schüll 2019. These ethnographic studies offer nuanced accounts of participants' tentative, exploratory, and often self-critical stance toward self-tracking and the data that it yields. For a theoretically sophisticated account of self-quantification practices in the context of the cultural and economic uncertainties of late modernity, see Vormbusch 2022.

39 Horning 2012a. On the redefinition of self-knowledge in an environment of superabundant, individualized data, see Hong 2020: 76ff. For an early critique of the limits of self-knowledge through numbers, see Morozov 2013a, chapter 7.

40 The wide range of contemporary self-tracking devices and practices is described in Lupton 2016: 16–30; see also Mau 2019, chapter 6.

41 Rettberg 2014, chapter 1; Cardell 2018.

42 Franklin 1904: 188–95.

43 Crawford et al. 2015.

44 On the converging technological and social developments that have enabled self-tracking to flourish, see Wolf 2010. On sharing, social support, and gamification, see Lupton 2016: 23.

45 Hull and Pasquale (2018: 191) suggest that corporate wellness programs, including those that involve self-tracking technologies, do not reduce employers' costs but rather discipline and condition workers.

46 On "pushed" and "imposed" self-tracking, see Lupton 2016: 121–5. On "surveillance creep" in connection with health tracking, see Frischmann and Selinger 2018: 20–8. For a nuanced discussion of the issue of autonomy, see Sharon 2017.

47 Quantification is of course a much more general tendency that goes well beyond social media platforms; see for example Muller 2018; Mau 2019; Mennicken and Salais 2022.

48 This is true even in the domain of scholarship. For a critical analysis of Academia.edu and the quantified scholarly self, see Duffy and Pooley 2017.

49 Artist Benjmain Grosser created the "Facebook Demetricator" (https://bengrosser.com/ projects/facebook-demetricator/) in response to the pervasiveness of Facebook's metrics (Grosser 2014).

50 On the option to hide "like" counts on Facebook and Instagram, see Perez 2021.

51 On commensuration, see Espeland and Stevens 1998.

52 On the "like economy" and the role of the like button in reorganizing the fabric of the Web, see Gerlitz and Helmond 2013. On the contribution of the like button to platform interoperability and the creation of an integrated platform ecosystem, see van Dijck 2013a, chapters 3, 8.

53 On quantified and objectified social ties as a new form of generalized social capital, see Schwarz 2021, chapter 4.

54 MacKenzie 2006.

55 On quantification as gamification, with reference to Twitter, see C. T. Nguyen 2021.

56 On positional goods, see Hirsch 1978.

57 The term "data doubles" was introduced by Haggerty and Ericson (2000) in their account, drawing on Deleuze and Guattari, of "surveillant assemblages"; it has subsequently been widely adopted.

58 On the data trails from which digital representations of the self are constructed, see Gillespie 2014: 173–4; Harcourt 2015; Cheney-Lippold 2017; Zuboff 2019, especially chapter 9.

59 Kosinski et al. (2013: 5802) showed that Facebook likes could be used "to automatically and accurately predict a range of highly sensitive personal attributes including: sexual orientation, ethnicity, religious and political views, personality traits, intelligence, happiness, use of addictive substances, parental separation, age, and gender."

60 Wang and Kosinski 2018. For a recent review of how "machines can infer information about our psychological traits or mental states by observing samples of our behaviour gathered from our online activities," see Burr and Cristianini 2019.

61 On errors in the algorithmic construction of our identities, see Cheney-Lippold 2017: 5–8.

62 On self-editing in asynchronous communication, see Schwarz 2011; Turkle 2011; Bullingham and Vasconcelos 2013. On the absence of the full range of body-behavioral cues, see Zhao 2005. On the ambivalent affordances of anonymity, see Suler 2004. On context collapse, see Marwick and boyd 2011a.

63 On self-entrepreneurship and neoliberalism, see Foucault 2008: 226, translation modified; McGuigan 2014.

64 On the enterprising self in the context of the post-Fordist economy, see du Gay 1996: 180–4; Rose 1998, chapter 7; Pongratz and Voß 2003.

65 On the practice of constructing a digital self to be consumed by others, see Marwick and boyd 2011b: 140; Ibrahim 2018, chapter 3.

66 On the influencer or lifestyle blogger as entrepreneur of the self, see Hearn and Schoenhoff 2016; Duffy 2017; Khamis et al. 2017; McRae 2017.

67 The vast majority of aspiring influencers, of course, do not strike it rich. See Duffy 2017 for a study of the largely unpaid or underpaid "aspirational labor" of fashion and style bloggers. I return to the theme of aspirational labor in chapter 4 (see p. 121).

68 On transformations of celebrity under digital hyperconnectivity, see Marwick 2010, 2016; Driessens 2015.

69 On digital micro-celebrity, see Marwick 2010: 223–6; the quotation is from p. 287.

70 Although self-branding was popularized before the rise of social media, the Web was an important point of reference; see the key statement by Peters 1997. On self-branding in the context of the transformation of capitalism, see Hearn 2008. On self-branding in social media, see Marwick 2010. On self-branding as a form of affective labor, see Genz 2015. On the democratization and universalization of self-branding, see Khamis et al. 2017.

71 On the threat of invisibility, see Bucher 2012.

72 On the integration of expressive individualism into consumerist capitalism, see Frank 1997; McGuigan 2009; Genz 2015. On the longstanding tension in American culture between "utilitarian individualism," epitomized by Benjamin Franklin's maxims about getting ahead through thrift, diligence, discipline, and calculation, and "expressive individualism," epitomized by Walt Whitman's expansive sense of self, identification with nature and the universe, and embrace of broad experience, deep feeling, unconstrained sensuality, and self-expression, see Bellah et al. 1985: 32–5.

73 On the "authenticity work" of lifestyle bloggers and the chronic risk of being perceived as inauthentic, see McRae 2017. On the labor involved in "branding the authentic self" in the context of fashion blogging, see Duffy 2017, chapter 4. The term "authenticity work" goes back to sociologist of culture Richard Peterson's (1997) work on country music.

74 For the notion of "communicative abundance," see Keane 1999.

75 As McRae 2017 notes, fans have substantial genre knowledge that enables them to identify standard moves which they then deem inauthentic.

76 Horning 2012c; on authenticity in the context of social media, see also Horning 2012b.

77 On algorithmic personalization, see Weinberg 2018; Lury and Day 2019. As Weinberg notes (2018: 47), such personalization is itself homogenizing – a form of "mass production by other means."

78 On algorithmic "digital mirroring," see Schwarz 2021: 42f.

79 On music as a technology of self, see DeNora 2000; the quotations are from pp. 46, 53, and 56.

80 On ASMR and "distant intimacy," see Andersen 2015.

81 Barratt and Davis 2015.

82 Gallagher 2016.

83 Andersen 2015: 691.

84 The same holds for the burgeoning array of mindfulness, meditation, and wellness apps. On the paradoxes of digital detox apps that rely on the very logic of "data-driven optimization" from which they promise to free us, see Hong 2022.

85 In one widely used instrument for assessing "problematic internet use," "mood regulation" – captured by agreement with such statements as "I have used the Internet to make myself feel better when I was down" – is one of four conceptual components (the others being "preference for online social interaction," "deficient self-regulation," and "negative outcomes") (Caplan 2010).

86 "Identifiable, addressable and manipulable": Lynden 2018. On "sentiment analysis," see Andrejevic 2013, chapter 3; Zuboff 2019: 282ff.

87 For music, see Wang et al. 2015; for analogous work on video, see Wang and Ji 2015; Tripathi et al. 2019. On the automated detection of boredom from patterns of smartphone usage, enabling "boredom-triggered proactive recommender systems," see Pielot et al. 2015. On "affective computing," "emotion analytics," and "sentiment analysis" more generally, see Zuboff 2019: 282ff.

88 On the disruption of the sense of time, analogous to the trancelike psychosomatic state induced by compulsive machine gambling (Schüll 2012), see Seymour 2020: 64–5, 199–201. On disruption of sleep patterns, see Billari et al. 2018; Robb 2019. On the reorganization of time under hyperconnectivity more broadly, see my discussion in chapter 2, pp. 50–6.

89 On the role of dopamine in the "hub of reward, anticipation, and motivation," see Sapolsky 2017: 64–76 (the quotation is from p. 76). On dopamine and social media, see Weinschenk 2012; Haynes 2018.

90 On the controversy over internet addiction as a distinct diagnostic category, see Pies 2009. For a bracing polemic against social media that embraces the language of "addiction," see Seymour 2020.

91 Foucault (1988: 18) discussed technologies of the self and technologies of power in connection with two other types of "technologies," conceptualizing each as a "matrix of practical reason": technologies of production and technologies of sign systems. Digital hyperconnectivity involves all four: for a preliminary canvassing of their interrelations, see Bakardjieva and Gaden 2012.

92 Foucault 1988: 19; Foucault 1987: 113, 117.

93 While Turkle (1995) does not use the Foucauldian language of "technologies of self," her pioneering study shows how people can use anonymous online role-playing games as a way of working on the self. On blogging as a technology of self, see Bakardjieva and Gaden 2012; on academic blogging during the writing of a dissertation, see Mewburn and Thomson 2018. For Foucauldian perspectives on life-logging and self-tracking, see Buongiorno 2016 and Schüll 2019; for a Foucauldian perspective on self-writing on Facebook as a successor to earlier forms of self-writing, see Sauter 2014. On digital content curation as a modern analog of the ancient Greek hupomnemata, characterized by Foucault as a "material record of things read, heard, or thought," see Weisgerber and Butler 2016.

94 Miller and Rose 2008: 212.

95 Rose 1999b: 87.

96 Miller and Rose 2008: 82.

97 On the shaping and governing of choice on the Web, see Graham 2016.

98 On the notion of "empty choice," see Kingori 2015; on technology and choice-making more generally, framed as a critique of "technological liberalism," see Dotson 2012.

99 As Mittelstadt et al. (2016: 9) note, personalization algorithms might be claimed to enhance decision-making autonomy, in a context of information overload, by filtering out irrelevant information. But since it is the algorithm that decides what information is irrelevant, such algorithmic filtering may in fact abridge decision-making autonomy and nudge individuals toward "institutionally preferred action."

100 Sunstein and Thaler 2003: 1159.

101 Schüll 2016: 328. The tension comes into sharp relief when one considers similarities of structure, if not of scope, between Sunstein- and Thaler-style nudging in liberal democratic settings and the much more comprehensive system of authoritarian digital nudging embodied in China's emerging "social credit" system, which likewise seeks to "responsibilize" individuals so as to create more "social trust" and likewise governs individuals "at a distance," through the choices they make. On the social credit system, see Creemers 2018; Liu 2019; Knight 2021.

102 Quito 2015.

103 On "predictive shopping" generally, see Sunstein 2015, chapter 7. On the outsourcing of taste to algorithms through retail subscription boxes, see Hu 2019. On the crucial role of algorithms that learn from experience and improve over time, making better predictions about which items the consumer is likely to keep, see Sinha et al. 2016.

104 On "societies of control," see the prescient though sketchy remarks of Deleuze (1992). I return to this notion – and to the theme of control more generally – in the Conclusion; see pp. 165–8.

105 On "governing the soul," see Rose 1999a; on techno-social engineering, see Frischmann and Selinger 2018.

106 On new forms of behaviorist conditioning, see Zuboff 2019, chapter 10.

107 On the history of concerns about the use of techniques of persuasion in the advertising industry, see Nelson 2008.

108 The case for this view is made most forcefully by Zuboff 2019.

109 For an analysis of "data colonialism," suggesting, at p. xi, that colonialism is not just a metaphor, see Couldry and Mejias 2019.

110 Zuboff 2019; Couldry and Mejias 2019.

111 Zuboff 2019.

Chapter 2: Interactions

1 On the tethered self and autonomy, see Turkle 2011: 172–9. On the paradox of being more connected when apart, yet less connected when together, see Turkle 2015: 160.

2 Chambers 2013: 124.

3 For rich, historically informed treatments of the reorganization of space and time in connection with media and information technology, see Thompson 1995: 31–7; Castells 2010 [1996]: 407–99; Couldry and Hepp 2017: 81–121.

4 For an historically informed perspective on technologically mediated "indirect relationships" as a key part of the "infrastructure of modernity," see Calhoun 1992. On new forms of "action at a distance" enabled by new communications media, see Thompson 1995: 82, 100ff.

5 On texting with physically copresent others, see Tjora 2011.

6 For sustained and sophisticated discussions of the ways in which interaction with copresent others can suffer, see Turkle 2011, 2015.

7 Such practices are not universally accepted; they remain sites of friction, uncertainty, and contestation. See for example Cahir and Lloyd 2015.

8 On absent presence, see Gergen 2002. On the complementary notion of "networked absence" – "a form of network connection with a perceived lack of engagement" – see Burchell 2017. On the emergence of a mediated "there and now" zone, see Zhao 2006.

9 On mediated copresence, see Zhao 2003; Zhao and Elesh 2008. On the hope that advances in augmented reality and virtual reality will create richer and more convincing forms of mediated copresence, see the coda to this chapter and the Conclusion. On the ways in which parents are routinely absent even when physically present with their children, see Turkle 2015: 103–26.

10 This point has been cogently made by Zhao 2006: 470–2. On face-to-face interaction as the "primordial real thing," see Goffman 1983: 2, echoing Berger and Luckmann 1967: 28.

11 On the far-reaching implications of the "self-documenting" quality of digitally mediated interaction, see Schwarz 2021, chapter 2; this paragraph is based on Schwarz's illuminating discussion.

12 On the distinction between concrete place and abstract space, see Agnew 2011. See also Castells' (2010 [1996], chapter 6) discussion of the relation between the "space of places" and the "space of flows."

13 On the social affordances of "locative media," which alert one's contacts to one's current location, see Saker and Frith 2018. Although GPS is ineffective indoors, Bluetooth and other systems provide high-precision indoor tracking, enabling stores to adjust push notifications to customers' proximity to particular items on the shelves (on Bluetooth beacons, see Kwet 2019).

14 On the Walkman, see Bull 2000. Puro (2002: 23) notes the twofold privatization of public space effected by mobile phones: "users sequester themselves non-verbally and then fill the air with private matters." On transformations of public space, see also Turkle 2011: 155–6. For a broader historical and theoretical argument about the ways in which "private life ... is carried into the public realm" in late modernity, see Kumar and Makarova 2008.

15 On the significance of earlier electronic media, especially television, in opening up the home to public developments, see Meyrowitz 1985: vii, 125.

16 On the inversion of public and private, see Austin 2020c.

17 On the blurring of boundaries between home and work, see Wajcman 2015: 139ff. This blurring, to be sure, antedates digital hyperconnectivity: see Nippert-Eng 1996; Hochschild 1997. (The subtitle of Hochschild's book *The Time Bind* is "when work becomes home and home becomes work.")

18 On the digitally mediated penetration of private life into the workplace, see Broadbent 2016.

19 Rigidly surveilled workers may not be able to attend to private matters during working hours; surveillance technologies thus seek to maintain the boundary between work and non-work. Yet other forms of digital surveillance of the labor force – notably fitness tracking and biomedical surveillance – erode that boundary by extending their reach into private life and non-working time.

20 On the surge in digital nomadism, see Kelly 2021.

21 On difficulties of coordination, synchronization, timing, and scheduling as standard times decline, see Shove 2012: 298f; Wajcman 2015: 76.

22 On the fragmentation of activity with respect to digitally mediated shopping, see Couclelis 2004. On temporal fragmentation in broader historical and theoretical perspective, see Rosa 2013: 124, 129, 130, 193.

23 On the interstitial nature of digitally mediated activity, see Carlson 2020: 239 (on news consumption) and Hjorth and Richardson 2011 (on casual mobile gaming). For a fine-grained empirical study of how a driver sustained a dual orientation toward driving and checking Facebook, see Licoppe and Figeac 2015.

24 For a broad historical and theoretical treatment of acceleration, in which digital connectivity figures only in passing, see Rosa 2013 (this is the translation of a book published in German in 2005, before the era of digital hyperconnectivity).

25 On "near-synchrony" in digitally mediated interaction, see Rettie 2009b. On synchrony and asynchrony as shaped by social norms and expectations in addition to technical affordances, see also Rettie 2009a.

26 On temporal autonomy in the context of digital connectivity, see Wajcman 2015: 62, 103, 107, 169.

27 On social media's privileging of the immediate and the new, see Gehl 2014: 48–50.

28 For a broadly Foucauldian analysis of Facebook's attempt to inculcate a "participatory subjectivity," see Bucher 2018: 88–9.

29 On the "liveliness" of the "like economy," see Gerlitz and Helmond 2013: "By prompting users to engage with Facebook features on the web and showing what their contacts have engaged with, Social Plugins [such as "like" or "share" buttons] seek to set a chain of interaction in motion, moving across numerous spaces within and outside the platform" (p. 1359).

30 On the "social photo" shared in a digitally networked environment as a "unit of

communication" and a form of "visual language," see Jurgenson 2019: 8–9, 13–17. A similar argument could also be made, as Jurgenson notes in the coda to his book, about the social video, since "speaking with images is increasingly done through video" (p. 114). On the use of stickers – images, more elaborate than emojis, that represent characters, actions, and/or emotions – to express emotions and achieve "communicative fluidity" in messaging and social media, see Lim 2015. On the increasing use of the full range of graphical communication devices in Facebook comment threads, see Herring and Dainas 2017. On the communicative affordances and cultural practices responsible for the resurgence of GIFs (very short, soundless, looping, low-resolution videos, often relying on humor, that lend themselves to the "performance of affect" and the "demonstration of cultural knowledge") in contemporary social media, messaging, and workplace contexts, see Miltner and Highfield 2017.

31 On the ways in which a temporally fragmented string of micro-interactions can come to be experienced as a quasi-continuous form of "connected presence" or "everyday dwelling," see Licoppe 2004, especially pp. 141 and 152, and, extending Licoppe's analysis to newer forms of digital media, Cui 2016 and Ling and Lai 2016. On the uses of WhatsApp to sustain a sense of "everyday dwelling" among friends, see O'Hara et al. 2014.

32 Battestini et al. 2010: 237.

33 Rettie 2009b.

34 Kannan et al. 2016.

35 On Malinowski's notion of "phatic communion," see Senft 2014: 104ff. Etymologically, and in Malinowski's usage, "phatic" refers to speech. Thus Malinowski refers to "phatic communion" – social bonding effected through speech – not to "phatic communication." In later usage, however, "phatic communication" has come to mean the kind of communication that serves a social bonding function; I follow this usage.

36 Licoppe and Smoreda 2005: 331. On the importance of phatic communication in digital contexts, see also Miller 2008; Schandorf 2013.

37 In highly politicized contexts, actions as seemingly trivial as liking a friend's post may turn out to be anything but trivial. This is a consequence of the extended accountability enabled by the self-documenting nature of digitally mediated interaction. For an analysis of "political defriending" on Facebook, in which people are held accountable for their "likes" and "shares," see Schwarz and Shani 2016: 403ff.

38 Turkle 2011: 11, 187–209.

39 Burchell 2015: 47. On social media and messaging app indicators as "connection cues" that trigger the constant checking and rechecking of devices, see Bayer et al. 2016a.

40 Liu 2018.

41 Hulick 2016.

42 Bucher 2013: 485.

43 Ling and Lai 2016: 844, 847.

44 On "soft coercion," see Ling 2016. On the social expectations that extend the "reach of in-the-moment accountability to others," see Bayer et al. 2016a: 130. On teenagers' anxieties about disconnection, their concerns about failing to keep up, and their fear of missing out on potentially important interaction, see Mascheroni and Vincent 2016: 318ff.

45 Burchell 2015: 36, 38, italics omitted; see also p. 47. To shield themselves from the burdens of superabundant micro-sociality, users also develop ways of controlling and limiting their availability for interaction at certain times, on certain channels, or with certain persons, even while they remain connected: availability for interaction does not follow automatically from connectivity but can be modulated as a way of managing the potentially overwhelming flow of interaction. Burchell (2017) sees these practices as broadly analogous to the "blasé attitude"

that, on Simmel's famous account, served as a "protective organ" against the relentless bombardment of stimuli in the metropolis. See also Schrock 2015: 1237 on availability as socially negotiated rather than technologically given, and Mannell 2019 on the "disconnective affordances" of mobile messaging.

46 I am indebted to Ori Schwarz for this suggestion.

47 On "persistent-pervasive community," see Hampton 2016; the quotation in the text is from p. 103.

48 On the "rise of mediated visibility," contrasting the "situated visibility of copresence" with the stretching out of the field of vision in space and time through different forms of communication media, see Thompson 2005: 35ff.

49 On digitally mediated visibility generally, see Harcourt 2015.

50 I address government surveillance in the Conclusion. As the example of "real-time facial recognition" (Amazon 2017) suggests, government surveillance depends increasingly on tools developed in the private sector; it also depends increasingly on data collected by private companies. On the erosion of the "boundaries between governing, commerce, and private life," see Harcourt 2015: 187ff.

51 Cegłowski 2014; on surveillance as the dominant business model of the internet, see also Zuckerman 2014; Couldry and Mejias 2019; Zuboff 2019. I address commercial surveillance in chapter 4.

52 On interpersonal digital surveillance – which has also been called "social searching," "lateral surveillance," "participatory surveillance," and "social surveillance" – see Marwick 2012; Trottier 2012. Interpersonal digital surveillance has also been conceptualized as the many watching the many, as distinguished from ways in which the few watch the many, as in classical models of top-down surveillance, or the many the few, as in new forms of bottom-up digital "sousveillance" or the mass media (or social media) monitoring of celebrities (Jurgenson 2013). On bottom-up forms of digital "sousveillance," see Mann and Ferenbok 2013.

53 For a lightfooted, wide-ranging study of eavesdropping in historical perspective, see Locke 2010.

54 On the objectification of digitally mediated interaction, see Schwarz 2011: 72 and, for a rich development of the implications of this idea for the rethinking of the basic premises of symbolic interactionism, Schwarz 2021, chapter 2.

55 For a key early statement on the affordances of digitally mediated interaction on social network sites, highlighting persistence and searchability in addition to replicability and scalability, see boyd 2011.

56 "To make the world more open and connected" was long Facebook's semi-official "mission." On Mark Zuckerberg's "you have one identity" quip as indicative of social media platforms' interest in maximizing one-way transparency, see van Dijck 2013b. (Zuckerberg went on to say that "having two identities for yourself is an example of a lack of integrity.") For a critique of the "ideology of openness" in connection with the use of social media in organizational contexts, see Gibbs et al. 2013.

57 Bucher 2012; Bucher 2018: 84ff.

58 It is not always surreptitious: the watcher may reveal the watching, for example by commenting on or liking a post by the target.

59 While the expression "Facebook stalking" registers a certain unease about behavior like the sustained surreptitious monitoring of a former romantic partner, the term is widely used without the negative connotations applied to "stalking" in other contexts. "Facebook stalking" often has an ironic meaning; it is used in a way that acknowledges the universality of the practice. So while "stalking" registers a persisting unease, the term has lost its strong

previous connotations of illegitimacy. Still, there are of course deeply disturbing forms of surreptitious social media stalking.

60 Marwick 2012: 388; see also pp. 384–5. The definition of eavesdropping is from Locke 2010: 3 (italics omitted). On the mutuality of social media surveillance, see Albrechtslund 2008.

61 On the distinction between deliberately "giving" and unconsciously "giving off" information in face-to-face interaction, see Goffman 1959: 2.

62 On the association between longer-term and more intensive Facebook use and the perception that others are happier and have better lives, see Chou and Edge 2012.

63 On social media, upward social comparison, and envy, see Krasnova et al. 2015. For a broader argument about the deleterious effects of social media (especially Instagram) on the mental health of teens, and of adolescent girls in particular, see Haidt 2021.

64 On the legal notion of "practical obscurity," see Kotfila 2014.

65 On fraudulent uses of information assembled by "people finder" sites, see Chen 2019; Rohrlich 2019.

66 On forms of digitally mediated over-visibility and excessive transparency, see Morozov 2013a: 63ff.

67 On the surveillance of romantic partners, see Tokunaga 2011, 2016; Fox and Warber 2014. On the broader phenomenon of the "quantified relationship," comprising the surveillance of a partner but also the tracking or gamification of behavior in intimate relationships, see Danaher et al. 2018.

68 On Facebook and jealousy, see Muise et al. 2009.

69 On the full range of interpersonal surveillance software and the advertising practices that promote it, see Chatterjee et al. 2018.

70 On the association between intimacy and transparency and its implications for partner surveillance, see Gregg 2013.

71 Some couples (and others), often with the support of religious groups, enlist phone and computer surveillance software as a tool for overcoming a pornography habit; see for example https://www.covenanteyes.com/how-it-works/.

72 Negotiations and struggles between parents and children are not confined to surveillance: they also concern limits on times, places, and contexts in which phones and other devices may be used.

73 On GPS tracking devices for pre-smartphone children, see Bettany and Kerrane 2016. Some devices include a "panic button" and enable parents to listen in unobtrusively on their child's environment and communicate with the child if necessary.

74 On this contract and, more generally, the tight digital "tethering" of children and parents and its implications for children's developmental need to separate from their parents, see Turkle 2011: 173f. On children's varied experience of this contract – some accepting its terms, others testing its limits or resisting the obligation to be reachable at any time – see Lachance 2020.

75 On surveillance-related struggles over boundaries between parents and children, see Erickson et al. 2016.

76 On surveillance creep generally, see Marx 1988: 2. Surveillance creep extends not only parents' monitoring of children, but children's monitoring of aged parents – and the care workers who tend to them – in nursing homes. On the ethical issues raised by this practice, see Berridge et al. 2019.

77 The *Black Mirror* episode "Arkangel" extrapolates this family surveillance creep into a future in which an implanted chip enables a parent not only to remotely monitor a child's experience but to intervene and filter that experience so as to shelter the child from putatively distressing experiences. Dystopian aspects of hyper-visibility and complete transparency are also explored in Dave Eggers' 2013 novel *The Circle*.

78 On Facebook's "privacy-focused vision for social networking," see Zuckerberg 2019.

79 For a more general discussion of the "multiplication of occasions where people will be exposed to diverse traces, tracks, representations and models of their own practices," see Cahour and Licoppe 2010. On digitalization and new ecologies of memory, see Schwarz 2014; Schwarz 2021: 73ff. For reflections on the "fully archived life," see Turkle 2011: 299–305.

80 On the pleasures of ephemeral communication in Snapchat, see Bayer et al. 2016b; on the limits of ephemerality in Snapchat, noting how the company has quietly adopted longer-lasting and archival functionality as well, see Hall 2017.

81 On the myth of platform neutrality, see Langlois and Elmer 2013: 2–4, 10–11; Morozov 2013a: 142ff; Gillespie 2018: 24ff.

82 Van Dijck 2013a: 12.

83 Facebook's experiments were reported in Bond et al. 2012 and Kramer et al. 2014. For a critique of the lack of consent, and an analysis of the problem of consent in large-scale internet experiments, see Flick 2016. For a broader critical discussion of the experiments, see Zuboff 2019: 299–309.

84 On continuous, automated experimentation, see Zuboff 2019: 298.

85 Ledvina 2014.

86 On behavior modification, and the connections between classical behavioral psychology and the "tuning" and "herding" of behavior through predictive analytics, see Zuboff 2019, especially chapter 10.

87 On Facebook's shift in 2016 from a single all-purpose "like" button to six "reaction" buttons, see Horning 2016.

88 Gehl 2014: 82–9.

89 This paragraph draws primarily on Bucher's analysis of "programmed sociality" on Faceboook. The quotations are from Bucher 2013: 484 and 487; see also Bucher 2018. On the incitement to activity through metrics, see Grosser 2014.

90 Gehl and Bakardjieva 2017: 2.

91 Ibid. On social bots and the Turing test, see Gehl 2014: 36–7.

92 Gehl 2014: 22, 23. For a philosophical analysis that inverts the Turing test and asks whether humans might become more machine-like in environments in which more and more tasks are outsourced to machines, see Frischmann and Selinger 2018: 175–208.

93 For an overview of strategies of bot detection, see Ferrara et al. 2016.

94 Shao et al. 2018.

95 I return to this issue in chapter 5; see p. 136.

96 On the ethical implications of this experiment, see Frischmann and Selinger 2018: 157–9.

97 http://www.skipser.com/p/2/p/automatic-facebook-birthday-wishes.html.

98 Frischmann and Selinger 2018: 157.

99 Dewey 2016; Stadil 2016. On the starkly differing behavior of men and women on Tinder, see Tyson et al. 2016.

100 Jackson 2017.

101 Markowitz 2017.

102 Pignataro 2017.

103 Bullock 2017. Complementing Smart Reply is Smart Compose, a kind of auto-complete on steroids. "From your greeting to your closing (and common phrases in between), Smart Compose suggests complete sentences in your emails so that you can draft them with ease." When the user sees a suggestion they like, they simply click the "tab" button to accept it. Smart Compose promises not only to "save you time by cutting back on repetitive writing" but to reduce spelling and grammatical errors and even "suggest relevant contextual

phrases": "if it's Friday it may suggest 'Have a great weekend!' as a closing phrase" (Lambert 2018).

104 Wen et al. 2015; the quotations are from pp. 86–7 and 91. Computer-generated humor systems have not been very successful, so the paper proposes instead "computer-aided humor" in which computer and human draw on different strengths in collaboration.

105 For doubts about Smart Reply, see Maxwell 2017; Syme 2018. For more general reflections on the social implications of machine-generated language, see Munger 2021; for a critique of the ideology of convenience, see Wu 2018b. On the virtues of inefficiency, see Morozov 2013a: 163–4, 314.

106 For a critique of the "techno-social engineering of human sociality," see Frischmann and Selinger 2018, chapter 9. The quotation is from p. 148; the pertinence of Habermas is noted at p. 162. For a critique of the corporate-driven automation of emojis and GIFs, see Hess 2016.

107 On Woebot, a chatbot developed at Stanford University that delivers cognitive-behavioral therapy, see Brown 2021. For an historical analysis of the development of automated forms of therapy, see Zeavin 2021, chapter 4. On "socially assistive robotics," see Matarić 2017; Clabaugh and Matarić 2018. On the temptations and dilemmas of "robotic companionship," see Turkle 2011.

108 The *Black Mirror* episode "Be Right Back" explores the possibility of replicating a lost loved one on three levels, through text, voice, and a full-scale silicon robot.

109 "AI companion who cares": https://replika.ai/. "If you're feeling down …": https://apps. apple.com/us/app/replika-virtual-ai-friend/id1158555867.

110 For a survey of recent research in the development of emotionally aware chatbots, see Pamungkas 2019.

111 On digitally mediated narcissism, see Barber 2018; on Replika as an "experiment in human-bot interaction," see Pardes 2017.

112 On machine empathy, see McStay 2018: 4–5. For a different perspective on empathy in connection with social robots, see Turkle 2011: 55.

113 For a philosophical perspective on these questions, arguing for the value of effort and against a one-sided emphasis on efficiency, see Frischmann and Selinger 2018, chapter 9; the quotation is from p. 157. For a psychoanalytically informed psychological perspective, see Turkle 2011, part one.

114 On this ironic reversal, see Austin 2020b.

115 On the experience of the body in Zoom, see Sacasas 2020. My account of Zoom fatigue draws also on Bailenson 2021.

116 On the "age of excarnation" and the digitally mediated accentuation of the shift "from tactile contact to optical vision," see Kearney 2021: 113ff. On virtual embodiment as a kind of "secondary embodiment," by analogy to Walter Ong's notion of "secondary orality," see Carr 2021. Even if we feel ourselves to be embodied in a virtual reality environment, we do not experience others as fully embodied beings; virtual embodiment is thus for Carr "essentially and inescapably solipsistic."

117 On "untact" in South Korea, see Lee 2020; Rashid 2021.

118 As Robin Sloan (2015) put it, writing about the ultra-fast food delivery app Sprig, "This is the Amazon move: absolute obfuscation of labor and logistics behind a friendly buy button. The experience for a Sprig customer is super convenient, almost magical; the experience for a chef or courier …? We don't know. We don't get to know. We're just here to press the button."

Chapter 3: Culture

1 On universal access to culture, see Lessig 2008: 42, 47. On digital museums, see Udell 2019, focusing on Google Arts and Culture.

2 On the "long tail," see Anderson 2006.

3 On giving things away as a business strategy, see Anderson 2009; Fourcade and Kluttz 2020.

4 On "commons-based peer production," see Benkler 2006: 60.

5 On the "high tech gift economy," see Barbrook 1998.

6 On the revitalization of amateur cultural production, see DiMaggio 2013; for a broad, historically informed account of vernacular creativity and new media, see Burgess 2007.

7 "Cutting, pasting, rendering, annotating, and commenting": Benkler 2006: 294. On "semiotic democracy," see Fiske 1987. Fiske was writing about the way television viewers were not simply passive recipients but active participants in the making of meaning, capable of rearticulating and subverting intended or "preferred" meanings.

8 On remix culture, see Lessig 2008: 26, 68ff.

9 On the prosumer, see Toffler 1980; Ritzer and Jurgenson 2010. For a critique of the celebration of interactivity, see Andrejevic 2007.

10 My definition of cultural goods is similar to that of Hirsch 1972: 641–2. The reference to "symbolic, expressive, or aesthetic gratifications" might seem at first glance to skew this definition toward "high" rather than popular culture. But the gratifications afforded by popular culture are every bit as symbolic, expressive, and aesthetic as those afforded by high culture. See for example Jenkins 2005 on new aesthetic possibilities offered by computer and video games.

11 Running counter to the dematerialization of cultural goods are certain forms of rematerialization, notably in connection with the steady revival in vinyl records over the course of the last decade or so (Magaudda 2011; Bartmanski and Woodward 2015).

12 Exceptions would include coffee table books, children's books, and other books for which the material envelope – its size, paper quality, tactility, and so on – is understood as central to the cultural good itself rather than simply as a delivery vehicle. And for book collectors, of course, the value and meaning of the cultural good – a rare first edition, a unique signed or annotated copy – lie in the indissoluble synthesis of cultural content and material substrate. On the dematerialization of the book and the transformation of publishing, see Thompson 2021: 10ff.

13 For early statements on the affordances of digital objects, see Negroponte 1995; boyd 2011.

14 Digital cultural goods, to be sure, are not always non-excludable. Paywalls can limit access to paying customers, and digital rights management (DRM) software can make copying difficult (though it also interferes with legitimate uses and does not necessarily prevent determined users from making copies). See Ocean 2017.

15 Although the *marginal* cost is negligible, the *total* costs of aggregating, storing, and distributing vast stocks of digital content are very high (Hindman 2018: 12–13). As Hindman underscores, and as I discuss in the final section of the chapter, this contributes to the continued concentration of power in digital cultural industries.

16 Property rights in professionally produced cultural goods complicate the picture. But they have not stood in the way of digital abundance. Napster, the first popular incarnation of digital musical abundance, which made some 4 million songs freely available, was shut down for copyright infringement; but Spotify has managed to make twenty times as much music available. Spotify must pay for the music it offers, but its vast market power has enabled it to do so on favorable terms, and its success in converting free to paid subscribers has generated a substantial revenue stream. On the limited sense in which digital abundance has led to the decommodification of culture, see the next section of this chapter.

17 On the addictive properties of the infinite scroll, see Eyal 2012.
18 On TikTok as a form of micro-entertainment characterized by its high "content density," see Constine 2020.
19 On internet memes as collections, see Shifman 2014: 41.
20 On the "experience economy," see Pine and Gilmore 1998; Hutter 2018.
21 The "blurring of contents" resulting from shared codes and from the "integration of all messages in a common cognitive pattern" was already noted by Castells 2010 [1996]: 402. See also Carr 2020 on "content collapse," the blurring of "distinctions of form, register, sense, and importance" once all content is delivered "through a single, universal medium."
22 On ubiquitous listening, see Kassabian 2013; on mobile sonic bubbles, which go back to the pre-digital Sony Walkman, see Bull 2000, 2006, 2015.
23 Highly immersive video games, to be sure, are a major exception.
24 On changing habits, expectations, and capacities, see Carr 2010.
25 On new forms of cultural literacy, see Greenfeld 2014; Miltner and Highfield 2017.
26 The option to accelerate has been challenged by some creators, noting for example that subtleties of timing in podcasts are thereby lost (Lagomarsino 2015). More recently, Netflix too decided to allow for playback at speeds up to 1.5 times the original, provoking a flurry of opposition from Hollywood (Weisenstein 2019).
27 For concerns about the effects of superabundance on musical desire, see Drott 2018: 330–6.
28 The non-fungible tokens (NFTs) that came to wide public attention in 2021 when a purely digital work of art sold at auction for $69 million (Reyburn 2021) represent another effort to recreate scarcity in a context of digital abundance. For a broader account of the use of blockchain technology to recreate scarcity in the context of infinitely replicable and therefore abundant digital art, see O'Dwyer 2020. I address the new techno-utopian discourse about cryptocurrencies, NFTs, and blockchain technology in the coda to chapter 4.
29 On the paradox of choice, see Schwartz 2004. On the shaping of choice in online contexts, see Graham 2018.
30 As DiMaggio (2013: 34) put it, "the Internet lays a table before us of unprecedented abundance, and then tries to keep us from that table by constantly showing us reflections of ourselves." On "automated culture," see Andrejevic 2020: 44ff.
31 Drott 2018: 335–6, quoting the co-founder and Chief Technology Officer of Echo Nest, a music data analysis service.
32 Even those who resist this temptation and actively seek out digital cultural materials of their own choosing cannot escape algorithms altogether. Digital cultural superabundance makes algorithmic navigation tools indispensable, just as the superabundance of information, consumer products, and potential partners makes algorithmic mediation unavoidable for Google, Amazon, and Tinder. Without algorithmic filtering and ordering, we would be completely lost in the digital wilderness (Gillespie 2016). Even when we actively search online for a cultural item, rather than simply acquiesce in what is recommended to us, the search results are filtered and presented to us in an order determined by algorithms. Inevitably, then, the horizons of our cultural attention – what we see and what remains invisible to us – are increasingly governed by algorithms.
33 On this tension – and the corresponding tension between the neoliberal self, governed in and through its choices, and an incipient post-neoliberal self, governed through its data – see chapter 1, pp. 44–8.
34 Simmel 1950 [1903]: 422.
35 Simon 1971: 40.
36 On price signals as a coordinating mechanism in a context of scarcity, see Abbott 2014: 12.
37 In this environment, as Stewart Brand famously put it, "information wants to be free." But it

is often forgotten that Brand was identifying a tension: "Information wants to be free because it has become so cheap to distribute, copy, and recombine – too cheap to meter. It wants to be expensive because it can be immeasurably valuable to the recipient. That tension will not go away" (Brand 1987: 202).

38 The phrase "free culture" was popularized by Lawrence Lessig in his 2004 book by that title. For Lessig, however, "free culture" was not about price: it was not about "'free' as in 'free beer,'" and not against intellectual property rights, but about "limiting the reach of those rights" so that "follow-on creators and innovators remain *as free as possible* from the control of the past" (2004: 4). And "free culture" was an ideal, not a reality: Lessig argued that culture had become *less* free – and more of a "permissions culture" – in the US, notably as a result of the Sonny Bono Copyright Term Extension Act of 1998, which had extended copyright protection for an additional twenty years.

39 On the commodification of the subscription rather than the individual digital cultural item, with reference to Spotify, see Fleischer 2017.

40 Anderson 2009.

41 Benkler 2006: 29, 32–3.

42 On open-source software, see Bauwens et al. 2019.

43 Benkler 2019: 82.

44 On the increasingly central role of commercial platforms in the mediation of amateur cultural creativity, see Nieborg and Poell 2018; van Dijck et al. 2018: 8, 12–20, 37ff.

45 On "small acts of engagement," see Picone et al. 2019.

46 I address this debate in chapter 4.

47 Cunningham and Craig 2017: 72.

48 Cunningham and Craig 2019: 45–6.

49 Stokel-Walker 2018. This has contributed to the growth of new subscription-based platforms such as Substack and Patreon, which can be lucrative for content creators with large and loyal followings (Austin 2021a). It has also contributed to the interest in non-fungible tokens (NFTs) and other blockchain-based initiatives; I address these in the coda to chapter 4.

50 On the "aspirational labor" of those who hope to get paid to do what they love, see Duffy 2017. On the emerging proto-industry, see Cunningham and Craig 2017: 71. On commercial intermediaries, see Cunningham and Craig 2019, chapter 3. I return to the theme of aspirational labor in chapter 4, situating it in the broader context of transformations of labor generated by digital platforms.

51 On empowerment, see especially Cunningham and Craig 2019: 65ff. On the tension between empowering and disempowering aspects, see van Dijck et al. 2018: 37. On contingency, see Nieborg and Poell 2018.

52 The majority of these of course have relatively modest numbers of followers. But brands have shown increasing interest in working with such micro-influencers; they are seen as better able to sustain the kind of perceived authenticity vis-a-vis their followers that is crucial for being an effective influencer. See Manzerolle and Daubs 2021: 6.

53 On the move toward frictionless shoppability on Instagram and Snapchat, see Manzerolle and Daubs 2021; on "ambient shopping," see T. Nguyen 2021.

54 The quotation is from Schwartz 2008. "Lulz" derives from LOL or "Laugh out Loud." On the centrality of lulz to subcultural trolling, see Phillips 2015, chapter 2. On the commercial appropriation of initially subcultural memetic language, see ibid. 137ff; Milner 2016: 202ff.

55 Frank 1997. x. On "cool capitalism," see McGuigan 2009; the quotation is from p. 1.

56 Nieborg and Poell 2018: 4279.

57 Wu 2016: 6.

58 See especially Benkler 2006; Lessig 2008.

59 On the "end of cultural elitism," see for example Gabler 2011.

60 On access to the means of cultural production, see DiMaggio 2013: 13.

61 Hanrahan 2013: 83. On the limitations of a focus on participation per se, see also Gillespie 2012.

62 For Pew Research Center statistics of social media use from a nationwide random sample, see Auxier and Anderson 2021. The figure on uploading TikToks should be taken as only broadly indicative; it is from a market research firm (Beer 2019), and methodological details about the survey are not provided. The figure, moreover, is from 2018, early in the TikTok craze; it may well be lower now that the user base has expanded so dramatically. Still, academic research supports the view that TikTok is distinctly participatory (Guinaudeau et al. 2022).

63 On the creativity of TikTok users, see Wei 2021.

64 On "circumscribed creativity," see Kaye et al. 2021.

65 This was part of an earlier TikTok "mission statement," quoted in Collie and Wilson-Barnao 2020: 177.

66 Burgess 2007: 89; Burgess 2012. Elaborating, Burgess notes that usability facilitates "popular access without the need for esoteric knowledge, by creating pleasurable surface interfaces that automate operations on the underlying layers of technology." Hackability, by contrast, celebrates "rational mastery and understanding of the technical 'reality' of machines." The tension between usability and hackability thus exemplifies a broader tension between "postmodern populism" and "critical modernism" (2007: 89).

67 On the "Kodak moment" and the "mass amateurization" of photography, see the illuminating discussion in Burgess 2007: 93ff, drawing on a rich body of historical scholarship on the subject.

68 On the "triumph of seamless usability," see Burgess et al. 2018. In her earlier analysis of "the iPhone moment" (2012: 40), Burgess offered a more nuanced appraisal of the iPhone, emphasizing its open-ended cultural "generativity," notwithstanding the fact that the iPhone itself is a "'closed,' tightly controlled device." An analogous point could be made about the generativity of TikTok, notwithstanding its opting for extreme usability.

69 On the "tyranny of convenience," see Wu 2018b.

70 Kelly 2005.

71 https://www.ampermusic.com/.

72 Silverstein 2019.

73 On the marketing of Apple devices, see Burgess 2007: 110ff; Burgess 2012.

74 For a critical analysis of the manner in which TikTok has channeled vernacular play and creativity, including that of children, "into the data-driven and commercial logic of the digital economy," see Collie and Wilson-Barnao 2020: 173. See also Horning's analysis of TikTok algorithms as "aggressively programming users" – by appealing to their fear of social exclusion – to compulsively "make and consume specific kinds of content" (2020a).

75 Gillespie 2018 provides a cogent and eloquent analysis of content moderation.

76 On hopeful Twitch streamers, who may stream for years without a single viewer, see Hernandez 2018.

77 As Hesmondhalgh observes, circulation has "remained the central locus of power in the cultural industries" (2019: 279).

78 Hindman 2018, chapter 5. On the persisting relevance of the winner-take-all logic in digital contexts, see also Elberse 2013, especially chapter 5. On trending algorithms, broadly understood, which bring potentially relevant bits of culture to our attention in ways that simultaneously register and reinforce popularity, see Gillespie 2016.

79 This is notably the case in the art world. See for example the video promoting the art app

"Magnus," billed as "Shazam for Art": https://www.youtube.com/watch?v=ofbWttwaoQ4. On the democratization of access more generally, see Smith Maguire 2018: 7.

80 For a popular version of this argument, focused on the art world, see Resch and Heidenreich 2019.

81 Robinson 2017: 19–27, 49–54; the quotation is from p. 25. Robinson was addressing the reconfiguration of television viewing in the context of digital hyperconnectivity, but her argument applies more broadly. See also the pioneering essay of Jenkins (2002) on the interactive audiences that have formed around digital cultural artifacts, emerging in part through the diffusion, generalization, and transformation of pre-digital forms of fandom. For a more skeptical argument about the promise of interactivity, see Andrejevic 2007: 28ff, 137ff.

82 Robinson 2017: 44–5, 46.

83 Critics of Frankfurt School cultural theory have long emphasized – in response to that school's characterization of the passivity of mass culture audiences – that audiences are in fact active in various ways. On "active audience theory," see for example Morley 1993.

84 Benkler 2019: 83.

85 On combinations of algorithmic and human curation, see Bhaskar 2016, 2017.

86 See for example DiMaggio 1991.

87 On digital media and the decline of elite culture, see Bolter 2019.

88 Horning 2020b.

89 For a sustained critique of the promise of "personalized" culture, see Weinberg 2018.

Chapter 4: Economics

1 Turner's (2006) account focuses on Stewart Brand and the various networks in which he was a key figure. The quotation in the text is from p. 4. On the legitimization of information technology, see especially pp. 247–9. As Turner observes, Brand and his networks transformed "the lingering ideals of the New Communalists into ideological resources for the technologists of the computer and software industries" (p. 246). On the countercultural roots of techno-utopian visions of decentralization, see also Schrape 2019; on the legacy of the counterculture in early articulations of the notion of virtual communities, see Matei 2005.

2 For critical analysis of early Web 2.0-era discourse, see van Dijck and Nieborg 2009 (building expressly on Turner) and Scholz 2008.

3 This tweaked mission statement – the previous longstanding mission statement promised to "give people the power to share and make the world more open and connected" – was adopted in 2017 in response to widespread criticism of Facebook's role in the 2016 US election (Constine 2017).

4 My discussion of the rhetoric of "sharing" draws especially on John 2013b; see also Belk 2014 and, for a recent review, Schor and Vallas 2021. On the way sharing-talk mobilizes values associated with therapeutic culture, see John 2013b: 122ff. Schor and Attwood-Charles, however, note that "sharing" may be "losing its semiotic potency" as once-novel forms of exchange captured by the term "become more normalized and 'conventionalized'" (2017: 4).

5 John 2013b: 125.

6 Influential accounts include books by Benkler 2006; Tapscott and Williams 2006; Leadbeater 2007; Lessig 2008 (the first to use the phrase "sharing economy"); Shirky 2008; Botsman and Rogers 2010; Gansky 2010; Rifkin 2014; Sundararajan 2016. Among these, the books by Tapscott and Williams and Leadbeater stand closest to the popular pole, that of Benkler closest to the scholarly pole (see also the two foundational articles by Benkler on shared creative labor [2002] and shareable goods [2004]). On the connection between popular business literature and broader theoretical accounts, see van Dijck and Nieborg 2009. The corporate rhetoric of sharing is epitomized in Mark Zuckerberg's claim – in a letter

accompanying Facebook's IPO in 2012 – that "sharing more … creates a more open culture and leads to a better understanding of the lives and perspectives of others" (quoted in John 2013b: 117).

7 Schor and Attwood-Charles 2017.
8 Belk 2014.
9 John 2013a: 177ff.
10 On online sharing as preparation for offline sharing, see Botsman and Rogers 2010: xx.
11 German journalist Sascha Lobo (2014) first proposed the notion of "platform capitalism" as a direct critique of the notion of the "sharing economy."
12 Andreessen 2007.
13 Gillespie 2010: 352, 349–50. The definitions in the penultimate sentence are quoted by Gillespie from the Oxford English Dictionary.
14 More specifically, as Gillespie (2010) argues, the term has been used strategically by tech firms – especially those that circulate user-generated content – to position themselves vis-a-vis "users, clients, advertisers and policymakers" in a complex and shifting economic, cultural, political, and regulatory environment.
15 The analytical literature on platforms crystallized in the second half of the 2010s; see notably Bratton 2015: 41ff; Srnicek 2017; Plantin et al. 2018; van Dijck et al. 2018; Cohen 2019: 37–46.
16 I take up the theme of populism in the next chapter.
17 See for example Gellman 1996.
18 Van Dijck et al. 2018: 1–2.
19 Not all forms of disintermediation, to be sure, involve re-intermediation. When a manufacturer adopts a "direct-to-consumer" model rather than marketing its goods through retail stores, this involves disintermediation but not re-intermediation.
20 For an early critical dissection of the myth that digital connectivity eliminates intermediaries, see Morozov 2013a: 164–6. On platform business models as a form of re-intermediation, see Parker et al. 2016: 70–1.
21 Platforms' mediation between different categories of users has spawned a literature in economics on "multisided platforms" and the "multisided markets" they bring into being, going back to the seminal paper of Rochet and Tirole (2003). For a non-technical account, see Evans and Schmalensee 2016.
22 On the centrality of APIs to the programmability of platforms, with particular reference to Facebook, see Helmond 2015; Nieborg and Helmond 2019.
23 On industrial platforms, see Pauli et al. 2021.
24 On matching as central to the work of platforms, see Evans and Schmalensee 2016.
25 Cusumano et al. 2020 distinguish two broad kinds of platforms. "Transaction platforms" (including what I have called content-hosting or content-organizing platforms) serve as intermediaries for the exchange of goods, services, or information. "Innovation platforms" enlist third-party companies (called "complementors" in the literature) to develop complementary products and services that are built on top of a programmable platform like a smartphone, desktop operating system, or game console. Many of the most successful platforms, they note, have been hybrids, facilitating transactions but also opening up their architectures to third-party developers.
26 Lobel 2016: 106. For a transaction cost perspective on platforms, see Nagle et al. 2020.
27 On market aggregation, see Parker et al. 2016: 73, 262.
28 Lobel 2016: 108.
29 Ibid. 107–8.
30 Ibid. 109; italics in the original. Blockchain technology, which I address in the coda to this chapter, carries the process of universal transactionalization and monetization even further.

31 Van Dijck 2013a: 29.
32 On the "designed core architecture that governs the interaction possibilities" on platforms, see Srnicek 2017: 48. On platforms as regulatory structures and governance systems, see Zysman and Kenney 2018: 54, 62; also Khan 2019: 976.
33 "Code is law": Lessig 1999: 6. I take up the theme of algorithmically mediated platform governance in the next chapter.
34 Bucher 2013.
35 On platforms as "generative mechanisms," see Bratton 2015: 44; on the tension between generativity and control in the platform economy, see Williams 2015 and Schwarz 2017: 378–9.
36 See the lucid and sophisticated analysis of content moderation on social media platforms in Gillespie 2018.
37 On datafication, see Mayer-Schönberger and Cukier 2013, chapter 5 and van Dijck et al. 2018; on "dataism," see van Dijck 2014.
38 *The Economist* 2017.
39 For doubts about the usefulness of superabundant data in the advertising context, see MacKenzie 2021. On the data imperative, see Fourcade and Healy 2017: "Organizations believe they should be in the data collection business, even when they do not yet know what to do with what they collect. That is the ceremonial aspect of the data imperative. If a firm is not sure how to extract its value, there are other organizations that know, or claim to know" (p. 16).
40 Zuboff 2019: 63–97. Other accounts conceptualize platform-extracted data as a form of capital (Sadowski 2019) or as integral to "platform capitalism" (Srnicek 2017: 39ff) or "data colonialism" (Thatcher et al. 2016; Couldry and Mejias 2019).
41 On the assetization of personal data, see Beauvisage and Mellet 2020. On data as an ingredient in platform capitalization, see Langley and Leyshon 2017. For an amusing and scathing account of "investor storytime" – investor storytime being "when someone pays you to tell them how rich they'll get when you finally put ads on your site," given the kinds of data you will be collecting – see Cegłowski 2014.
42 Evans and Schmalensee 2016: 44.
43 A similar logic applies to social media networks. A key reason people continue to use Facebook is that so many other people use it, which makes it easier to find people or keep in touch.
44 For an analysis of indirect network effects in the emergence of Open Table and YouTube, see Evans and Schmalensee 2016: 7–14, 69–76. Of course there are many complications. For example, indirect network effects may be asymmetrical, positive for one party, negative for the other. On advertising-based platforms such as Google and Facebook, advertisers benefit from the growth of users, but users may be irritated by an increase in advertising (even if some appreciate the "personalized" advertisements made possible by user data).
45 Ibid. 36. Achieving a critical mass is not automatic or easy, since it is difficult to induce participation from either side before sufficient numbers are participating on the other side (ibid. 69ff). To get past this "chicken-and-egg problem," platforms often find it necessary to subsidize one category of users, which then makes the platform attractive to the other category. Advertising-based platforms like Google or Facebook, for example, have subsidized users by providing their services for free. Having attracted large numbers of users in this way, they were then in a position to attract advertisers. On cross-subsidization, see ibid. 31ff, 93ff; Srnicek 2017: 46.
46 Van Dijck et al. 2018: 12–16.
47 On "large technological systems," see Hughes 1987.

48 Star 1999: 380, 382; Sandvig 2013: 11.

49 Public goods are non-rivalrous and non-excludable; clean air and national defense are frequently adduced examples. Club goods are non-rivalrous but excludable; films shown in movie theaters (assuming the theater is not full) would be an example. A good is non-excludable if it is technically impossible or economically infeasible to exclude others from consuming or using it once it is provided to some. On the economics of infrastructural goods, see Frischmann 2012.

50 On the "broad, multipurpose functionality" of infrastructure, see Frischmann 2012: 65.

51 Edwards 2002: 187. Like all "family-resemblance" characterizations, the one I have offered is fuzzy. Some systems may be infrastructural in some respects but not in all. And all of the elements can be understood as continua. Infrastructure is therefore a matter of degree. What counts as infrastructure, moreover, changes over time, as prevailing understandings of what is indispensable change.

52 On the "internet as infrastructure," see Sandvig 2013.

53 On the tech giants as "infrastructural platforms," offering an array of infrastructural services, see van Dijck et al. 2018: 13–15; I have taken this discussion as the starting point for the enumeration offered in the text. On the fruitful intersection of "platform studies" and "infrastructure studies" perspectives, see Plantin et al. 2018; Plantin and Punathambekar 2019.

54 For a legal argument conceptualizing platform power in terms of control over infrastructural goods, see Rahman 2018.

55 Khan 2017; Guggenberger 2021; Kenney et al. 2021.

56 Khan 2017: 754–5, quoting a 2012 business research report by Sucharita Kodali and Brian K. Walker.

57 Guggenberger 2021: 258–9.

58 On Amazon's exploitation of its power to pressure vendors, see Mattioli and Flint 2021.

59 For the logic of this competition, and an argument for banning it, see Khan 2019. Amazon has claimed that the company does not use the detailed sales data it collects about products sold by the platform's third-party vendors to decide which products to produce and sell itself. But the *Wall Street Journal* reported that Amazon employees in fact commonly used such data for this purpose. This enabled the company to undercut third-party vendors by copying popular products and producing them under its private label brands (Mattioli 2020).

60 On Amazon's immense investments in logistics and delivery capacity, see Greene 2020.

61 On Amazon's 80 percent increase in capital expenditures during the pandemic, see Palmer 2021.

62 This reflects a return of "patient capital," oriented to long-term dominance, rather than insisting on short-term profit. See for example Rahman and Thelen 2019: 178–80.

63 Lovink 2008. A few years later, Hillis et al. (2012) emphasized the "astonishing naturaliz-ation" of search in everyday life: "to search has become so natural and obvious a condition of using the Web, and the Web such a natural and obvious feature of the internet, that the specific contingency of these everyday practices has become obscured. ... Often it will take a technical breakdown to expose the myriad moments of your everyday life almost instinctively or autonomously given over to some kind of search activity or device" (p. 2).

64 Zuboff 2019: 74ff.

65 On the infrastructural ambitions and achievements of Facebook, see Nieborg and Helmond 2019; Bucher 2021, chapter 2. On the privacy-infringing aspect of Facebook's data-gathering, see Srinivasan 2019.

66 User data for Facebook itself ("monthly active users") and for all of the company's apps together are from the fourth quarter of 2021 (Meta 2022). Facebook hasn't released numbers

for Instagram users since 2018, but an anonymous employee reported the number reached 2 billion in fall 2021 (Roth 2021). Figures for WhatsApp and Messenger are widely reported estimates.

67 Facebook 2013.

68 Zuckerberg 2019. This has major implications for Facebook/Meta's business model: the company will need to shift from advertising to commissions and micro-payments. See Yuan 2019.

69 The figures for businesses and advertisers are from Facebook 2020.

70 On Facebook's partnerships with news and fact-checking organizations – formed after the 2016 election – as a "political speech infrastructure," see Ananny 2020.

71 Vaidhyanathan 2018: 99.

72 On enclosure within a single platform ecosystem as a key business strategy of giant platforms, not only Facebook, see Srnicek 2017: 110.

73 Vaidhyanathan 2018: 98–105; Statt and Liao 2019.

74 Facebook 2016.

75 I return to Facebook's pivot to the metaverse in the Conclusion; see pp. 158–9.

76 "Platformed masses": Lovink and Tkacz 2015: 14. " Leveling of the governed": Weber 1978 [1922]: 985.

77 The tech giants have faced a considerably tougher regulatory environment in Europe, notably with respect to the European Union's General Data Protection Regulation (GDPR). On the GDPR, see Hoofnagle et al. 2019.

78 For a review of acquisitions by the giant platforms, see Alcantara et al. 2021.

79 For the thesis that the giant platforms are converging as they compete on these frontiers, see Srnicek 2017: 107–10. As Srnicek notes, tech giants like Amazon and Facebook compete even in search, not by trying to construct an alternative general search engine to rival Google, but by seeking to internalize search within their platforms (p. 105). On competition among major platforms as a source of innovation, see Hemphill 2019. This is not to say that tech giants don't engage in anticompetitive behavior: there is abundant evidence that they do. It is rather to acknowledge that they do face effective competition from other tech giants, though not, increasingly, from smaller companies.

80 On consumers as political allies of platforms in the context of attempts at platform regulation, see Rahman and Thelen 2019.

81 Khan 2017; the quotation is from p. 744. Another factor is that digital markets have been seen as "exceptionally dynamic and self-correcting," with exceptionally low barriers to entry; this has favored a "highly permissive approach to regulation and antitrust enforcement" (Khan 2019: 1074).

82 Khan 2017: 717.

83 For a sympathetic account of the neo-Brandeisan approach, see Khan 2020.

84 Rahman 2018: 1629.

85 On regulating platforms as public utilities, see Rahman 2018; on the "essential facilities" doctrine, see Guggenberger 2021.

86 Wu 2018a.

87 Khan 2019.

88 Biden also appointed legal scholar Tim Wu as special assistant to the president for technology and competition policy; Wu's 2018 book *The Curse of Bigness* argued for reviving an aggressive antitrust policy that would not shy away from breaking up giant firms. And Biden appointed Jonathan Kanter, a longtime critic of Google, to lead the antitrust division of the Department of Justice.

89 For broad discussions of platformization, see especially van Dijck et al. 2018 and Nieborg

and Poell 2018. On Github as "a platform where platforms are assembled and configured," see Mackenzie 2018: 37.

90 On the decomposition of jobs into tasks, see Davis 2016: 167; Sundararajan 2016: 173ff; Casilli and Posada 2019. To be sure, some platforms do match persons with positions; on such automated hiring platforms, see Ajunwa and Greene 2019. My focus here, however, is on the matching of persons with tasks or projects.

91 Newman 2019.

92 A key driver of demand for crowdsourced microtasks is the need for staggering amounts of training data for the development of autonomous vehicles. This has called into being several new specialized crowdsourced microtask platforms that have differentiated themselves from Amazon Mechanical Turk and other generalist platforms by offering quality control, AI-enhanced production tools, and training and management of crowdworkers. These have offered more reliable work to their hundreds of thousands of workers, but not necessarily higher pay: workers make just $1–$2 per hour. As Schmidt (2019: 12) notes in his analysis of these new platforms, the growth of AI – in this case the development of autonomous vehicles – increases the demand for human labor to train the AI. But the volume of human labor is so great that there is great pressure to use AI tools to assist with the human labor of training AI: "The goal of the manual labour is the training of AI models, while at the same time similar algorithms are used to support the manual labour and make it more reliable and cost efficient. Humans and AI train each other." On the centrality of poorly paid microtasks to the development and functioning of AI more generally, see Crawford 2021: 63ff.

93 Ravenelle 2019; Schor 2020.

94 On sector-specific professional platforms, see Sundararajan 2017: 8 and Fuller et al. 2020.

95 https://www.upwork.com/resources/what-is-flexible-talent-management.

96 Drahokoupil and Piasna 2017.

97 On opportunities for independent micro-entrepreneurs in emerging economies, see Lehdonvirta et al. 2018; for a broader discussion of digital labor and development, see Graham et al. 2017.

98 Sundararajan 2016: 176; "the end of employment" is from the subtitle of that book. Though not an unqualified platform enthusiast, Sundararajan is broadly optimistic about the developments he describes; see for a concise statement Sundararajan 2017.

99 Schor 2020.

100 Ravenelle 2019: 1–2.

101 On the structural and cognitive constraints faced by online pieceworkers in managing their putatively flexible work schedules, see Lehdonvirta 2018. On the degree of workers' dependence on platforms for their living as a key to the differentiated experience of platform workers, see ibid. 23–4; Vallas and Schor 2020: 280–1.

102 Cunningham and Craig 2019, chapter 2.

103 The concept of "algorithmic management" was first used by Lee et al. (2015) in connection with the governance of work on ride-hailing platforms; it has been developed by Mateescu and Nguyen 2019, Kellogg et al. 2020, and Wood 2021.

104 Kellogg et al. 2020; see also Wood 2021.

105 The algorithmic micromanagement of workers on platforms such as Uber and Instacart, which goes well beyond the assignment of orders, is in tension with platforms' classification of workers as independent contractors, a classification that typically depends, in part, on the workers' labor not being controlled by the hiring company. The stakes of struggles over this classification are high, since classification as employees would entitle gig workers to a range of protections and benefits that are not made available to independent contractors. Still, most surveyed Uber and Lyft drivers prefer not to be defined as employees. For an

analysis of workers' ambivalence toward employee status, see Dubal 2020. On algorithmic control and information asymmetry in the case of Uber, see Rosenblat and Stark 2016. On information asymmetry in food delivery apps, see Wood 2021: 2. On algorithmic governance in food delivery apps, see Griesbach et al. 2019, noting cross-platform variation in modes of algorithmic management, and Chen and Sun 2020 for an ethnographic study of how Chinese food couriers deal with algorithmically governed expectations of delivery times.

106 On algorithm-driven flexible scheduling as a form of "flexible despotism," see Wood 2020.

107 Customers are enlisted in the evaluation process not only directly (as when passengers rate Uber drivers) but also indirectly (as when managers use customer tracking data to evaluate retail sales staff or comments on TripAdvisor to evaluate hotel staff). On the use of TripAdvisor reviews by hotel management, see Orlikowski and Scott 2014. On "monitoring customers to manage workers" more generally, as an instance of "refractive surveillance," see Levy and Barocas 2018.

108 Kellogg et al. 2020; Wood 2021. On Amazon warehouse work, see Delfanti 2021.

109 On the promise of people analytics from a business point of view, see Gal et al. 2019; for critical reflections on risks of people analytics, see Giermindl et al. 2022.

110 On automated hiring platforms, see Ajunwa and Greene 2019.

111 On such "algorithmic replacement," see Kellogg et al. 2020: 380–1.

112 Wood 2021.

113 On the monitoring of employee health and fitness – the most striking example of the extension of surveillance outside the workplace itself – see Ajunwa et al. 2017: 763–9; Manokha 2019. On algorithmically governed rewards and gamification, see Kellogg et al. 2020: 381–2; on gamification in Chinese food delivery apps, see Lei 2021: 291, 292.

114 Taylor 1911: 39. On digital Taylorism, see Delfanti and Frey 2021.

115 Kalleberg and Vallas 2018: 1.

116 Ibid. 5.

117 On the lower transaction costs of outsourcing, see Vallas 2019: 51, 53. On "algorithmic insecurity" as a distinctive form of precarity experienced on digital platforms, see Wood and Lehdonvirta 2021. The authors argue that the algorithmic insecurity associated with sometimes arbitrary and capricious reputational systems is experienced even by workers who have not (yet) received a bad rating.

118 Terranova (2000: 33) saw "free labor" in this double sense – both "voluntarily given and un-waged, enjoyed and exploited" – as an aspect of the "social factory," a phrase used by Italian autonomist Marxists to designate the shift of labor from distinct and enclosed workplaces to society at large. On the emergence of related notions of "immaterial labor" in autonomist Marxism, see Hesmondhalgh 2010: 272ff.

119 See for example Casilli 2016.

120 Hesmondhalgh (2010), for example, accepts the idea of unpaid labor but criticizes the claim that such labor is exploited. Writing from a Marxist perspective, Srnicek is more sharply critical of the idea of subsuming platform-based social interaction under the rubric of "labor," since such activity is not subject to the rationalizing pressures that apply to other parts of the capitalist productive process (2017: 53–6). For a recent review of the debate that draws a sharp distinction between the experience-near category of work and the experience-distant category of labor and develops the notion of "workless labor," see Schwarz 2021, chapter 6.

121 Duffy 2017: 8.

122 On consignment labor, see Kenney and Zysman 2019: 27–31; the quotation is from p. 27. On "aspirational labor," see Duffy 2017; the quotation is from p. 4 (italics omitted). See also the related notion of "hope labor," which refers to "un- or under-compensated [online]

work carried out in the present, often for experience or exposure, in the hope that future employment opportunities may follow" (Kuehn and Corrigan 2013).

123 Platforms such as Facebook, Twitter, and Pinterest that had been slow to offer creators opportunities to monetize have sought recently to catch up (Isaac and Lorenz 2021).

124 Casilli and Posada 2019: 299.

125 Cunningham and Craig 2019: 91f.

126 Duffy 2017: 211.

127 On the distinctive precarity of creative labor, dependent as it is on algorithmically mediated visibility, see Duffy et al. 2021.

128 For a collection of resources on cryptocurrency and related subjects, curated by Evgeny Morozov from a broadly critical perspective, see https://the-crypto-syllabus.com/. The site includes bibliographies on NFTs, DeFi, DAOs, and more. For a collection of boosterish analyses, hosted by the venture capitalist firm Andreessen Horowitz, see https://future.a16z.com/category/crypto-web3/. On DeFi specifically, see Gogel 2021 and – for concern about a new "shadow banking system" emerging under the umbrella of DeFi – Allen 2022.

129 For an accessible account of the essential work done by ledgers in establishing a consensual reality and the fundamental transformation in the nature of ledgers enabled by blockchain, see Berg et al. 2017; for a more formal account, see Davidson et al. 2018.

130 Sklaroff (2017) has argued that the use of smart contracts to automate contracting and eliminate human intermediaries introduces new inefficiencies and that the flexibility occasioned by the linguistic ambiguity and enforcement discretion that are central to traditional "semantic contracts" actually makes for greater efficiency.

131 On the populist appeal of Bitcoin, see Atkins 2022. On what I have called transactionalization – the proliferation of market transactions through the reduction of transaction costs – see Berg et al. 2017: "The blockchain, through smart contracts, lowers the information costs and transactions costs associated with many incomplete contracts and so expands the scale and scope of economic activity. … It allows markets to operate where before only large firms could operate, and it allows business and markets to operate where before only government could operate."

132 On anarcho-capitalist elements in blockchain discourse, see Flood and Robb 2017. On the crystallization of libertarian claims in response to the Canadian government's obstruction of Bitcoin transactions during the 2022 truckers' occupation of Ottawa, see Silverman 2022.

133 The opposition to centralized platforms, to be sure, is much sharper in rhetoric than in reality. Marc Andreessen, for example, continues to sit on the Board of Directors of Facebook/Meta even as the venture capital firm he cofounded, Andreessen Horowitz, has been investing heavily in crypto startups.

134 On the internet as a "low-trust society," see Tufekci 2019.

135 For influential and unabashedly evangelical accounts, see Tapscott and Tapscott 2018 and (for a focus on "technologies of freedom") Allen et al. 2020.

136 The energy costs result from the enormous computational power required to solve the cryptographic problems that are used to ensure – in Bitcoin's "proof-of-work" system – the integrity of the ledger. The evident unsustainability of proof-of-work validation on a larger scale has led other cryptocurrencies to adopt "proof-of-stake" systems as an alternative, but those face their own technical challenges. On the failure of cryptocurrencies to meet the basic criteria of a currency, see Diehl 2021b. On the broader phenomenon of digital currencies, including the digital wallets operated by WeChat and Alipay that are widely used in China, see Brunnermeier et al. 2021.

137 On the myth of complete disintermediation and the reality of re-intermediation, see Caliskan 2020: 552–3; Leveneur and Heudebert 2020: 282ff; Allen 2022.

138 Diehl 2021a.

139 Morozov 2022.

140 On the smooth absorption of blockchain into the existing order, see Kohl 2021: 9–11. As Kohl observes, "dominant political and economic actors will look to new technology for opportunities for maintaining, reinforcing and enhancing the status quo, and some of these ways may produce the very opposite outcomes to those articulated in utopian narratives" (p. 11).

Chapter 5: Politics

1 The cartoon is reprinted in *Public Domain Review*, n.d.

2 On the similarities between hopes and fears aroused by radio in its early decades and those aroused by the internet today, see Smith 2014.

3 For a sharp critique of the limitations of the "minimal effects" literature, even in the American context, see Zaller 1996; on the limitations in comparative perspective, with reference to Mexico, see Lawson and McCann 2005. On television and personalistic populist leaders in Latin America, see Weyland 2001: 16; Boas 2005. On the intertwined personalization and television-focused mediatization of politics in Italy and France, focusing on Berlusconi and Sarkozy, see Campus 2010. On Netanyahu and "telepopulism" in Israel, see Peri 2004.

4 On "mass self-communication," see Castells 2013 [2009]: xix–xxiii, 58–71. On the internet's contribution to a more robustly democratic "networked public sphere," see Benkler 2006, chapter 7.

5 For a sophisticated though on balance celebratory account of the "new species of social movement" created by networked digital communications technology, see Castells 2012. On digital media and the "logic of connective action," which bypasses formal organization and mobilizes using broad, personalizable, meme-like appeals rather than tighter, more exclusive collective identities, see Bennett and Segerberg 2013; Schwarz 2021: 63–73. For a nuanced appraisal of "networked protest," underscoring the ambivalent affordances of social media for social movements, see Tufekci 2014b, 2017. For a recent account that remains optimistic about the possibilities of digital democracy, see Deseriis 2021.

6 On forms of "computational politics" that are guided by micro-targeting, see Tufekci 2014a; on the significance of targeted advertising during the 2016 American election, see Vaidhyanathan 2018: 161–74. In response to massive criticism about its role during that election – especially the criticism that targeted ads, unlike publicly visible broadcast ads, were invisible to all but the targeted – Facebook created an Ad Archive in 2018 (expanded and rechristened as its Ad Library in 2019). In principle, this allows anyone to see and search for currently running and past advertisements. But researchers have sharply criticized the Ad Library's many limitations; see for example Dubois et al. 2022.

7 For a nuanced account of the role of WhatsApp in the 2019 election in Nigeria, see Cheeseman et al. 2020; on WhatsApp during the 2018 election in Brazil, see Evangelista and Bruno 2019.

8 For a powerful critique of a narrow focus on technology, see Benkler et al. 2018; their argument for a more historical and institutional approach is summarized at pp. 20–3. For a nuanced, historically and institutionally grounded account of transformations of the public, understood in consistently relational terms, see Starr 2021b.

9 The notion of a "structure of feeling" was developed in a number of writings by Raymond Williams; see notably Williams 1961. On "feeling rules," see Hochschild 1983.

10 See for example Andrejevic 2013 on "infoglut"; Benkler et al. 2018 on "network propaganda" and "epistemic crisis"; Eyal 2019 on the "crisis of expertise"; Rauch 2021 on the "constitution of knowledge"; and Edenberg and Hannon 2021 on the emerging academic subfield of "political epistemology."

11 On the democratic implications of citizen journalism and the related phenomenon of "social journalism," see Goode 2009.

12 On the (unfulfilled) promise of "liquid feedback," an online polling system developed for the German Pirate Party to allow the party to more accurately understand the views of its members, see Morozov 2013a: 102–3.

13 On the dynamics of circulation of misinformation, see Shao et al. 2018; Vosoughi et al. 2018.

14 For a lucid recent overview, see Starr 2021a. For a sophisticated approach to the sharing of fake news on social media platforms, informed by a broad "sociotechnical" approach to media effects, see Marwick 2018.

15 On the "participatory turn," see Mede and Schäfer 2020: 477–8.

16 On lay expertise, see Epstein 1995; Callon 1999; Prior 2003.

17 On the "proliferation and diversification of cultural authority" in the domain of medicine and health, see Epstein and Timmermans 2021. On the idea that parents are experts on the health of their own children, an idea that is prevalent in well-educated vaccine-hesitant milieux, see Reich 2016, chapter 2.

18 See Toff and Nielsen's (2018) empirical study of "folk theories of distributed discovery" in digitally mediated environments, focusing on individuals who do not regularly engage directly with media producers. The authors highlight the recurring refrain, "I just google it" (p. 647).

19 On the folk theory underlying this sense of paralysis, the sense that "I just don't know what to believe," see ibid. 649–53. On the contribution of digital hyperconnectivity to the crisis of public knowledge more broadly, see Brubaker 2017a; Sacasas 2021a.

20 Tufekci 2017: 228–41; the quotations are from pp. 228, 231, and 241. On the critical importance of trusted intermediaries, see pp. 231, 240, and 244. China has developed particularly sophisticated capacities for distracting citizens at key junctures through coordinated high-volume social media posts. On "flooding" as a technique of distraction in China, see Roberts 2018, chapter 6. On digital authoritarianism and disinformation in the Middle East, see Jones 2022.

21 Bannon is quoted in Lewis 2018.

22 Quandt's observation from a decade ago – that widespread distrust of what appears to be a "produced" and manipulated "media reality" is often accompanied by trust in a seemingly more authentic "user-generated reality" (2012: 8) – remains pertinent today. See also Toff and Nielsen 2018.

23 On epistemic hubris in contemporary American politics, though not in connection with digital hyperconnectivity, see Barker et al. 2022.

24 This and the next two paragraphs draw on Brubaker 2021.

25 "Greatest threat": New York Times Editorial Board 2020.

26 Flaxman et al. 2020.

27 Gorvett 2020.

28 The claim that the vaccines have caused more deaths than they have prevented can be found not only in fringe milieux but in a peer-reviewed journal article (Kostoff et al. 2021), though that article was retracted in May 2022 after a post-publication review.

29 On the proliferation of channels and the "end of mass communication," see Chaffee and Metzger 2001.

30 On the boost given to conspiracy thinking by the internet, see Aupers 2012: 26–7; Harambam 2017: 173ff; Boullier et al. 2021.

31 On epistemic individualism in relation to conspiracy theories, see Guillon 2018; on epistemic populism, see Saurette and Gunster 2011; on counter-knowledge, see Ylä-Anttila 2018.

32 See for example Conrad 2021. For a bracingly skeptical view of the purported "crisis of truth," see Shapin 2019.

33 The quotations are drawn from Sacasas 2021a, written in the aftermath of the January 2021 attack on the Capitol.

34 For the concern that the AI-powered natural language-generating model GPT-3 – trained on a vast corpus of internet text data and capable of producing convincing new text on any topic – could radically disrupt human communication by making it impossible to infer anything about human intentionality from textual data, see Munger 2020a.

35 On the contribution of large language models like GPT-3 to the automation of disinformation, see DiResta 2020. Since such models can generate plausible new essays on any subject, they will also pose a major challenge to practices designed to ensure academic integrity; see Dehouche 2021.

36 Conceptualizations of affect and of the "affective turn" vary widely. For some, "affect" designates the realm of feeling and emotions; for others, it refers to pre-linguistic bodily states and disturbances as distinguished from culturally codified and linguistically expressed emotions; for still others, the term "loses its mooring in studies of human emotion and expands to signify disturbance and influence in their most global senses" (Wetherell 2012: 2). I use "affect," "feeling," and "emotion" in broadly synonymous ways.

37 For a wide-ranging review of work on emotions in protest and social movements, see Jasper 2011. Much work on emotions and politics – including that of Jasper, a sociologist – has been done by scholars outside political science, which remains dominated by rationalist approaches.

38 For pioneering discussions of parasocial relationships, see Horton and Wohl 1956; Horton and Strauss 1957. On "mediated quasi-interaction" and "non-reciprocal intimacy at a distance," see Thompson 1995: 84, 219ff. More recently, scholars have discussed parasocial relationships developed in social media contexts. On the political significance of parasocial bonds with Trump, formed through exposure to *The Apprentice* and other media, see Gabriel et al. 2018; on the political significance of the parasocial relationships fostered by YouTube, see Munger and Phillips 2022; on parasocial relationships with talk radio and cable TV hosts, see Berry and Sobieraj 2014: 133. On social media and the informalization of politics, which may foster parasocial relationships, see Manning et al. 2017.

39 For overviews, see Mazzoleni and Schulz 1999; Mazzoleni 2008; Esser 2013.

40 For a broad discussion of the relation between emotions, media, and politics, see Wahl-Jorgensen 2019. On the role of TikTok in mobilizing political identity and affect via information-rich visual cues and embodied memes, see Munger 2020b.

41 Castells 2012: 15.

42 Papacharissi 2015: 6, 130–1. For a broader critique of austere Habermasian deliberative rationality in favor of invoking "the imaginary, the poetic, the capacity to ridicule, the ethical and the emotional in striking new ways," see Watts's sympathetic account of the capacity of the unruly politics of Anonymous and 4chan to suggest "new conceptions of the political" (2019: 85).

43 See for example Massanari (2017) on Reddit as a breeding ground for "toxic technocultures."

44 On the political ambivalence of anger, one of the key components of moral outrage, see Wahl-Jorgensen 2019: 12. On anger dynamics in protest movements, see Jasper 2014.

45 On the positive role of outrage, see Castells 2012; Spring et al. 2018. In their critique of the latter, Brady and Crockett (2019) note that while outrage can mobilize and energize collective action, it can also undermine the capacity to act strategically, focus attention on immediately salient issues, limit the ability to take account of complexity, foster blame and distrust, and discourage marginalized groups – those most vulnerable, especially in an online environment, to coordinated outraged harassment – from participating in the public sphere.

46 On this association, see Darley and Pittman 2003: 332f; Salerno and Peter-Hagene 2013;

Brady et al. 2020a: 985–6. On the "other-condemning" emotions in the broader context of an account of the moral emotions as a whole, see Haidt 2003.

47 On the processes through which people who engage in harassment may come to believe that their actions are justified, see Lewis et al. 2021. The reported prevalence of online harassment in the US is high. A Pew Research Center study reported that 41 percent of Americans had personally experienced online harassment in 2020, while two-thirds had observed others being harassed (Vogels 2021). Of course, not all harassment is prompted by moral outrage, just as not all expressions of moral outrage issue in harassment.

48 On outrage as a business model in talk radio and cable news, see Berry and Sobieraj 2014; on the regulatory changes that enabled this business model to flourish, see pp. 75–80.

49 In a study of Twitter, Brady et al. 2017 found that adding a single moral-emotional word (a word with both moral and emotional resonance) to a tweet increases the frequency of retweets by 20 percent, even after controlling for the effects of moral and emotional language on their own. In an environment in which the rapid scanning of superabundant content leaves one only milliseconds to decide, quasi-automatically, whether to engage or move on to the next post or tweet, content that captures our attention has a much greater chance of spreading (Brady et al. 2020a: 993). On social media engagement with attention-capturing moral and emotional content, see also Brady et al. 2020b.

50 The incentives to produce *engaging* content, of course, do not always translate into incentives to produce *outrageous* content. During the mid-century era of network television dominance in the US, commercial incentives – deriving from the need to assemble the broadest possible audiences – pointed *away* from the production of outrage (Berry and Sobieraj 2014: 80).

51 For evidence of the "reinforcement learning" through which social media metrics encourage the expression of outrage, see Brady et al. 2021.

52 On the affective dimensions of misinformation and "junk news," see Boler and Davis 2020; Savolainen et al. 2020; Serrano-Puche 2021.

53 The popular and influential Libs of Tiktok Twitter account, for example, reposts (and of course decontextualizes and tendentiously reframes) TikToks and social media posts in a manner calculated to incite outrage among its devoted conservative followers; its modus operandi depends on the abundance of easily accessible outrage-inducing material.

54 On the nationalization of news and its relation to the nationalization of politics in the US, see Hopkins 2018; Moskowitz 2021.

55 On the abundance of outrage-provoking material in a big country with a highly integrated and centralized media system, see Yglesias 2021.

56 On selective editing in outrage-mobilizing "response videos" on YouTube, see Lewis et al. 2021.

57 On digitally mediated interaction as "self-documenting," see Schwarz 2021, chapter 2; on context collapse, outrage, and political de-friending on Facebook, see Schwarz and Shani 2016.

58 On outrage and counter-outrage and the interactive logic of "digital political performativity," see De Kosnik 2019.

59 Haidt and Rose-Stockwell (2019) highlight specific changes made by social media platforms that accelerated the circulation of outrage, especially the Retweet button introduced by Twitter in 2009 and the equivalent Share button introduced on Facebook's mobile app in 2012.

60 On the lower costs of expressing moral outrage online, see Crockett 2017: 770. On the general process of "concept creep" through which concepts of harm have been expanding, see Haslam 2016. For an analysis and critique of "political hobbyism," a form of political participation driven by voracious, hyper-partisan, and often outrage-energized consumption of and engagement with political news, chiefly in online contexts, see Hersh 2020.

61 On the reputational benefits of expressing outrage in online environments, see Crockett 2017: 770.

62 On moral grandstanding, see Tosi and Warmke 2020.

63 On the transformation of public shaming, see Koganzon 2015.

64 For a broader theoretical discussion of how digital objectification extends the scope of accountability in space and time, see Schwarz 2021: 33–5.

65 On hyper-politics, see Jäger 2022.

66 On affective polarization, see Iyengar et al. 2019. The related concept of "negative partisanship" emphasizes that increased antipathy toward the other party is not accompanied by stronger positive feelings for one's own party; see Abramowitz and Webster 2016. Affective polarization has emerged over several decades in response to long-term causes, including increased alignment between partisan, ideological, religious, and racial identities. Here as elsewhere, hyperconnectivity – and social media in particular – serves as an intensifier rather than as a prime cause. Whether affective polarization and negative partisanship have been accompanied by increased ideological polarization among ordinary citizens remains under debate.

67 On false polarization in the US, see Levendusky and Malhotra 2016. On affective polarization as a consequence of exaggerated views of issue polarization, see Levendusky and Malhotra 2014, who attribute false polarization to media coverage of politics, but without discussing social media. On the contribution of social media to false polarization, see Settle 2018: 97, 173–283; Brady et al. 2020a: 989; Bail 2021: 67, 75–6, 99–102.

68 On the inescapability of politics on Facebook, even for those who are not interested in politics, see Settle 2018: 1–16, 44, 64, 134–5.

69 Kim et al. 2021.

70 Bail 2021: 68–83.

71 On false polarization as self-fulfilling, see Ahler 2014, arguing that mistaken beliefs about the degree of ideological polarization of others' views lead people to adopt slightly more ideologically polarized positions themselves.

72 Morozov 2014.

73 For a survey of the wide range of public sector algorithmic governance in the US, see Engstrom et al. 2020. On the "dataist state," see Fourcade and Gordon 2020: 81. On "dataism" as an ideology, see van Dijck 2014.

74 On algorithmic risk assessment in the criminal justice context, see Stevenson 2018. For an accessible overview of controversies this has provoked, see Tashea 2017.

75 On predictive policing, see Bennett Moses and Chan 2018.

76 On algorithmic prediction of risk of abuse to children, see Eubanks 2018, chapter 4. On algorithmic identification of those at risk of suicide by the Veterans Administration, see Carey 2020.

77 Engstrom et al. 2020: 22ff.

78 Ibid. 39ff.

79 Ibid. 60ff.

80 Although China's social credit system has been characterized as an "epitome" of the global trend toward algorithmic governance (Zou 2021: 140), this characterization seems at best premature, and it seems to conflate governance through data with algorithmic governance. As China scholars Adam Knight and Rogier Creemers, authors of the sharpest historically informed accounts of the origins and development of the social credit system (Creemers 2018; Knight 2021) observe, it is "notable that big data analytics, artificial intelligence and machine learning are absent from social credit mechanisms" (Knight and Creemers 2021: 6). The social credit system – keeping in mind that it is not a single coherent all-encompassing system, but

a congeries of variously scaled and differently designed initiatives, some directly implemented by branches of the central state, others introduced by municipalities, still others by giant tech firms under government sponsorship (Liu 2019) – is extremely interesting from the point of view of the development of what Cheung and Chen (2021) call a "data state." But machine learning and algorithmic governance are at present much more centrally implicated in other aspects of China's formidable surveillance capacities – notably in its immense investments in facial recognition technology (Mozur 2019; Standaert 2021) – than they are in the social credit system.

81 On the ways in which platforms govern – while at the same time being themselves subject to governance – see Gorwa 2019: 856ff.

82 I add the qualification "in some measure" in reference to the perennial problem of attempting to specify media effects: it is difficult to distinguish empirically between selection effects (self-selection onto a particular platform, for example, or a particular media provider) and causal effects (as in the claim that YouTube radicalizes viewers). For a review of this difficulty, with respect to the question of whether patterns of partisan media use *reflect* or *cause* polarization, see de Benedictis-Kessner et al. 2020.

83 On the increased commingling of public and private in digital governance, see Harcourt 2015, chapter 7; Tréguer 2019; Fourcade and Gordon 2020.

84 On the nineteenth-century "avalanche of printed numbers," see Hacking 1982. For an appreciation of the literature on the relation between politics and numbers, likewise broadly Foucauldian in inspiration, that distinguishes a European strand more focused on bureaucracy, surveillance, and domination from a more optimistic and pluralist American strand, see Rose 1991. For a recent analysis of informational power and informational politics in the first half of the twentieth century – this too, broadly Foucauldian – see Koopman 2019. For a broad American take on the relation between politics and numbers, more eclectic in theoretical inspiration, see Starr 1987.

85 For a concise and accessible account of the "machine learning revolution," see Domingos 2015, chapter 1; on the importance of the sheer volume of data, see especially pp. 7, 12. The dependence of machine learning on huge volumes of data also accounts for the enormous advantages in the race to develop machine learning (and artificial intelligence more broadly) enjoyed by Google, Facebook, and other giant data-intensive platforms.

86 For the classic discussion of "high modernist" ways of "seeing like a state," see Scott 1998. On "new ways of seeing like a state" in the developing world that differ from the high modernist style, see Johns 2019. For a wide-ranging discussion of new algorithmic ways of "learning like a state," see Fourcade and Gordon 2020.

87 For an argument that pervasive digital mediation per se has made the social world both more knowable and more governable, see Schwarz 2021: 123ff.

88 Zuboff 2020.

89 On the concentrated control over digital data as a key form of power and source of inequality and a fundamental challenge to democratic citizenship, see Andrejevic 2013: 154.

90 These are among the key controversies and concerns identified in slightly different terms in Katzenbach and Ulbricht's (2019) concise overview of algorithmic governance.

91 For a legal perspective on the "paradox of automation" – that automation introduced in an effort to prevent discrimination may contribute to reproducing discrimination – see Ajunwa 2019. For an argument that algorithms can serve as a helpful corrective to cognitive or other biases, see Sunstein 2019. For evidence that automation reduced racial disparities in access to small business credit in a program designed to support employment in small businesses during the pandemic, see Howell et al. 2021.

92 For a systematic discussion of the many choices involved in preparing and training machine

learning algorithms, see Lehr and Ohm 2017. On the "problem of tainted training data" in connection with predictive policing algorithms, see Huq 2019: 1076ff. On sources of discriminatory treatment in the design of algorithms more generally, see Kroll 2017: 678ff. For a broad discussion of race and technology from the perspective of "race critical code studies," see Benjamin 2019.

93　On strategies for assuring algorithmic fairness, see Kroll 2017. On algorithms as a means of detecting and combating discrimination, see Kleinberg et al. 2019.

94　On the tension between normative expectations of transparent and accountable governance and algorithmic opacity, see Engstrom and Ho 2021: 6off. For an accessible account of the algorithmically governed "black box society," with proposals for increased transparency, see Pasquale 2015.

95　On problems of gaming in the context of algorithmic governance, see Engstrom and Ho 2021: 67–9.

96　For these and other ways of addressing challenges of transparency and accountability, see ibid. 60–2. On the limits to transparency as an ideal, focusing specifically on the limits of transparency as a means of assuring algorithmic accountability, see Ananny and Crawford 2018.

97　Virginia Eubanks, for example, found that when workers in a child protection agency encountered a discrepancy between their own assessments of risk of abuse and those of an algorithmic model, they were inclined to second-guess their own judgment (2018: 141–2).

98　On the human costs of automation, see Carr 2014.

99　Schwarz 2021, chapter 5, drawing on Lash's (2007) distinction between regulative and generative rules.

100　Zuboff (2019: 212–21) notes that it was Google's chief economist, Hal Varian, who observed that digitally mediated remote control could transform the meaning of contracting.

101　On "tuning" and "herding," see Zuboff 2019, chapter 10.

102　Content moderation is analyzed with exemplary lucidity by Gillespie 2018. On the changing regulatory and discursive environment that has fostered the turn to automated content moderation, see Katzenbach 2021; on the sudden turn to automated moderation during the pandemic, see Scott and Kayali 2020.

103　Facebook has reported in recent years on rates of "proactivity" (the share of violating content discovered by algorithms before being flagged by users). Proactivity has increased most dramatically for hate speech, from 24 percent in 2017 to 98 percent in 2021. Proactivity for bullying – hard to detect algorithmically because it is often context-specific – increased from just 13 percent in the second quarter of 2020 to 54 percent nine months later. Increases were much smaller for other categories, but only because proactivity was already high by the time rates began to be reported, in 2017 or 2018. For example, proactivity increased for "organized hate" from 89 percent in 2018 to 98 percent in 2021, and for terrorism from 97 percent in 2017 to 99.7 percent in 2021. The data – specifically for the Facebook platform; Instagram data are reported separately – can be downloaded from https://transparency.fb.com/data/community-standards-enforcement/.

104　In 2018, Facebook officials noted that the company automatically removes suspected terrorist content "in some cases" yet "still rel[ies] on specialized reviewers to evaluate most posts" (Gorwa et al. 2020: 9). By 2021, the message was different: the company reported that it removes millions of posts that violate its policies every day, and that "most of this happens automatically, with technology working behind the scenes to remove violating content— often before anyone sees it" (https://transparency.fb.com/enforcement/detecting-violations/technology-detects-violations/; retrieved November 3, 2021). In most cases, it is "a simple matter" to ascertain whether a post violates Facebook policies; it is only when this is more

difficult – "perhaps [because] the sentiment of the post is unclear, its language is particularly complex or its imagery too context-dependent" – that the post is referred to human
reviewers (https://transparency.fb.com/policies/improving/prioritizing-content-review/;
retrieved November 3, 2021). Some content is not simply removed before anyone flags it
or even before anyone sees it; it is prevented from being uploaded at all. In the twenty-four
hours after the 2019 live-streamed massacre at a mosque in Christchurch, New Zealand, for
example, Facebook was able to automatically block 80 percent of some 1.5 million attempts
to upload versions of the video. For this "incredible technical and computational feat" to
be possible, every video that all Facebook users tried to upload had to be instantly matched
against a hastily assembled database of some 800 versions of the attack video (Gorwa et al.
2020: 2).

105 "Every time reviewers make a decision, we use that information to train our technology. Over
time, across millions of decisions, our technology gets better, allowing us to remove more
violating content." https://transparency.fb.com/policies/improving/prioritizing-content-
review/. On the psychological stresses of the work of content moderation, see Roberts 2019:
111–23. For skepticism about the possibility of thoroughly automated content moderation,
see Gillespie 2018: 97–110.

106 On the additional power automated ex ante content moderation would confer on platforms'
already great power over speech, see Cobbe 2021.

107 On the danger of the algorithmic depoliticization of fundamentally political issues about
what counts as appropriate speech, see Gorwa et al. 2020: 11–12.

108 On the materiality of digitally mediated power, see Schwarz 2021, chapters 4 and 5.

109 On populism as a deeply contested concept, see Brubaker 2017b: 358ff; on the decades-
spanning structural transformations fostering a chronic populism in late modern liberal
democratic contexts, see ibid. 369ff. For purposes of the present argument, I understand by
"populism" a discursive and stylistic repertoire that features direct appeals to "the people,"
understood as "ordinary" people, against elites and against the mediating institutions and
modes of expression of the "establishment."

110 On the promise of "disintermediating politics" by cutting out party bureaucrats through
forms of intra-party digital direct democracy, see Gerbaudo 2019: 70f, 75f, 183f.

111 For a critique of the "myth of the neutral platform," see Gillespie 2018, chapter 2.

112 On the hostility of populism to intermediary bodies, see Urbinati 2015.

113 On the connotations of "platform," see Gillespie 2010.

114 On the affinities between the affordances of social media and populist political appeals, see
Gerbaudo 2018; see also Tucker et al. 2017. On the ways in which the affordances of YouTube
have made the platform a hospitable space for the emergence of an alternative right-wing
ecosystem appealing to the disaffected, see Munger and Phillips 2022: 193–8.

115 On digital democracy initiatives, see Gerbaudo 2019; Deseriis 2021.

116 On "calculated publics," see Gillespie 2014. On the ways in which trending algorithms
both record and reinforce popularity, providing an "invitation to value" the items they
visibilize, see Gillespie 2016. As Gillespie notes, popularity-reinforcing cultural metrics (such
as best-seller lists or "Top 40" songs) have a long pre-digital history, but they have become
ubiquitous and much more granular under digital hyperconnectivity.

117 On new modalities of "algorithmic populism," and specifically on strategies of "algorithmic
activism" that use the affordances of digital media in an effort to boost the popularity of
digital political messaging, see Maly 2022.

118 On "low" style as central to populism, see Ostiguy 2009.

119 On attention as a scarce political resource, see Tufekci 2013b.

120 Morozov (2013a: 5) defines solutionism as the habit of "recasting complex social situations

either as neatly defined problems with definite, computable solutions or as transparent and self-evident processes that can be easily optimized – if only the right algorithms are in place." On Silicon Valley's "technological imaginary," see Ferrari 2020.

121 Sætra 2020: 2. For an accessible critique of the logic of optimization, see Reich et al. 2021, chapter 1.

122 Oakeshott 1991: 9.

123 On antagonistic re-politicization as an element of the populist repertoire, see Brubaker 2017b: 364.

124 Bickerton and Invernizzi Accetti 2015, 2021. On the concept of "party democracy" and the long-term erosion in the capacity of political parties to organize and mediate the links between voters and governments, see also Mair 2002: 84ff.

125 Bickerton and Invernizzi Accetti 2021: 18. The internet and digital technology are mentioned only in connection with the Italian Five Star Movement; they do not figure at all in the authors' general account of the origins, logic, or consequences of technopopulism. For an alternative understanding of technopopulism as "the belief that the 'government of the people, by the people, for the people' … is achievable by means of information communications technology," see Deseriis 2017.

126 Bickerton and Invernizzi Accetti 2021: 218.

Conclusion

1 Bogost 2020.

2 The extent and quality of this digital infrastructure are of course highly variable, both between and within countries.

3 Austin 2020a.

4 On the "pandemic shock doctrine" or "screen new deal," see Klein 2020.

5 Schmidt 2020. On Schmidt's central position in the powerful networks pushing for public–private partnerships in which "public schools, hospitals, doctor's offices, police, and military [would] all outsourc[e] (at a high cost) many of their core functions to private tech companies," see Klein 2020.

6 On tech platforms' moves into medical research and the broader health field as part of the emergence of a "platform society," see van Dijck et al. 2018: 97–116.

7 On pre-pandemic restrictions on telemedicine, see Keesara et al. 2020. On Amazon Care, focused on virtual services but offering in-person mobile care at patients' homes as well, see Black 2021, who notes that the ambitions of Amazon to "disrupt" healthcare build on the fact that the company has long ceased to be primarily an online retailer and is fundamentally "a logistics, cloud technology, and analytics company."

8 For critical discussions of the joint Google–Apple initiative to develop the technical basis for an automated Bluetooth-based, privacy-preserving, decentralized contact tracing app, see Sharon 2020; Mann et al. 2021; Storeng and de Bengy Puyvallée 2021. For concerns about digital surveillance during Covid, see Sekalala et al. 2020.

9 On conspicuous platform philanthropy during the pandemic, see Cinnamon 2020; Sharon 2020. On the harnessing of the platforms' "infrastructural power" for public health surveillance purposes, see Tréguer 2021 (drawing on Michael Mann's distinction between "despotic" and "infrastructural" power).

10 On platforms' efforts to highlight their "public value" during the pandemic, see Cinnamon 2020; on the retrospective re-legitimation of platform surveillance practices, see Tréguer 2021: 30.

11 On edtech initiatives in response to the pandemic, see especially the reports of Williamson and Hogan (2020, 2021), the former focused on K-12 education, the latter on higher

education. The quotations are from Williamson and Hogan 2020: 3, 1. On tech-promoted visions of a data-driven "learnification" of education, in which holistic understandings of education are displaced by a focus on discrete and measurable instances of learning, see van Dijck et al. 2018: 124f. Premised on decomposition, quantification, and miniaturization, the learnification of education is similar in certain respects to the taskification of work that I discussed in chapter 4; see pp. 114–15.

12 On the notion of digital liveness in historical and philosophical perspective, see Auslander 2012; for interesting pre-pandemic reflections on "liveness in the digital age," see Sanden 2019.

13 On Fortnite as a social space, especially a space for kids to hang out together, see Hassan 2018.

14 On the rise of game live streaming as a new form of "networked broadcasting," see Taylor 2018.

15 On new forms of digital "liveness," see Vandenberg et al. 2021 (although the authors note that for the virtual rave concerts they studied, participants felt the essence of the experience – dancing in the physical copresence of others – was lost). On the ways in which virtual reality can create a sense of "presence," see Bolter et al. 2021: 71ff, 141ff. VR did not have a breakthrough moment for live music during the pandemic; VR headsets, though getting cheaper and better, were simply not widely enough available. But the pandemic did spur all kinds of VR music initiatives; see Roettgers 2021.

16 On the hybrid, interactive future of live events, see Damiani 2021b.

17 On the market opportunities of virtual concerts, see Steele and Needleman 2021. For broader reflections on the possibilities of the digital experience economy, see Horning 2020c.

18 On Zoom fatigue, see Sacasas 2020; Bailenson 2021.

19 On remote work using AR and VR tools, see Estes 2020; Bolter et al. 2021: 117–18; Damiani 2021a. "Better experience": Zoom CEO Eric Yuan, quoted in Zahn and Serwer 2021. (Zoom has been investing heavily in AR and VR tools.)

20 Microsoft posted a public-facing video entitled "What is Microsoft's Metaverse?" (Microsoft 2021a) just a week after Facebook's name change, in evident response to the public discussion and attention that move had created. But Microsoft had positioned itself as a leader in the emerging metaverse business before Facebook's public metaverse pivot (Microsoft 2021b). Perhaps because Microsoft's AR-focused metaverse undertakings addressed business clients rather than consumers, or perhaps simply because this was not presented as a fundamental turning point for the company, this garnered much less public attention. Epic Games and Roblox had likewise been talking up the metaverse before Facebook's pivot. Epic Games framed its legal case against the rents extracted by Apple for in-game purchases through its App Store in terms of its efforts to build an open metaverse (Griffith 2021), while Roblox CEO David Baszucki observed that the metaverse "started to feel very real in 2020" as the pandemic brought people onto gaming platforms for a widening range of experiences – including birthday parties, job interviews, concerts, and movie premieres – beyond the games for which they had been designed (Baszucki 2021). For an argument that Epic Games' Fortnite is best positioned to take the lead in this area, see Park 2020; for an argument that Microsoft's vision of the metavese is "much more grounded and realistic" than that of Facebook, see Campa 2021. Google and Apple have eschewed talking about the metaverse per se, but they too have made immense investments in AR and VR.

21 Zuckerberg, quoted in Newton 2021.

22 The massive selloff precipitated by slowing growth in its user base – the company lost a quarter of its value in a single day in February 2022 – has made Facebook/Meta's huge bet on the metaverse all the more vital to the long-term success of the company. On the demand from flush venture capital investors for a big new idea to invest in, see Merchant 2021b.

23 Horning 2021. For a short film that explores the dystopian possibilities of hyper-commercialized AR, see Matsuda 2016.

24 On the origins of the metaverse concept in dystopian fiction – Neal Stephenson's *Snow Crash* and Ernest Cline's *Ready Player One* – see Merchant 2021a. Quotations in this paragraph are from this article.

25 For the interview, a mixture of often satirical questions and serious answers, see Soldo 2021. For a thoughtful reflection on Andreessen, see Sacasas 2021b. For a philosophical defense of virtual reality, arguing that "in the long run, virtual worlds may have most of what is good about the nonvirtual world," see Chalmers 2022: 330.

26 For an influential early survey of the digital divide and digital inequality more broadly, see DiMaggio et al. 2004; for a recent collection, see Hargittai 2021.

27 Bowles 2018, 2019.

28 On the "post-Orwellian surveillance state," see Giroux 2015. On the surge of interest in Orwell prompted by the Snowden revelations, see Harcourt 2015: 31f.

29 On the camps, see Amnesty International 2021; Byler 2021. For estimates on numbers interned, see the sources cited in the Amnesty report, p. 48.

30 On the surveillance state in Xinjiang, see Leibold 2020; Byler 2021.

31 On the connections between Covid, intensifying surveillance, and the longer-term development of data-driven "social governance" in China, see Bernot et al. 2021 and (for a focus on the social credit system) Knight and Creemers 2021.

32 On the health code system and its contribution to broader systems of social control and discipline, see Cong 2021; the quotation is from p. 6. For the use of the health code in controlling dissent, see Buckley et al. 2022.

33 For a discussion of the social credit system as "merely one manifestation of the global age of the algorithm," see Loubere and Brehm 2018. On the social credit system, see also Creemers 2018; Liu 2019; Knight 2021. On the intensification of surveillance and social control during the pandemic as indicative of a drift toward "authoritarian liberalism" in the West, see Tréguer 2021.

34 On the limitations of Orwell's vision for understanding the present, see Harcourt 2015: 39–53.

35 Huxley 1958: 44.

36 Huxley 1950 [1932]: 66–7, 282.

37 Huxley 1958: 46, 45.

38 Ibid. 45–6.

39 The quotations are from Huxley's 1946 foreword to *Brave New World* (Huxley 1950 [1932], no page number). Huxley expressed similar ideas in his letter to Orwell (Huxley 1949) and in the reflections collected in *Brave New World Revisited* (Huxley 1958).

40 As critics have noted, Zuboff tends to take at face value the hyperbolic claims made to investors and advertisers about the effectiveness of surveillance-guided micro-targeting (Doctorow 2020; MacKenzie 2021). And when Zuboff writes, as she does recurrently, about behavioral modification efforts achieving "heightened probability that approximates certainty" (2019: 295) or about "a market project of total certainty" (379ff), this should be understood as a speculative projection about the future – that is, as a form of social science fiction – rather than an analysis of the present.

41 Zuboff 2020.

42 Zuboff 2019: 8.

43 "Instrumentarian power": ibid. 352, 376ff; "creature of the market": ibid. 326.

44 "Meanings and motives": ibid. 360; "engineering of souls" and "engineering of behavior": ibid. 376.

45 Ibid. 377; "ubiquitous sensate, networked, computational infrastructure": ibid. 20.

46 On "architectures of control," the influential contribution of Lessig (1999) remains relevant, as does Castells' account of the dialectical relationship between "technologies of freedom" and "technologies of control" (2001, chapter 6). For a broader historical perspective on the centrality of information processing to the "control revolution," see Beniger 1986: 8–11.

47 Deleuze 1992: 6, 8, italics in the original.

48 For an argument that control and discipline are not antithetical, see Williams 2015: 212. On digital enclosure, see especially Andrejevic 2007: 1ff, 105ff.

49 "Well-funded army": Shirky 2014; on "distraction by design," see also Williams 2018: 7–37. On the distinction between automatic, "bottom-up" and deliberate, "top-down" modes of selective visual attention, emphasizing that the former precede the latter in time, see Theeuwes 2010. On the internet as a "powerful mind-altering technology" that reinforces bottom-up, stimulus-driven modes of attention, see Carr 2010: 115ff (the quotation is from p. 116). On the ways in which digital technology has accentuated the brain's natural vulnerability to interference, including "both *distractions* from irrelevant information and *interruptions* by our attempts to simultaneously pursue multiple goals," see Gazzaley and Rosen 2016: 3 (italics in the original).

50 Eliot 1971: 120. The phrase is from the "Burnt Norton" section of *Four Quartets*; a few lines below, Eliot refers to "this twittering world."

51 On "the gentle power of nudges" in the context of the "emerging science of choice," see Thaler and Sunstein 2008 (the quotations are from pp. 8 and 7). On "tuning" and "herding," see Zuboff 2019: 294ff. On conditioning, an updated version of what B. F. Skinner made famous in the mid-twentieth century, see ibid. 296; on continuous, automated experimentation, see ibid. 297ff. Behavioral modification more generally is a theme that runs throughout Zuboff's book. For critiques of Zuboff's focus on behavior modification, see Morozov 2019; Doctorow 2020. For a broader critique of the "myth of the digital propaganda wizard," questioning the efficacy of the kind of "computational politics" analyzed by Tufekci (2014a), see Karpf 2019.

52 On asymmetries of knowledge and the resulting asymmetries of power, see Zuboff 2019: 11, 187, 192, 203. "*About* us, but ... not *for* us": p. 187. "Epistemic inequality": Zuboff 2020. "Means to others' ends" is a recurrent motif in Zuboff 2019 (see for example pp. 9, 88, 94, 352, 377, 469).

53 On "techno-social engineering" as a project of "designing environments and designing the people who live in them," see Frischmann and Selinger 2018; the quotation is from p. 5. On tech companies' interest in "designing users," see also Williams 2018: 10.

54 On automation, see Andrejevic 2020; on platformization, van Dijck et al. 2018; on infrastructuralization, Plantin et al. 2018.

55 For critical perspectives on the resilience of forms of digital utopianism that recurrently envision a future of technology-enabled decentralization, see Dickel and Schrape 2017; Schrape 2019. On the tension between utopian and dystopian possibilities generated by digital technologies, see Torpey 2020.

56 On the discourse of inevitability, see Zuboff 2019: 221ff.

57 Starr 2004. For a concise account of the importance of "design choices" in the original structuring and successive restructurings of the internet, see Benkler 2016.

58 For a rueful retrospective discussion by the inventor of the pop-up ad, see Zuckerman 2014. On the emergence of the advertising–surveillance nexus, see Zuboff 2019, chapter 3.

59 For this suggestion, see the brilliant and amusing talk by Cegłowski 2014.

60 On the origin of these "safe harbor" provisions, see Gillespie 2018: 30–3.

61 Romer 2019.

62 Zuckerman 2020. One experiment in constructing such an alternative social media platform, by sociologist Chris Bail, found that an anonymous discussion platform, which paired people of opposing political views to discuss an assigned controversial topic, reduced polarization and fostered civil engagement. While acknowledging the often toxic nature of anonymous online exchanges, Bail argues that anonymity here served a useful purpose by "disrupt[ing] the feedback loop between [political] identity, status seeking, and political polarization" (Bail 2021: 122ff; the quotation is from p. 122).

References

Abbott, Andrew. 2014. "The Problem of Excess." *Sociological Theory* 32(1):1–26. doi: 10.1177/0735275114523419.

Abramowitz, Alan I., and Steven Webster. 2016. "The Rise of Negative Partisanship and the Nationalization of U.S. Elections in the 21st Century." *Electoral Studies* 41:12–22. doi: 10.1016/j.electstud.2015.11.001.

Agnew, John A. 2011. "Space and Place." Pp. 316–30 in *The SAGE Handbook of Geographical Knowledge*, edited by John A. Agnew and David N. Livingstone. Los Angeles; London: Sage.

Ahler, Douglas J. 2014. "Self-Fulfilling Misperceptions of Public Polarization." *The Journal of Politics* 76(3):607–20. doi: 10.1017/S0022381614000085.

Ajunwa, Ifeoma. 2019. "The Paradox of Automation as Anti-Bias Intervention." *Cardozo Law Review* 41(5):1671–742.

Ajunwa, Ifeoma, Kate Crawford, and Jason Schultz. 2017. "Limitless Worker Surveillance." *California Law Review* 105(3):735–76.

Ajunwa, Ifeoma, and Daniel Greene. 2019. "Platforms at Work: Automated Hiring Platforms and Other New Intermediaries in the Organization of Work." Pp. 61–91 in *Work and Labor in the Digital Age*, edited by S. P. Vallas and A. Kovalainen. Bingley: Emerald Publishing.

Albrechtslund, Anders. 2008. "Online Social Networking as Participatory Surveillance." *First Monday* 13(3). https://doi.org/10.5210/fm.v13i3.2142.

Alcantara, Chris, Kevin Schaul, Gerrit De Vynck, and Reed Albergotti. 2021. "How Big Tech Got So Big: Hundreds of Acquisitions." *Washington Post*, April 21.

Allen, Darcy W. E., Chris Berg, and Sinclair Davidson. 2020. *The New Technologies of Freedom*. Great Barrington, MA: American Institute for Economic Research.

Allen, Hilary J. 2022. "DeFi: Shadow Banking 2.0?" Forthcoming, *William & Mary Law Review*. Available at SSRN: https://papers.ssrn.com/abstract=4038788.

Altheide, David L. 1994. "An Ecology of Communication." *The Sociological Quarterly* 35(4):665–83. doi: 10.1111/j.1533-8525.1994.tb00422.x.

Amazon. 2017. "Amazon Rekognition Announces Real-Time Face Recognition, Support for Recognition of Text in Image, and Improved Face Detection." *AWS Machine Learning Blog*. Retrieved March 9, 2022. https://aws.amazon.com/blogs/machine-learning/amazon -rekognition-announces-real-time-face-recognition-support-for-recognition-of-text-in -image-and-improved-face-detection/.

Amnesty International. 2021. *"Like We Were Enemies in a War": China's Mass Internment, Torture and Persecution of Muslims in Xinjiang.* https://www.amnesty.org/en/documents /asa17/4137/2021/en/.

Ananny, Mike. 2020. "Making up Political People: How Social Media Create the Ideals, Definitions, and Probabilities of Political Speech." *Georgetown Law Technology Review* 4:351–66. doi: 10.31219/osf.io/7pd62.

Ananny, Mike, and Kate Crawford. 2018. "Seeing without Knowing: Limitations of the Transparency Ideal and its Application to Algorithmic Accountability." *New Media & Society* 20(3):973–89. doi: 10.1177/1461444816676645.

Andersen, Joceline. 2015. "Now You've Got the Shiveries: Affect, Intimacy, and the ASMR Whisper Community." *Television & New Media* 16(8):683–700. https://doi.org/10.1177/1527476414556184.

Anderson, Chris. 2006. *The Long Tail: Why the Future of Business is Selling Less of More.* New York: Hyperion.

Anderson, Chris. 2009. *Free: The Future of a Radical Price.* New York: Hyperion.

Andreessen, Marc. 2007. "The Three Kinds of Platforms You Meet on the Internet." *Pmarchive.* Retrieved May 13, 2021. https://pmarchive.com/three_kinds_of_platforms_you_meet_on_the_internet.html.

Andrejevic, Mark. 2007. *iSpy: Surveillance and Power in the Interactive Era.* Lawrence, KS: University Press of Kansas.

Andrejevic, Mark. 2013. *Infoglut: How Too Much Information is Changing the Way We Think and Know.* New York: Routledge.

Andrejevic, Mark. 2020. *Automated Media.* New York: Routledge.

Atkins, Ed. 2022. "Populist Ecologies of Bitcoin." *Political Geography* 94:102535. doi: 10.1016/j.polgeo.2021.102535.

Aupers, Stef. 2012. "'Trust No One': Modernization, Paranoia and Conspiracy Culture." *European Journal of Communication* 27(1):22–34. doi: 10.1177/0267323111433566.

Auslander, Philip. 2012. "Digital Liveness: A Historico-Philosophical Perspective." *PAJ: A Journal of Performance and Art* 34(3):3–11. doi: 10.1162/PAJJ_a_00106.

Austin, Drew. 2020a. "Home Screens: Quarantine is the Future Big Tech Wanted Us to Want. How Long Before We Want Out?" *Real Life*, April 27.

Austin, Drew. 2020b. "Indoor Kids." *Kneeling Bus.* Retrieved January 20, 2022. https://kneelingbus.substack.com/p/110-indoor-kids.

Austin, Drew. 2020c. "Rainbow in the Dark." *Kneeling Bus.* Retrieved January 25, 2022. https://kneelingbus.substack.com/p/143-rainbow-in-the-dark.

Austin, Drew. 2021a. "Paid in Full." *Real Life*, April 19.

Austin, Drew. 2021b. "Running Up That Hill." *Kneeling Bus.* Retrieved January 20, 2022. https://kneelingbus.substack.com/p/172-running-up-that-hill.

Auxier, Brooke, and Monica Anderson. 2021. *Social Media Use in 2021.* Washington, DC: Pew Research Center.

Bail, Chris. 2021. *Breaking the Social Media Prism: How to Make Our Platforms Less Polarizing.* Princeton, NJ: Princeton University Press.

Bailenson, Jeremy N. 2021. "Nonverbal Overload: A Theoretical Argument for the Causes of Zoom Fatigue." *Technology, Mind, and Behavior* 2(1). doi: 10.1037/tmb0000030.

Bakardjieva, Maria, and Georgia Gaden. 2012. "Web 2.0 Technologies of the Self." *Philosophy & Technology* 25(3):399–413. https://doi.org/10.1007/s13347-011-0032-9.

Barbrook, Richard. 1998. "The Hi-Tech Gift Economy." *First Monday* 3(12). doi: 10.5210/fm.v3i12.631.

Bar-Gill, Oren. 2019. "Algorithmic Price Discrimination When Demand is a Function of Both Preferences and (Mis)Perceptions." *The University of Chicago Law Review* 86(2):217–54.

Barber, Trudy. 2018. "Do We Want to Live in a World Where Our 'Best Friends' Are AI Chatbots?" *The Conversation.* http://theconversation.com/do-we-want-to-live-in-a-world-where-our-best-friends-are-ai-chatbots-91451.

Barker, David C., Ryan Detamble, and Morgan Marietta. 2022. "Intellectualism, Anti-Intellectualism, and Epistemic Hubris in Red and Blue America." *American Political Science Review* 116(1):38–53. doi: 10.1017/S0003055421000988.

Barratt, Emma L., and Nick J. Davis. 2015. "Autonomous Sensory Meridian Response (ASMR): A Flow-like Mental State." *PeerJ* 3(March). https://doi.org/10.7717/peerj.851.

Bartmanski, Dominik, and Ian Woodward. 2015. "Vinyl: The Analogue Medium in the Age of Digital Reproduction." *Journal of Consumer Culture* 15(1):3–27. doi: 10.1177/1469540513488403.

Baszucki, David. 2021. "The Metaverse is Coming." *Wired*, January 2.

Battestini, Agathe, Vidya Setlur, and Timothy Sohn. 2010. "A Large Scale Study of Text-Messaging Use." Pp. 229–38 in *Proceedings of the 12th International Conference on Human Computer Interaction with Mobile Devices and Services – MobileHCI '10*. Lisbon, Portugal: ACM Press.

Bauwens, Michel, Vasilis Kostakis, and Alex Pazaitis. 2019. *Peer to Peer: The Commons Manifesto*. London: University of Westminster Press.

Bayer, Joseph B., Scott W. Campbell, and Rich Ling. 2016a. "Connection Cues: Activating the Norms and Habits of Social Connectedness." *Communication Theory* 26(2):128–49. https://doi.org/10.1111/comt.12090.

Bayer, Joseph B., Nicole B. Ellison, Sarita Y. Schoenebeck, and Emily B. Falk. 2016b. "Sharing the Small Moments: Ephemeral Social Interaction on Snapchat." *Information, Communication & Society* 19(7):956–77. https://doi.org/10.1080/1369118X.2015.1084349.

Beauvisage, Thomas, and Kevin Mellet. 2020. "Datassets: Assetizing and Marketizing Personal Data." Pp. 75–95 in *Assetization: Turning Things into Assets in Technoscience Capitalism*, edited by K. Birch and F. Muniesa. Cambridge, MA: The MIT Press.

Beck, Ulrich, and Elisabeth Beck-Gernsheim. 2002. *Individualization: Institutionalized Individualism and its Social and Political Consequences*. London; Thousand Oaks, CA: Sage.

Beck, Ulrich, Anthony Giddens, and Scott Lash. 1994. *Reflexive Modernization: Politics, Tradition and Aesthetics in the Modern Social Order*. Cambridge: Polity.

Beer, Chris. 2019. "Is TikTok Setting the Scene for Music on Social Media?" *GWI*. Retrieved April 23, 2021. https://blog.globalwebindex.com/trends/tiktok-music-social-media/.

Belk, Russell. 2014. "Sharing Versus Pseudo-Sharing in Web 2.0." *The Anthropologist* 18(1):7–23. doi: 10.1080/09720073.2014.11891518.

Bell, Beth T., Jennifer A. Cassarly, and Lucy Dunbar. 2018. "Selfie-Objectification: Self-Objectification and Positive Feedback ('Likes') Are Associated with Frequency of Posting Sexually Objectifying Self-Images on Social Media." *Body Image* 26(September):83–9. https://doi.org/10.1016/j.bodyim.2018.06.005.

Bell, David. 2001. *An Introduction to Cybercultures*. London; New York: Routledge.

Bellah, Robert N., Richard Madsen, William M. Sullivan, Ann Swidler, and Steven M. Tipton. 1985. *Habits of the Heart: Individualism and Commitment in American Life*. Berkeley: University of California Press.

Beniger, James. 1986. *The Control Revolution: Technological and Economic Origins of the Information Society*. Cambridge, MA: Harvard University Press.

Benjamin, Ruha. 2019. *Race after Technology: Abolitionist Tools for the New Jim Code*. Cambridge: Polity.

Benkler, Yochai. 2002. "Coase's Penguin, or, Linux and 'The Nature of the Firm.'" *The Yale Law Journal* 112(3):369–446. doi: 10.2307/1562247.

Benkler, Yochai. 2004. "Sharing Nicely: On Shareable Goods and the Emergence of Sharing as a Modality of Economic Production." *The Yale Law Journal* 114(2):273–358. doi: 10.2307/4135731.

Benkler, Yochai. 2006. *The Wealth of Networks: How Social Production Transforms Markets and Freedom*. New Haven, CT: Yale University Press.

Benkler, Yochai. 2016. "Degrees of Freedom, Dimensions of Power." *Daedalus* 145(1):18–32.

Benkler, Yochai. 2019. "A Political Economy of Utopia?" *Duke Law & Technology Review* 18:78–84.

Benkler, Yochai, Robert Faris, and Hal Roberts. 2018. *Network Propaganda: Manipulation, Disinformation, and Radicalization in American Politics*. Oxford: Oxford University Press.

Bennett, W. Lance, and Alexandra Segerberg. 2013. *The Logic of Connective Action: Digital Media and the Personalization of Contentious Politics*. Cambridge: Cambridge University Press.

Bennett Moses, Lyria, and Janet Chan. 2018. "Algorithmic Prediction in Policing: Assumptions, Evaluation, and Accountability." *Policing and Society* 28(7):806–22. doi: 10.1080/10439463.2016.1253695.

Berg, Chris, Sinclair Davidson, and Jason Potts. 2017. "The Blockchain Economy: A Beginner's Guide to Institutional Cryptoeconomics." *Cryptoeconomics Australia*. Retrieved February 23, 2022. https://medium.com/cryptoeconomics-australia/the-blockchain -economy-a-beginners-guide-to-institutional-cryptoeconomics-64bf2f2beec4.

Berger, Peter L., and Thomas Luckmann. 1967. *The Social Construction of Reality: A Treatise in the Sociology of Knowledge*. New York: Doubleday.

Berlin, Isaiah. 1953. *The Hedgehog and the Fox; An Essay on Tolstoy's View of History*. New York: Simon & Schuster.

Bernot, Ausma, Alexander Trauth-Goik, and Susan Trevaskes. 2021. "Handling COVID-19 with Big Data in China: Increasing 'Governance Capacity' or 'Function Creep'?" *Australian Journal of International Affairs* 75(5):480–6. doi: 10.1080/10357718.2021.1956430.

Berridge, Clara, Jodi Halpern, and Karen Levy. 2019. "Cameras on Beds: The Ethics of Surveillance in Nursing Home Rooms." *AJOB Empirical Bioethics* 10(1):55–62. doi: 10.1080/23294515.2019.1568320.

Berry, Jeffrey M., and Sarah Sobieraj. 2014. *The Outrage Industry: Political Opinion Media and the New Incivility*. Oxford; New York: Oxford University Press.

Bettany, Shona M., and Ben Kerrane. 2016. "The Socio-Materiality of Parental Style." *European Journal of Marketing* 50(11):2041–66. https://doi.org/10.1108/EJM-07-2015-0437.

Bhaskar, Michael. 2016. "In the Age of the Algorithm, the Human Gatekeeper is Back." *The Guardian*. Retrieved April 25, 2021. http://www.theguardian.com/technology/2016/sep/30 /age-of-algorithm-human-gatekeeper.

Bhaskar, Michael. 2017. *Curation*. Piatkus Books.

Bickerton, Christopher, and Carlo Invernizzi Accetti. 2015. "Populism and Technocracy: Opposites or Complements?" *Critical Review of International Social and Political Philosophy* 20(2):186–206. doi: 10.1080/13698230.2014.995504.

Bickerton, Christopher J., and Carlo Invernizzi Accetti. 2021. *Technopopulism: The New Logic of Democratic Politics*. Oxford: Oxford University Press.

Billari, Francesco C., Osea Giuntella, and Luca Stella. 2018. "Broadband Internet, Digital Temptations, and Sleep." *Journal of Economic Behavior & Organization* 153(September):58–76. https://doi.org/10.1016/j.jebo.2018.07.001.

Black, Ryan. 2021. "How Amazon is Working to Disrupt Healthcare." *MDLinx*, September 17.

Boas, Taylor C. 2005. "Television and Neopopulism in Latin America: Media Effects in Brazil and Peru." *Latin American Research Review* 40(2):27–49. doi: 10.1353/lar.2005.0019.

Bogost, Ian. 2020. "You Already Live in Quarantine." *The Atlantic*, March 4.

Boler, Megan, and Elizabeth Davis. 2020. "Introduction: Propaganda by Other Means." Pp. 1–49 in *Affective Politics of Digital Media*, edited by M. Boler and E. Davis. New York; Abingdon: Routledge.

Bolter, Jay David. 2019. *The Digital Plenitude: The Decline of Elite Culture and the Rise of Digital Media*. Cambridge, MA: The MIT Press.

Bolter, Jay David, Maria Engberg, and Blair MacIntyre. 2021. *Reality Media: Augmented and Virtual Reality*. Cambridge, MA: The MIT Press.

Bolter, Jay David, and Richard A. Grusin. 1999. *Remediation: Understanding New Media*. Cambridge, MA: The MIT Press.

Bond, Robert M., Christopher J. Fariss, Jason J. Jones, Adam D. I. Kramer, Cameron Marlow, Jaime E. Settle, and James H. Fowler. 2012. "A 61-Million-Person Experiment in Social Influence and Political Mobilization." *Nature* 489(7415). https://doi.org/10.1038/nature11421.

Botsman, Rachel, and Roo Rogers. 2010. *What's Mine is Yours: The Rise of Collaborative Consumption*. London: Harper Collins.

Boullier, Henri, Baptiste Kotras, and Ignacio Siles. 2021. "Uncertain Knowledge. Studying 'Truth' and 'Conspiracies' in the Digital Age." *RESET. Recherches en Sciences Sociales Sur Internet* 10. doi: 10.4000/reset.2750.

Bowles, Nellie. 2018. "Silicon Valley Nannies Are Phone Police for Kids." *The New York Times*, October 26.

Bowles, Nellie. 2019. "Human Contact as a Luxury Good." *New York Times*, March 24.

boyd, danah. 2011. "Social Network Sites as Networked Publics: Affordances, Dynamics, and Implications." Pp. 39–58 in *A Networked Self: Identity, Community and Culture on Social Network Sites*, edited by Zizi Papacharissi. New York: Routledge.

Brady, William J., and M. J. Crockett. 2019. "How Effective is Online Outrage?" *Trends in Cognitive Sciences* 23(2):79–80. doi: 10.1016/j.tics.2018.11.004.

Brady, William J., M. J. Crockett, and Jay J. Van Bavel. 2020a. "The MAD Model of Moral Contagion: The Role of Motivation, Attention, and Design in the Spread of Moralized Content Online." *Perspectives on Psychological Science* 15(4):978–1010. doi: 10.1177/1745691620917336.

Brady, William J., Ana P. Gantman, and Jay J. Van Bavel. 2020b. "Attentional Capture Helps Explain Why Moral and Emotional Content Go Viral." *Journal of Experimental Psychology: General* 149(4):746–56. doi: http://dx.doi.org/10.1037/xge0000673.

Brady, William J., Killian McLoughlin, Tuan N. Doan, and Molly J. Crockett. 2021. "How Social Learning Amplifies Moral Outrage Expression in Online Social Networks." *Science Advances* 7:eabe5641. doi: 10.1126/sciadv.abe5641.

Brady, William J., Julian A. Wills, John T. Jost, Joshua A. Tucker, and Jay J. Van Bavel. 2017. "Emotion Shapes the Diffusion of Moralized Content in Social Networks." *Proceedings of the National Academy of Sciences* 114(28):7313–18. doi: 10.1073/pnas.1618923114.

Brand, Stewart. 1987. *The Media Lab: Inventing the Future at MIT*. New York: Viking.

Bratton, Benjamin H. 2015. *The Stack: On Software and Sovereignty*. Cambridge, MA: The MIT Press.

Broadbent, Stefana. 2016. *Intimacy at Work: How Digital Media Bring Private Life to the Workplace*. Walnut Creek, CA: Left Coast Press.

Brown, Karen. 2021. "Something Bothering You? Tell It to Woebot." *The New York Times*, June 1.

Brubaker, Rogers. 2017a. "Forget Fake News. Social Media is Making Democracy Less Democratic." *Zócalo Public Square*. https://www.zocalopublicsquare.org/2017/11/29/forget -fake-news-social-media-making-democracy-less-democratic/ideas/essay/.

Brubaker, Rogers. 2017b. "Why Populism?" *Theory and Society* 46(5):357–85. doi: 10.1007/s11186-017-9301-7.

Brubaker, Rogers. 2021. "Paradoxes of Populism during the Pandemic." *Thesis Eleven* 164(1):73–87. doi: 10.1177/0725513620970804.

Brunnermeier, Markus, Harold James, and Jean-Pierre Landau. 2021. "The Digitalisation of Money." Bank for International Settlements, BIS Working Papers 41.

Bucher, Taina. 2012. "Want to Be on the Top? Algorithmic Power and the Threat of Invisibility on Facebook." *New Media & Society* 14(7):1164–80. https://doi.org/10.1177 /1461444812440159.

Bucher, Taina. 2013. "The Friendship Assemblage: Investigating Programmed Sociality on Facebook." *Television & New Media* 14(6):479–93. doi: 10.1177/1527476412452800.

Bucher, Taina. 2018. *If...Then: Algorithmic Power and Politics*. Oxford: Oxford University Press.

Bucher, Taina. 2021. *Facebook*. Chichester: John Wiley & Sons.

Buckley, Chris, Vivian Wang, and Keith Bradsher. 2022. "Living by the Code: In China, Covid-Era Controls May Outlast the Virus." *The New York Times*, January 30.

Bull, Michael. 2000. *Sounding out the City: Personal Stereos and the Management of Everyday Life*. Oxford; New York: Berg.

Bull, Michael. 2006. "Investigating the Culture of Mobile Listening: From Walkman to iPod." Pp. 131–49 in *Consuming Music Together*, edited by K. O'Hara and B. Brown. Berlin; Heidelberg: Springer-Verlag.

Bull, Michael. 2015. *Sound Moves: iPod Culture and Urban Experience*. Abingdon: Routledge.

Bullingham, L., and A. C. Vasconcelos. 2013. "'The Presentation of Self in the Online World': Goffman and the Study of Online Identities." *Journal of Information Science* 39(1):101–12. https://doi.org/10.1177/0165551512470051.

Bullock, Greg. 2017. "Save Time with Smart Reply in Gmail." *The Keyword*. Retrieved March 25, 2022. https://blog.google/products/gmail/save-time-with-smart-reply-in-gmail/.

Buongiorno, Federica. 2016. "The Digital Self: The Construction of Self and Social Recognition in the Global Digital Society." Athens Institute for Education and Research, ATINER'S Conference Paper Series No. CBC2016-2189.

Burchell, Kenzie. 2015. "Tasking the Everyday: Where Mobile and Online Communication Take Time." *Mobile Media & Communication* 3(1):36–52. https://doi.org/10.1177 /2050157914546711.

Burchell, Kenzie. 2017. "Finding Time for Goffman: When Absence is More Telling than Presence." Pp. 186–95 in *Conditions of Mediation: Phenomenological Perspectives on Media*, edited by Tim Markham and Scott Rodgers. New York: Peter Lang.

Burgess, Jean. 2007. "Vernacular Creativity and New Media." PhD Dissertation, Queensland University of Technology.

Burgess, Jean. 2012. "The IPhone Moment, the Apple Brand and the Creative Consumer: From 'Hackability and Usability' to Cultural Generativity." Pp. 28–42 in *Studying Mobile Media: Cultural Technologies, Mobile Communication, and the iPhone*, edited by L. Hjorth, J. Burgess, and I. Richardson. New York: Routledge.

Burgess, Jean, Peta Mitchell, and Tim Highfield. 2018. "Automating the Digital Everyday: An Introduction." *Media International Australia* 166(1):6–10. doi: 10.1177/1329878X17739020.

Burr, Christopher, and Nello Cristianini. 2019. "Can Machines Read Our Minds?" *Minds and Machines* 29: 461–94. https://doi.org/10.1007/s11023-019-09497-4.

Byler, Darren. 2021. *In the Camps: Life in China's High-Tech Penal Colony*. Columbia Global Reports.

Cahir, Jayde, and Justine Lloyd. 2015. "'People Just Don't Care': Practices of Text Messaging in the Presence of Others." *Media, Culture & Society* 37(5):703–19. https://doi.org/10.1177/0163443715577242.

Cahour, Béatrice, and Christian Licoppe. 2010. "Confrontations with Traces of One's Own Activity: Understanding, Development and Regulation of Action in an Increasingly Reflexive World." *Revue d'anthropologie des connaissances* 4(2):a-k. https://doi.org/10.3917/rac.010.000a.

Calhoun, Craig. 1992. "The Infrastructure of Modernity: Indirect Social Relationships, Information Technology, and Social Integration." Pp. 205–36 in *Social Change and Modernity*, edited by H. Haferkamp and N. Smelser. Berkeley: University of California Press.

Calhoun, Craig. 1998. "Community without Propinquity Revisited: Communications Technology and the Transformation of the Urban Public Sphere." *Sociological Inquiry* 68(3):373–97. doi: 10.1111/j.1475-682X.1998.tb00474.x.

Caliskan, Koray. 2020. "Data Money: The Socio-Technical Infrastructure of Cryptocurrency Blockchains." *Economy and Society* 49(4):540–61. doi: 10.1080/03085147.2020.1774258.

Callon, Michel. 1999. "The Role of Lay People in the Production and Dissemination of Scientific Knowledge." *Science, Technology and Society* 4(1):81–94. doi: 10.1177/097172189900400106.

Campa, Emilio. 2021. "Why Microsoft May Beat Zuckerberg to the Metaverse." *VentureBeat*. Retrieved November 28, 2021. https://venturebeat.com/2021/11/12/why-microsoft-may-beat-zuckerberg-to-the-metaverse/.

Campbell, Heidi, and Ruth Tsuria, eds. 2021. *Digital Religion: Understanding Religious Practice in Digital Media*. Abingdon: Routledge.

Campus, Donatella. 2010. "Mediatization and Personalization of Politics in Italy and France: The Cases of Berlusconi and Sarkozy." *The International Journal of Press/Politics* 15(2):219–35. doi: 10.1177/1940161209358762.

Caplan, Scott E. 2010. "Theory and Measurement of Generalized Problematic Internet Use: A Two-Step Approach." *Computers in Human Behavior* 26(5):1089–97. https://doi.org/10.1016/j.chb.2010.03.012.

Cardell, Kylie. 2018. "Is a Fitbit a Diary? Self-Tracking and Autobiography." *M/C Journal* 21(2). http://journal.media-culture.org.au/index.php/mcjournal/article/view/1348.

Carey, Benedict. 2020. "Can an Algorithm Prevent Suicide?" *The New York Times*, November 23.

Carlson, Matt. 2020. "Journalistic Epistemology and Digital News Circulation: Infrastructure, Circulation Practices, and Epistemic Contests." *New Media & Society* 22(2):230–46. doi: 10.1177/1461444819856921.

Carr, Nicholas G. 2010. *The Shallows: What the Internet is Doing to Our Brains*. New York: W. W. Norton & Company.

Carr, Nicholas G. 2014. *The Glass Cage: Automation and Us*. New York: W. W. Norton & Company.

Carr, Nicholas. 2020. "From Context Collapse to Content Collapse." *Rough Type*. Retrieved April 9, 2022. https://www.roughtype.com/?p=8724.

Carr, Nicholas. 2021. "Meanings of the Metaverse: Secondary Embodiment." *Rough Type*. Retrieved March 15, 2022. https://www.roughtype.com/?p=8998.

Casilli, Antonio. 2016. "Is There a Global Digital Labor Culture? Marginalization of Work, Global Inequalities, and Coloniality." In *2nd Symposium of the Project for Advanced Research in Global Communication (PARGC)*, Philadelphia. https://halshs.archives -ouvertes.fr/halshs-01387649.

Casilli, Antonio A., and Julian Posada. 2019. "The Platformization of Labor and Society." Pp. 293–306 in *Society and the Internet*, edited by M. Graham and W. Dutton. Second edition. Oxford: Oxford University Press.

Castells, Manuel. 2001. *The Internet Galaxy: Reflections on the Internet, Business, and Society*. Oxford: Oxford University Press.

Castells, Manuel. 2010 [1996]. *The Rise of the Network Society*. Chichester: John Wiley & Sons.

Castells, Manuel. 2012. *Networks of Outrage and Hope: Social Movements in the Internet Age*. Cambridge, UK; Malden, MA: Polity.

Castells, Manuel. 2013 [2009]. *Communication Power*. Oxford: Oxford University Press.

Cegłowski, Maciej. 2014. "The Internet with a Human Face." *Idle Words*. Retrieved August 14, 2021. https://idlewords.com/talks/internet_with_a_human_face.htm.

Chaffee, Steven H., and Miriam J. Metzger. 2001. "The End of Mass Communication?" *Mass Communication and Society* 4(4):365–79. doi: 10.1207/S15327825MCS0404_3.

Chalmers, David J. 2022. *Reality+: Virtual Worlds and the Problem of Philosophy*. London: Penguin.

Chambers, Deborah. 2013. *Social Media and Personal Relationships: Online Intimacies and Networked Friendship*. Basingstoke: Palgrave Macmillan.

Chatterjee, R., P. Doerfler, H. Orgad, S. Havron, J. Palmer, D. Freed, K. Levy, N. Dell, D. McCoy, and T. Ristenpart. 2018. "The Spyware Used in Intimate Partner Violence." Pp. 441–58 in *2018 IEEE Symposium on Security and Privacy (SP)*. https://doi.org/10.1109/SP. 2018.00061.

Cheeseman, Nic, Jonathan Fisher, Idayat Hassan, and Jamie Hitchen. 2020. "Social Media Disruption: Nigeria's WhatsApp Politics." *Journal of Democracy* 31(3):145–59. doi: 10.1353/ jod.2020.0037.

Chen, Brian X. 2019. "I Shared My Phone Number. I Learned I Shouldn't Have." *The New York Times*, August 15.

Chen, Julie Yujie, and Ping Sun. 2020. "Temporal Arbitrage, Fragmented Rush, and Opportunistic Behaviors: The Labor Politics of Time in the Platform Economy." *New Media & Society* 22(9):1561–79. doi: 10.1177/1461444820913567.

Cheney-Lippold, John. 2017. *We Are Data: Algorithms and the Making of Our Digital Selves*. New York: New York University Press.

Cheung, Anne S.Y., and Yongxi Chen. 2021. "From Datafication to Data State: Making Sense of China's Social Credit System and its Implications." *Law and Social Inquiry*. doi: 10.1017/lsi.2021.56.

Chou, Hui-Tzu Grace, and Nicholas Edge. 2012. "'They Are Happier and Having Better Lives than I Am': The Impact of Using Facebook on Perceptions of Others' Lives." *Cyberpsychology, Behavior, and Social Networking* 15(2).117–21. https://doi.org/10.1089 /cyber.2011.0324.

Cinnamon, Jonathan. 2020. "Platform Philanthropy, 'Public Value', and the COVID-19 Pandemic Moment." *Dialogues in Human Geography* 10(2):242–5. doi: 10.1177/2043820620933860.

Clabaugh, Caitlyn, and Maja Matarić. 2018. "Robots for the People, by the People: Personalizing Human–Machine Interaction." *Science Robotics* 3(21). doi: 10.1126/scirobotics.aat7451.

Cobbe, Jennifer. 2021. "Algorithmic Censorship by Social Platforms: Power and Resistance." *Philosophy & Technology* 34:739–66. doi: 10.1007/s13347-020-00429-0.

Cohen, Julie E. 2013. "What Privacy is For." *Harvard Law Review* 126:1904–33.

Cohen, Julie. 2019. *Between Truth and Power: The Legal Constructions of Informational Capitalism*. Oxford; New York: Oxford University Press.

Collie, Natalie, and Caroline Wilson-Barnao. 2020. "Playing with TikTok: Algorithmic Culture and the Future of Creative Work." Pp. 172–88 in *The Future of Creative Work*, edited by Greg Hearn. Cheltenham: Edward Elgar.

Cong, Wanshu. 2021. "From Pandemic Control to Data-Driven Governance: The Case of China's Health Code." *Frontiers in Political Science* 3. doi: 10.3389/fpos.2021.627959.

Conrad, Maximilian. 2021. "Post-Truth Politics, Digital Media, and the Politicization of the Global Compact for Migration." *Politics and Governance* 9(3):301–11. doi: 10.17645/pag.v9i3.3985.

Constine, Josh. 2017. "Facebook Now Has 2 Billion Monthly Users… and Responsibility." *TechCrunch*. Retrieved August 14, 2021. https://social.techcrunch.com/2017/06/27/facebook-2-billion-users/.

Constine, Josh. 2020. "Content Density: Why TikToks Trounce Stories." *Josh Constine's Press Club*. Retrieved February 6, 2021. https://constine.substack.com/p/content-density-why-tiktoks-trounce.

Cooley, Charles Horton. 1902. *Human Nature and the Social Order*. New York: Charles Scribner's Sons.

Couclelis, Helen. 2004. "Pizza over the Internet: E-Commerce, the Fragmentation of Activity and the Tyranny of the Region." *Entrepreneurship & Regional Development* 16:41–54. https://doi.org/10.1080/0898562042000205027.

Couldry, Nick, and Andreas Hepp. 2017. *The Mediated Construction of Reality*. Cambridge: Polity.

Couldry, Nick, and Ulises A. Mejias. 2019. *The Costs of Connection: How Data is Colonizing Human Life and Appropriating it for Capitalism*. Stanford, CA: Stanford University Press.

Crawford, Kate. 2021. *Atlas of AI: Power, Politics, and the Planetary Costs of Artificial Intelligence*. New Haven, CT: Yale University Press.

Crawford, Kate, Jessa Lingel, and Tero Karppi. 2015. "Our Metrics, Ourselves: A Hundred Years of Self-Tracking from the Weight Scale to the Wrist Wearable Device." *European Journal of Cultural Studies* 18(4–5):479–96. https://doi.org/10.1177/1367549415584857.

Creemers, Rogier. 2018. "China's Social Credit System: An Evolving Practice of Control." Available at SSRN. doi: 10.2139/ssrn.3175792.

Crockett, M. J. 2017. "Moral Outrage in the Digital Age." *Nature Human Behaviour* 1(11):769–71. doi: 10.1038/s41562-017-0213-3.

Cui, Di. 2016. "Beyond 'Connected Presence': Multimedia Mobile Instant Messaging in Close Relationship Management." *Mobile Media & Communication* 4(1):19–36. https://doi.org/10.1177/2050157915583925.

Cunningham, Stuart, and David Craig. 2017. "Being 'Really Real' on YouTube: Authenticity, Community and Brand Culture in Social Media Entertainment." *Media International Australia* 164(1):71–81. doi: 10.1177/1329878X17709098.

Cunningham, Stuart, and David Craig. 2019. *Social Media Entertainment: The New Intersection of Hollywood and Silicon Valley*. New York: New York University Press.

Cusumano, Michael A., David B. Yoffie, and Annabelle Gawer. 2020. "The Future of Platforms." *MIT Sloan Management Review*, Spring:46–54.

Damiani, Jesse. 2021a. "Facebook Wants Your Next Meeting to Take Place in its New VR App." *Freethink*. Retrieved November 12, 2021. https://www.freethink.com/technology /facebook-vr-meetings.

Damiani, Jesse. 2021b. "The Future of 'Live' is Hybrid, Real-Time, and Interactive." *Freethink*. Retrieved November 12, 2021. https://www.freethink.com/culture/virtual-events.

Danaher, John, Sven Nyholm, and Brian D. Earp. 2018. "The Quantified Relationship." *The American Journal of Bioethics* 18(2):3–19. doi: 10.1080/15265161.2017.1409823.

Danby, Susan J., Marilyn Fleer, Christina Davidson, and Maria Hatzigianni, eds. 2018. *Digital Childhoods*. Singapore: Springer Singapore.

Darley, John M., and Thane S. Pittman. 2003. "The Psychology of Compensatory and Retributive Justice." *Personality and Social Psychology Review* 7(4):324–36. doi: 10.1207/ S15327957PSPR0704_05.

Davidson, Sinclair, Primavera De Filippi, and Jason Potts. 2018. "Blockchains and the Economic Institutions of Capitalism." *Journal of Institutional Economics* 14(4):639–58. doi: 10.1017/S1744137417000200.

Davis, Gerald F. 2016. *The Vanishing American Corporation: Navigating the Hazards of a New Economy*. Oakland, CA: Berrett-Koehler Publishers.

de Benedictis-Kessner, Justin, Matthew A. Baum, and Adam J. Berinsky. 2020. "Polarization and Media Usage: Disentangling Causality." Pp. 553–71 in *The Oxford Handbook of Electoral Persuasion*, edited by E. Suhay, B. Grofman, and A. H. Trechsel. Oxford: Oxford University Press.

De Kosnik, Abigail. 2019. "#CancelColbert: Popular Outrage, Divo Citizenship, and Digital Political Performativity." Pp. 203–17 in *#identity: Hashtagging Race, Gender, Sexuality, and Nation*, edited by A. De Kosnik and K. P. Feldman. Ann Arbor: University of Michigan Press.

De Swaan, Abram. 1988. *In Care of the State: Health Care, Education, and Welfare in Europe and the USA in the Modern Era*. Cambridge: Polity.

Dehouche, Nassim. 2021. "Plagiarism in the Age of Massive Generative Pre-Trained Transformers (GPT-3)." *Ethics in Science and Environmental Politics* 21:17–23. doi: 10.3354/ esep00195.

Deleuze, Gilles. 1992. "Postscript on the Societies of Control." *October* 59:3–7.

Delfanti, Alessandro. 2021. "Machinic Dispossession and Augmented Despotism: Digital Work in an Amazon Warehouse." *New Media & Society* 23(1):39–55. doi: 10.1177/1461444819891613.

Delfanti, Alessandro, and Bronwyn Frey. 2021. "Humanly Extended Automation or the Future of Work Seen through Amazon Patents." *Science, Technology, & Human Values* 46(3):655–82. doi: 10.1177/0162243920943665.

DeNora, Tia. 2000. *Music in Everyday Life*. Cambridge; New York: Cambridge University Press.

Deseriis, Marco. 2017. "Technopopulism: The Emergence of a Discursive Formation." *TripleC: Communication, Capitalism & Critique* 15(2):441–58. doi: 10.31269/triplec. v15i2.770.

Deseriis, Marco. 2021. "Rethinking the Digital Democratic Affordance and its Impact on Political Representation: Toward a New Framework." *New Media & Society* 23(8):2452–73. doi: 10.1177/1461444820929678.

Deutsch, Nathaniel. 2009. "The Forbidden Fork, the Cell Phone Holocaust, and Other Haredi Encounters with Technology." *Contemporary Jewry* 29(1):3–19. https://doi.org/10.1007/s12397-008-9002-7.

Dewey, Caitlin. 2016. "This Guy Has Swiped Right on 200,000 Women, without Much Success." *Washington Post*, August 1.

Dickel, M. H. 1995. "Bent Gender: Virtual Disruptions of Gender and Sexual Identity." *Electronic Journal of Communication* 5(4). http://www.cios.org/EJCPUBLIC/005/4/00545.HTML.

Dickel, Sascha, and Jan-Felix Schrape. 2017. "The Logic of Digital Utopianism." *NanoEthics* 11(1):47–58. doi: 10.1007/s11569-017-0285-6.

Didžiokaitė, Gabija, Paula Saukko, and Christian Greiffenhagen. 2018. "The Mundane Experience of Everyday Calorie Trackers: Beyond the Metaphor of Quantified Self." *New Media & Society* 20(4):1470–87. https://doi.org/10.1177/1461444817698478.

Diehl, Stephen. 2021a. "The Intellectual Incoherence of Cryptoassets." *Stephen Diehl*. Retrieved February 20, 2022. https://www.stephendiehl.com/blog/crypto-absurd.html.

Diehl, Stephen. 2021b. "The Non-Innovation of Cryptocurrency." *Stephen Diehl*. Retrieved March 3, 2022. https://www.stephendiehl.com/blog/non-innovation.html.

DiMaggio, Paul. 1991. "Social Structure, Institutions, and Cultural Goods: The Case of the United States." Pp. 133–55 in *Social Theory for a Changing Society*, edited by P. Bourdieu and J. S. Coleman. Boulder, CO: Westview Press; New York: Russell Sage Foundation.

DiMaggio, Paul. 2013. "The Internet's Influence on the Production and Consumption of Culture: Creative Destruction and New Opportunities." Pp. 364–94 in *Change: 19 Key Essays on How Internet is Changing Our Lives*. Madrid: BBVA.

DiMaggio, Paul, Eszter Hargittai, Coral Celeste, and Steven Shafer. 2004. "Digital Inequality: From Unequal Access to Differentiated Use." Pp. 355–400 in *Social Inequality*, edited by K. M. Neckerman. New York: Russell Sage Foundation.

DiResta, Renée. 2020. "The Supply of Disinformation Will Soon be Infinite." *The Atlantic*, September 20.

Doctorow, Cory. 2020. "How to Destroy 'Surveillance Capitalism.'" *OneZero*, August 25.

Domingos, Pedro. 2015. *The Master Algorithm: How the Quest for the Ultimate Learning Machine Will Remake Our World*. New York: Basic Books.

Dotson, Taylor. 2012. "Technology, Choice and the Good Life: Questioning Technological Liberalism." *Technology in Society* 34(4):326–36. doi: 10.1016/j.techsoc.2012.10.004.

Drahokoupil, Jan, and Agnieszka Piasna. 2017. "Work in the Platform Economy: Beyond Lower Transaction Costs." *Intereconomics* 52(6):335–40. doi: 10.1007/s10272-017-0700-9.

Driessens, Olivier. 2015. "The Democratization of Celebrity: Mediatization, Promotion, and the Body." Pp. 371–84 in *A Companion to Celebrity*, edited by P. David Marshall and Sean Redmond. Hoboken, NJ: John Wiley & Sons. https://doi.org/10.1002/9781118475089.ch20.

Drott, Eric. 2018. "Why the Next Song Matters: Streaming, Recommendation, Scarcity." *Twentieth-Century Music* 15(3):325–57. https://doi.org/10.1017/S1478572218000245.

Du Gay, Paul. 1996. *Consumption and Identity at Work*. London; Thousand Oaks, CA: Sage.

Dubal, V. B. 2020. "An Uber Ambivalence: Employee Status, Worker Perspectives, & Regulation in the Gig Economy." Pp. 33–56 in *Beyond the Algorithm: Qualitative Insights for Gig Work Regulation*, edited by D. Das Acevedo. Cambridge: Cambridge University Press.

Dubois, Philippe R., Camille Arteau-Leclerc, and Thierry Giasson. 2022. "Micro-Targeting, Social Media, and Third Party Advertising: Why the Facebook Ad Library Cannot Prevent Threats to Canadian Democracy." Pp. 236–69 in *Cyber-Threats to Canadian Democracy*, edited by H. A. Garnett and M. Pal. Montreal: McGill-Queen's University Press.

Duffy, Brooke Erin. 2017. *(Not) Getting Paid to Do What You Love: Gender, Social Media, and Aspirational Work*. New Haven, CT: Yale University Press.

Duffy, Brooke Erin, Annika Pinch, Shruti Sannon, and Megan Sawey. 2021. "The Nested Precarities of Creative Labor on Social Media." *Social Media + Society* 7(2). doi: 10.1177/20563051211021368.

Duffy, Brooke Erin, and Jefferson D. Pooley. 2017. "'Facebook for Academics': The Convergence of Self-Branding and Social Media Logic on Academia.Edu." *Social Media + Society* 3(1). doi: 10.1177/2056305117696523.

Edenberg, Elizabeth, and Michael Hannon. 2021. *Political Epistemology*. Oxford: Oxford University Press.

Edwards, Paul N. 2002. "Infrastructure and Modernity: Force, Time, and Social Organization in the History of Sociotechnical Systems." Pp. 185–225 in *Modernity and Technology*, edited by P. Brey, A. Feenberg, and T. J. Misa. Cambridge, MA: MIT Press.

Eggers, Dave. 2013. *The Circle*. New York: Alfred A. Knopf.

Elberse, Anita. 2013. *Blockbusters: Hit-Making, Risk-Taking, and the Big Business of Entertainment*. New York: Henry Holt and Company.

Eliot, T. S. 1971. *The Complete Poems and Plays, 1909–1950*. New York: Harcourt, Brace & World.

Engstrom, David Freeman, and Daniel E. Ho. 2021. "Artificially Intelligent Government: A Review and Agenda." Pp. 57–86 in *Research Handbook on Big Data Law*, edited by Roland Vogl. Cheltenham: Edward Elgar.

Engstrom, David Freeman, Daniel E. Ho, Catherine M. Sharkey, and Mariano-Florentino Cuéllar. 2020. "Government by Algorithm: Artificial Intelligence in Federal Administrative Agencies." NYU School of Law, Public Law Research Paper No. 20-54. Available at SSRN. https://papers.ssrn.com/sol3/papers.cfm?abstract_id=3551505.

Epifanova, Alena. 2020. *Deciphering Russia's 'Sovereign Internet Law': Tightening Control and Accelerating the Splinternet*. Berlin: Forschungsinstitut der Deutschen Gesellschaft für Auswärtige Politik.

Epstein, Steven. 1995. "The Construction of Lay Expertise: AIDS Activism and the Forging of Credibility in the Reform of Clinical Trials." *Science, Technology, & Human Values* 20(4):408–37. doi: 10.1177/016224399502000402.

Epstein, Steven, and Stefan Timmermans. 2021. "From Medicine to Health: The Proliferation and Diversification of Cultural Authority." *Journal of Health and Social Behavior* 62(3):240–54. doi: 10.1177/00221465211010468.

Erickson, Lee B., Pamela Wisniewski, Heng Xu, John M. Carroll, Mary Beth Rosson, and Daniel F. Perkins. 2016. "The Boundaries Between: Parental Involvement in a Teen's Online World." *Journal of the Association for Information Science and Technology* 67(6):1384–403. https://doi.org/10.1002/asi.23450.

Erk, Corina. 2019. "Phänomenologie der Briefkultur gestern und heute." Pp. 394–416 in *Von der Idee zum Medium: Resonanzfelder zwischen Aufklärung und Gegenwart*, edited by Christine Schramm and Felix Lenz. Paderborn, Germany: Wilhelm Fink.

Espeland, Wendy Nelson, and Mitchell L. Stevens. 1998. "Commensuration as a Social Process." *Annual Review of Sociology* 24(1):313–43. https://doi.org/10.1146/annurev.soc.24.1.313.

Esser, Frank. 2013. "Mediatization as a Challenge: Media Logic versus Political Logic." Pp. 155–76 in *Democracy in the Age of Globalization and Mediatization*, edited by H. Kriesi. London: Palgrave Macmillan.

Estes, Adam Clark. 2020. "We're Closer to Holographic Meetings than You Think." *Vox*, September 15.

Eubanks, Virginia. 2018. *Automating Inequality: How High-Tech Tools Profile, Police, and Punish the Poor*. New York: St. Martin's Press.

Evangelista, Rafael, and Fernanda Bruno. 2019. "WhatsApp and Political Instability in Brazil: Targeted Messages and Political Radicalisation." *Internet Policy Review* 8(4):1–23. doi: 10.14763/2019.4.1434.

Evans, David S., and Richard Schmalensee. 2016. *Matchmakers: The New Economics of Multisided Platforms*. Boston, MA: Harvard Business Review Press.

Eyal, Gil. 2019. *The Crisis of Expertise*. Cambridge, UK; Medford, MA: Polity.

Eyal, Nir. 2012. "Infinite Scroll: The Web's Slot Machine." *Psychology Today*, August 29.

Facebook. 2013. "Facebook Q2 2013 Earnings Call." Zuckerberg Transcripts. https://epublications.marquette.edu/zuckerberg_files_transcripts/238.

Facebook. 2016. "Facebook Q1 2016 Earnings Call." Zuckerberg Transcripts. https://epublications.marquette.edu/zuckerberg_files_transcripts/227.

Facebook. 2020. "Facebook Q3 2020 Earnings Call." Zuckerberg Transcripts. https://epublications.marquette.edu/zuckerberg_files_transcripts/1320.

Fader, Ayala. 2017a. "The Counterpublic of the J(Ewish) Blogosphere: Gendered Language and the Mediation of Religious Doubt among Ultra-Orthodox Jews in New York." *Journal of the Royal Anthropological Institute* 23(4):727–47. https://doi.org/10.1111/1467-9655.12697.

Fader, Ayala. 2017b. "Ultra-Orthodox Jewish Interiority, the Internet, and the Crisis of Faith." *HAU: Journal of Ethnographic Theory* 7(1):185–206. https://doi.org/10.14318/hau7.1.016.

Ferrara, Emilio, Onur Varol, Clayton Davis, Filippo Menczer, and Alessandro Flammini. 2016. "The Rise of Social Bots." *Communications of the ACM* 59(7):96–104. https://doi.org/10.1145/2818717.

Ferrari, Elisabetta. 2020. "Technocracy Meets Populism: The Dominant Technological Imaginary of Silicon Valley." *Communication, Culture and Critique* 13(1):121–4. doi: 10.1093/ccc/tcz051.

Fiske, John. 1987. *Television Culture: Popular Pleasures and Politics*. London; New York: Methuen.

Flaxman, Seth et al. 2020. "Estimating the Effects of Non-Pharmaceutical Interventions on COVID-19 in Europe." *Nature* 584:257–61. doi: 10.1038/s41586-020-2405-7.

Fleischer, Rasmus. 2017. "If the Song Has No Price, is it Still a Commodity? Rethinking the Commodification of Digital Music." *Culture Unbound* 9(2):146–62. doi: 10.3384/cu.2000.1525.1792146.

Flick, Catherine. 2016. "Informed Consent and the Facebook Emotional Manipulation Study." *Research Ethics* 12(1):14–28. doi: 10.1177/1747016115599568.

Flood, John, and Lachlan Robb. 2017. "Trust, Anarcho-Capitalism, Blockchain and Initial Coin Offerings." Griffith Law School Research Paper No. 17-23. Available at SSRN. https://papers.ssrn.com/sol3/papers.cfm?abstract_id=3074263.

Floridi, Luciano. 2014. *The Fourth Revolution: How the Infosphere is Reshaping Human Reality*. Oxford: Oxford University Press.

Ford, Matthew, and Andrew Hoskins. 2022. *Radical War: Data, Attention and Control in the Twenty-First Century*. London: Hurst Publishers.

Foucault, Michel. 1983. "Self-writing." [Translation of "L'écriture de soi," *Corps Écrit* 5:3–23]. https://foucault.info/documents/foucault.hypomnemata.en/.

Foucault, Michel. 1987. "The Ethic of Care for the Self as a Practice of Freedom: An Interview with Michel Foucault on January 20, 1984." *Philosophy & Social Criticism* 12(2–3):112–31. https://doi.org/10.1177/019145378701200202.

Foucault, Michel. 1988. "Technologies of the Self." Pp. 16–49 in *Technologies of the Self: A Seminar with Michel Foucault*, edited by Luther H. Martin, Huck Gutman, and Patrick H. Hutton. Amherst, MA: University of Massachusetts Press.

Foucault, Michel. 1995. *Discipline and Punish: The Birth of the Prison*. London: Vintage Books.

Foucault, Michel. 2008. *The Birth of Biopolitics: Lectures at the Collège de France, 1978–79*. Edited by Michel Senellart, translated by Graham Burchell. Basingstoke; New York: Palgrave Macmillan.

Fourcade, Marion, and Jeffrey Gordon. 2020. "Learning Like a State: Statecraft in the Digital Age." *Journal of Law and Political Economy* 1(1):78–108.

Fourcade, Marion, and Kieran Healy. 2017. "Seeing like a Market." *Socio-Economic Review* 15(1):9–29. doi: 10.1093/ser/mww033.

Fourcade, Marion, and Daniel N. Kluttz. 2020. "A Maussian Bargain: Accumulation by Gift in the Digital Economy." *Big Data & Society* 7(1). doi: 10.1177/2053951719897092.

Fox, Jesse, and Katie M. Warber. 2014. "Social Networking Sites in Romantic Relationships: Attachment, Uncertainty, and Partner Surveillance on Facebook." *Cyberpsychology, Behavior, and Social Networking* 17(1):3–7. doi: 10.1089/cyber.2012.0667.

Frank, Thomas. 1997. *The Conquest of Cool: Business Culture, Counterculture, and the Rise of Hip Consumerism*. Chicago, IL: University of Chicago Press.

Franklin, Benjamin. 1904. "The Autobiography of Benjamin Franklin." Pp. 1–313 in *Works of Benjamin Franklin*, Vol. 1, edited by John Bigelow. New York: Putnam.

Frischmann, Brett M. 2012. *Infrastructure: The Social Value of Shared Resources*. New York: Oxford University Press.

Frischmann, Brett, and Evan Selinger. 2018. *Re-Engineering Humanity*. Cambridge; New York: Cambridge University Press.

Frith, Jordan. 2019. *A Billion Little Pieces: RFID and Infrastructures of Identification*. Cambridge, MA: The MIT Press.

Fuller, Joseph B. et al. 2020. *Building the On-Demand Workforce*. Cambridge, MA: Harvard Business School and BCG.

Gabler, Neal. 2011. "The End of Cultural Elitism." *Boston Globe*, January 6.

Gabriel, Shira, Elaine Paravati, Melanie C. Green, and Jason Flomsbee. 2018. "From *Apprentice* to President: The Role of Parasocial Connection in the Election of Donald Trump." *Social Psychological and Personality Science* 9(3):299–307. doi: 10.1177/1948550617722835.

Gal, Uri et al. 2019. *People Analytics – Using Data and Algorithms to Shape the Employee Experience*. University of Sydney, Business School and Capgemini.

Gallagher, Rob. 2016. "Eliciting Euphoria Online: The Aesthetics of 'ASMR' Video Culture." *Film Criticism* 40(2). https://doi.org/10.3998/fc.13761232.0040.202.

Gansky, Lisa. 2010. *The Mesh: Why the Future of Business is Sharing*. New York: Penguin.

Gazzaley, Adam, and Larry D. Rosen. 2016. *The Distracted Mind: Ancient Brains in a High-Tech World*. Cambridge, MA: The MIT Press.

Gehl, Robert W. 2014. *Reverse Engineering Social Media: Software, Culture, and Political Economy in New Media Capitalism*. Philadelphia, PA: Temple University Press.

Gehl, Robert W., and Maria Bakardjieva, eds. 2017. *Socialbots and Their Friends: Digital Media and the Automation of Sociality*. New York: Routledge.

Gellman, Robert. 1996. "Disintermediation and the Internet." *Government Information Quarterly* 13(1):1–8. doi: 10.1016/S0740-624X(96)90002-7.

Genz, Stéphanie. 2015. "My Job is Me: Postfeminist Celebrity Culture and the Gendering of Authenticity." *Feminist Media Studies* 15(4):545–61. https://doi.org/10.1080/14680777.2014.952758.

Gerbaudo, Paolo. 2018. "Social Media and Populism: An Elective Affinity?" *Media, Culture & Society* 40(5):745–53. doi: 10.1177/0163443718772192.

Gerbaudo, Paolo. 2019. *The Digital Party: Political Organisation and Online Democracy*. London: Pluto Press.

Gergen, Kenneth J. 1991. *The Saturated Self: Dilemmas of Identity in Contemporary Life*. New York: Basic Books.

Gergen, Kenneth J. 2002. "The Challenge of Absent Presence." Pp. 227–41 in *Perpetual Contact: Mobile Communication, Private Talk, Public Performance*, edited by James E. Katz and Mark Aakhus. Cambridge: Cambridge University Press.

Gerlitz, Carolin, and Anne Helmond. 2013. "The Like Economy: Social Buttons and the Data-Intensive Web." *New Media & Society* 15(8):1348–65. https://doi.org/10.1177/1461444812472322.

Gibbs, Jennifer L., Nik Ahmad Rozaidi, and Julia Eisenberg. 2013. "Overcoming the 'Ideology of Openness': Probing the Affordances of Social Media for Organizational Knowledge Sharing." *Journal of Computer-Mediated Communication* 19(1):102–20. https://doi.org/10.1111/jcc4.12034.

Giddens, Anthony. 1991. *Modernity and Self-Identity: Self and Society in the Late Modern Age*. Stanford, CA: Stanford University Press.

Giddens, Anthony. 1995. *Affluence, Poverty and the Idea of a Post-Scarcity Society*. Geneva, Switzerland: United Nations Research Institute for Social Development.

Giermindl, Lisa Marie et al. 2022. "The Dark Sides of People Analytics: Reviewing the Perils for Organisations and Employees." *European Journal of Information Systems* 31(3):410–35. doi: 10.1080/0960085X.2021.1927213.

Gillespie, Ryan. 2012. "The Art of Criticism in the Age of Interactive Technology: Critics, Participatory Culture, and the Avant-Garde." *International Journal of Communication* 6:56–75.

Gillespie, Tarleton. 2010. "The Politics of 'Platforms.'" *New Media & Society* 12(3):347–64. doi: 10.1177/1461444809342738.

Gillespie, Tarleton. 2014. "The Relevance of Algorithms." Pp. 167–93 in *Media Technologies: Essays on Communication, Materiality, and Society*, edited by T. Gillespie, P. Boczkowski, and K. Foot. Cambridge, MA: The MIT Press.

Gillespie, Tarleton. 2016. "#trendingistrending: When Algorithms Become Culture." Pp. 52–75 in *Algorithmic Cultures: Essays on Meaning, Performance and New Technologies*, edited by R. Seyfert and J. Roberge. Abingdon; New York: Routledge.

Gillespie, Tarleton. 2018. *Custodians of the Internet: Platforms, Content Moderation, and the Hidden Decisions that Shape Social Media*. New Haven, CT: Yale University Press.

Giroux, Henry A. 2015. "Totalitarian Paranoia in the Post-Orwellian Surveillance State." *Cultural Studies* 29(2):108–40. doi: 10.1080/09502386.2014.917118.

Goffman, Erving. 1956. "The Nature of Deference and Demeanor." *American Anthropologist* 58(3):473–502.

Goffman, Erving. 1959. *The Presentation of Self in Everyday Life*. Garden City, NY: Doubleday.

Goffman, Erving. 1983. "The Interaction Order." *American Sociological Review* 48(1):1–17. https://doi.org/10.2307/2095141.

Gogel, David. 2021. *DeFi Beyond the Hype: The Emerging World of Decentralized Finance*. Wharton School, University of Pennsylvania, Wharton Blockchain and Digital Asset Project.

Goode, Luke. 2009. "Social News, Citizen Journalism and Democracy." *New Media & Society* 11(8):1287–305. doi: 10.1177/1461444809341393.

Gorski, Philip S. 2003. *The Disciplinary Revolution: Calvinism and the Rise of the State in Early Modern Europe*. Chicago, IL: University of Chicago Press.

Gorvett, Zaria. 2020. "Why Most Covid-19 Deaths Won't Be from the Virus." *BBC Future*, May 28.

Gorwa, Robert. 2019. "What is Platform Governance?" *Information, Communication & Society* 22(6):854–71. doi: 10.1080/1369118X.2019.1573914.

Gorwa, Robert, Reuben Binns, and Christian Katzenbach. 2020. "Algorithmic Content Moderation: Technical and Political Challenges in the Automation of Platform Governance." *Big Data & Society* 7(1):1–15. doi: 10.1177/2053951719897945.

Graham, Mark, Isis Hjorth, and Vili Lehdonvirta. 2017. "Digital Labour and Development: Impacts of Global Digital Labour Platforms and the Gig Economy on Worker Livelihoods." *Transfer: European Review of Labour and Research* 23(2):135–62. doi: 10.1177/1024258916687250.

Graham, Timothy. 2016. "Technologies of Choice: The Shaping of Choice on the World Wide Web." PhD Thesis, The University of Queensland. https://doi.org/10.14264/uql.2016.865.

Graham, Timothy. 2018. "Platforms and Hyper-Choice on the World Wide Web." *Big Data & Society* 5(1). doi: 10.1177/2053951718765878.

Greene, Jay. 2020. "Amazon's Big Holiday Shopping Advantage: An In-House Shipping Network Swollen by Pandemic-Fueled Growth." *Washington Post*, November 27.

Greenfeld, Karl Taro. 2014. "Faking Cultural Literacy." *The New York Times*, May 24.

Greetly. 2020. "What is Touchless Technology? No-Touch Visitor Management System." Retrieved January 29, 2022. https://www.greetly.com/blog/what-is-touchless-technology.

Gregg, Melissa. 2013. "Spouse-Busting: Intimacy, Adultery, and Surveillance Technology." *Surveillance & Society* 11(3):301–10. https://doi.org/10.24908/ss.v11i3.4514.

Griesbach, Kathleen, Adam Reich, Luke Elliott-Negri, and Ruth Milkman. 2019. "Algorithmic Control in Platform Food Delivery Work." *Socius* 5:1–15. doi: 10.1177/2378023119870041.

Griffith, Erin. 2021. "Apple and Epic Trial Opens With a Tour of the Fortnite 'Metaverse.'" *The New York Times*, May 3.

Grosser, Benjamin. 2014. "What Do Metrics Want? How Quantification Prescribes Social Interaction on Facebook." *Computational Culture* 4. http://computationalculture.net/what-do-metrics-want/.

Guggenberger, Nikolas. 2021. "Essential Platforms." *Stanford Technology Law Review* 24(2):237–343. doi: 10.2139/ssrn.3703361.

Guillon, Jean-Baptiste. 2018. "Les théories du complot et le paradoxe de l'individualisme épistémique." *Diogène* 261–262:54–87.

Guinaudeau, Benjamin, Fabio Votta, and Kevin Munger. 2022. "Fifteen Seconds of Fame:

TikTok and the Democratization of Mobile Video on Social Media." *Computational Communication Research*. Forthcoming.

Hacking, Ian. 1982. "Biopower and the Avalanche of Printed Numbers." *Humanities in Society* 5:279–95.

Haggerty, Kevin D., and Richard V. Ericson. 2000. "The Surveillant Assemblage." *The British Journal of Sociology* 51(4):605–22. https://doi.org/10.1080/00071310020015280.

Haidt, Jonathan. 2003. "The Moral Emotions." Pp. 852–70 in *Handbook of Affective Sciences*, edited by Richard J. Davidson, Klaus R. Sherer, and H. Hill Goldsmith. New York: Oxford University Press.

Haidt, Jonathan. 2021. "The Dangerous Experiment on Teen Girls." *The Atlantic*, November 21.

Haidt, Jonathan, and Tobias Rose-Stockwell. 2019. "The Dark Psychology of Social Networks." *The Atlantic*, November 12.

Hall, James. 2014. *The Self-Portrait: A Cultural History*. New York: Thames & Hudson.

Hall, Kimberly. 2017. "Snapchat's Failed Ephemerality." *Amodern* 7, December.

Hampton, Keith N. 2016. "Persistent and Pervasive Community: New Communication Technologies and the Future of Community." *American Behavioral Scientist* 60(1):101–24. doi: 10.1177/0002764215601714.

Hampton, Keith N., and Barry Wellman. 2018. "Lost and Saved . . . Again: The Moral Panic about the Loss of Community Takes Hold of Social Media." *Contemporary Sociology: A Journal of Reviews* 47(6):643–51.

Hanrahan, Nancy Weiss. 2013. "If the People Like It, It Must Be Good: Criticism, Democracy and the Culture of Consensus." *Cultural Sociology* 7(1):73–85. doi: 10.1177/1749975512453656.

Harambam, Jaron. 2017. "'The Truth is Out There': Conspiracy Culture in an Age of Epistemic Instability." PhD Dissertation, Erasmus University Rotterdam.

Harcourt, Bernard E. 2015. *Exposed: Desire and Disobedience in the Digital Age*. Cambridge, MA: Harvard University Press.

Hargittai, Eszter, ed. 2021. *Handbook of Digital Inequality*. Cheltenham; Northampton, MA: Edward Elgar.

Haslam, Nick. 2016. "Concept Creep: Psychology's Expanding Concepts of Harm and Pathology." *Psychological Inquiry* 27(1):1–17. doi: 10.1080/1047840X.2016.1082418.

Hassan, Aisha. 2018. "Fortnite is a Social Space the Way Skateparks and Facebook Used to Be." *Quartz*. Retrieved November 29, 2021. https://qz.com/quartzy/1493147/fortnite -a-social-space-like-facebook-and-skateparks-once-were/.

Haynes, Trevor. 2018. "Dopamine, Smartphones & You: A Battle for Your Time." *Science in the News*. Retrieved July 7, 2019. http://sitn.hms.harvard.edu/flash/2018/dopamine -smartphones-battle-time/.

Hearn, Alison. 2008. "'Meat, Mask, Burden': Probing the Contours of the Branded 'Self'." *Journal of Consumer Culture* 8(2):197–217. https://doi.org/10.1177/1469540508090086.

Hearn, Alison, and Stephanie Schoenhoff. 2016. "From Celebrity to Influencer." Pp. 194–212 in *A Companion to Celebrity*, edited by P. David Marshall and Sean Redmond. Chichester: John Wiley & Sons.

Heehs, Peter. 2013. *Writing the Self: Diaries, Memoirs, and the History of the Self*. New York: Bloomsbury Academic.

Helmond, Anne. 2015. "The Platformization of the Web: Making Web Data Platform Ready." *Social Media + Society* 1(2). doi: 10.1177/2056305115603080.

Hemphill, C. Scott. 2019. "Disruptive Incumbents: Platform Competition in an Age of Machine Learning." *Columbia Law Review* 119(7):1973–2000.

Hernandez, Patricia. 2018. "The Twitch Streamers Who Spend Years Broadcasting to No One." *The Verge*, July 16.

Herring, Susan, and Ashley Dainas. 2017. "'Nice Picture Comment!' Graphicons in Facebook Comment Threads." Pp. 2185–94 in *Proceedings of the 50th Hawaii International Conference on System Sciences*, edited by T. Bui and R. Sprague. University of Hawaii. https://doi.org /10.24251/HICSS.2017.264.

Hersh, Eitan. 2020. *Politics is for Power*. New York: Scribner.

Hesmondhalgh, David. 2010. "User-Generated Content, Free Labour and the Cultural Industries." *Theory & Politics in Organization* 10(3/4):267–84.

Hesmondhalgh, David. 2019. *The Cultural Industries*. 4th ed. London: Sage.

Hess, Amanda. 2016. "Hands Off My Smiley Face: Emoji Become Corporate Tools." *The New York Times*, June 20.

Hillis, Ken, Michael Petit, and Kylie Jarrett. 2012. *Google and the Culture of Search*. Abingdon: Routledge.

Hindman, Matthew Scott. 2018. *The Internet Trap: How the Digital Economy Builds Monopolies and Undermines Democracy*. Princeton, NJ: Princeton University Press.

Hirsch, Fred. 1978. *Social Limits to Growth*. Cambridge, MA: Harvard University Press.

Hirsch, Paul M. 1972. "Processing Fads and Fashions: An Organization-Set Analysis of Cultural Industry Systems." *American Journal of Sociology* 77(4):639–59.

Hjorth, Larissa, and Ingrid Richardson. 2011. "Playing the Waiting Game: Complicating Notions of (Tele)Presence and Gendered Distraction in Casual Mobile Gaming." Pp. 111–26 in *Cultures of Participation: Media Practices, Politics and Literacy*, edited by H. Greif, L. Hjorth, and A. Lasén. Frankfurt am Main: Peter Lang.

Hochschild, Arlie Russell. 1983. *The Managed Heart: Commercialization of Human Feeling*. Berkeley; Los Angeles; London: University of California Press.

Hochschild, Arlie Russell. 1997. *The Time Bind: When Work Becomes Home and Home Becomes Work*. New York: Metropolitan Books/Henry Holt and Co.

Hong, Sun-ha. 2020. *Technologies of Speculation: The Limits of Knowledge in a Data-Driven Society*. New York: New York University Press.

Hong, Sun-ha. 2021. "Technofutures in Stasis: Smart Machines, Ubiquitous Computing, and the Future That Keeps Coming Back." *International Journal of Communication* 15.

Hong, Sun-ha. 2022. "Antiseptic Machine Life." In *Relative Intimacies*, Vol. 3: *Intersubjectivity*, edited by L. Cantor and E. Watlington. Cambridge, MA: The MIT Press.

Hoofnagle, Chris Jay, Bart van der Sloot, and Frederik Zuiderveen Borgesius. 2019. "The European Union General Data Protection Regulation: What it Is and What it Means." *Information & Communications Technology Law* 28(1):65–98. doi: 10.1080/13600834.2019.1573501.

Hopkins, Dan. 2018. "All Politics is National Because All Media is National." *FiveThirtyEight*. Retrieved February 27, 2021. https://fivethirtyeight.com/features/all-politics-is-national -because-all-media-is-national/.

Horning, Rob. 2012a. "The Rise of the Data Self." *PopMatters*, January 25. https://www. popmatters.com/153721--2495892321.html.

Horning, Rob. 2012b. "Facebook in the Age of Facebook." *The New Inquiry*, April 19. https:// thenewinquiry.com/facebook-in-the-age-of-facebook/.

Horning, Rob. 2012c. "Hi Haters!" *The New Inquiry*, November 27. https://thenewinquiry .com/hi-haters/.

Horning, Rob. 2016. "Reacting to Reactions." *The New Inquiry*, March 11. https:// thenewinquiry.com/blog/reacting-to-reactions/.

Horning, Rob. 2020a. "How TikTok Turns Status Games into Spectator Sports." *Internal Exile*. Retrieved April 1, 2022. https://robhorningreallife.tumblr.com/post/617384205542998016 /how-tiktok-turns-status-games-into-spectator.

Horning, Rob. 2020b. "I Write the Songs." *Real Life*, September 2. https://reallifemag.com /i-write-the-songs/.

Horning, Rob. 2020c. "Significant Flavor." *Verso Books*. Retrieved March 6, 2021. https:// www.versobooks.com/blogs/4656-significant-flavor.

Horning, Rob. 2021. "'This Feeling That You're Really There'." *TinyLetter*. Retrieved November 7, 2021. https://tinyletter.com/reallifemag/letters/this-feeling-that-you-re-really-there.

Horton, Donald, and Anselm Strauss. 1957. "Interaction in Audience-Participation Shows." *American Journal of Sociology* 62(6):579–87.

Horton, Donald, and Richard Wohl. 1956. "Mass Communication and Para-Social Interaction." *Psychiatry* 19(3):215–29. doi: 10.1080/00332747.1956.11023049.

Howell, Sabrina T., Theresa Kuchler, David Snitkof, Johannes Stroebel, and Jun Wong. 2021. "Racial Disparities in Access to Small Business Credit: Evidence from the Paycheck Protection Program." Available at SSRN. doi: 10.2139/ssrn.3939384.

Hu, Cherie. 2019. "Give Me What You Want." *Real Life*, February 21. https://reallifemag. com/give-me-what-you-want/.

Hughes, Thomas Parke. 1987. "The Evolution of Large Technological Systems." Pp. 51–82 in *The Social Construction of Technological Systems: New Directions in the Sociology and History of Technology*, edited by W. E. Bijker, T. P. Hughes, and T. Pinch. Cambridge, MA: The MIT Press.

Hulick, Samuel. 2016. "Slack, I'm Breaking Up with You." *UserOnboard*. Retrieved March 24, 2022. https://ux.useronboard.com/slack-i-m-breaking-up-with-you-54600aceo3ea.

Hull, Gordon, and Frank Pasquale. 2018. "Toward a Critical Theory of Corporate Wellness." *BioSocieties* 13(1):190–212. https://doi.org/10.1057/s41292-017-0064-1.

Huq, Aziz Z. 2019. "Racial Equity in Algorithmic Criminal Justice." *Duke Law Journal* 68:1043–144.

Hutchby, Ian. 2001. "Technologies, Texts and Affordances." *Sociology* 35(2):441–56. doi: 10.1177/S0038038501000219.

Hutter, Michael. 2018. "The Role of Newness in the Experience Economy." Pp. 149–64 in *Innovation Society Today: Perspectives, Fields, and Cases*, edited by W. Rammert, A. Windeler, H. Knoblauch, and M. Hutter. Wiesbaden: Springer Fachmedien.

Huxley, Aldous. 1949. "Letter to George Orwell." Retrieved December 15, 2021. https://www. openculture.com/2018/08/aldous-huxley-george-orwell-hellish-vision-future-better-1949. html.

Huxley, Aldous. 1950 [1932]. *Brave New World*. New York: Harper.

Huxley, Aldous. 1958. *Brave New World Revisited*. New York: Harper.

Ibrahim, Yasmin. 2018. *Production of the "Self" in the Digital Age*. Berlin: Springer.

Inglehart, Ronald. 1977. *The Silent Revolution: Changing Values and Political Styles among Western Publics*. Princeton, NJ: Princeton University Press.

Isaac, Mike, and Taylor Lorenz. 2021. "Facebook Wants to Court Creators. It Could be a Tough Sell." *The New York Times*, July 12.

Iyengar, Shanto, Yphtach Lelkes, Matthew Levendusky, Neil Malhotra, and Sean J. Westwood. 2019. "The Origins and Consequences of Affective Polarization in the United States." *Annual Review of Political Science* 22(1):129–46. doi: 10.1146/annurev-polisci-051117-073034.

Jackson, James. 2017. "How a Matchmaking AI Conquered (and Was Exiled) from Tinder." *Vice*, November 6.

Jäger, Anton. 2022. "How the World Went from Post-Politics to Hyper-Politics." *Tribune*, January 3.

Jasper, James M. 2011. "Emotions and Social Movements: Twenty Years of Theory and Research." *Annual Review of Sociology* 37:285–303. doi: 10.1146/annurev-soc-081309-150015.

Jasper, James M. 2014. "Constructing Indignation: Anger Dynamics in Protest Movements." *Emotion Review* 6(3):208–13. doi: 10.1177/1754073914522863.

Jenkins, Henry. 2002. "Interactive Audiences? The 'Collective Intelligence' of Media Fans." Pp. 157–82 in *The New Media Book*, edited by D. Harries. London: British Film Institute.

Jenkins, Henry. 2005. "Games, the New Lively Art." Pp. 175–92 in *Handbook of Computer Game Studies*, edited by J. Raessens and J. H. Goldstein. Cambridge, MA: The MIT Press.

John, Nicholas A. 2013a. "Sharing and Web 2.0: The Emergence of a Keyword." *New Media & Society* 15(2):167–82. doi: 10.1177/1461444812450684.

John, Nicholas A. 2013b. "The Social Logics of Sharing." *The Communication Review* 16(3):113–31. doi: 10.1080/10714421.2013.807119.

Johns, Fleur. 2019. "From Planning to Prototypes: New Ways of Seeing Like a State." *The Modern Law Review* 82(5):833–63. doi: 10.1111/1468-2230.12442.

Jones, Marc Owen. 2022. *Digital Authoritarianism in the Middle East: Deception, Disinformation and Social Media*. London: C. Hurst.

Joseff, Katie, Anastasia Goodwin, and Samuel Woolley. 2020. "Nanoinfluencers Are Slyly Barnstorming the 2020 Election." *Wired*, August 15.

Jurgenson, Nathan. 2012. "The Facebook Eye." *The Atlantic*, January 13. https://www.theatlantic.com/technology/archive/2012/01/the-facebook-eye/251377/.

Jurgenson, Nathan. 2013. "Review of Bauman and Lyon's Liquid Surveillance: A Conversation." *Surveillance & Society* 11(1/2):204–7. https://doi.org/10.24908/ss.v11i1/2.4725.

Jurgenson, Nathan. 2019. *The Social Photo: On Photography and Social Media*. New York: Verso Books.

Kalleberg, Arne L., and Steve P. Vallas. 2018. "Probing Precarious Work: Theory, Research, and Politics." *Research in the Sociology of Work* 31:1–30. doi: 10.1108/S0277-283320170000031017.

Kannan, Anjuli et al. 2016. "Smart Reply: Automated Response Suggestion for Email." Pp. 955–64 in *Proceedings of the 22nd ACM SIGKDD International Conference on Knowledge Discovery and Data Mining – KDD '16*. San Francisco, CA: ACM Press. https://doi.org/10.1145/2939672.2939801.

Karpf, David. 2019. "On Digital Disinformation and Democratic Myths." *MediaWell, Social Science Research Council*. Retrieved December 15, 2021. https://mediawell.ssrc.org/expert-reflections/on-digital-disinformation-and-democratic-myths/.

Karpf, David. 2020. "Two Provocations for the Study of Digital Politics in Time." *Journal of Information Technology & Politics* 17(2):87–96. doi: 10.1080/19331681.2019.1705222.

Kassabian, Anahid. 2013. *Ubiquitous Listening: Affect, Attention, and Distributed Subjectivity*. Berkeley: University of California Press.

Katzenbach, Christian. 2021. "'AI Will Fix This' – The Technical, Discursive, and Political Turn to AI in Governing Communication." *Big Data & Society* 8(2). doi: 10.1177/20539517211046182.

Katzenbach, Christian, and Lena Ulbricht. 2019. "Algorithmic Governance." *Internet Policy Review* 8(4). doi: 10.14763/2019.4.1424.

Kaye, D. Bondy Valdovinos, Xu Chen, and Jing Zeng. 2021. "The Co-Evolution of Two Chinese Mobile Short Video Apps: Parallel Platformization of Douyin and TikTok." *Mobile Media & Communication* 9(2):229–53. doi: 10.1177/2050157920952120.

Keane, John. 1999. *On Communicative Abundance.* Centre for the Study of Democracy Perspectives. London: University of Westminster Press.

Kearney, Richard. 2021. *Touch: Recovering Our Most Vital Sense.* New York: Columbia University Press.

Keesara, Sirina, Andrea Jonas, and Kevin Schulman. 2020. "Covid-19 and Health Care's Digital Revolution." *New England Journal of Medicine* 382:e82. doi: 10.1056/NEJMp2005835.

Kellogg, Katherine C., Melissa A. Valentine, and Angèle Christin. 2020. "Algorithms at Work: The New Contested Terrain of Control." *Academy of Management Annals* 14(1):366–410. doi: 10.5465/annals.2018.0174.

Kelly, Jack. 2021. "The New Trend of Wanderlust, Work-From-Anywhere Digital Nomads." *Forbes*, June 20. https://www.forbes.com/sites/jackkelly/2021/06/20/the-new-trend-of-wanderlust-work-from-anywhere-digital-nomads/.

Kelly, Kevin. 2005. "We Are the Web." *Wired*, August 1.

Kenney, Martin, and John Zysman. 2019. "Work and Value Creation in the Platform Economy." *Research in the Sociology of Work* 33:13–41.

Kenney, Martin, Dafna Bearson, and John Zysman. 2021. "The Platform Economy Matures: Measuring Pervasiveness and Exploring Power." *Socio-Economic Review* 19(4):1451–83. doi: 10.1093/ser/mwab014.

Khamis, Susie, Lawrence Ang, and Raymond Welling. 2017. "Self-Branding, 'Micro-Celebrity' and the Rise of Social Media Influencers." *Celebrity Studies* 8(2):191–208. https://doi.org/10.1080/19392397.2016.1218292.

Khan, Lina M. 2017. "Amazon's Antitrust Paradox." *The Yale Law Journal* 126(3):710–805.

Khan, Lina M. 2019. "The Separation of Platforms and Commerce." *Columbia Law Review* 119:973–1093.

Khan, Lina M. 2020. "The End of Antitrust History Revisited." *Harvard Law Review* 133:1655–82.

Kim, Jin Woo, Andrew Guess, Brendan Nyhan, and Jason Reifler. 2021. "The Distorting Prism of Social Media: How Self-Selection and Exposure to Incivility Fuel Online Comment Toxicity." *Journal of Communication* 71(6):922–46. doi: 10.1093/joc/jqab034.

Kingori, Patricia. 2015. "The 'Empty Choice': A Sociological Examination of Choosing Medical Research Participation in Resource-Limited Sub-Saharan Africa." *Current Sociology* 63(5):763–78. https://doi.org/10.1177/0011392115590093.

Klein, Naomi. 2020. "Screen New Deal: Under Cover of Mass Death, Andrew Cuomo Calls in the Billionaires to Build a High-Tech Dystopia." *The Intercept.* Retrieved November 12, 2021. https://theintercept.com/2020/05/08/andrew-cuomo-eric-schmidt-coronavirus-tech-shock-doctrine/.

Kleinberg, Jon, Jens Ludwig, Sendhil Mullainathan, and Cass R. Sunstein. 2019. "Discrimination in the Age of Algorithms." *Journal of Legal Analysis* 10:113–74.

Knight, Adam. 2021. "Technologies of Risk and Discipline in China's Social Credit System." Pp. 237–62 in *Law and the Party in China: Ideology and Organisation*, edited by R. Creemers and S. Trevaskes. Cambridge: Cambridge University Press.

Knight, Adam, and Rogier Creemers. 2021. "Going Viral: The Social Credit System and COVID-19." Available at SSRN. doi: 10.2139/ssrn.3770208.

Koganzon, Rita. 2015. "The Politics of Digital Shaming." *The New Atlantis* 45:118–26.

Kohl, Uta. 2021. "Blockchain Utopia and its Governance Shortfalls." Pp. 13–39 in *Blockchain and Public Law: Global Challenges in the Era of Decentralisation*, edited by O. Pollicino and G. De Gregorio. Cheltenham: Edward Elgar.

Koopman, Colin. 2019. *How We Became Our Data: A Genealogy of the Informational Person.* University of Chicago Press.

Kosinski, Michal, David Stillwell, and Thore Graepel. 2013. "Private Traits and Attributes Are Predictable from Digital Records of Human Behavior." *Proceedings of the National Academy of Sciences* 110(15):5802–5. https://doi.org/10.1073/pnas.1218772110.

Kosoff, Maya. 2015. "The Vision Uber's CEO Has for His $50 Billion Company Suggests the Startup is Only Beginning to Scratch the Surface." *Business Insider.* Retrieved January 26, 2022. https://www.businessinsider.com/travis-kalanicks-vision-for-uber-2015-6.

Kostoff, Ronald N., Daniela Calina, Darja Kanduc, Michael B. Briggs, Panayiotis Vlachoyiannopoulos, Andrey A. Svistunov, and Aristidis Tsatsakis. 2021. "Why Are We Vaccinating Children against COVID-19?" *Toxicology Reports* 8:1665–84. doi: 10.1016/j. toxrep.2021.08.010.

Kotfila, Christopher. 2014. "This Message Will Self-Destruct: The Growing Role of Obscurity and Self-Destructing Data in Digital Communication." *Bulletin of the Association for Information Science and Technology* 40(2):12–16. https://doi.org/10.1002/bult.2014. 1720400206.

Kramer, Adam D. I., Jamie E. Guillory, and Jeffrey T. Hancock. 2014. "Experimental Evidence of Massive-Scale Emotional Contagion through Social Networks." *Proceedings of the National Academy of Sciences* 111(24):8788–90. https://doi.org/10.1073/pnas.1320040111.

Krasnova, Hanna et al. 2015. "Why Following Friends Can Hurt You: An Exploratory Investigation of the Effects of Envy on Social Networking Sites among College-Age Users." *Information Systems Research* 26(3):585–605. https://doi.org/10.1287/isre.2015.0588.

Kroll, Joshua. 2017. "Accountable Algorithms." *University of Pennsylvania Law Review* 165:633–705.

Kuehn, Kathleen, and Thomas F. Corrigan. 2013. "Hope Labor: The Role of Employment Prospects in Online Social Production." *The Political Economy of Communication* 1(1): 9–25.

Kumar, Krishan, and Ekaterina Makarova. 2008. "The Portable Home: The Domestication of Public Space." *Sociological Theory* 26(4):324–43.

Kwet, Michael. 2019. "Retail Stores Track Your Every Move." *New York Times*, June 16.

Lachance, Jocelyn. 2020. "Parental Surveillance of Teens in the Digital Era: The 'Ritual of Confession' to the 'Ritual of Repentance.'" *International Journal of Adolescence and Youth* 25(1):355 63. https://doi.org/10.1080/02673843.2019.1651351.

Lagomarsino, John. 2015. "You're Listening to Podcasts Too Fast." *The Verge.* Retrieved April 2, 2021. https://www.theverge.com/2015/2/17/8043077/stop-listening-to-podcasts -fast-speed.

Lambert, Paul. 2018. "SUBJECT: Write Emails Faster with Smart Compose in Gmail." *The Keyword.* Retrieved March 25, 2022. https://blog.google/products/gmail/subject-write -emails-faster-smart-compose-gmail/.

Langley, P., and A. Leyshon. 2017. "Platform Capitalism: The Intermediation and Capitalization of Digital Economic Circulation." *Finance and Society* 3(1):11–31. doi: 10.2218/finsoc.v3i1.1936.

Langlois, Ganaele, and Greg Elmer. 2013. "The Research Politics of Social Media Platforms." *Culture Machine* 14:1–17.

Lash, Scott. 2007. "Power after Hegemony: Cultural Studies in Mutation?" *Theory, Culture & Society* 24(3):55–78. doi: 10.1177/0263276407075956.

Lawson, Chappell, and James A. McCann. 2005. "Television News, Mexico's 2000 Elections and Media Effects in Emerging Democracies." *British Journal of Political Science* 35(1):1–30. doi: 10.1017/S0007123405000013.

Leadbeater, Charles. 2007. *We-Think: The Power of Mass Creativity.* London: Profile.

Ledvina, Andrew. 2014. "10 Ways Facebook is Actually the Devil." *Andrewledvina.com.* Retrieved March 25, 2022. https://andrewledvina.com/blog/2014-07-04-10-ways-facebook -is-the-devil/.

Lee, Julie Yoonnyung. 2020. "The South Koreans Left behind in a Contact-Free Society." *BBC Worklife*, August 5.

Lee, Min Kyung, Daniel Kusbit, Evan Metsky, and Laura Dabbish. 2015. "Working with Machines: The Impact of Algorithmic and Data-Driven Management on Human Workers." Pp. 1603–12 in *Proceedings of the 33rd Annual ACM Conference on Human Factors in Computing Systems.* New York: Association for Computing Machinery.

Lehdonvirta, Vili. 2018. "Flexibility in the Gig Economy: Managing Time on Three Online Piecework Platforms." *New Technology, Work and Employment* 33(1):13–29. doi: 10.1111/ ntwe.12102.

Lehdonvirta, Vili, Otto Kässi, Isis Hjorth, Helena Barnard, and Mark Graham. 2018. "The Global Platform Economy: A New Offshoring Institution Enabling Emerging-Economy Microproviders." *Journal of Management Studies* 45(2):567–99.

Lehr, David, and Paul Ohm. 2017. "Playing with the Data: What Legal Scholars Should Learn About Machine Learning." *U.C. Davis Law Review* 51:653–717.

Lei, Ya-Wen. 2021. "Delivering Solidarity: Platform Architecture and Collective Contention in China's Platform Economy." *American Sociological Review* 86(2):279–309. doi: 10.1177/0003122420979980.

Leibold, James. 2020. "Surveillance in China's Xinjiang Region: Ethnic Sorting, Coercion, and Inducement." *Journal of Contemporary China* 29(121):46–60. doi: 10.1080/10670564.2019.1621529.

Lessig, Lawrence. 1999. *Code: And Other Laws of Cyberspace.* New York: Basic Books.

Lessig, Lawrence. 2004. *Free Culture: How Big Media Uses Technology and the Law to Lock Down Culture and Control Creativity.* New York: Penguin Press.

Lessig, Lawrence. 2008. *Remix: Making Art and Commerce Thrive in the Hybrid Economy.* New York: Penguin Press.

Levendusky, Matthew, and Neil Malhotra. 2014. "The Media Make Us Think We're More Polarized than We Really Are." *The Monkey Cage*, February 5.

Levendusky, Matthew S., and Neil Malhotra. 2016. "(Mis)Perceptions of Partisan Polarization in the American Public." *Public Opinion Quarterly* 80(S1):378–91. doi: 10.1093/poq/ nfv045.

Leveneur, Claire, and Paola Heudebert. 2020. "Blockchain, Disintermediation and the Future of Legal Professions." *Cardozo International & Comparative Law Review* 4(1):275–319.

Levy, Karen, and Solon Barocas. 2018. "Refractive Surveillance: Monitoring Customers to Manage Workers." *International Journal of Communication* 12:1166–88.

Lewis, Michael. 2018. "Has Anyone Seen the President?" *Bloomberg*, February 9.

Lewis, Rebecca, Alice E. Marwick, and William Clyde Partin. 2021. "'We Dissect Stupidity and Respond to It': Response Videos and Networked Harassment on YouTube." *American Behavioral Scientist* 65(5):735–56. doi: 10.1177/0002764221989781.

Licoppe, Christian. 2004. "'Connected' Presence: The Emergence of a New Repertoire for Managing Social Relationships in a Changing Communication Technoscape." *Environment and Planning D: Society and Space* 22(1):135–56. https://doi.org/10.1068 /d323t.

Licoppe, Christian, and Julien Figeac. 2015. "Direct Video Observation of the Uses of Smartphone on the Move: Reconceptualizing Mobile Multi-Activity." Pp. 48–64 in *Mobility and Locative Media: Mobile Communication in Hybrid Spaces*, edited by A. de Souza e Silva and M. Sheller. Abingdon: Routledge

Licoppe, Christian, and Zbigniew Smoreda. 2005. "Are Social Networks Technologically Embedded? How Networks Are Changing Today with Changes in Communication Technology." *Social Networks* 27(4):317–35. https://doi.org/10.1016/j.socnet.2004.11.001.

Lim, Sun Sun. 2015. "On Stickers and Communicative Fluidity in Social Media." *Social Media + Society* 1(1). https://doi.org/10.1177/2056305115578137.

Ling, Rich. 2016. "Soft Coercion: Reciprocal Expectations of Availability in the Use of Mobile Communication." *First Monday* 21(9). https://doi.org/10.5210/fm.v21i9.6814.

Ling, Rich, and Chih-Hui Lai. 2016. "Microcoordination 2.0: Social Coordination in the Age of Smartphones and Messaging Apps." *Journal of Communication* 66(5):834–56. https://doi.org/10.1111/jcom.12251.

Liu, Alicia. 2018. "Death By a Thousand Pings: The Hidden Side of Using Slack." *Counter Intuition*. Retrieved March 24, 2022. https://medium.com/counter-intuition/the-hidden -side-of-using-slack-2443d9b66f8a.

Liu, Chuncheng. 2019. "Multiple Social Credit Systems in China." *Economic Sociology: The European Electronic Newsletter* 21(1):22–32.

Lobel, Orly. 2016. "The Law of the Platform." *Minnesota Law Review* 101:87–166.

Lobo, Sascha. 2014. "Auf dem Weg in die Dumpinghölle." *Der Spiegel*, September 3.

Locke, John L. 2010. *Eavesdropping: An Intimate History*. Oxford; New York: Oxford University Press.

Loubere, Nicholas, and Stefan Brehm. 2018. "The Global Age of Algorithm: Social Credit and the Financialisation of Governance in China." *Chinoiresie*, May 8. https:// www.chinoiresie.info/the-global-age-of-algorithm-social-credit-and-the-financialisation -of-governance-in-china/.

Lovink, Geert. 2008. "Society of the Query: The Googlization of Our Lives." *Future Non Stop*. Retrieved June 28, 2021. http://future-nonstop.org/c/4449020673d4bb73efe4bbfb d49f45ca.

Lovink, Geert, and Nathaniel Tkacz. 2015. "Moneylab: Sprouting New Digital-Economic Forms." Pp. 14–18 in *Moneylab Reader: An Intervention in Digital Economy*, edited by G. Lovink, N. Tkacz, and P. de Vries. Amsterdam: Institute of Network Cultures.

Lupton, Deborah. 2016. *The Quantified Self*. Malden, MA: Polity.

Lury, Celia, and Sophie Day. 2019. "Algorithmic Personalization as a Mode of Individuation." *Theory, Culture & Society* 36(2):17–37. https://doi.org/10.1177/0263276418818888.

Lynden, James. 2018. "Why Mood Matters in a Digital World." *Medium*, October 9. https:// medium.com/@jameslynden/markets of mood in a digital-world-f71b67c38a29

Mackenzie, Adrian. 2018. "48 Million Configurations and Counting: Platform Numbers and Their Capitalization." *Journal of Cultural Economy* 11(1):36–53. doi: 10.1080/17530350.2017.1393443.

MacKenzie, Donald A. 2006. *An Engine, Not a Camera: How Financial Models Shape Markets.* Cambridge, MA: The MIT Press.

MacKenzie, Donald. 2021. "Cookies, Pixels and Fingerprints." *London Review of Books*, April 1.

MacKenzie, Donald. 2022. "Blink, Bid, Buy." *London Review of Books*, May 12.

Magaudda, Paolo. 2011. "When Materiality 'Bites Back': Digital Music Consumption Practices in the Age of Dematerialization." *Journal of Consumer Culture* 11(1):15–36. doi: 10.1177/1469540510390499.

Mair, Peter. 2002. "Populist Democracy vs Party Democracy." Pp. 81–98 in *Democracies and the Populist Challenge*, edited by Y. Mény and Y. Surel. London: Palgrave Macmillan.

Maly, Ico. 2022. "Populism as a Mediatized Communicative Relation: The Birth of Algorithmic Populism." Pp. 33–58 in *Applied Linguistics and Politics*, edited by C. W. Chun. London: Bloomsbury Academic.

Mann, Monique, Peta Mitchell, and Marcus Foth. 2021. "Between Surveillance and Technological Solutionism: A Critique of 'Privacy-Preserving' Apps for COVID-19 Contact-Tracing." Available at SSRN. https://papers.ssrn.com/abstract=3717370

Mann, Steve, and Joseph Ferenbok. 2013. "New Media and the Power Politics of Sousveillance in a Surveillance-Dominated World." *Surveillance & Society* 11(1/2):18–34.

Mannell, Kate. 2019. "A Typology of Mobile Messaging's Disconnective Affordances." *Mobile Media & Communication* 7(1):76–93. https://doi.org/10.1177/2050157918772864.

Manning, Nathan, Ruth Penfold-Mounce, Brian D. Loader, Ariadne Vromen, and Michael Xenos. 2017. "Politicians, Celebrities and Social Media: A Case of Informalisation?" *Journal of Youth Studies* 20(2):127–44. doi: 10.1080/13676261.2016.1206867.

Manokha, Ivan. 2019. "New Means of Workplace Surveillance." *Monthly Review*, February 1.

Manzerolle, Vincent, and Michael Daubs. 2021. "Friction-Free Authenticity: Mobile Social Networks and Transactional Affordances." *Media, Culture & Society* 43(7):1279–96. doi: 10.1177/0163443721999953.

Markowitz, Dale. 2017. "The Future of Online Dating is Unsexy and Brutally Effective." *Gizmodo.* https://gizmodo.com/the-future-of-online-dating-is-unsexy-and-brutally-effe -1819781116.

Markus, Hazel, and Paula Nurius. 1986. "Possible Selves." *American Psychologist* 41(9):954–69. https://doi.org/10.1037/0003-066X.41.9.954.

Marwick, Alice. 2005. "Selling Your Self: Online Identity in the Age of a Commodified Internet." MA Thesis, University of Washington.

Marwick, Alice. 2010. "Status Update: Celebrity, Publicity and Self-Branding in Web 2.0." PhD Dissertation, University of Washington.

Marwick, Alice. 2012. "The Public Domain: Social Surveillance in Everyday Life." *Surveillance & Society* 9(4):378–93.

Marwick, Alice. 2016. "You May Know Me From YouTube: (Micro)-Celebrity in Social Media." Pp. 333–50 in *A Companion to Celebrity*, edited by P. David Marshall and Sean Redmond. Chichester: John Wiley & Sons.

Marwick, Alice. 2018. "Why Do People Share Fake News? A Sociotechnical Model of Media Effects." *Georgetown Law Technology Review* 2:474–512.

Marwick, Alice, and danah boyd. 2011a. "I Tweet Honestly, I Tweet Passionately: Twitter Users, Context Collapse, and the Imagined Audience." *New Media & Society* 13(1):114–33.

Marwick, Alice, and danah boyd. 2011b. "To See and Be Seen: Celebrity Practice on Twitter." *Convergence* 17(2):139–58. https://doi.org/10.1177/1354856510394539.

Marx, Gary T. 1988. *Undercover: Police Surveillance in America*. Berkeley: University of California Press.

Mascheroni, Giovanna, and Jane Vincent. 2016. "Perpetual Contact as a Communicative Affordance: Opportunities, Constraints, and Emotions." *Mobile Media & Communication* 4(3):310–26. https://doi.org/10.1177/2050157916639347.

Mascheroni, Giovanna, Jane Vincent, and Estefanía Jimenez. 2015. "'Girls Are Addicted to Likes So They Post Semi-Naked Selfies': Peer Mediation, Normativity and the Construction of Identity Online." *Cyberpsychology: Journal of Psychosocial Research on Cyberspace* 9(1). https://doi.org/10.5817/CP2015-1-5.

Massanari, Adrienne. 2017. "#Gamergate and The Fappening: How Reddit's Algorithm, Governance, and Culture Support Toxic Technocultures." *New Media & Society* 19(3):329–46. doi: 10.1177/1461444815608807.

Matarić, Maja J. 2017. "Socially Assistive Robotics: Human Augmentation versus Automation." *Science Robotics* 2(4). doi: 10.1126/scirobotics.aam5410.

Mateescu, Alexandra, and Aiha Nguyen. 2019. "Workplace Monitoring & Surveillance." Data & Society Research Institute. https://datasociety.net/wp-content/uploads/2019/02/DS_Workplace_Monitoring_Surveillance_Explainer.pdf.

Matei, Sorin. 2005. "From Counterculture to Cyberculture: Virtual Community Discourse and the Dilemma of Modernity." *Journal of Computer-Mediated Communication* 10(3). doi: 10.1111/j.1083-6101.2005.tb00262.x.

Matsuda, Keiichi. 2016. "Hyper-Reality." Retrieved November 19, 2021. http://hyper-reality.co/.

Mattioli, Dana. 2020. "Amazon Scooped Up Data From its Own Sellers to Launch Competing Products." *Wall Street Journal*, April 24.

Mattioli, Dana, and Joe Flint. 2021. "Amazon Coerces Partners by Using its Broad Reach – Technology Giant Strong-Arms Vendors in One Market to Engage with it in Others." *Wall Street Journal*, April 15.

Mau, Steffen. 2019. *The Metric Society: On the Quantification of the Social*. Cambridge, UK: Medford, MA: Polity.

Mauss, Marcel. 2002 [1925]. *The Gift: The Form and Reason for Exchange in Archaic Societies*. London: Routledge.

Maxwell, Samantha. 2017. "Google's Smart Reply: Convenience Over Connection." *The Technoskeptic*, December 20.

Mayer-Schönberger, Viktor, and Kenneth Cukier. 2013. *Big Data: A Revolution That Will Transform How We Live, Work, and Think*. Boston, MA: Houghton Mifflin Harcourt.

Mazzoleni, Gianpietro. 2008. "Mediatization of Politics." Pp. 3047–51 in *The International Encyclopedia of Communication*, Vol. vii, edited by W. Donsbach. Malden, MA: Blackwell.

Mazzoleni, Gianpietro, and Winfried Schulz. 1999. "'Mediatization' of Politics: A Challenge for Democracy?" *Political Communication* 16(3):247–61. doi: 10.1080/105846099198613.

McCabe, David, and Adam Satariano. 2022. "The Era of Borderless Data is Ending." *The New York Times*, May 23.

McGuigan, Jim. 2009. *Cool Capitalism*. London: Pluto.

McGuigan, Jim. 2014. "The Neoliberal Self." *Culture Unbound: Journal of Current Cultural Research* 6(1):223–40. https://doi.org/10.3384/cu.2000.1525.146223.

McRae, Sarah. 2017. "'Get Off My Internets': How Anti-Fans Deconstruct Lifestyle Bloggers' Authenticity Work." *Persona Studies* 3(1):13. https://doi.org/10.21153/ps2017vol3no1art640.

McStay, Andrew. 2018. *Emotional AI: The Rise of Empathic Media*. London: Sage.

Mead, George Herbert. 1934. *Mind, Self, and Society: From the Standpoint of a Social Behaviorist*. Edited by Charles W. Morris. Chicago, IL: University of Chicago Press.

Mede, Niels G., and Mike S. Schäfer. 2020. "Science-Related Populism: Conceptualizing Populist Demands toward Science." *Public Understanding of Science* 29(5):473–91. doi: 10.1177/0963662520924259.

Mennicken, Andrea, and Wendy Nelson Espeland. 2019. "What's New with Numbers? Sociological Approaches to the Study of Quantification." *Annual Review of Sociology* 45:223–45. doi: 10.1146/annurev-soc-073117-041343.

Mennicken, Andrea, and Robert Salais, eds. 2022. *The New Politics of Numbers: Utopia, Evidence and Democracy*. Cham: Springer International.

Merchant, Brian. 2021a. "The Metaverse Has Always Been a Dystopian Idea." *Vice*. Retrieved September 12, 2021. https://www.vice.com/en/article/v7eqbb/the-metaverse-has-always -been-a-dystopia.

Merchant, Brian. 2021b. "The Real Reason Facebook Changed its Name." *The Atlantic*, October 28.

Meta. 2022. "Meta Reports Fourth Quarter and Full Year 2021 Results." https://s21. q4cdn.com/399680738/files/doc_financials/2021/q4/FB-12.31.2021-Exhibit-99.1-Final. pdf.

Mewburn, Inger, and Pat Thomson. 2018. "Towards an Academic Self?: Blogging during the Doctorate." Pp. 20–35 in *The Digital Academic: Critical Perspectives on Digital Technologies in Higher Education*, edited by Deborah Lupton, Inger Mewburn, and Pat Thomson. Abingdon; New York: Routledge.

Meyrowitz, Joshua. 1985. *No Sense of Place: The Impact of Electronic Media on Social Behavior*. New York: Oxford University Press.

Microsoft. 2021a. "Converging the Physical and Digital with Digital Twins, Mixed Reality, and Metaverse Apps." Retrieved November 28, 2021. https://azure.microsoft.com /en-us/blog/converging-the-physical-and-digital-with-digital-twins-mixed-reality-and -metaverse-apps/.

Microsoft. 2021b. "What is Microsoft's Metaverse?" Retrieved November 28, 2021. https:// www.youtube.com/watch?v=Qw6UCwCt4bE.

Miller, Peter, and Nikolas S. Rose. 2008. *Governing the Present: Administering Economic, Social and Personal Life*. Cambridge, UK; Malden, MA: Polity.

Miller, Vincent. 2008. "New Media, Networking and Phatic Culture." *Convergence* 14(4):387–400. https://doi.org/10.1177/1354856508094659.

Milner, Ryan M. 2016. *The World Made Meme: Public Conversations and Participatory Media*. Cambridge, MA: The MIT Press.

Miltner, Kate M., and Tim Highfield. 2017. "Never Gonna GIF You Up: Analyzing the Cultural Significance of the Animated GIF." *Social Media + Society* 3(3). doi: 10.1177/2056305117725223.

Mittelstadt, Brent Daniel, Patrick Allo, Mariarosaria Taddeo, Sandra Wachter, and Luciano Floridi. 2016. "The Ethics of Algorithms: Mapping the Debate." *Big Data & Society* 3(2). https://doi.org/10.1177/2053951716679679.

Monserrate, Steven Gonzalez. 2022. "The Cloud is Material: On the Environmental Impacts of Computation and Data Storage." *MIT Case Studies in Social and Ethical Responsibilities of Computing*, January 27. doi: 10.21428/2c646de5.031d4553.

Morley, David. 1993. "Active Audience Theory: Pendulums and Pitfalls." *Journal of Communication* 43(4):13–19. doi: 10.1111/j.1460-2466.1993.tb01299.x.

Morozov, Evgeny. 2013a. *To Save Everything, Click Here: The Folly of Technological Solutionism*. New York: Public Affairs.

Morozov, Evgeny. 2013b. "Machines of Laughter and Forgetting." *The New York Times*, March 30.

Morozov, Evgeny. 2014. "The Rise of Data and the Death of Politics." *The Guardian*, July 19.

Morozov, Evgeny. 2019. "Capitalism's New Clothes." *The Baffler*. Retrieved December 26, 2021. https://thebaffler.com/latest/capitalisms-new-clothes-morozov.

Morozov, Evgeny. 2020. "The Tech 'Solutions' for Coronavirus Take the Surveillance State to the Next Level." *The Guardian*, April 15.

Morozov, Evgeny. 2022. "Web3: A Map in Search of Territory." *The Crypto Syllabus*. Retrieved January 17, 2022. https://the-crypto-syllabus.com/web3-a-map-in-search-of-territory/.

Moskowitz, Daniel J. 2021. "Local News, Information, and the Nationalization of U.S. Elections." *American Political Science Review* 115(1):114–29. doi:10.1017/S0003055420000829.

Mozur, Paul. 2019. "One Month, 500,000 Face Scans: How China is Using A.I. to Profile a Minority." *The New York Times*, April 14.

Muise, Amy, Emily Christofides, and Serge Desmarais. 2009. "More Information than You Ever Wanted: Does Facebook Bring Out the Green-Eyed Monster of Jealousy?" *Cyberpsychology & Behavior: The Impact of the Internet, Multimedia and Virtual Reality on Behavior and Society* 12(4):441–4. https://doi.org/10.1089/cpb.2008.0263.

Muller, Jerry Z. 2018. *The Tyranny of Metrics*. Princeton, NJ: Princeton University Press.

Munger, Kevin. 2020a. "GPT-3: Informational Hyper-Inflation." *Never Met a Science*, August 20. https://kevinmunger.substack.com/p/gpt-3-informational-hyper-inflation?s=r.

Munger, Kevin. 2020b. "Theorizing TikTok." *Never Met a Science*, July 26. https://kevinmunger.substack.com/p/theorizing-tiktok?s=r.

Munger, Kevin. 2021. "Hello Goodbye." *Real Life*, April 12.

Munger, Kevin, and Joseph Phillips. 2022. "Right-Wing YouTube: A Supply and Demand Perspective." *The International Journal of Press/Politics* 27(1):186–219. doi:10.1177/1940161220964767.

Nafus, Dawn, and Jamie Sherman. 2014. "This One Does Not Go Up to 11: The Quantified Self Movement as an Alternative Big Data Practice." *International Journal of Communication* 8:1784–94.

Nagle, Angela. 2017. *Kill All Normies: Online Culture Wars From 4Chan and Tumblr To Trump and the Alt-Right*. Winchester, UK; Washington, US: Zero Books.

Nagle, Frank, Robert Seamans, and Steven Tadelis. 2020. "Transaction Cost Economics in the Digital Economy: A Research Agenda." Available at SSRN. doi: 10.2139/ssrn.3661856.

Nakamura, Lisa. 2002. *Cybertypes: Race, Ethnicity, and Identity on the Internet*. London: Routledge.

Nash, Catherine J., and Andrew Gorman-Murray, eds. 2019. *The Geographies of Digital Sexuality*. Singapore: Springer Singapore.

Negroponte, Nicholas. 1995. *Being Digital*. New York: Knopf.

Nelson, Michelle R. 2008. "The Hidden Persuaders: Then and Now." *Journal of Advertising* 37(1):113–26. https://doi.org/10.2753/JOA0091-3367370109.

New York Times Editorial Board. 2020. "The Most Patriotic Thing You Can Do Right Now." *The New York Times*, May 24.

Newman, Andy. 2019. "I Found Work on an Amazon Website. I Made 97 Cents an Hour." *The New York Times*, November 15.

Newton, Casey. 2021. "Mark in the Metaverse: Facebook's CEO on Why the Social Network

Is Becoming 'a Metaverse Company.'" *The Verge*. Retrieved November 11, 2021. https://www.theverge.com/22588022/mark-zuckerberg-facebook-ceo-metaverse-interview.

Nguyen, C. Thi. 2021. "How Twitter Gamifies Communication." Pp. 410–36 in *Applied Epistemology*, edited by J. Lackey. Oxford: Oxford University Press.

Nguyen, Terry. 2021. "Online Shopping Changed, and We Barely Noticed." *Vox*. Retrieved May 11, 2021. https://www.vox.com/the-goods/22412098/social-commerce-explainer.

Nguyen, Terry. 2022. "The Empty Promise of Instant Delivery." *Vox*. Retrieved January 20, 2022. https://www.vox.com/the-goods/22880345/pandemic-shopper-convenience-instant-delivery.

Nieborg, David B., and Anne Helmond. 2019. "The Political Economy of Facebook's Platformization in the Mobile Ecosystem: Facebook Messenger as a Platform Instance." *Media, Culture & Society* 41(2):196–218. doi: 10.1177/0163443718818384.

Nieborg, David B., and Thomas Poell. 2018. "The Platformization of Cultural Production: Theorizing the Contingent Cultural Commodity." *New Media & Society* 20(11):4275–92. doi: 10.1177/1461444818769694.

Nippert-Eng, Christena E. 1996. *Home and Work: Negotiating Boundaries through Everyday Life*. Chicago, IL: University of Chicago Press.

O'Dwyer, Rachel. 2020. "Limited Edition: Producing Artificial Scarcity for Digital Art on the Blockchain and its Implications for the Cultural Industries." *Convergence* 26(4):874–94. doi: 10.1177/1354856518795097.

O'Hara, Kenton P., Michael Massimi, Richard Harper, Simon Rubens, and Jessica Morris. 2014. "Everyday Dwelling with WhatsApp." Pp. 1131–43 in *Proceedings of the 17th ACM Conference on Computer Supported Cooperative Work & Social Computing – CSCW '14*. Baltimore: ACM Press. https://doi.org/10.1145/2531602.2531679.

O'Reilly, Séamas. 2019. "How Smart Are Gmail's 'Smart Replies'?" *The Guardian*, February 17. https://www.theguardian.com/technology/2019/feb/17/gmail-smart-replies-seamas-o-reilly.

Oakeshott, Michael. 1991. *Rationalism in Politics and Other Essays*. Indianapolis, IN: Liberty Fund.

Ocean, Neel. 2017. "Digital Goods as Public Goods." *Neelocean.com*. Retrieved March 1, 2021. https://www.neelocean.com/digital-goods-as-public-goods/.

Orlikowski, Wanda J., and Susan V. Scott. 2014. "What Happens When Evaluation Goes Online? Exploring Apparatuses of Valuation in the Travel Sector." *Organization Science* 25(3):868–91. doi: 10.1287/orsc.2013.0877.

Ostiguy, Pierre. 2009. "The High and the Low in Politics: A Two-Dimensional Political Space for Comparative Analysis and Electoral Studies." Kellogg Institute, Working Paper No. 360.

Palmer, Annie. 2021. "Amazon is Spending Big to Take on UPS and FedEx." *CNBC*, April 30.

Pamungkas, Endang Wahyu. 2019. "Emotionally-Aware Chatbots: A Survey." *ArXiv*. http://arxiv.org/abs/1906.09774.

Papacharissi, Zizi. 2015. *Affective Publics: Sentiment, Technology, and Politics*. Oxford: Oxford University Press.

Pardes, Arielle. 2017. "What My Personal Chat Bot is Teaching Me About AI's Future." *Wired*, November 12.

Park, Gene. 2020. "Silicon Valley is Racing to Build the next Version of the Internet. Fortnite Might Get There First." *Washington Post*, April 17.

Parker, Geoffrey G., Marshall W. Van Alstyne, and Sangeet Paul Choudary. 2016. *Platform*

Revolution: How Networked Markets Are Transforming the Economy and How to Make Them Work for You. New York: W. W. Norton & Company.

Pasquale, Frank. 2015. *The Black Box Society: The Secret Algorithms That Control Money and Information*. Cambridge, MA: Harvard University Press.

Pauli, Tobias, Erwin Fielt, and Martin Matzner. 2021. "Digital Industrial Platforms." *Business & Information Systems Engineering* 63(2):181–90. doi: 10.1007/s12599-020-00681-w.

Pendergrast, Kelly. 2019. "Ill at Ease." *Real Life*. Retrieved January 26, 2022. https://reallifemag.com/ill-at-ease/.

Perez, Sarah. 2021. "Facebook and Instagram Will Now Allow Users to Hide 'Like' Counts on Posts." *TechCrunch*. Retrieved April 3, 2022. https://social.techcrunch.com/2021/05/26/facebook-and-instagram-will-now-allow-users-to-hide-like-counts-on-posts/.

Peri, Yoram. 2004. *Telepopulism: Media and Politics in Israel*. Stanford, CA: Stanford University Press.

Peters, Tom. 1997. "The Brand Called You." *Fast Company*, August 31. https://www.fastcompany.com/28905/brand-called-you.

Peterson, Richard A. 1997. *Creating Country Music: Fabricating Authenticity*. Chicago, IL: University of Chicago Press.

Phillips, Whitney. 2015. *This is Why We Can't Have Nice Things: Mapping the Relationship between Online Trolling and Mainstream Culture*. Cambridge, MA: The MIT Press.

Picone, Ike, Jelena Kleut, Tereza Pavlíčková, Bojana Romic, Jannie Møller Hartley, and Sander De Ridder. 2019. "Small Acts of Engagement: Reconnecting Productive Audience Practices with Everyday Agency." *New Media & Society* 21(9):2010–28. doi: 10.1177/1461444819837569.

Pielot, Martin, Tilman Dingler, Jose San Pedro, and Nuria Oliver. 2015. "When Attention is Not Scarce – Detecting Boredom from Mobile Phone Usage." Pp. 825–36 in *Proceedings of the 2015 ACM International Joint Conference on Pervasive and Ubiquitous Computing – UbiComp '15*. Osaka, Japan: ACM Press. https://dl.acm.org/doi/10.1145/2750858.2804252.

Pies, Ronald. 2009. "Should DSM-V Designate 'Internet Addiction' a Mental Disorder?" *Psychiatry (Edgmont)* 6(2):31–7.

Pignataro, Juliana Rose. 2017. "Artificial Intelligence Dating is the Future, Tinder Co-Founder Says." *International Business Times*, April 3.

Pine, Joseph P., II, and James H. Gilmore. 1998. "Welcome to the Experience Economy." *Harvard Business Review*, August.

Plantin, Jean-Christophe, Carl Lagoze, Paul N. Edwards, and Christian Sandvig. 2018. "Infrastructure Studies Meet Platform Studies in the Age of Google and Facebook." *New Media & Society* 20(1):293–310. doi: 10.1177/1461444816661553.

Plantin, Jean-Christophe, and Aswin Punathambekar. 2019. "Digital Media Infrastructures: Pipes, Platforms, and Politics." *Media, Culture & Society* 41(2):163–74. doi: 10.1177/0163443718818376.

Pongratz, Hans J., and G. Günter Voß. 2003. "From Employee to 'Entreployee': Towards a 'Self-Entrepreneurial' Work Force?" *Concepts and Transformation* 8(3):239–54. https://doi.org/10.1075/cat.8.3.04pon.

Prior, Lindsay. 2003. "Belief, Knowledge and Expertise: The Emergence of the Lay Expert in Medical Sociology." *Sociology of Health & Illness* 25(3):41 57. doi: 10.1111/1467-9566.00339.

Public Domain Review. n.d. "Yellow Journalism: The 'Fake News' of the 19th Century." *The Public Domain Review*. Retrieved November 5, 2021. https://publicdomainreview.org/collection/yellow-journalism-the-fake-news-of-the-19th-century/.

Puro, Jukka-Pekka. 2002. "Finland: A Mobile Culture." Pp. 19–29 in *Perpetual Contact: Mobile Communication, Private Talk, Public Performance*, edited by James E. Katz and Mark Aakhus. Cambridge; New York: Cambridge University Press.

Quandt, Thorsten. 2012. "What's Left of Trust in a Network Society? An Evolutionary Model and Critical Discussion of Trust and Societal Communication." *European Journal of Communication* 27(1):7–21.

Quito, Anne. 2015. "The Next Design Trend is One That Eliminates All Choices." *Quartz*. Retrieved April 19, 2020. https://qz.com/429929/the-next-design-trend-is-one-that -eliminates-all-choices/.

Rahman, K. Sabeel. 2018. "The New Utilities: Private Power, Social Infrastructure, and the Revival of the Public Utility Concept." *Cardozo Law Review* 39:1621–89.

Rahman, K. Sabeel, and Kathleen Thelen. 2019. "The Rise of the Platform Business Model and the Transformation of Twenty-First-Century Capitalism." *Politics & Society* 47(2):177–204. doi: 10.1177/0032329219838932.

Rainie, Harrison, and Barry Wellman. 2012. *Networked: The New Social Operating System*. Cambridge, MA: The MIT Press.

Rashid, Raphael. 2021. "South Korea Cuts Human Interaction in Push to Build 'Untact' Society." *The Guardian*, December 10.

Rauch, Jonathan. 2021. *The Constitution of Knowledge: A Defense of Truth*. Washington, DC: Brookings Institution Press.

Ravenelle, Alexandrea J. 2019. *Hustle and Gig: Struggling and Surviving in the Sharing Economy*. Oakland, CA: University of California Press.

Reich, Jennifer A. 2016. *Calling the Shots: Why Parents Reject Vaccines*. New York: New York University Press.

Reich, Rob, Mehran Sahami, and Jeremy M. Weinstein. 2021. *System Error: Where Big Tech Went Wrong and How We Can Reboot*. New York: HarperCollins.

Resch, Magnus, and Stefan Heidenreich. 2019. "What the Art World Can Do to Make Art Accessible to More People." *Artsy*. Retrieved April 26, 2021. https://www.ashartsy.net /article/artsy-editorial-art-art-accessible-people.

Rettberg, Jill Walker. 2014. *Seeing Ourselves Through Technology: How We Use Selfies, Blogs and Wearable Devices to See and Shape Ourselves*. Basingstoke: Palgrave Macmillan.

Rettie, Ruth. 2009a. "Mobile Phone Communication: Extending Goffman to Mediated Interaction." *Sociology* 43(3):421–38. https://doi.org/10.1177/0038038509103197.

Rettie, Ruth. 2009b. "SMS: Exploiting the Interactional Characteristics of Near-Synchrony." *Information, Communication & Society* 12(8):1131–48. https://doi.org/10.1080 /13691180902786943.

Reyburn, Scott. 2021. "JPG File Sells for $69 Million, as 'NFT Mania' Gathers Pace." *The New York Times*, March 11.

Rheingold, Howard. 2008. "Virtual Communities – Exchanging Ideas through Computer Bulletin Boards." *Journal for Virtual Worlds Research* 1(1). https://doi.org/10.4101/jvwr.v1i1. 293.

Rifkin, Jeremy. 2014. *The Zero Marginal Cost Society: The Internet of Things, the Collaborative Commons, and the Eclipse of Capitalism*. New York: Palgrave Macmillan.

Ritzer, George, and Nathan Jurgenson. 2010. "Production, Consumption, Prosumption: The Nature of Capitalism in the Age of the Digital 'Prosumer.'" *Journal of Consumer Culture* 10(1):13–36. doi: 10.1177/1469540509354673.

Robb, Michael B. 2019. "Screens and Sleep: The New Normal: Parents, Teens, Screens, and Sleep in the United States." San Francisco: Common Sense Media. https://www. commonsensemedia.org/research/the-new-normal-parents-teens-screens-and-sleep.

Roberts, Margaret E. 2018. *Censored: Distraction and Diversion Inside China's Great Firewall.* Princeton, NJ: Princeton University Press.

Roberts, Sarah T. 2019. *Behind the Screen: Content Moderation in the Shadows of Social Media.* New Haven, CT: Yale University Press.

Robinson, Laura. 2007. "The Cyberself: The Self-Ing Project Goes Online, Symbolic Interaction in the Digital Age." *New Media & Society* 9(1):93–110. https://doi.org/10.1177 /1461444807072216.

Robinson, M. J. 2017. *Television on Demand: Curatorial Culture and the Transformation of TV.* New York: Bloomsbury Academic.

Rochet, Jean-Charles, and Jean Tirole. 2003. "Platform Competition in Two-Sided Markets." *Journal of the European Economic Association* 1(4):990–1029. doi: 10.1162/154247603322493212.

Roettgers, Janko. 2021. "VR Wants to Save the Live Music Business, One Avatar at a Time." *Protocol*, March 26.

Rohrlich, Justin. 2019. "Online 'People Finder' Sites Are a Blessing for Identity Thieves." *Quartz.* Retrieved March 25, 2022. https://qz.com/1690801/background-check-sites-like -truthfinder-are-great-for-identity-thieves/.

Romer, Paul. 2019. "A Tax to Fix Big Tech." *New York Times*, May 7.

Rona-Tas, Akos. 2020. "Predicting the Future: Art and Algorithms." *Socio-Economic Review* 18(3):893–911. doi: 10.1093/ser/mwaa040.

Roose, Kevin. 2018. "Is Tech Too Easy to Use?" *The New York Times*, December 12.

Rosa, Hartmut. 2013. *Social Acceleration: A New Theory of Modernity.* New York: Columbia University Press.

Rose, Nikolas S. 1991. "Governing by Numbers: Figuring out Democracy." *Accounting, Organizations and Society* 16(7):673–92. doi: 10.1016/0361-3682(91)90019-B.

Rose, Nikolas S. 1998. *Inventing Our Selves: Psychology, Power, and Personhood.* Cambridge; New York: Cambridge University Press.

Rose, Nikolas S. 1999a. *Governing the Soul: The Shaping of the Private Self.* 2nd ed. London; New York: Free Association Books.

Rose, Nikolas S. 1999b. *Powers of Freedom: Reframing Political Thought.* Cambridge; New York: Cambridge University Press.

Rosenblat, Alex, and Luke Stark. 2016. "Algorithmic Labor and Information Asymmetries: A Case Study of Uber's Drivers." *International Journal of Communication* 10:3758–84.

Roth, Emma. 2021. "Instagram Reportedly Hit 2 Billion Active Users but Probably Won't Admit It." *The Verge.* Retrieved April 1, 2022. https://www.theverge.com/2021/12/14 /22834571/instagram-2-billion-active-users.

Sacasas, L. M. 2011. "A Frictionless Life Is Also a Life Without Traction." *The Frailest Thing.* Retrieved January 29, 2022. https://thefrailestthing.com/2011/05/05/a-frictionless-life-is -also-a-life-without-traction/.

Sacasas, L. M. 2013. "From Memory Scarcity to Memory Abundance." *The Frailest Thing.* Retrieved January 2, 2022. https://thefrailestthing.com/2013/01/25/from-memory-scarcity -to-memory-abundance/.

Sacasas, L. M. 2020. "A Theory of Zoom Fatigue." *The Convivial Society.* Retrieved November 19, 2021. https://theconvivialsociety.substack.com/p/a-theory-of-zoom-fatigue.

Sacasas, L. M. 2021a. "The Insurrection Will Be Live Streamed: Notes Toward a Theory of Digitization." *The Convivial Society*, January 15.

Sacasas, L. M. 2021b. "Notes From the Metaverse." *The Convivial Society*. Retrieved September 12, 2021. https://theconvivialsociety.substack.com/p/notes-from-the-metaverse.

Sadowski, Jathan. 2019. "When Data is Capital: Datafication, Accumulation, and Extraction." *Big Data & Society* 6(1). doi: 10.1177/2053951718820549.

Sætra, Henrik Skaug. 2020. "A Shallow Defence of a Technocracy of Artificial Intelligence: Examining the Political Harms of Algorithmic Governance in the Domain of Government." *Technology in Society* 62:101283. doi: 10.1016/j.techsoc.2020.101283.

Saker, M., and J. Frith. 2018. "Locative Media and Sociability: Using Location-Based Social Networks to Coordinate Everyday Life." *Architecture_MPS* 14(1). doi: 10.14324/111.444. amps.2018v14i1.001.

Salerno, Jessica M., and Liana C. Peter-Hagene. 2013. "The Interactive Effect of Anger and Disgust on Moral Outrage and Judgments." *Psychological Science* 24(10):2069–78.

Sanden, Paul. 2019. "Rethinking Liveness in the Digital Age." Pp. 178–92 in *The Cambridge Companion to Music in Digital Culture*, edited by N. Cook, M. M. Ingalls, and D. Trippett. Cambridge: Cambridge University Press.

Sandvig, Christian. 2013. "The Internet as Infrastructure." In *The Oxford Handbook of Internet Studies*, edited by W. H. Dutton. Oxford: Oxford University Press.

Sapolsky, Robert M. 2017. *Behave: The Biology of Humans at Our Best and Worst*. New York: Penguin Press.

Saurette, Paul, and Shane Gunster. 2011. "Ears Wide Shut: Epistemological Populism, Argutainment and Canadian Conservative Talk Radio." *Canadian Journal of Political Science* 44(1):195–218. doi: 10.1017/S0008423910001095.

Sauter, Theresa. 2014. "'What's on Your Mind?' Writing on Facebook as a Tool for Self-Formation." *New Media & Society* 16(5):823–39. doi: 10.1177/1461444813495160.

Savolainen, Laura, Damian Trilling, and Dimitra Liotsiou. 2020. "Delighting and Detesting Engagement: Emotional Politics of Junk News." *Social Media + Society* 6(4). doi: 10.1177/2056305120972037.

Schandorf, Michael. 2013. "Mediated Gesture: Paralinguistic Communication and Phatic Text." *Convergence* 19(3):319–44. https://doi.org/10.1177/1354856512439501.

Schatzki, Theodore R., K. Knorr-Cetina, and Eike von Savigny, eds. 2001. *The Practice Turn in Contemporary Theory*. London; New York: Routledge.

Schmidt, Eric. 2020. "A Real Digital Infrastructure at Last." *Wall Street Journal*, March 27.

Schmidt, Florian Alexander. 2019. "Crowdsourced Production of AI Training Data: How Human Workers Teach Self-Driving Cars How to See." Hans-Böckler-Stiftung, Working Paper No. 155.

Scholz, Trebor. 2008. "Market Ideology and the Myths of Web 2.0." *First Monday* 3(3). doi: 10.5210/fm.v13i3.2138.

Schor, Juliet. 2020. *After the Gig: How the Sharing Economy Got Hijacked and How to Win it Back*. Oakland, CA: University of California Press.

Schor, Juliet B., and William Attwood-Charles. 2017. "The 'Sharing' Economy: Labor, Inequality, and Social Connection on for-Profit Platforms." *Sociology Compass* 11(8):e12493. doi: https://doi.org/10.1111/soc4.12493.

Schor, Juliet B., and Steven P. Vallas. 2021. "The Sharing Economy: Rhetoric and Reality." *Annual Review of Sociology* 47: 369–89. doi: 10.1146/annurev-soc-082620-031411.

Schrape, Jan-Felix. 2019. "The Promise of Technological Decentralization: A Brief Reconstruction." *Society* 56(1):31–7. doi: 10.1007/s12115-018-00321-w.

Schrock, Andrew Richard. 2015. "Communicative Affordances of Mobile Media: Portability, Availability, Locatability, and Multimediality." *International Journal of Communication* 9:1229–46.

Schüll, Natasha Dow. 2012. *Addiction by Design: Machine Gambling in Las Vegas*. Princeton, NJ: Princeton University Press.

Schüll, Natasha Dow. 2016. "Data for Life: Wearable Technology and the Design of Self-Care." *BioSocieties* 11(3):317–33. https://doi.org/10.1057/biosoc.2015.47.

Schüll, Natasha Dow. 2019. "Self in the Loop: Bits, Patterns, and Pathways in the Quantified Self." Pp. 25–38 in *A Networked Self and Human Augmentics, Artificial Intelligence, Sentience*, edited by Zizi Papacharissi. New York: Routledge.

Schwartz, Barry. 2004. *The Paradox of Choice: Why More is Less*. New York: Ecco.

Schwartz, Mattathias. 2008. "The Trolls Among Us." *The New York Times*, August 3. https://www.nytimes.com/2008/08/03/magazine/03trolls-t.html.

Schwarz, Jonas Andersson. 2017. "Platform Logic: An Interdisciplinary Approach to the Platform-Based Economy." *Policy & Internet* 9(4):374–94. doi: https://doi.org/10.1002/poi3.159.

Schwarz, Ori. 2011. "Who Moved My Conversation? Instant Messaging, Intertextuality and New Regimes of Intimacy and Truth." *Media, Culture & Society* 33(1):71–87. https://doi.org/10.1177/0163443710385501.

Schwarz, Ori. 2012. "The New Hunter-Gatherers: Making Human Interaction Productive in the Network Society." *Theory, Culture & Society* 29(6):78–98. https://doi.org/10.1177/0263276412452619.

Schwarz, Ori. 2014. "The Past Next Door: Neighbourly Relations with Digital Memory-Artefacts." *Memory Studies* 7(1):7–21. doi: 10.1177/1750698013490591.

Schwarz, Ori. 2021. *Sociological Theory for Digital Society: The Codes That Bind Us Together*. Cambridge, UK; Medford, MA: Polity.

Schwarz, Ori, and Guy Shani. 2016. "Culture in Mediated Interaction: Political Defriending on Facebook and the Limits of Networked Individualism." *American Journal of Cultural Sociology* 4(3):385–421. doi: 10.1057/s41290-016-0006-6.

Scott, James C. 1998. *Seeing like a State: How Certain Schemes to Improve the Human Condition Have Failed*. New Haven, CT: Yale University Press.

Scott, Mark, and Laura Kayali. 2020. "What Happened When Humans Stopped Managing Social Media Content." *POLITICO*, October 21.

Sekalala, Sharifah, Stéphanie Dagron, Lisa Forman, and Benjamin Mason Meier. 2020. "Analyzing the Human Rights Impact of Increased Digital Public Health Surveillance during the COVID-19 Crisis." *Health and Human Rights Journal* 22(2):7–20.

Senft, Gunter. 2014. *Understanding Pragmatics*. Abingdon: Routledge.

Serrano-Puche, Javier. 2021. "Digital Disinformation and Emotions: Exploring the Social Risks of Affective Polarization." *International Review of Sociology* 31(2):231–45. doi: 10.1080/03906701.2021.1947953.

Settle, Jaime E. 2018. *Frenemies: How Social Media Polarizes America*. Cambridge; New York: Cambridge University Press.

Seymour, Richard. 2020. *The Twittering Machine*. London: Verso

Shao, Chengcheng, Giovanni Luca Ciampaglia, Onur Varol, Kai-Cheng Yang, Alessandro Flammini, and Filippo Menczer. 2018. "The Spread of Low-Credibility Content by Social Bots." *Nature Communications* 9(1):1–9. doi: 10.1038/s41467-018-06930-7.

Shapin, Steven. 2019. "Is There a Crisis of Truth?" *Los Angeles Review of Books*, December 2.

Sharma, Bhakti, Susanna S. Lee, and Benjamin K. Johnson. 2022. "The Dark at the End of the Tunnel: Doomscrolling on Social Media Newsfeeds." *Technology, Mind, and Behavior* 3(1). doi: 10.1037/tmb0000059.

Sharon, Tamar. 2017. "Self-Tracking for Health and the Quantified Self: Re-Articulating Autonomy, Solidarity, and Authenticity in an Age of Personalized Healthcare." *Philosophy & Technology* 30(1):93–121. https://doi.org/10.1007/s13347-016-0215-5.

Sharon, Tamar. 2020. "Blind-Sided by Privacy? Digital Contact Tracing, the Apple/Google API and Big Tech's Newfound Role as Global Health Policy Makers." *Ethics and Information Technology* 23:45–57. doi: 10.1007/s10676-020-09547-x.

Shifman, Limor. 2014. *Memes in Digital Culture.* Cambridge, MA: The MIT Press.

Shirky, Clay. 2008. *Here Comes Everybody: The Power of Organizing Without Organizations.* New York: Penguin Books.

Shirky, Clay. 2014. "Why I Just Asked My Students To Put Their Laptops Away…." *Medium.* Retrieved February 8, 2015. https://medium.com/@cshirky/why-i-just-asked-my-students-to-put-their-laptops-away-7f5f7c50f368.

Shove, Elizabeth. 2012. "Comfort and Convenience: Temporality and Practice." Pp. 289–306 in *The Oxford Handbook of the History of Consumption,* edited by F. Trentmann. Oxford: Oxford University Press.

Silverman, Jacob. 2022. "Bitcoin Goes to War." *The New Republic*, March 3.

Silverstein, Drew. 2019. "How Technology Can Democratize Music." TEDx. https://www.ted.com/talks/drew_silverstein_how_technology_can_democratize_music.

Simmel, Georg. 1950 [1903]. "The Metropolis and Mental Life." Pp. 409–24 in *The Sociology of Georg Simmel,* edited by K. H. Wolff. New York: Free Press.

Simon, Herbert. 1971. "Designing Organizations for an Information-Rich World." Pp. 38–52 in *Computers, Communications, and the Public Interest,* edited by M. Greenberger. Baltimore, MD: Johns Hopkins University Press.

Sinha, Jay I., Thomas Foscht, and Thomas Fung. 2016. "How Analytics and AI Are Driving the Subscription E-Commerce Phenomenon." *MIT Sloan Management Review*, December 6. https://sloanreview.mit.edu/article/using-analytics-and-ai-subscription-e-commerce-has-personalized-marketing-all-boxed-up/.

Sklaroff, Jeremy M. 2017. "Smart Contracts and the Cost of Inflexibility." *University of Pennsylvania Law Review* 166(1):263–304.

Sloan, Robin. 2015. "Why I Quit Ordering From Uber-for-Food Start-Ups." *The Atlantic*, November 6.

Smith Maguire, Jennifer. 2018. "The Taste for the Particular: A Logic of Discernment in an Age of Omnivorousness." *Journal of Consumer Culture* 18(1):3–20. doi: 10.1177/1469540516634416.

Smith, Stephen. 2014. "Radio: The Internet of the 1930s." *APM Reports.* Retrieved August 13, 2021. https://www.apmreports.org/episode/2014/11/10/radio-the-internet-of-the-1930s.

Soldo, Niccolo. 2021. "The Dubrovnik Interviews: Marc Andreessen." *Fisted by Foucault.* Retrieved November 7, 2021. https://niccolo.substack.com/p/the-dubrovnik-interviews-marc-andreessen.

Spring, Victoria L., C. Daryl Cameron, and Mina Cikara. 2018. "The Upside of Outrage." *Trends in Cognitive Sciences* 22(12):1067–9. doi: 10.1016/j.tics.2018.09.006.

Srinivasan, Dina. 2019. "The Antitrust Case Against Facebook: A Monopolist's Journey

Towards Pervasive Surveillance in Spite of Consumers' Preference for Privacy." *Berkeley Business Law Journal* 16(1):39–101.

Srnicek, Nick. 2017. *Platform Capitalism*. Cambridge, UK; Malden, MA: Polity.

Stadil, Sebastian. 2016. "Looking for the One: How I Went on 150 Dates in 4 Months." *Mission.org*. Retrieved March 25, 2022. https://medium.com/the-mission/looking-for-the-one-how-i-went-on-150-dates-in-4-months-bf43a095516c.

Standaert, Michael. 2021. "Smile for the Camera: The Dark Side of China's Emotion-Recognition Tech." *The Guardian*, March 3.

Star, Susan Leigh. 1999. "The Ethnography of Infrastructure." *American Behavioral Scientist* 43(3):377–91. doi: 10.1177/00027649921955326.

Starr, Paul. 1987. "The Sociology of Official Statistics." Pp. 7–57 in *The Politics of Numbers: The Population of the United States in the 1980s*, edited by W. Alonso and P. Starr. New York: Russell Sage Foundation.

Starr, Paul. 2004. *The Creation of the Media: Political Origins of Modern Communications*. New York: Basic Books.

Starr, Paul. 2021a. "The Flooded Zone: How We Became More Vulnerable to Disinformation in the Digital Era." Pp. 67–91 in *The Disinformation Age: Politics, Technology, and Disruptive Communication in the United States*, edited by W. L. Bennett and S. Livingston. New York: Cambridge University Press.

Starr, Paul. 2021b. "The Relational Public." *Sociological Theory* 39(2):57–80. doi: 10.1177/07352751211004660.

Statt, Nick, and Shannon Liao. 2019. "Facebook Wants to Be WeChat." *The Verge*, March 8.

Steele, Anne, and Sarah E. Needleman. 2021. "Twenty One Pilots in Concert – As Roblox Avatars." *Wall Street Journal*, October 3.

Stevenson, Megan. 2018. "Assessing Risk Assessment in Action." *Minnesota Law Review* 103:303–84.

Stokel-Walker, Chris. 2018. "'Success' on YouTube Still Means a Life of Poverty." *BloombergQuint*, February 27.

Storeng, Katerini Tagmatarchi, and Antoine de Bengy Puyvallée. 2021. "The Smartphone Pandemic: How Big Tech and Public Health Authorities Partner in the Digital Response to Covid-19." *Global Public Health* 16(8–9):1482–98. doi: 10.1080/17441692.2021.1882530.

Strate, Lance. 2008. "Studying Media AS Media: McLuhan and the Media Ecology Approach." *MediaTropes* 1:127–42.

Suler, John. 2004. "The Online Disinhibition Effect." *Cyberpsychology & Behavior: The Impact of the Internet, Multimedia and Virtual Reality on Behavior and Society* 7(3):321–6. https://doi.org/10.1089/1094931041291295.

Sundararajan, Arun. 2016. *The Sharing Economy: The End of Employment and the Rise of Crowd-Based Capitalism*. Cambridge, MA: The MIT Press.

Sundararajan, Arun. 2017. "The Future of Work." *Finance & Development* 54(2):6–11.

Sunstein, Cass R. 2015. *Choosing Not to Choose: Understanding the Value of Choice*. New York: Oxford University Press.

Sunstein, Cass R. 2019. "Algorithms, Correcting Biases." *Social Research* 86(2):499–511.

Sunstein, Cass R., and Richard H. Thaler. 2003. "Libertarian Paternalism is Not an Oxymoron." *The University of Chicago Law Review* 70(4):1159–202.

Syme, Rachel. 2018. "Gmail Smart Replies and the Ever-Growing Pressure to E-Mail Like a Machine." *The New Yorker*, November 28.

Tapscott, Don, and Alex Tapscott. 2018. *Blockchain Revolution: How the Technology behind*

Bitcoin is Changing Money, Business, and the World. Updated edition. New York: Portfolio/ Penguin.

Tapscott, Don, and Anthony D. Williams. 2006. *Wikinomics: How Mass Collaboration Changes Everything*. New York: Portfolio.

Tashea, Jason. 2017. "Risk-Assessment Algorithms Challenged in Bail, Sentencing and Parole Decisions." *ABA Journal*, March 1.

Taylor, Frederick Winslow. 1911. *The Principles of Scientific Management*. New York; London: Harper.

Taylor, T. L. 2018. *Watch Me Play: Twitch and the Rise of Game Live Streaming*. Princeton, NJ: Princeton University Press.

Terranova, Tiziana. 2000. "Free Labor: Producing Culture for the Digital Economy." *Social Text* 18(2):33–58.

Thaler, Richard H., and Cass R. Sunstein. 2008. *Nudge: Improving Decisions about Health, Wealth, and Happiness*. New Haven, CT: Yale University Press.

Thatcher, Jim, David O'Sullivan, and Dillon Mahmoudi. 2016. "Data Colonialism through Accumulation by Dispossession: New Metaphors for Daily Data." *Environment and Planning D: Society and Space* 34(6):990–1006. doi: 10.1177/0263775816633195.

The Economist. 2017. "The World's Most Valuable Resource is No Longer Oil, but Data." May 6.

Theeuwes, Jan. 2010. "Top-Down and Bottom-Up Control of Visual Selection." *Acta Psychologica* 135(2):77–99. doi: 10.1016/j.actpsy.2010.02.006.

Thompson, John B. 1995. *The Media and Modernity: A Social Theory of the Media*. Stanford, CA: Stanford University Press.

Thompson, John B. 2005. "The New Visibility." *Theory, Culture & Society* 22(6):31–51. https:// doi.org/10.1177/0263276405059413.

Thompson, John B. 2021. *Book Wars: The Digital Revolution in Publishing*. Cambridge (UK) and Medford MA: Polity.

Tjora, Aksel H. 2011. "Invisible Whispers: Accounts of SMS Communication in Shared Physical Space." *Convergence* 17(2):193–211. https://doi.org/10.1177/1354856510394604.

Toff, Benjamin, and Rasmus Kleis Nielsen. 2018. "'I Just Google It': Folk Theories of Distributed Discovery." *Journal of Communication* 68(3):636–57. doi: 10.1093/joc/jqy009.

Toffler, Alvin. 1980. *The Third Wave*. New York: Morrow.

Tokunaga, Robert S. 2011. "Social Networking Site or Social Surveillance Site? Understanding the Use of Interpersonal Electronic Surveillance in Romantic Relationships." *Computers in Human Behavior* 27(2):705–13. https://doi.org/10.1016/j.chb.2010.08.014.

Tokunaga, Robert S. 2016. "Interpersonal Surveillance over Social Network Sites: Applying a Theory of Negative Relational Maintenance and the Investment Model." *Journal of Social and Personal Relationships* 33(2):171–90. doi: 10.1177/0265407514568749.

Torpey, John. 2020. "A Sociological Agenda for the Tech Age." *Theory and Society* 49(5):749–69. doi: 10.1007/s11186-020-09406-0.

Tosi, Justin, and Brandon Warmke. 2020. *Grandstanding: The Use and Abuse of Moral Talk*. New York: Oxford University Press.

Tréguer, Félix. 2019. "Seeing like Big Tech: Security Assemblages, Technology, and the Future of State Bureaucracy." Pp. 145–64 in *Data Politics: Worlds, Subjects, Rights*, edited by D. Bigo, E. Isin, and E. Ruppert. Abingdon: Routledge.

Tréguer, Félix. 2021. "The Virus of Surveillance: How the COVID-19 Pandemic is Fuelling Technologies of Control." *Political Anthropological Research on International Social Sciences* 2(1):16–46.

Tripathi, A., T. S. Ashwin, and R. M. R. Guddeti. 2019. "EmoWare: A Context-Aware Framework for Personalized Video Recommendation Using Affective Video Sequences." *IEEE Access* 7:51185–200. https://doi.org/10.1109/ACCESS.2019.2911235.

Trottier, Daniel. 2012. *Social Media as Surveillance: Rethinking Visibility in a Converging World*. Abingdon: Routledge.

Tucker, Joshua A., Yannis Theocharis, Margaret E. Roberts, and Pablo Barberá. 2017. "From Liberation to Turmoil: Social Media and Democracy." *Journal of Democracy* 28(4):46–59. doi: 10.1353/jod.2017.0064.

Tufekci, Zeynep. 2013a. "We Were Always Human." Pp. 33–47 in *Human No More: Digital Subjectivities, Unhuman Subjects, and the End of Anthropology*, edited by Neil L. Whitehead and Michael Wesch. Louisville, CO: University Press of Colorado.

Tufekci, Zeynep. 2013b. "'Not This One': Social Movements, the Attention Economy, and Microcelebrity Networked Activism." *American Behavioral Scientist* 57(7):848–70. doi: 10.1177/0002764213479369.

Tufekci, Zeynep. 2014a. "Engineering the Public: Big Data, Surveillance and Computational Politics." *First Monday* 19(7).

Tufekci, Zeynep. 2014b. "Social Movements and Governments in the Digital Age: Evaluating a Complex Landscape." *Journal of International Affairs* 68(1):1–18.

Tufekci, Zeynep. 2017. *Twitter and Tear Gas: The Power and Fragility of Networked Protest*. New Haven, CT: Yale University Press.

Tufekci, Zeynep. 2019. "The Internet Has Made Dupes – and Cynics – of Us All." *Wired*, June 24.

Turkle, Sherry. 1995. *Life on the Screen: Identity in the Age of the Internet*. New York: Simon & Schuster.

Turkle, Sherry. 1996. "Parallel Lives: Working on Identity in Virtual Space." Pp. 157–75 in *Constructing the Self in a Mediated World*, edited by Debra Grodin and Thomas R. Lindlof. Thousand Oaks, CA: Sage.

Turkle, Sherry. 2008. "Always-On/Always-On-You: The Tethered Self." Pp. 121–37 in *Handbook of Mobile Communication Studies*, edited by J. E. Katz. Cambridge, MA: The MIT Press.

Turkle, Sherry. 2011. *Alone Together: Why We Expect More from Technology and Less from Each Other*. New York: Basic Books.

Turkle, Sherry. 2015. *Reclaiming Conversation: The Power of Talk in a Digital Age*. New York: Penguin Press.

Turner, Fred. 2006. *From Counterculture to Cyberculture*. Chicago, IL: University of Chicago Press.

Twenge, Jean M. 2017. *IGen: Why Today's Super-Connected Kids Are Growing Up Less Rebellious, More Tolerant, Less Happy – and Completely Unprepared for Adulthood – and What That Means for the Rest of Us*. New York: Simon & Schuster.

Tyson, Gareth, Vasile C. Perta, Hamed Haddadi, and Michael C. Seto. 2016. "A First Look at User Activity on Tinder." *ArXiv* July. http://arxiv.org/abs/1607.01952.

Udell, Megan. 2019. "The Museum of the Infinite Scroll: Assessing the Effectiveness of Google Arts and Culture as a Virtual Tool for Museum Accessibility." MA Capstone project, University of San Francisco.

Urbinati, Nadia. 2015. "A Revolt against Intermediary Bodies." *Constellations* 22(4):477–86. doi: 10.1111/1467-8675.12188.

Vaidhyanathan, Siva. 2018. *Antisocial Media: How Facebook Disconnects Us and Undermines Democracy*. New York: Oxford University Press.

Vallas, Steven P. 2019. "Platform Capitalism: What's at Stake for Workers?" *New Labor Forum* 28(1):48–59. doi: 10.1177/1095796018817059.

Vallas, Steven, and Juliet B. Schor. 2020. "What Do Platforms Do? Understanding the Gig Economy." *Annual Review of Sociology* 46:273–94. doi: 10.1146/annurev-soc-121919-054857.

Van Dijck, José. 2013a. *The Culture of Connectivity: A Critical History of Social Media*. Oxford; New York: Oxford University Press.

Van Dijck, José. 2013b. "'You Have One Identity': Performing the Self on Facebook and LinkedIn." *Media, Culture & Society* 35(2):199–215.

Van Dijck, José. 2014. "Datafication, Dataism and Dataveillance: Big Data between Scientific Paradigm and Ideology." *Surveillance & Society* 12(2):197–208.

Van Dijck, José, and David Nieborg. 2009. "Wikinomics and its Discontents: A Critical Analysis of Web 2.0 Business Manifestos." *New Media & Society* 11(5):855–74. doi: 10.1177/1461444809105356.

Van Dijck, José, Thomas Poell, and Martijn de Waal. 2018. *The Platform Society: Public Values in a Connective World*. New York: Oxford University Press.

Vandenberg, Femke, Michaël Berghman, and Julian Schaap. 2021. "The 'Lonely Raver': Music Livestreams during COVID-19 as a Hotline to Collective Consciousness?" *European Societies* 23(suppl.1):S141–52. doi: 10.1080/14616696.2020.1818271.

Vogels, Emily A. 2021. *The State of Online Harassment*. Washington, DC: Pew Research Center.

Vormbusch, Uwe. 2022. "Accounting for Who We Are and Could Be: Inventing Taxonomies of the Self in an Age of Uncertainty." Pp. 97–133 in *The New Politics of Numbers: Utopia, Evidence and Democracy*, edited by A. Mennicken and R. Salais. Cham: Springer International.

Vosoughi, Soroush, Deb Roy, and Sinan Aral. 2018. "The Spread of True and False News Online." *Science* 359(6380):1146–51. doi: 10.1126/science.aap9559.

Wahl-Jorgensen, Karin. 2019. *Emotions, Media and Politics*. Cambridge, UK; Malden, MA: Polity.

Wajcman, Judy. 2015. *Pressed for Time: The Acceleration of Life in Digital Capitalism*. Chicago, IL: The University of Chicago Press.

Wang, Ju-Chiang, Yi-Hsuan Yang, and Hsin-Min Wang. 2015. "Affective Music Information Retrieval," February. https://arxiv.org/abs/1502.05131v1.

Wang, S., and Q. Ji. 2015. "Video Affective Content Analysis: A Survey of State-of-the-Art Methods." *IEEE Transactions on Affective Computing* 6(4):410–30. https://doi.org/10.1109/TAFFC.2015.2432791.

Wang, Yilun, and Michal Kosinski. 2018. "Deep Neural Networks Are More Accurate than Humans at Detecting Sexual Orientation from Facial Images." *Journal of Personality and Social Psychology* 114(2):246–57. https://doi.org/10.1037/pspa0000098.

Watts, Rob. 2019. "New Politics: The Anonymous Politics of 4chan, Outrage and the New Public Sphere." Pp. 73–89 in *Young People and the Politics of Outrage and Hope*, edited by P. Kelly, P. Campbell, L. Harrison, and C. Hickey. Leiden; Boston: Brill.

Weber, Max. 1978 [1922]. *Economy and Society: An Outline of Interpretive Sociology*. Edited by G. Roth and C. Wittich. Berkeley: University of California Press.

Wei, Eugene. 2021. "American Idle." *Remains of the Day*. Retrieved April 28, 2021. https://www.eugenewei.com/blog/2021/2/15/american-idle.

Weinberg, Lindsay A. 2018. "From Mass Culture to Personalization." PhD Dissertation, University of California, Santa Cruz.

Weinschenk, Susan. 2012. "Why We're All Addicted to Texts, Twitter and Google." *Psychology*

Today, September 11. http://www.psychologytoday.com/blog/brain-wise/201209/why-were-all-addicted-texts-twitter-and-google.

Weisenstein, Kara. 2019. "Who Watches Netflix at 1.5x Speed, and Why?" *Mic*. Retrieved April 2, 2021. https://www.mic.com/p/who-watches-netflix-at-15x-speed-why-19277720.

Weiser, Mark. 1991. "The Computer for the 21st Century." *Scientific American*, September:94-104.

Weisgerber, Corinne, and Shannan H. Butler. 2016. "Curating the Soul: Foucault's Concept of *Hupomnemata* and the Digital Technology of Self-Care." *Information, Communication & Society* 19(10):1340–55. https://doi.org/10.1080/1369118X.2015.1088882.

Wen, Miaomiao et al. 2015. "OMG UR Funny! Computer-Aided Humor with an Application to Chat." Pp. 86–93 in *Proceedings of the Sixth International Conference on Computational Creativity*. Provo, UT: Brigham Young University.

Wetherell, Margaret. 2012. *Affect and Emotion: A New Social Science Understanding*. London: Sage.

Weyland, Kurt. 2001. "Clarifying a Contested Concept: Populism in the Study of Latin American Politics." *Comparative Politics* 34(1):1–22. doi: 10.2307/422412.

Williams, Alex. 2015. "Control Societies and Platform Logic." *New Formations* 84–85:209–27. doi: 10.3898/neWf:84/85.10.2015.

Williams, James. 2018. *Stand Out of Our Light: Freedom and Resistance in the Attention Economy*. Cambridge: Cambridge University Press.

Williams, Raymond. 1961. *The Long Revolution*. London: Chatto and Windus.

Williamson, Ben. 2021. "Meta-Edtech." *Learning, Media and Technology* 46(1):1–5. doi: 10.1080/17439884.2021.1876089.

Williamson, Ben, and Anna Hogan. 2020. *Commercialisation and Privatisation in/of Education in the Context of Covid-19*. Brussels: Education International.

Williamson, Ben, and Anna Hogan. 2021. *Pandemic Privatisation in Higher Education: Edtech & University Reform*. Brussels: Education International.

Wolf, Gary. 2009. "Know Thyself: Tracking Every Facet of Life, from Sleep to Mood to Pain, 24/7/365." *Wired*, June 22. https://www.wired.com/2009/06/lbnp-knowthyself/.

Wolf, Gary. 2010. "The Data-Driven Life." *The New York Times*, April 28.

Wood, Alex J. 2020. *Despotism on Demand: How Power Operates in the Flexible Workplace*. Ithaca, NY: Cornell University Press.

Wood, Alex J. 2021. *Algorithmic Management: Consequences for Work Organisation and Working Conditions*. Brussels: European Commission.

Wood, Alex, and Vili Lehdonvirta. 2021. "Platform Precarity: Surviving Algorithmic Insecurity in the Gig Economy." Available at SSRN. doi: 10.2139/ssrn.3795375.

Wu, Tim. 2016. *The Attention Merchants: The Epic Scramble to Get inside Our Heads*. New York: Alfred A. Knopf.

Wu, Tim. 2018a. *The Curse of Bigness: Antitrust in the New Gilded Age*. New York: Columbia Global Reports.

Wu, Tim. 2018b. "The Tyranny of Convenience." *The New York Times*, February 20.

Yglesias, Matthew. 2021. "Why Everyone is so Crazy." *Slow Boring*, August 11.

Ylä-Anttila, Tuukka. 2018. "Populist Knowledge: 'Post-Truth' Repertoires of Contesting Epistemic Authorities." *European Journal of Cultural and Political Sociology* 5(4):356–88. doi: 10.1080/23254823.2017.1414620.

Yuan, Li. 2019. "Mark Zuckerberg Wants Facebook to Emulate WeChat. Can It?" *The New York Times*, March 8.

Zahn, Max, and Andy Serwer. 2021. "Zoom Meetings Will Offer 'Better Experience' than Face-to-Face: CEO." *Yahoo News*, October 25.

Zaller, John. 1996. "The Myth of Massive Media Impact Revived: New Support for a Discredited Idea." Pp. 17–78 in *Political Persuasion and Attitude Change*, edited by D. C. Mutz, P. M. Sniderman, and R. A. Brody. Ann Arbor: University of Michigan Press.

Zeavin, Hannah. 2021. *The Distance Cure: A History of Teletherapy*. Cambridge, MA: The MIT Press.

Zhao, Shanyang. 2003. "Toward a Taxonomy of Copresence." *Presence: Teleoperators and Virtual Environments* 12(5):445–55. https://doi.org/10.1162/105474603322761261.

Zhao, Shanyang. 2005. "The Digital Self: Through the Looking Glass of Telecopresent Others." *Symbolic Interaction* 28(3):387–405. https://doi.org/10.1525/si.2005.28.3.387.

Zhao, Shanyang. 2006. "The Internet and the Transformation of the Reality of Everyday Life: Toward a New Analytic Stance in Sociology." *Sociological Inquiry* 76(4):458–74. doi: 10.1111/j.1475-682X.2006.00166.x.

Zhao, Shanyang, and David Elesh. 2008. "Copresence as 'Being with': Social Contact in Online Public Domains." *Information, Communication & Society* 11(4):565–83. https://www.tandfonline.com/doi/full/10.1080/13691180801998995.

Zou, Sheng. 2021. "Disenchanting Trust: Instrumental Reason, Algorithmic Governance, and China's Emerging Social Credit System." *Media and Communication* 9(2):140–9. doi: 10.17645/mac.v9i2.3806.

Zuboff, Shoshana. 2019. *The Age of Surveillance Capitalism: The Fight for a Human Future at the New Frontier of Power*. New York: Public Affairs.

Zuboff, Shoshana. 2020. "You Are Now Remotely Controlled." *The New York Times*, January 24.

Zuckerberg, Mark. 2019. "A Privacy-Focused Vision for Social Networking." https://www.facebook.com/notes/mark-zuckerberg/a-privacy-focused-vision-for-social-networking/10156700570096634/.

Zuckerman, Ethan. 2014. "The Internet's Original Sin." *The Atlantic*. http://m.theatlantic.com/technology/archive/2014/08/advertising-is-the-internets-original-sin/376041/.

Zuckerman, Ethan. 2020. "The Case for Digital Public Infrastructure." Knight First Amendment Institute, Columbia University.

Zulli, Diana. 2018. "Capitalizing on the Look: Insights into the Glance, Attention Economy, and Instagram." *Critical Studies in Media Communication* 35(2):137–50. doi: 10.1080/15295036.2017.1394582.

Zysman, John, and Martin Kenney. 2018. "The Next Phase in the Digital Revolution: Intelligent Tools, Platforms, Growth, Employment." *Communications of the ACM* 61(2):54–63. doi: 10.1145/3173550.

Index

253